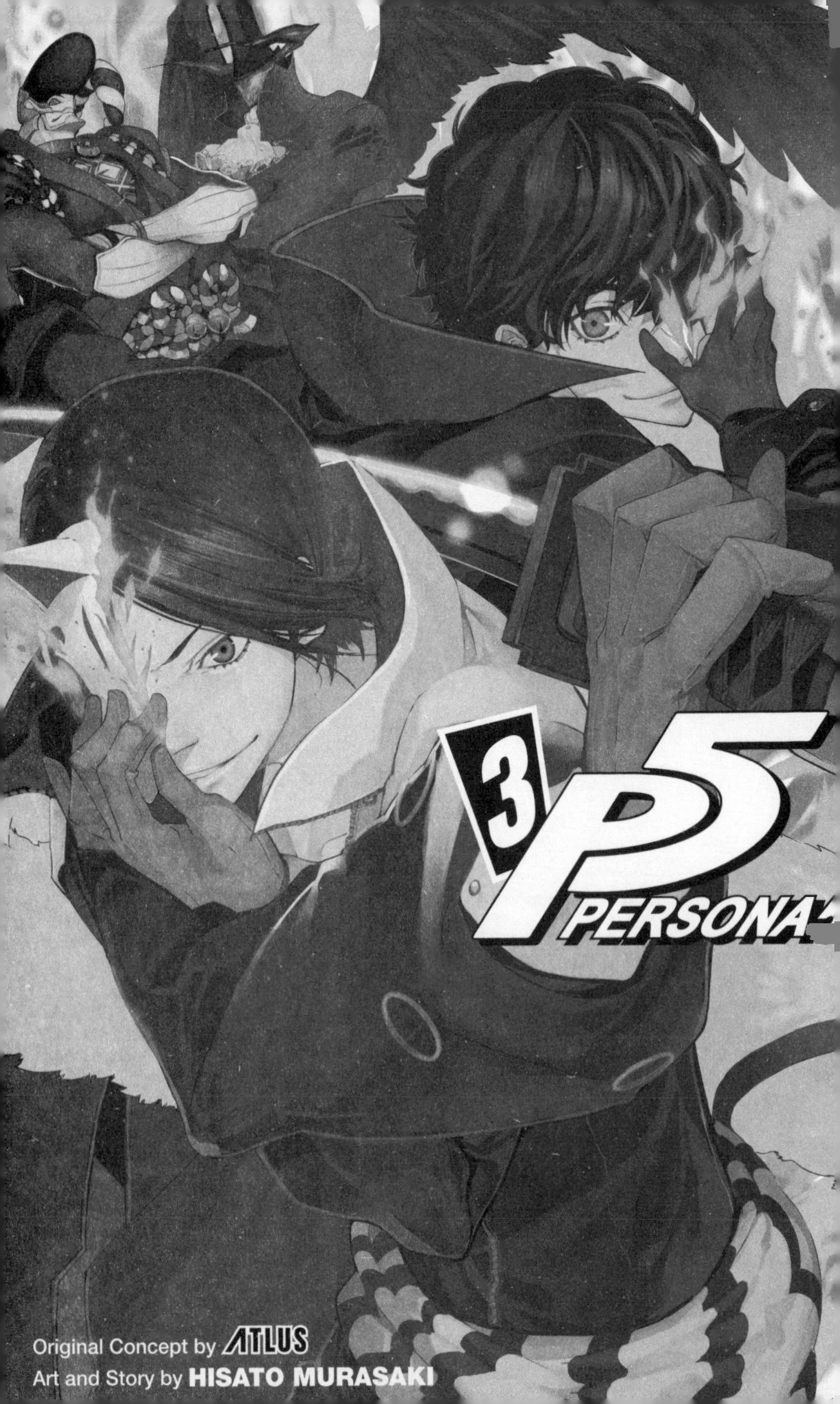
3
P5
PERSONA
Original Concept by ATLUS
Art and Story by HISATO MURASAKI

P5 PERSONA5

VOLUME 3

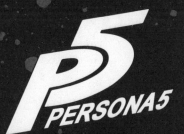

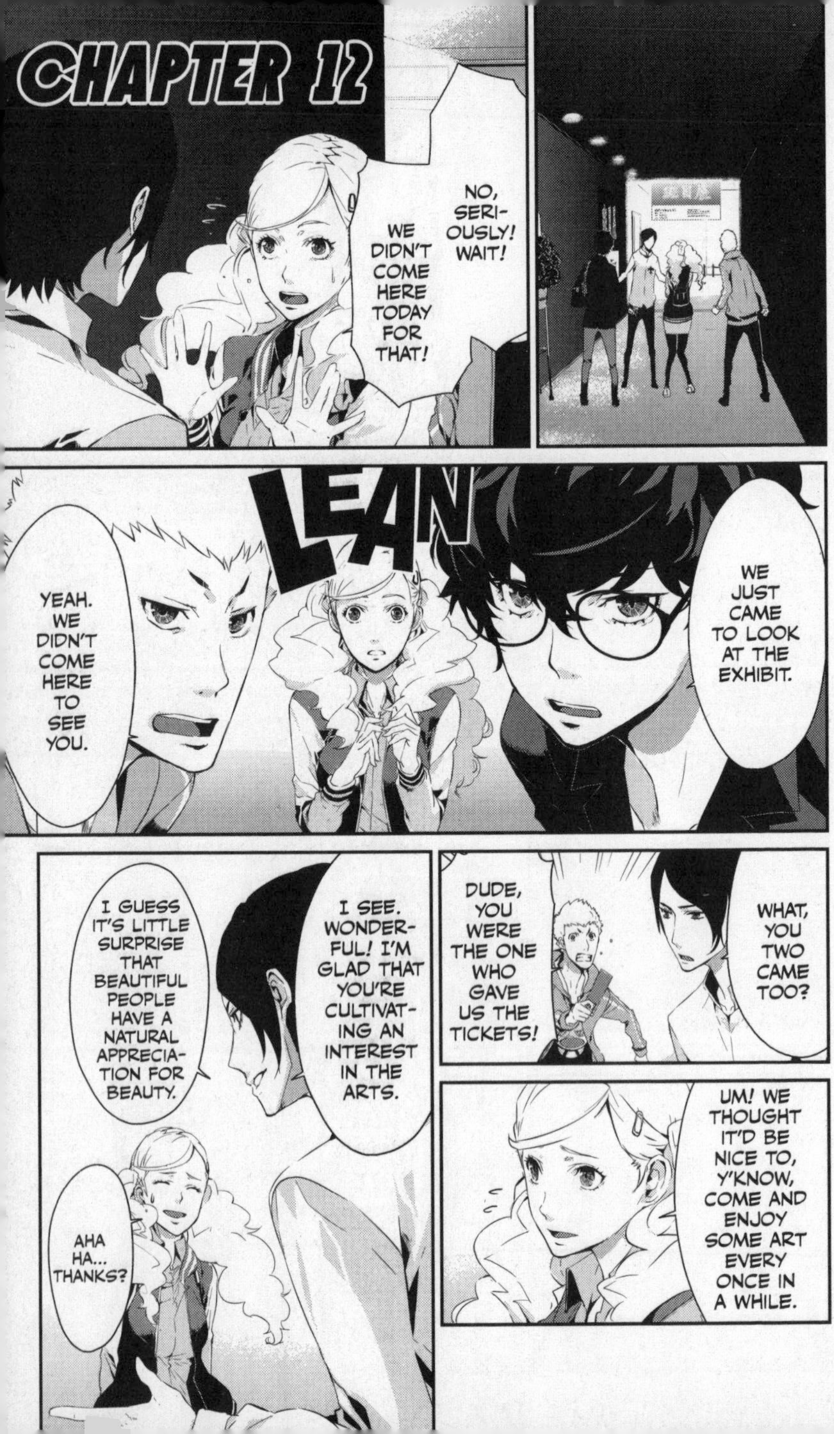
CHAPTER 12
NO, SERIOUSLY! WAIT!
WE DIDN'T COME HERE TODAY FOR THAT!
WE JUST CAME TO LOOK AT THE EXHIBIT.
LEAN
YEAH. WE DIDN'T COME HERE TO SEE YOU.
WHAT, YOU TWO CAME TOO?
DUDE, YOU WERE THE ONE WHO GAVE US THE TICKETS!
UM! WE THOUGHT IT'D BE NICE TO, Y'KNOW, COME AND ENJOY SOME ART EVERY ONCE IN A WHILE.
I SEE. WONDERFUL! I'M GLAD THAT YOU'RE CULTIVATING AN INTEREST IN THE ARTS.
I GUESS IT'S LITTLE SURPRISE THAT BEAUTIFUL PEOPLE HAVE A NATURAL APPRECIATION FOR BEAUTY.
AHA HA... THANKS?

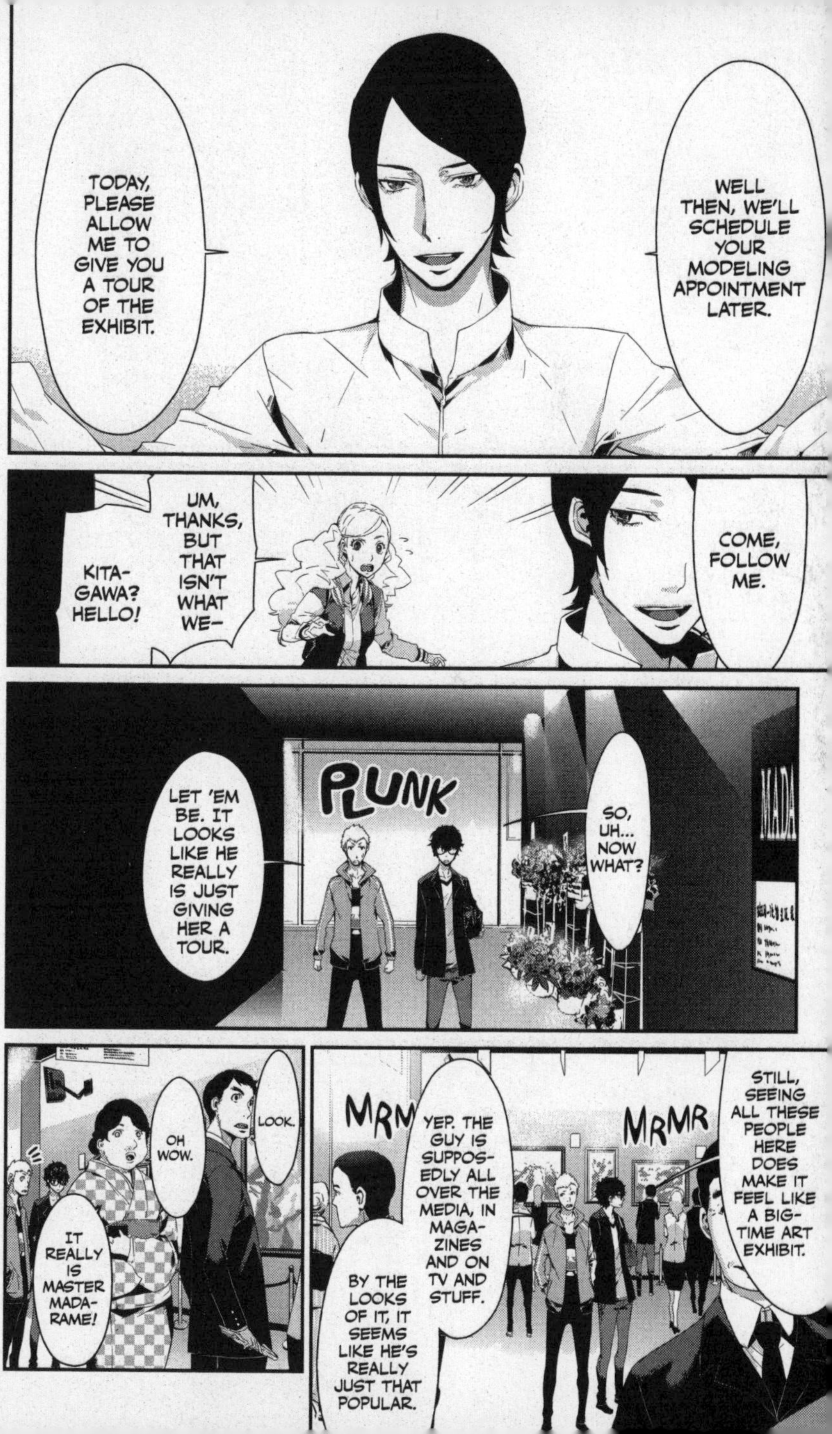
WELL THEN, WE'LL SCHEDULE YOUR MODELING APPOINTMENT LATER.
TODAY, PLEASE ALLOW ME TO GIVE YOU A TOUR OF THE EXHIBIT.
COME, FOLLOW ME.
UM, THANKS, BUT THAT ISN'T WHAT WE—
KITA-GAWA? HELLO!
SO, UH... NOW WHAT?
PLUNK
LET 'EM BE. IT LOOKS LIKE HE REALLY IS JUST GIVING HER A TOUR.
STILL, SEEING ALL THESE PEOPLE HERE DOES MAKE IT FEEL LIKE A BIG-TIME ART EXHIBIT.
MRMR
YEP. THE GUY IS SUPPOS-EDLY ALL OVER THE MEDIA, IN MAGA-ZINES AND ON TV AND STUFF.
MRM
BY THE LOOKS OF IT, IT SEEMS LIKE HE'S REALLY JUST THAT POPULAR.
LOOK.
OH WOW.
IT REALLY IS MASTER MADA-RAME!

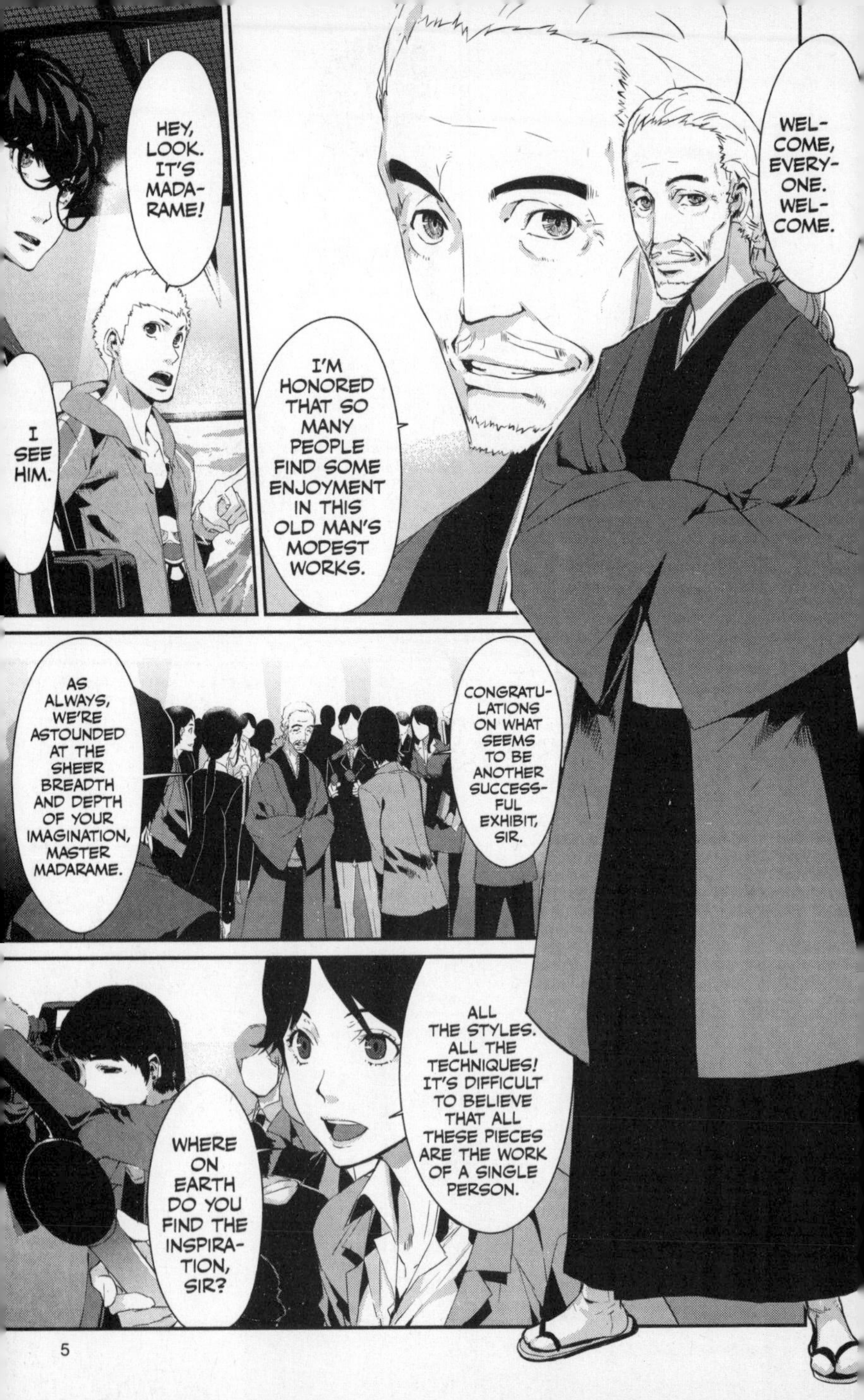
WEL-COME, EVERY-ONE. WEL-COME.
I'M HONORED THAT SO MANY PEOPLE FIND SOME ENJOYMENT IN THIS OLD MAN'S MODEST WORKS.
HEY, LOOK. IT'S MADA-RAME!
I SEE HIM.
CONGRATU-LATIONS ON WHAT SEEMS TO BE ANOTHER SUCCESS-FUL EXHIBIT, SIR.
AS ALWAYS, WE'RE ASTOUNDED AT THE SHEER BREADTH AND DEPTH OF YOUR IMAGINATION, MASTER MADARAME.
ALL THE STYLES. ALL THE TECHNIQUES! IT'S DIFFICULT TO BELIEVE THAT ALL THESE PIECES ARE THE WORK OF A SINGLE PERSON.
WHERE ON EARTH DO YOU FIND THE INSPIRA-TION, SIR?

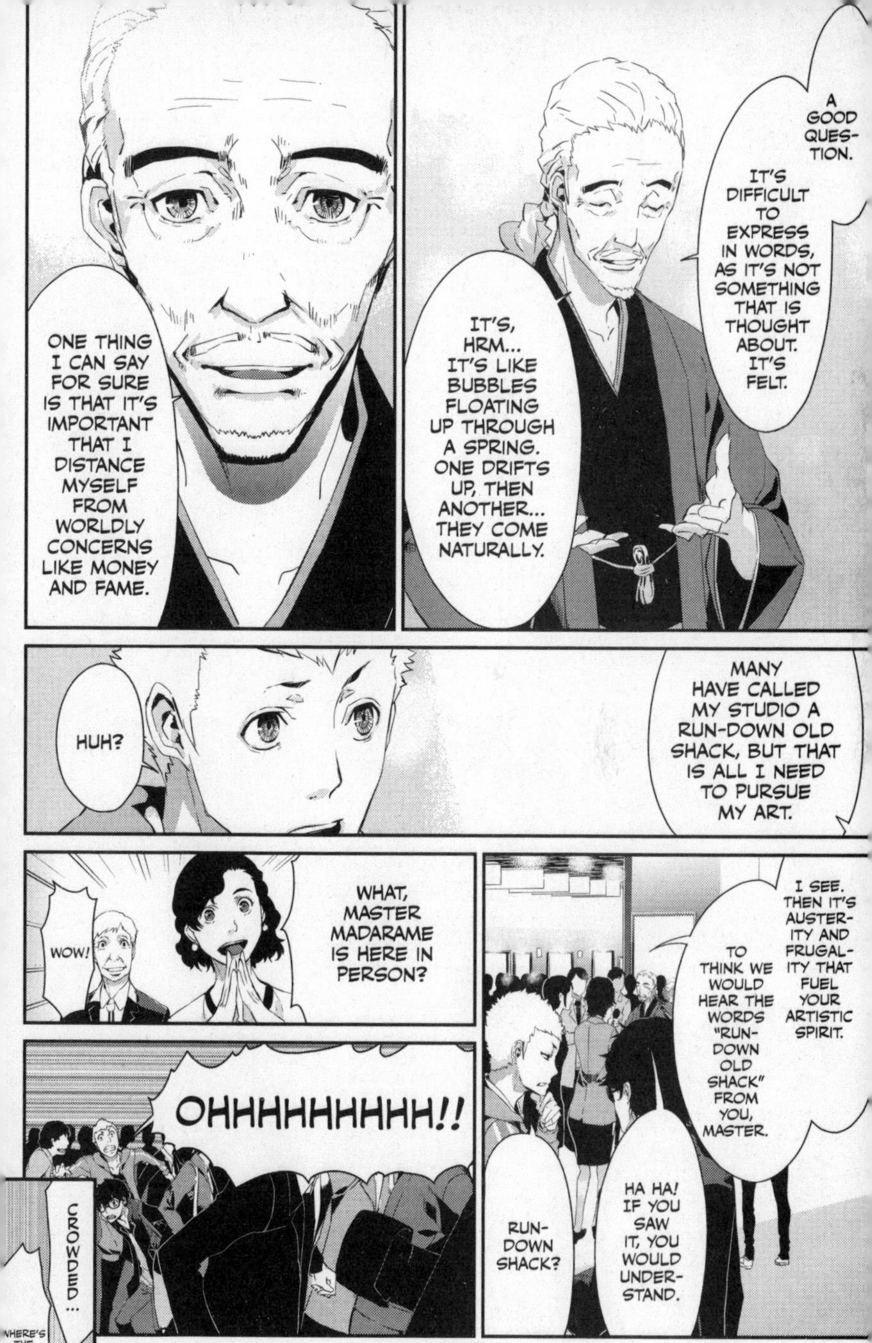
A GOOD QUES-TION.
IT'S DIFFICULT TO EXPRESS IN WORDS, AS IT'S NOT SOMETHING THAT IS THOUGHT ABOUT. IT'S FELT.
IT'S, HRM... IT'S LIKE BUBBLES FLOATING UP THROUGH A SPRING. ONE DRIFTS UP, THEN ANOTHER... THEY COME NATURALLY.
ONE THING I CAN SAY FOR SURE IS THAT IT'S IMPORTANT THAT I DISTANCE MYSELF FROM WORLDLY CONCERNS LIKE MONEY AND FAME.
MANY HAVE CALLED MY STUDIO A RUN-DOWN OLD SHACK, BUT THAT IS ALL I NEED TO PURSUE MY ART.
HUH?
I SEE. THEN IT'S AUSTER-ITY AND FRUGAL-ITY THAT FUEL YOUR ARTISTIC SPIRIT.
TO THINK WE WOULD HEAR THE WORDS "RUN-DOWN OLD SHACK" FROM YOU, MASTER.
HA HA! IF YOU SAW IT, YOU WOULD UNDER-STAND.
RUN-DOWN SHACK?
WHAT, MASTER MADARAME IS HERE IN PERSON?
WOW!
OHHHHHHHHH!!
CROWDED...
WHERE'S THE EXIT?!

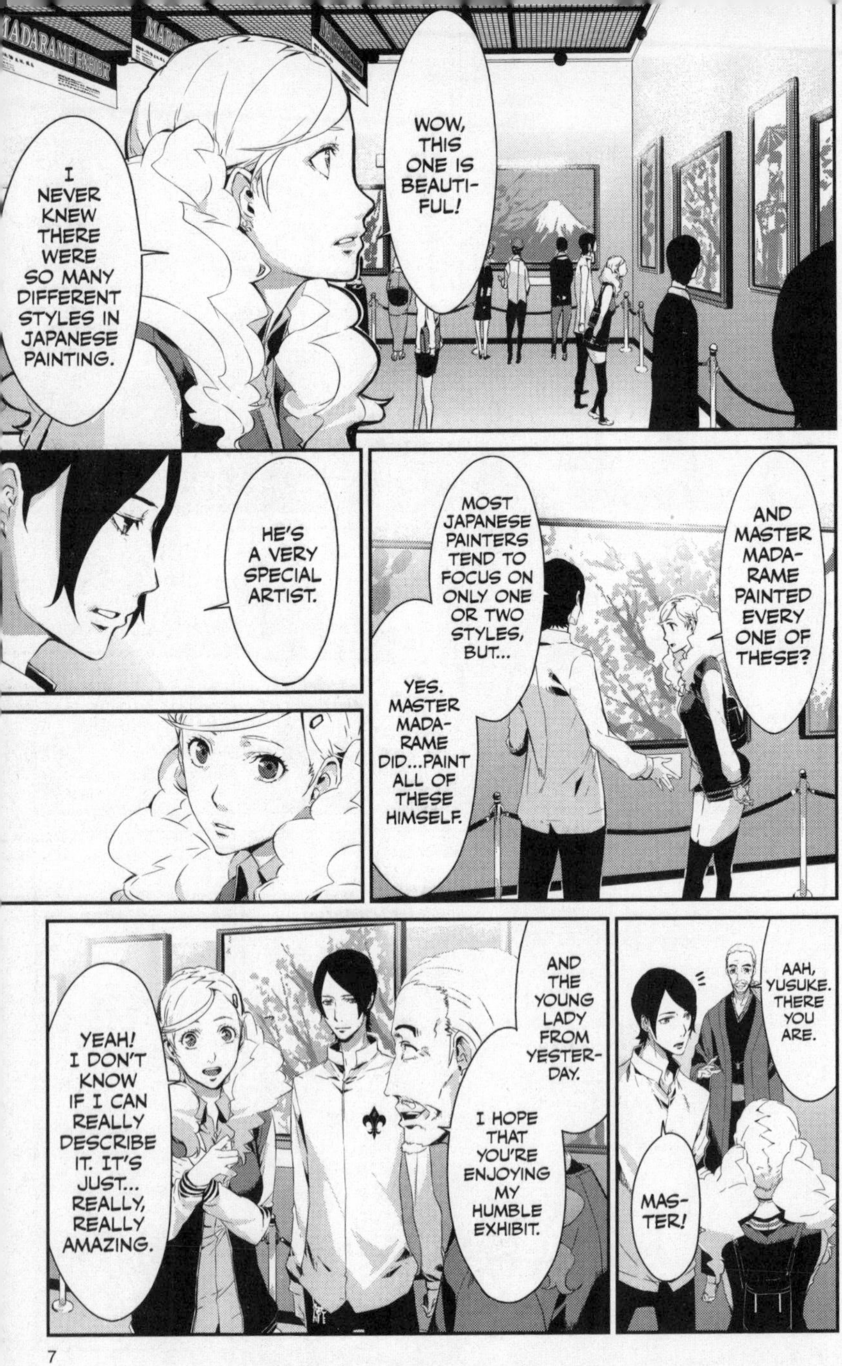
MADARAME EXHIBIT
WOW, THIS ONE IS BEAUTIFUL!
I NEVER KNEW THERE WERE SO MANY DIFFERENT STYLES IN JAPANESE PAINTING.
AND MASTER MADARAME PAINTED EVERY ONE OF THESE?
MOST JAPANESE PAINTERS TEND TO FOCUS ON ONLY ONE OR TWO STYLES, BUT...
YES. MASTER MADARAME DID...PAINT ALL OF THESE HIMSELF.
HE'S A VERY SPECIAL ARTIST.
AAH, YUSUKE. THERE YOU ARE.
MASTER!
AND THE YOUNG LADY FROM YESTERDAY.
I HOPE THAT YOU'RE ENJOYING MY HUMBLE EXHIBIT.
YEAH! I DON'T KNOW IF I CAN REALLY DESCRIBE IT. IT'S JUST... REALLY, REALLY AMAZING.

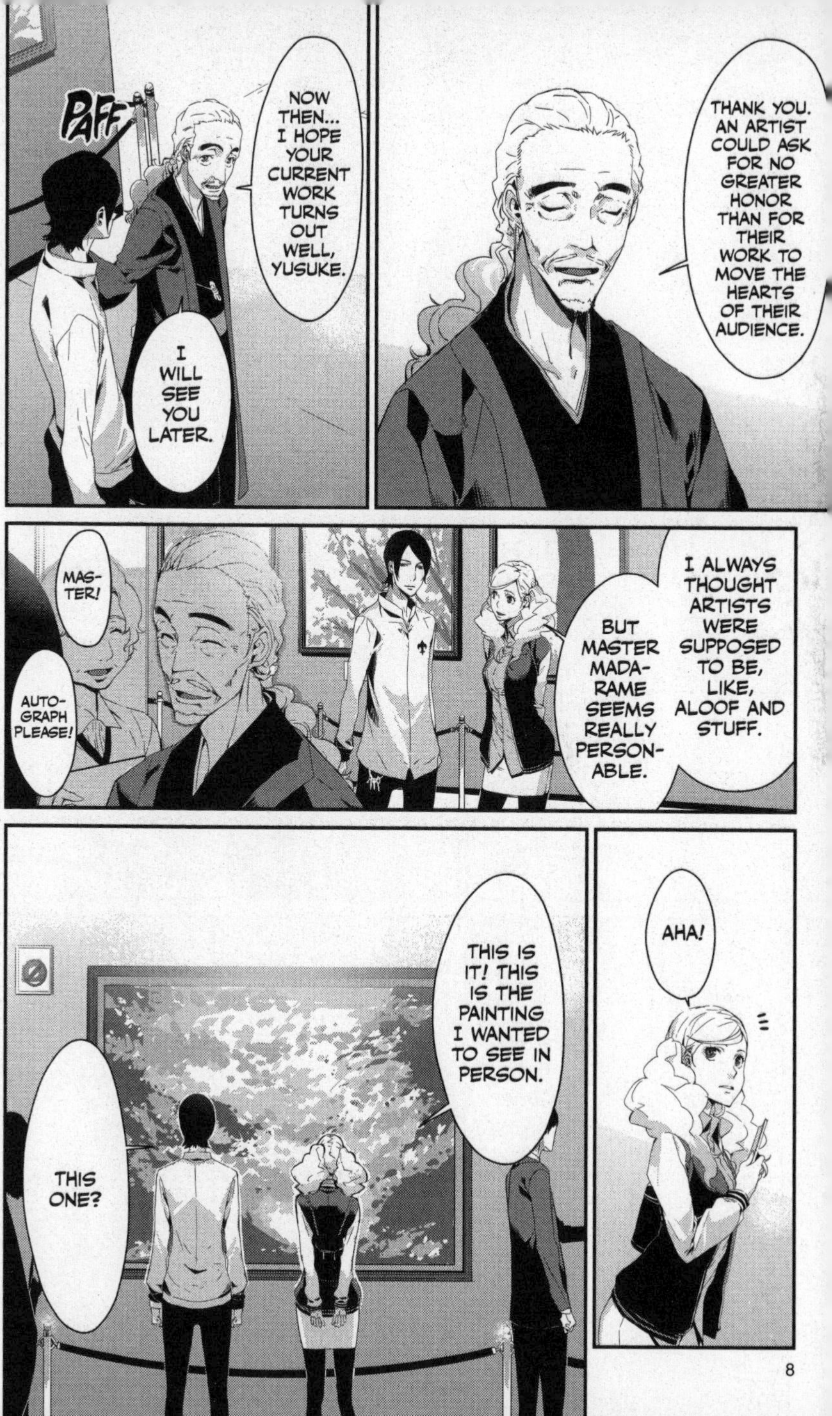
THANK YOU. AN ARTIST COULD ASK FOR NO GREATER HONOR THAN FOR THEIR WORK TO MOVE THE HEARTS OF THEIR AUDIENCE.
NOW THEN... I HOPE YOUR CURRENT WORK TURNS OUT WELL, YUSUKE.
PAFF
I WILL SEE YOU LATER.
I ALWAYS THOUGHT ARTISTS WERE SUPPOSED TO BE, LIKE, ALOOF AND STUFF.
BUT MASTER MADARAME SEEMS REALLY PERSONABLE.
MASTER!
AUTOGRAPH PLEASE!
AHA!
THIS IS IT! THIS IS THE PAINTING I WANTED TO SEE IN PERSON.
THIS ONE?

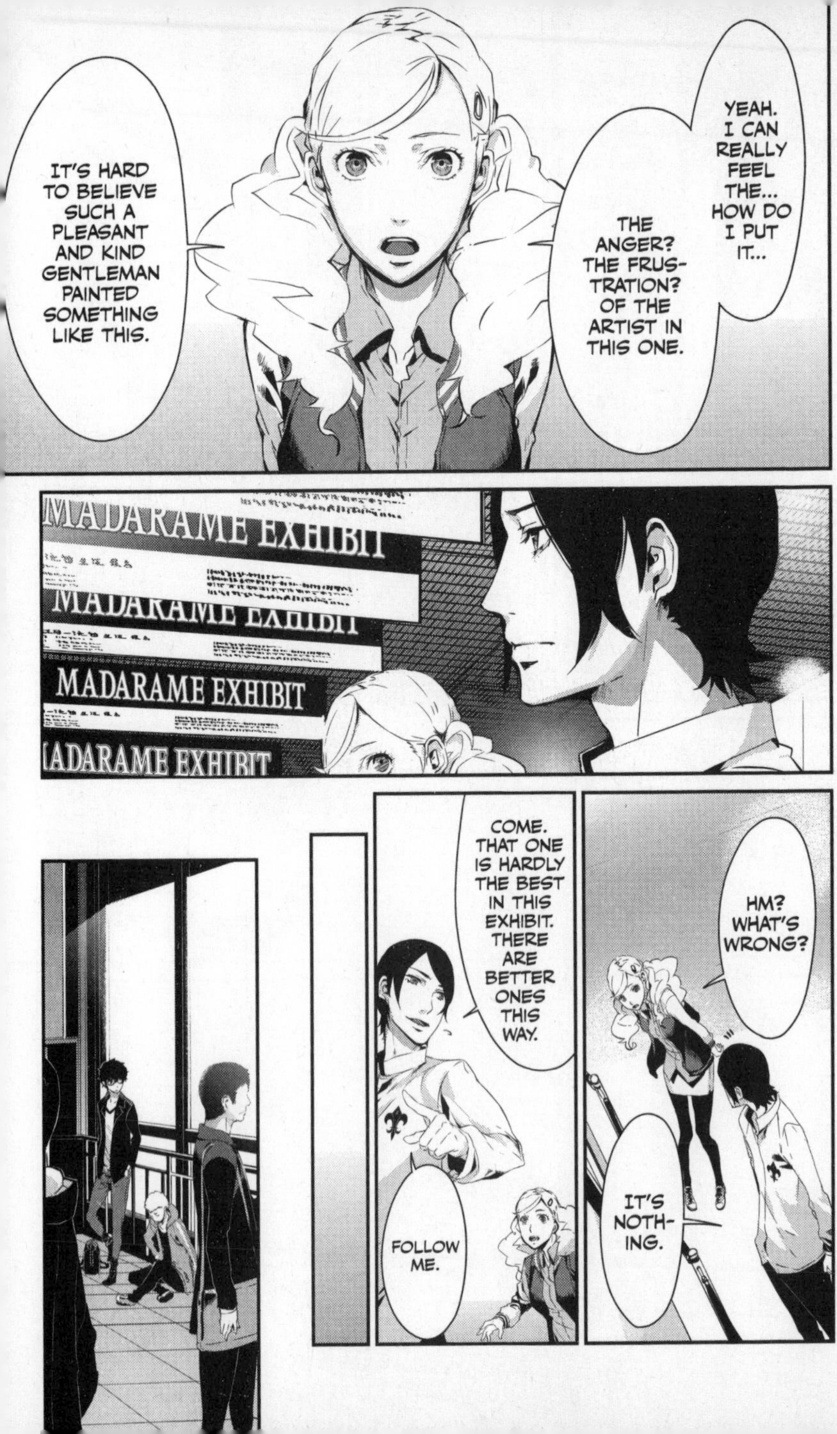
YEAH. I CAN REALLY FEEL THE... HOW DO I PUT IT...
THE ANGER? THE FRUS-TRATION? OF THE ARTIST IN THIS ONE.
IT'S HARD TO BELIEVE SUCH A PLEASANT AND KIND GENTLEMAN PAINTED SOMETHING LIKE THIS.
MADARAME EXHIBIT
HM? WHAT'S WRONG?
IT'S NOTH-ING.
COME. THAT ONE IS HARDLY THE BEST IN THIS EXHIBIT. THERE ARE BETTER ONES THIS WAY.
FOLLOW ME.

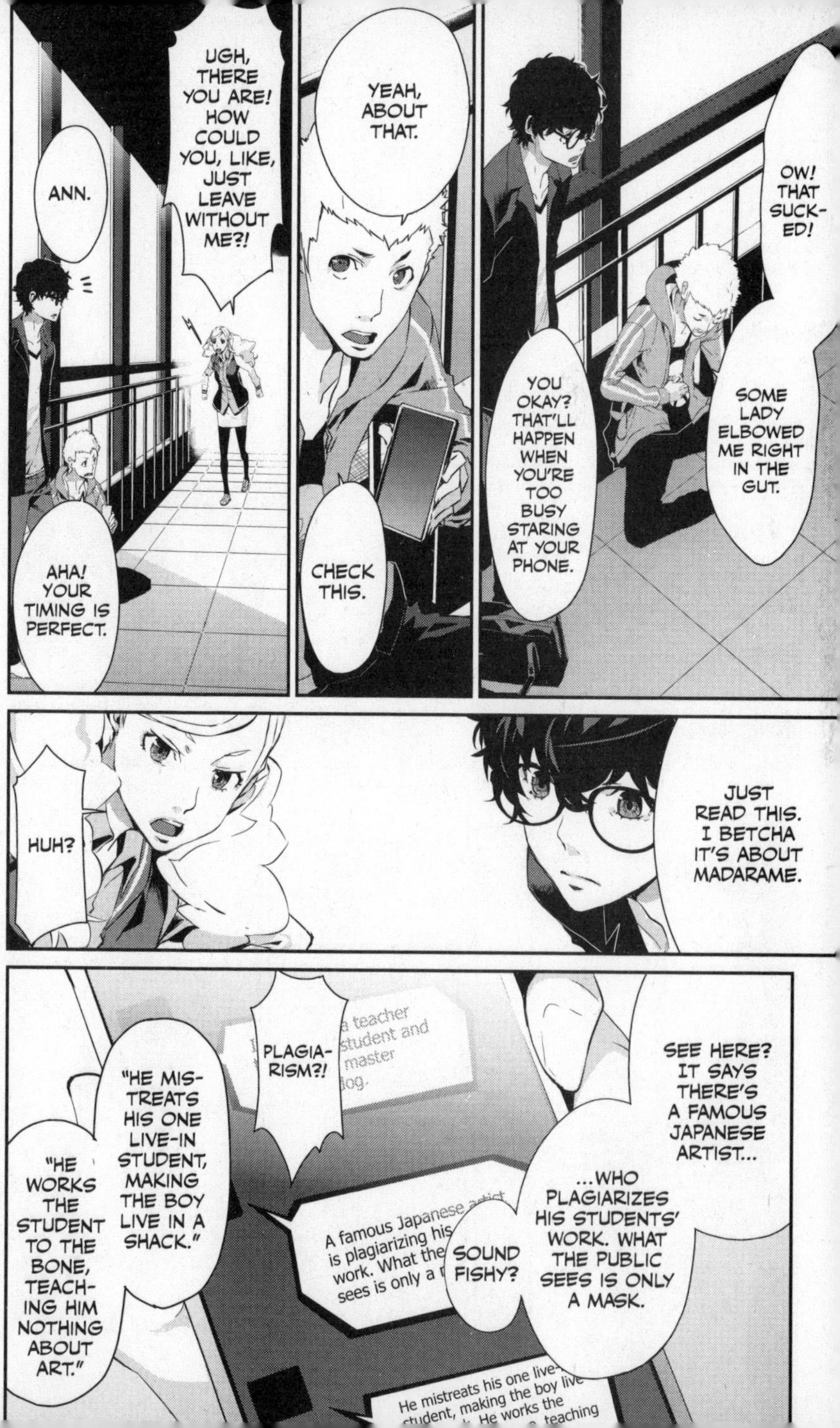
OW! THAT SUCK-ED!
SOME LADY ELBOWED ME RIGHT IN THE GUT.
YOU OKAY? THAT'LL HAPPEN WHEN YOU'RE TOO BUSY STARING AT YOUR PHONE.
YEAH, ABOUT THAT.
CHECK THIS.
UGH, THERE YOU ARE! HOW COULD YOU, LIKE, JUST LEAVE WITHOUT ME?!
ANN.
AHA! YOUR TIMING IS PERFECT.
JUST READ THIS. I BETCHA IT'S ABOUT MADARAME.
HUH?
SEE HERE? IT SAYS THERE'S A FAMOUS JAPANESE ARTIST...
...WHO PLAGIARIZES HIS STUDENTS' WORK. WHAT THE PUBLIC SEES IS ONLY A MASK.
SOUND FISHY?
PLAGIA-RISM?!
"HE MIS-TREATS HIS ONE LIVE-IN STUDENT, MAKING THE BOY LIVE IN A SHACK."
"HE WORKS THE STUDENT TO THE BONE, TEACHING HIM NOTHING ABOUT ART."

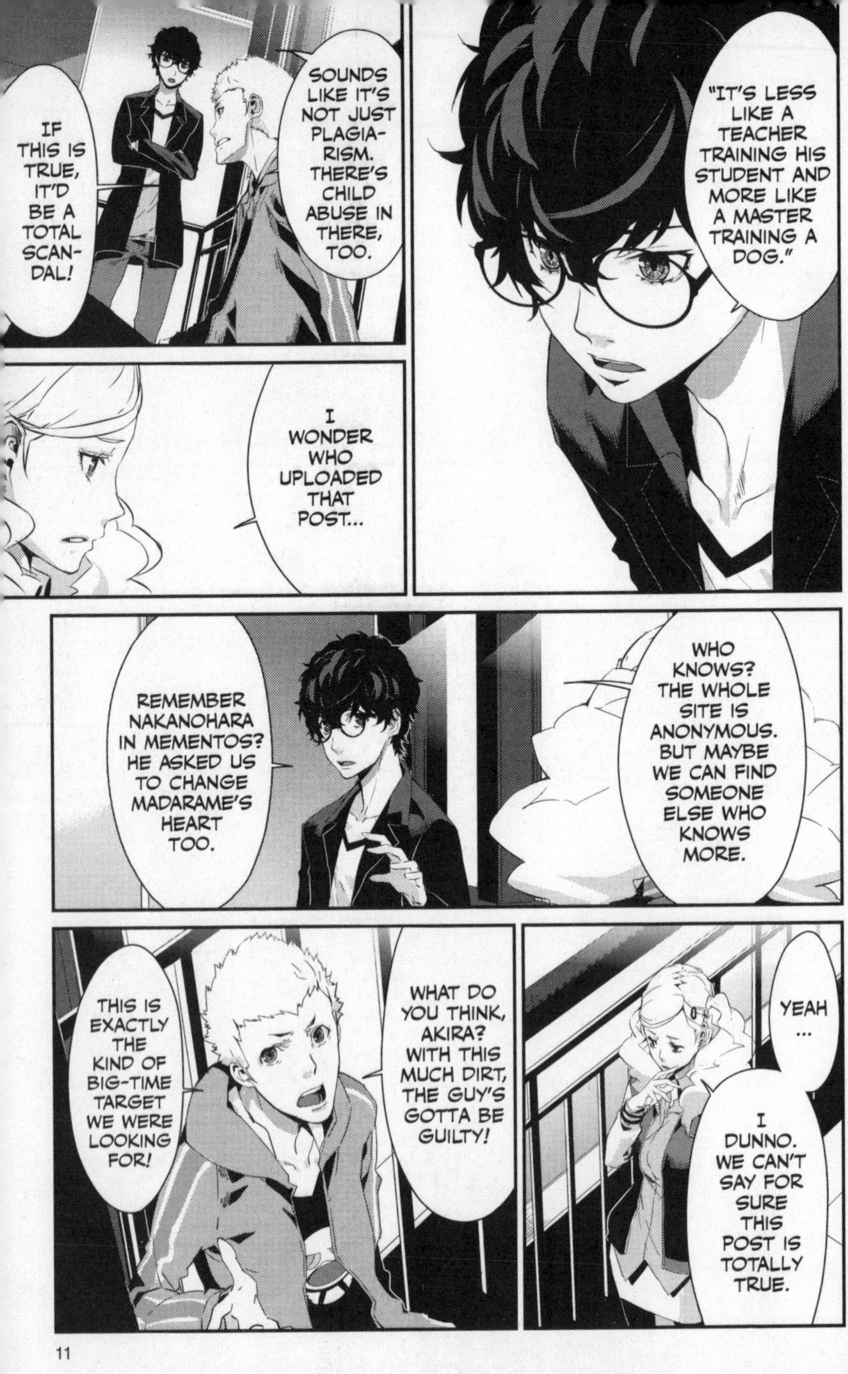
"IT'S LESS LIKE A TEACHER TRAINING HIS STUDENT AND MORE LIKE A MASTER TRAINING A DOG."
SOUNDS LIKE IT'S NOT JUST PLAGIA-RISM. THERE'S CHILD ABUSE IN THERE, TOO.
IF THIS IS TRUE, IT'D BE A TOTAL SCAN-DAL!
I WONDER WHO UPLOADED THAT POST...
WHO KNOWS? THE WHOLE SITE IS ANONYMOUS. BUT MAYBE WE CAN FIND SOMEONE ELSE WHO KNOWS MORE.
REMEMBER NAKANOHARA IN MEMENTOS? HE ASKED US TO CHANGE MADARAME'S HEART TOO.
YEAH...
I DUNNO. WE CAN'T SAY FOR SURE THIS POST IS TOTALLY TRUE.
WHAT DO YOU THINK, AKIRA? WITH THIS MUCH DIRT, THE GUY'S GOTTA BE GUILTY!
THIS IS EXACTLY THE KIND OF BIG-TIME TARGET WE WERE LOOKING FOR!

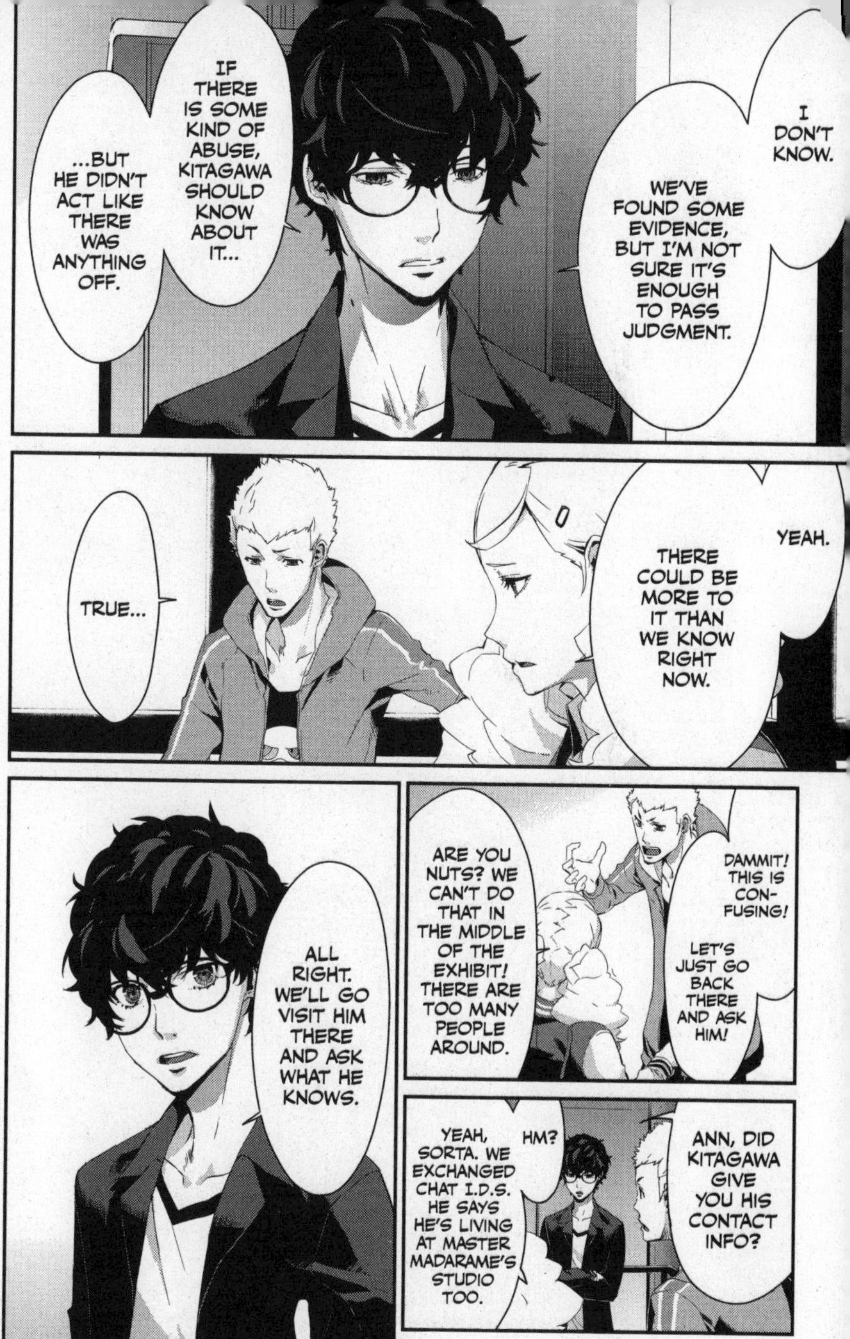
I DON'T KNOW.
WE'VE FOUND SOME EVIDENCE, BUT I'M NOT SURE IT'S ENOUGH TO PASS JUDGMENT.
IF THERE IS SOME KIND OF ABUSE, KITAGAWA SHOULD KNOW ABOUT IT...
...BUT HE DIDN'T ACT LIKE THERE WAS ANYTHING OFF.
YEAH.
THERE COULD BE MORE TO IT THAN WE KNOW RIGHT NOW.
TRUE...
DAMMIT! THIS IS CON-FUSING!
LET'S JUST GO BACK THERE AND ASK HIM!
ARE YOU NUTS? WE CAN'T DO THAT IN THE MIDDLE OF THE EXHIBIT! THERE ARE TOO MANY PEOPLE AROUND.
ANN, DID KITAGAWA GIVE YOU HIS CONTACT INFO?
HM?
YEAH, SORTA. WE EXCHANGED CHAT I.D.S. HE SAYS HE'S LIVING AT MASTER MADARAME'S STUDIO TOO.
ALL RIGHT. WE'LL GO VISIT HIM THERE AND ASK WHAT HE KNOWS.

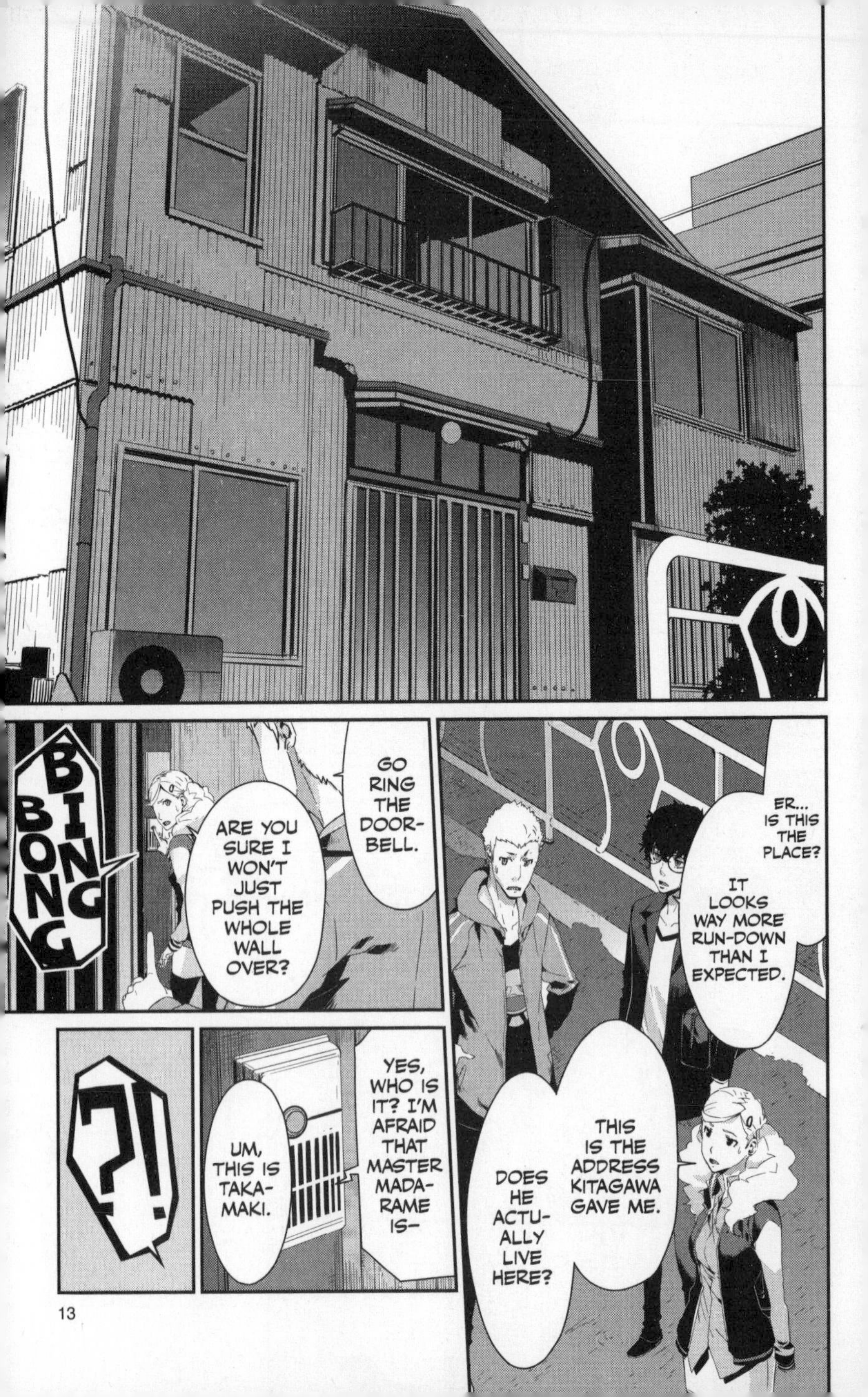
ER... IS THIS THE PLACE?
IT LOOKS WAY MORE RUN-DOWN THAN I EXPECTED.
THIS IS THE ADDRESS KITAGAWA GAVE ME.
DOES HE ACTUALLY LIVE HERE?
GO RING THE DOORBELL.
ARE YOU SURE I WON'T JUST PUSH THE WHOLE WALL OVER?
BING BONG
YES, WHO IS IT? I'M AFRAID THAT MASTER MADARAME IS—
UM, THIS IS TAKAMAKI.
?!

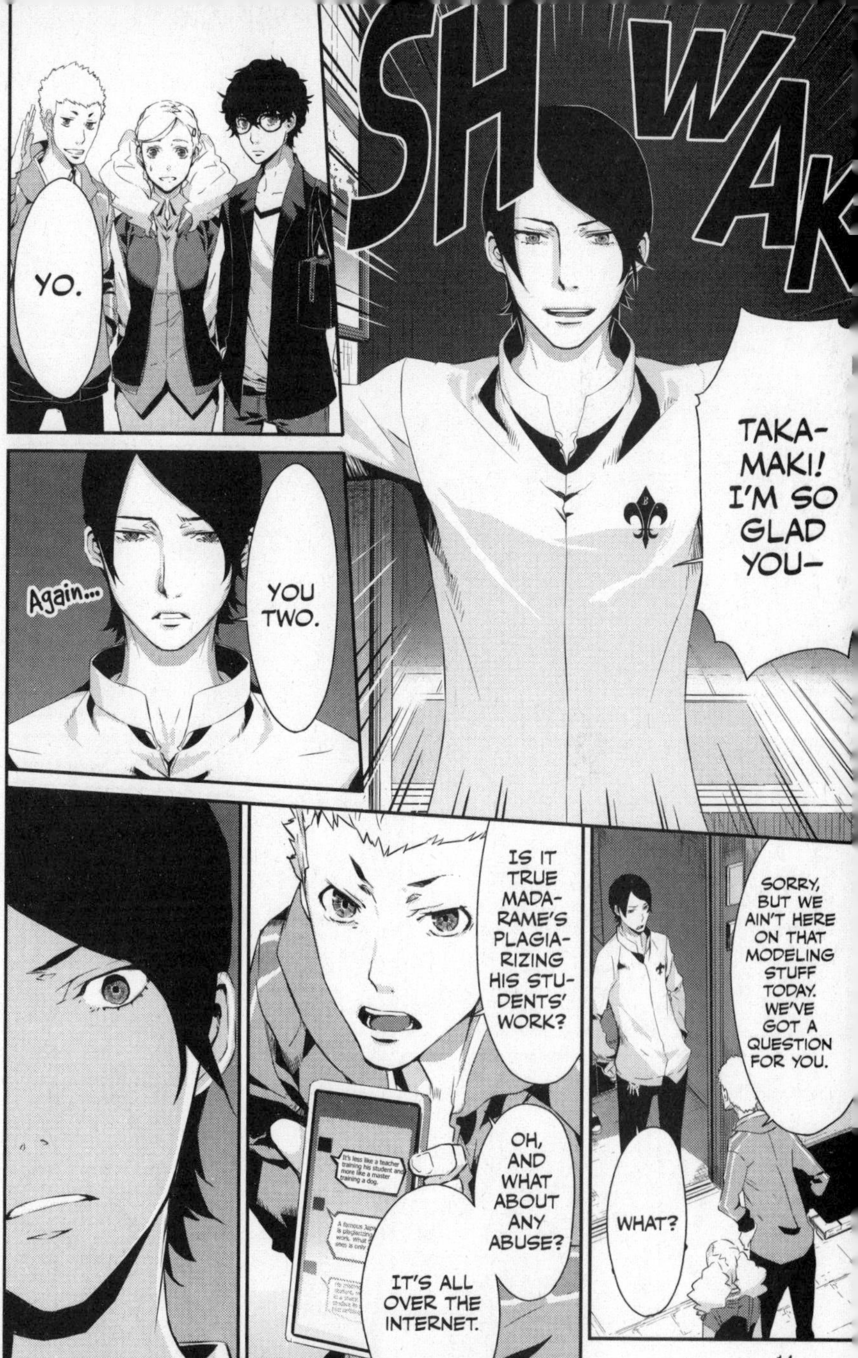
SHWAK
TAKA-MAKI! I'M SO GLAD YOU—
YO.
Again...
YOU TWO.
SORRY, BUT WE AIN'T HERE ON THAT MODELING STUFF TODAY. WE'VE GOT A QUESTION FOR YOU.
WHAT?
IS IT TRUE MADA-RAME'S PLAGIA-RIZING HIS STU-DENTS' WORK?
OH, AND WHAT ABOUT ANY ABUSE?
IT'S ALL OVER THE INTERNET.

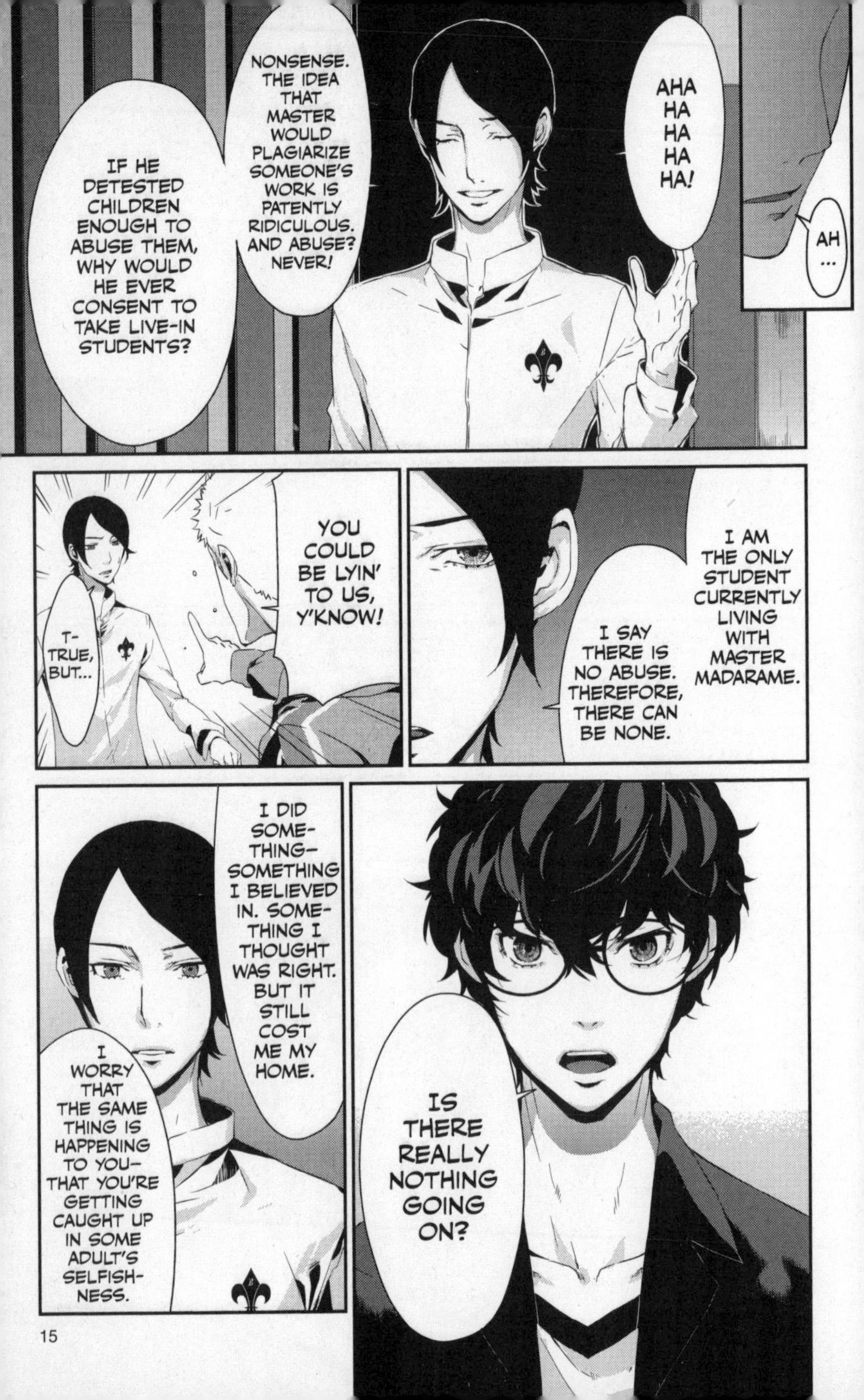
AH ...
AHA HA HA HA HA!
NONSENSE. THE IDEA THAT MASTER WOULD PLAGIARIZE SOMEONE'S WORK IS PATENTLY RIDICULOUS. AND ABUSE? NEVER!
IF HE DETESTED CHILDREN ENOUGH TO ABUSE THEM, WHY WOULD HE EVER CONSENT TO TAKE LIVE-IN STUDENTS?
I AM THE ONLY STUDENT CURRENTLY LIVING WITH MASTER MADARAME.
I SAY THERE IS NO ABUSE. THEREFORE, THERE CAN BE NONE.
YOU COULD BE LYIN' TO US, Y'KNOW!
T-TRUE, BUT...
IS THERE REALLY NOTHING GOING ON?
I DID SOME-THING—SOMETHING I BELIEVED IN. SOME-THING I THOUGHT WAS RIGHT. BUT IT STILL COST ME MY HOME.
I WORRY THAT THE SAME THING IS HAPPENING TO YOU—THAT YOU'RE GETTING CAUGHT UP IN SOME ADULT'S SELFISH-NESS.

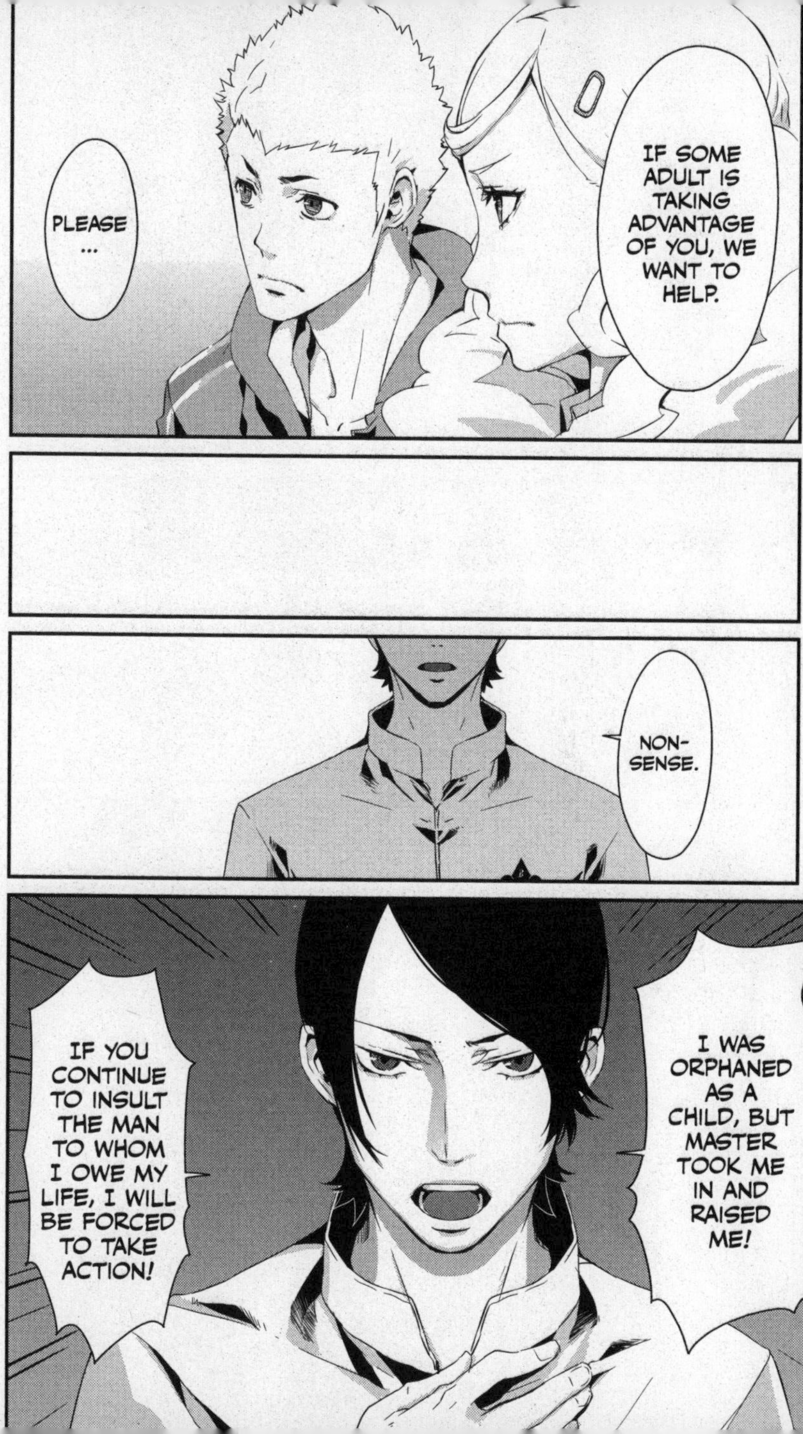
IF SOME ADULT IS TAKING ADVANTAGE OF YOU, WE WANT TO HELP.
PLEASE ...
NON-SENSE.
I WAS ORPHANED AS A CHILD, BUT MASTER TOOK ME IN AND RAISED ME!
IF YOU CONTINUE TO INSULT THE MAN TO WHOM I OWE MY LIFE, I WILL BE FORCED TO TAKE ACTION!

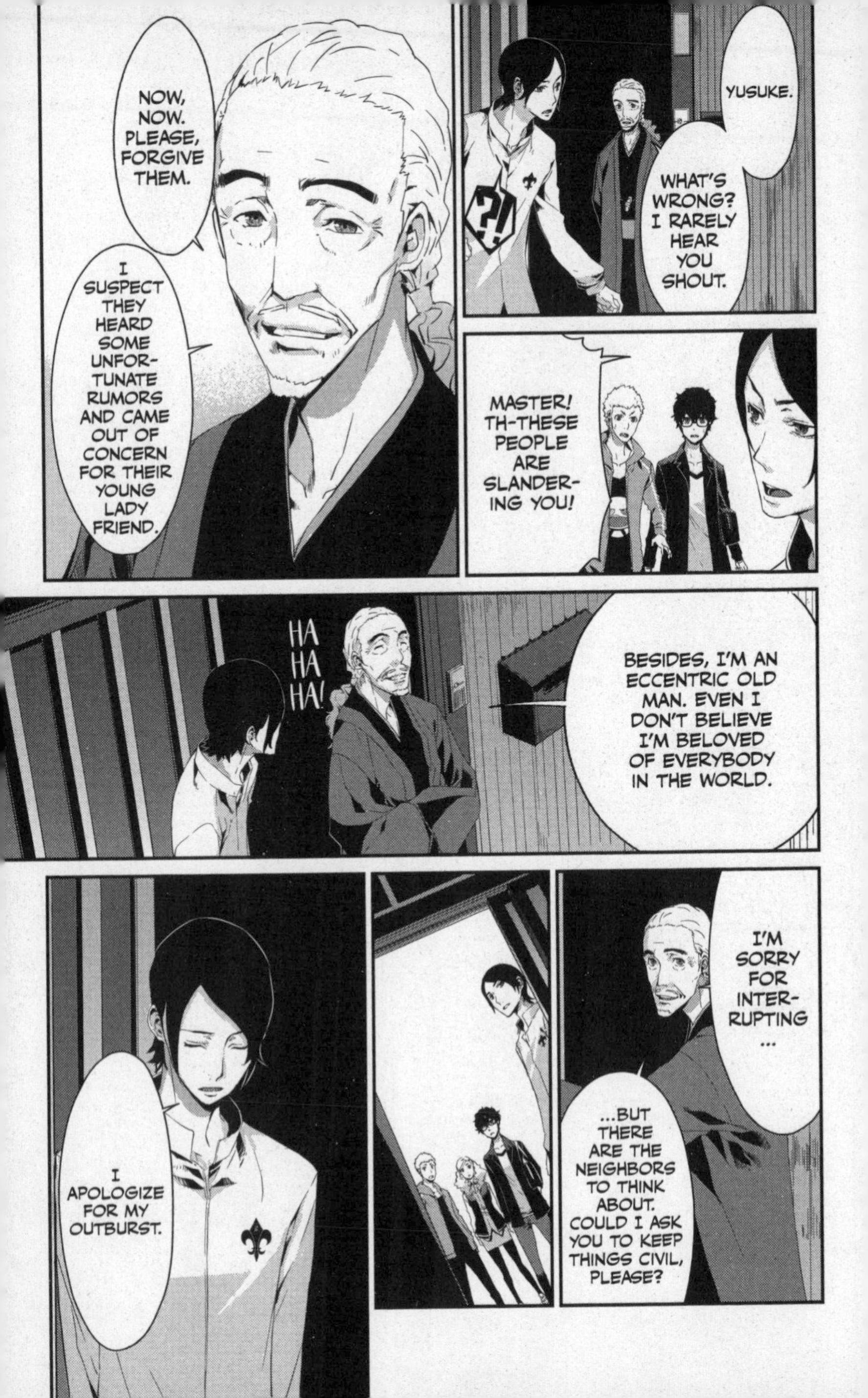
YUSUKE.
WHAT'S WRONG? I RARELY HEAR YOU SHOUT.
MASTER! TH-THESE PEOPLE ARE SLANDERING YOU!
NOW, NOW. PLEASE, FORGIVE THEM.
I SUSPECT THEY HEARD SOME UNFORTUNATE RUMORS AND CAME OUT OF CONCERN FOR THEIR YOUNG LADY FRIEND.
BESIDES, I'M AN ECCENTRIC OLD MAN. EVEN I DON'T BELIEVE I'M BELOVED OF EVERYBODY IN THE WORLD.
HA HA HA!
I'M SORRY FOR INTERRUPTING...
...BUT THERE ARE THE NEIGHBORS TO THINK ABOUT. COULD I ASK YOU TO KEEP THINGS CIVIL, PLEASE?
I APOLOGIZE FOR MY OUTBURST.

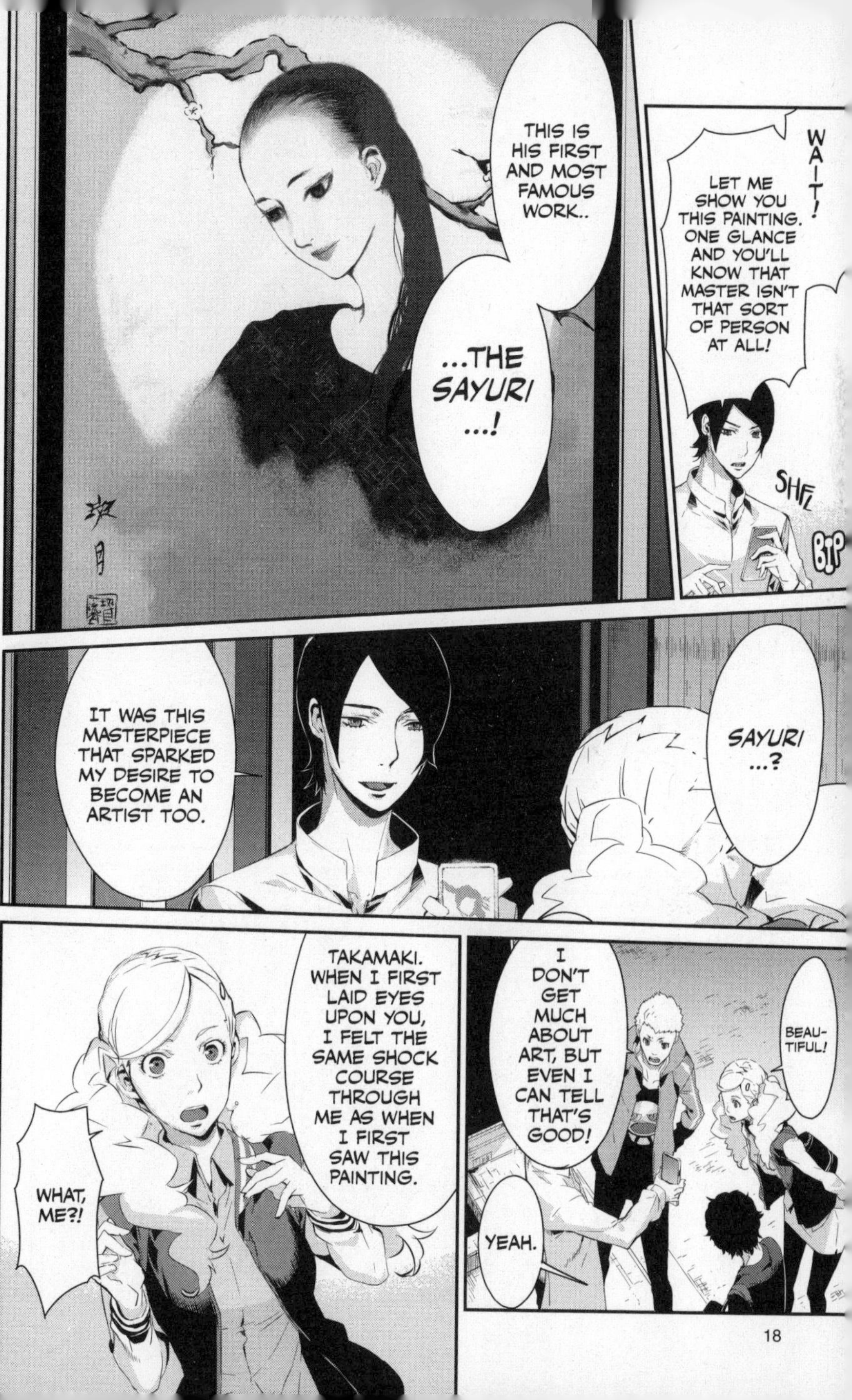
WAIT!
LET ME SHOW YOU THIS PAINTING. ONE GLANCE AND YOU'LL KNOW THAT MASTER ISN'T THAT SORT OF PERSON AT ALL!
SHFL
BIP
THIS IS HIS FIRST AND MOST FAMOUS WORK..
...THE SAYURI ...!
SAYURI ...?
IT WAS THIS MASTERPIECE THAT SPARKED MY DESIRE TO BECOME AN ARTIST TOO.
BEAU-TIFUL!
I DON'T GET MUCH ABOUT ART, BUT EVEN I CAN TELL THAT'S GOOD!
YEAH.
TAKAMAKI. WHEN I FIRST LAID EYES UPON YOU, I FELT THE SAME SHOCK COURSE THROUGH ME AS WHEN I FIRST SAW THIS PAINTING.
WHAT, ME?!

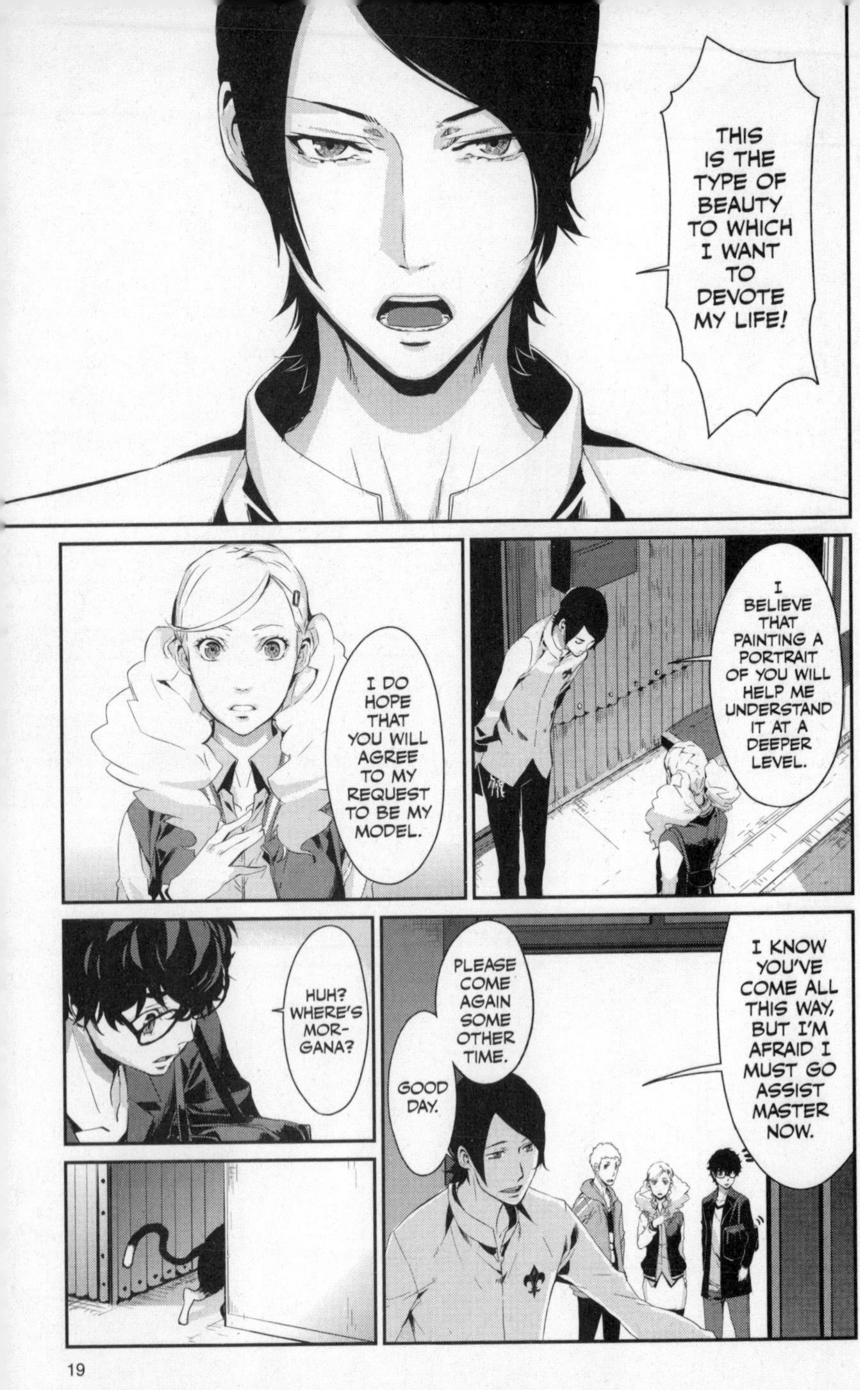
THIS IS THE TYPE OF BEAUTY TO WHICH I WANT TO DEVOTE MY LIFE!
I BELIEVE THAT PAINTING A PORTRAIT OF YOU WILL HELP ME UNDERSTAND IT AT A DEEPER LEVEL.
I DO HOPE THAT YOU WILL AGREE TO MY REQUEST TO BE MY MODEL.
I KNOW YOU'VE COME ALL THIS WAY, BUT I'M AFRAID I MUST GO ASSIST MASTER NOW.
PLEASE COME AGAIN SOME OTHER TIME.
GOOD DAY.
HUH? WHERE'S MOR-GANA?

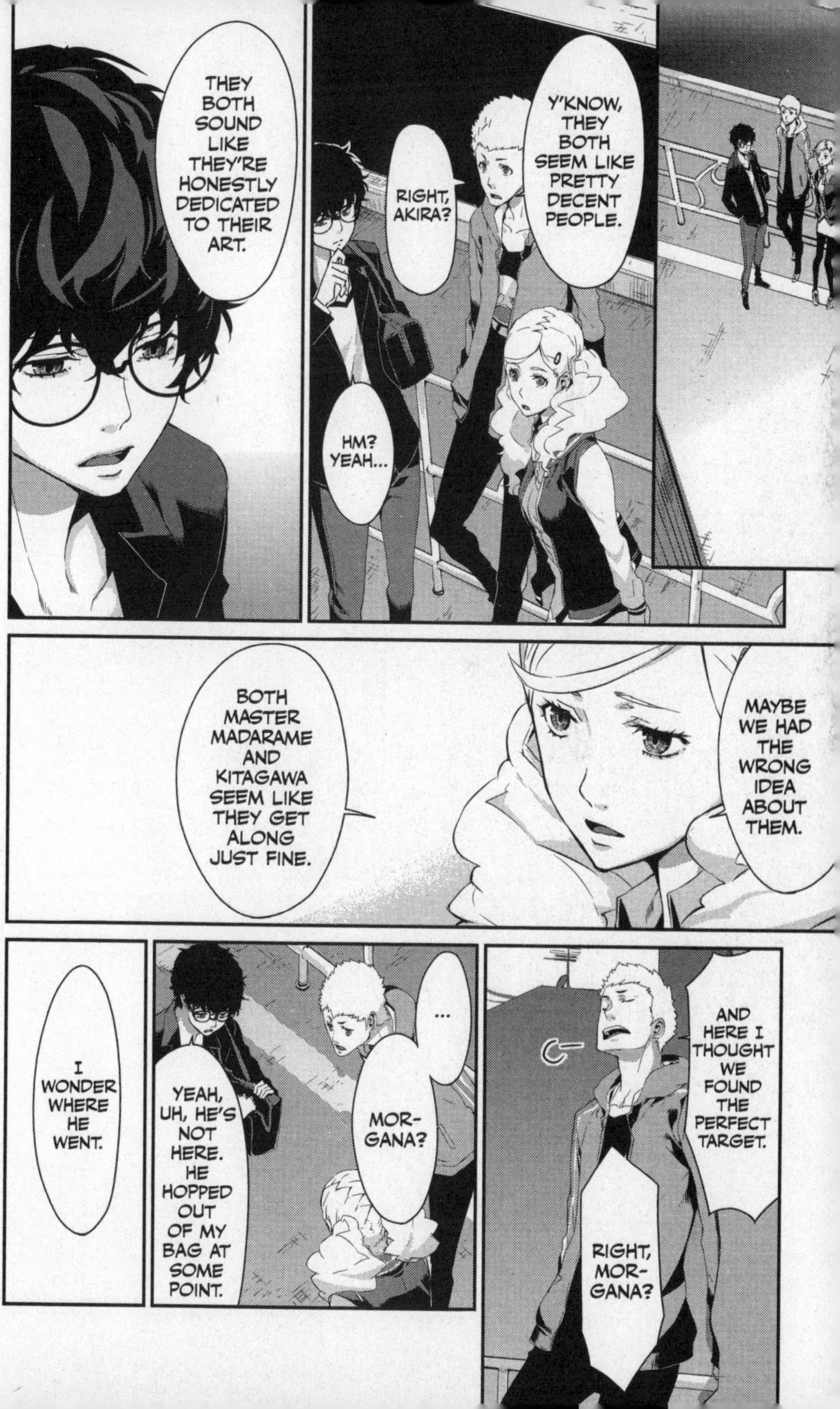
Y'KNOW, THEY BOTH SEEM LIKE PRETTY DECENT PEOPLE.
RIGHT, AKIRA?
HM? YEAH...
THEY BOTH SOUND LIKE THEY'RE HONESTLY DEDICATED TO THEIR ART.
MAYBE WE HAD THE WRONG IDEA ABOUT THEM.
BOTH MASTER MADARAME AND KITAGAWA SEEM LIKE THEY GET ALONG JUST FINE.
AND HERE I THOUGHT WE FOUND THE PERFECT TARGET.
RIGHT, MOR-GANA?
...
MOR-GANA?
YEAH, UH, HE'S NOT HERE. HE HOPPED OUT OF MY BAG AT SOME POINT.
I WONDER WHERE HE WENT.

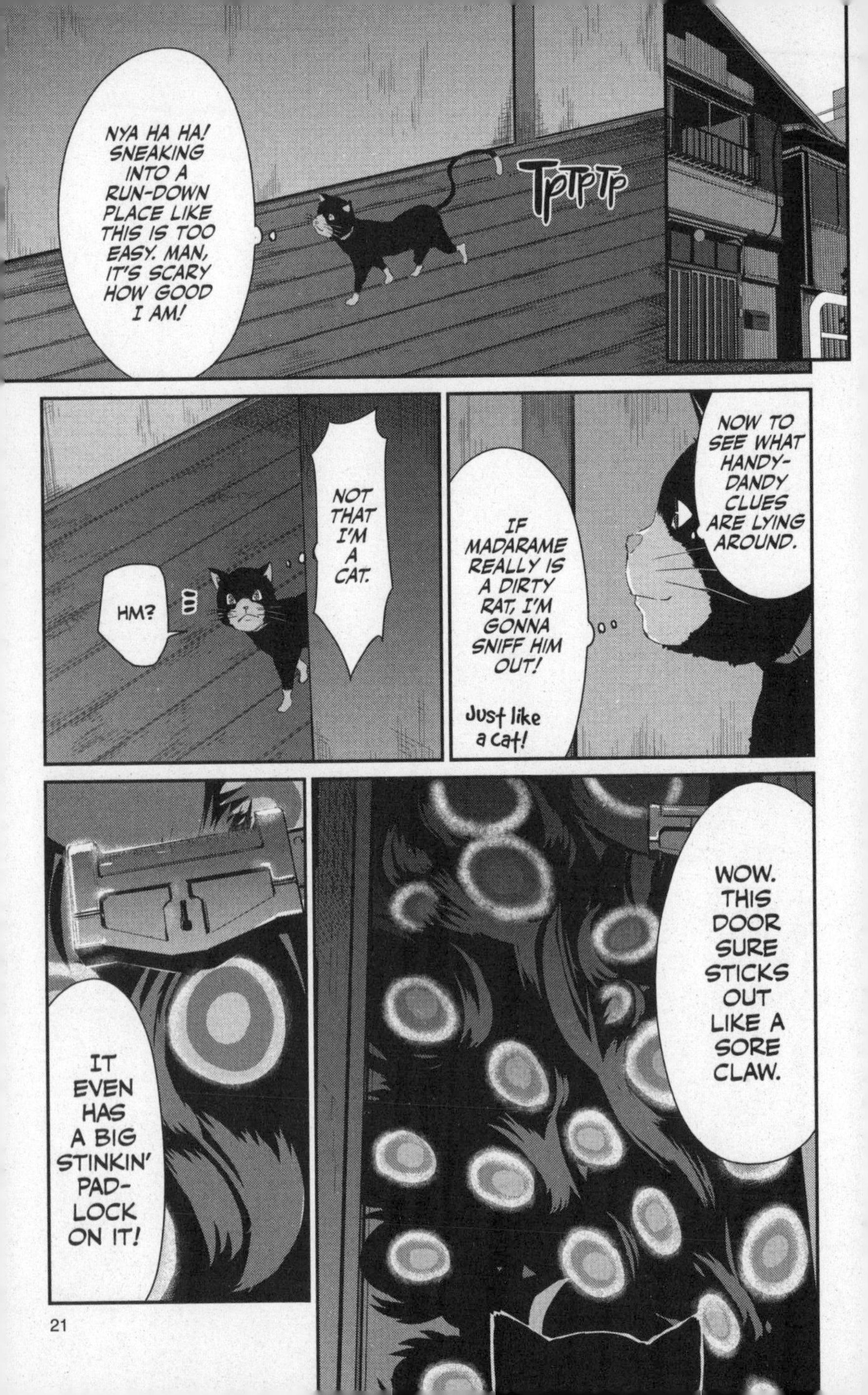
NYA HA HA! SNEAKING INTO A RUN-DOWN PLACE LIKE THIS IS TOO EASY. MAN, IT'S SCARY HOW GOOD I AM!
TPTPTP
NOW TO SEE WHAT HANDY-DANDY CLUES ARE LYING AROUND.
IF MADARAME REALLY IS A DIRTY RAT, I'M GONNA SNIFF HIM OUT!
Just like a cat!
NOT THAT I'M A CAT.
HM?
WOW. THIS DOOR SURE STICKS OUT LIKE A SORE CLAW.
IT EVEN HAS A BIG STINKIN' PAD-LOCK ON IT!

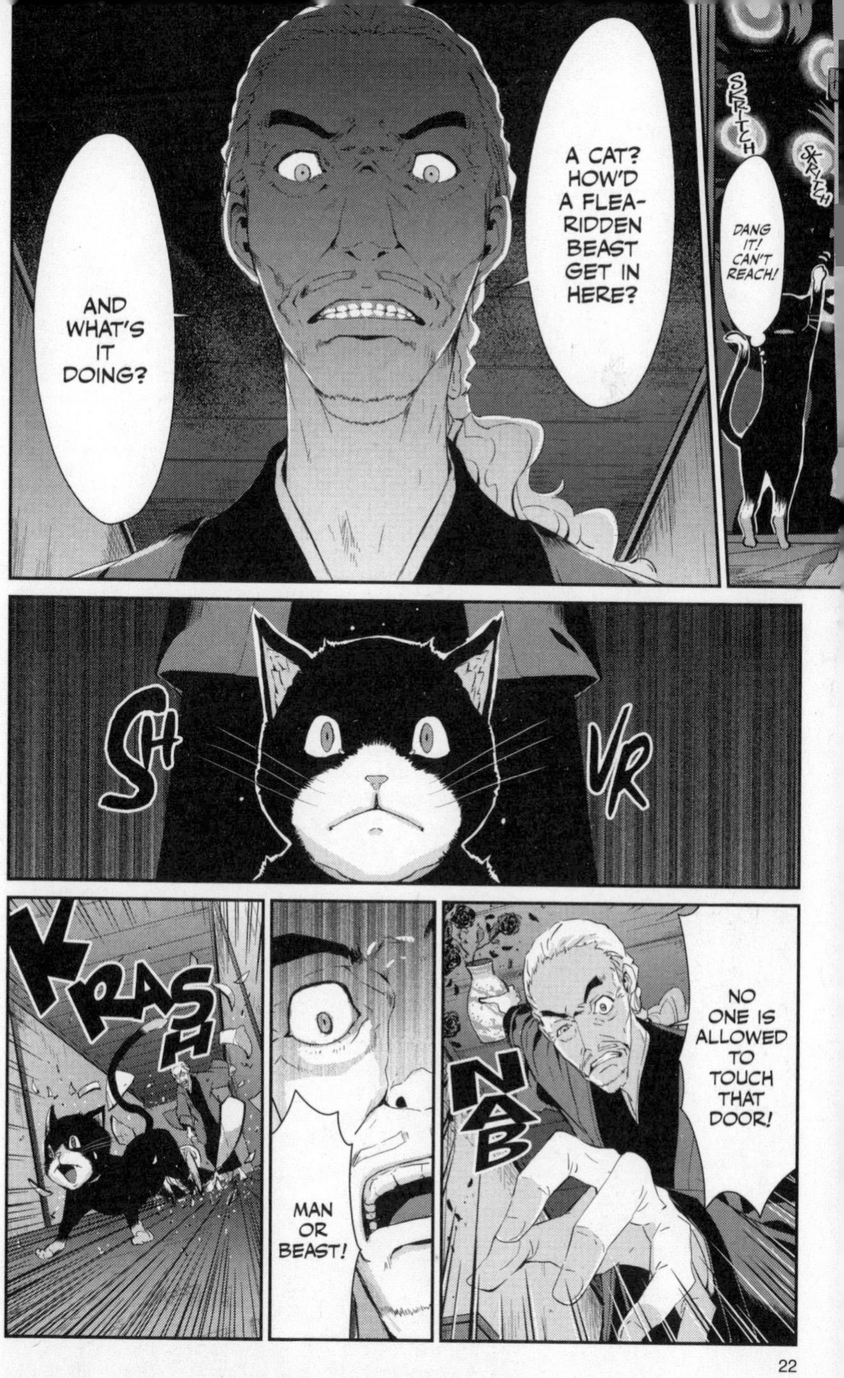
SKRITCH
SKRITCH
DANG IT! CAN'T REACH!
A CAT? HOW'D A FLEA-RIDDEN BEAST GET IN HERE?
AND WHAT'S IT DOING?
SHVR
NO ONE IS ALLOWED TO TOUCH THAT DOOR!
NAB
MAN OR BEAST!
KRASH

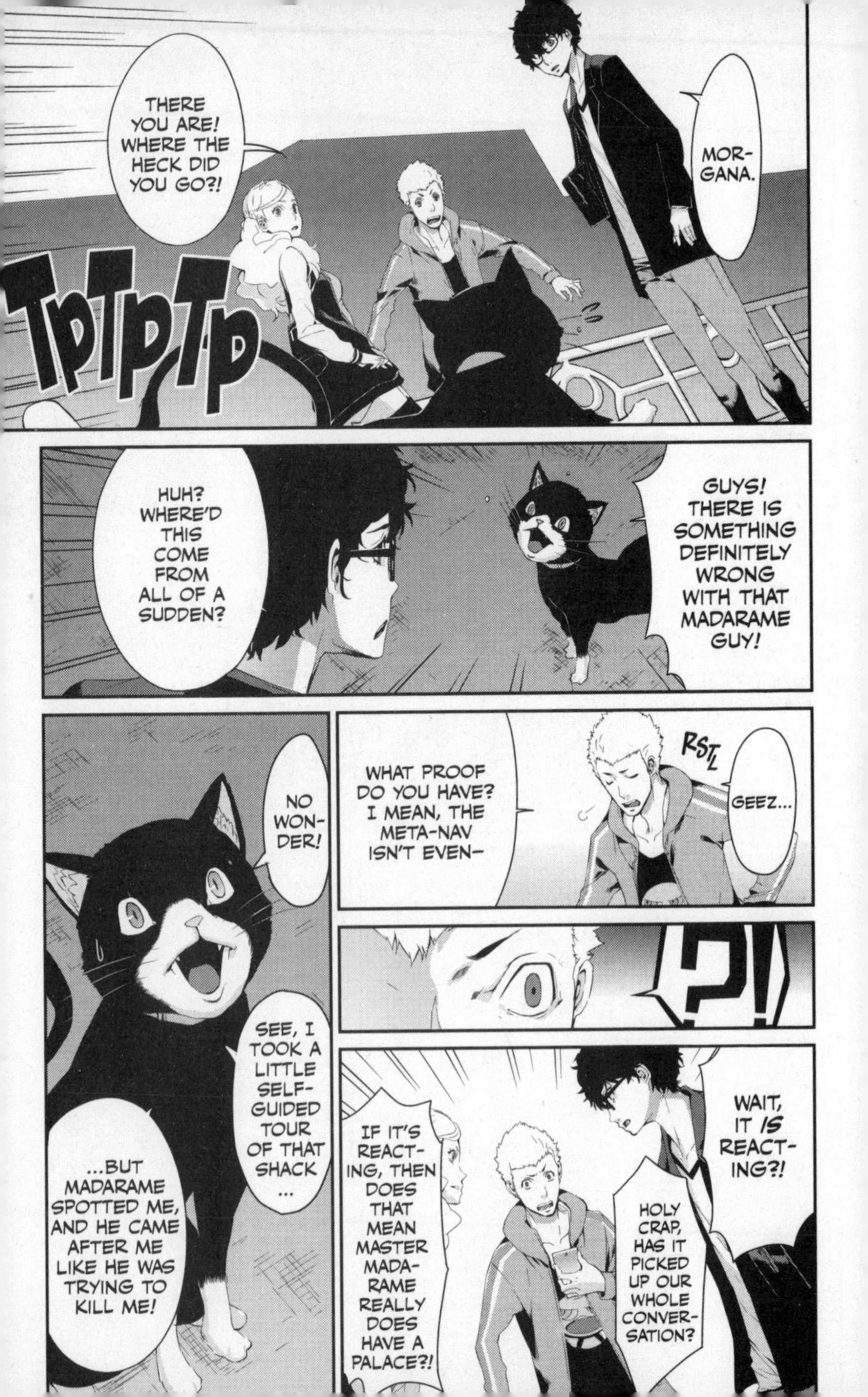
MORGANA.
THERE YOU ARE! WHERE THE HECK DID YOU GO?!
TpTpTpTp
GUYS! THERE IS SOMETHING DEFINITELY WRONG WITH THAT MADARAME GUY!
HUH? WHERE'D THIS COME FROM ALL OF A SUDDEN?
RSTL
GEEZ...
WHAT PROOF DO YOU HAVE? I MEAN, THE META-NAV ISN'T EVEN—
?!
WAIT, IT *IS* REACTING?!
HOLY CRAP, HAS IT PICKED UP OUR WHOLE CONVERSATION?
IF IT'S REACTING, THEN DOES THAT MEAN MASTER MADARAME REALLY DOES HAVE A PALACE?!
NO WONDER!
SEE, I TOOK A LITTLE SELF-GUIDED TOUR OF THAT SHACK...
...BUT MADARAME SPOTTED ME, AND HE CAME AFTER ME LIKE HE WAS TRYING TO KILL ME!

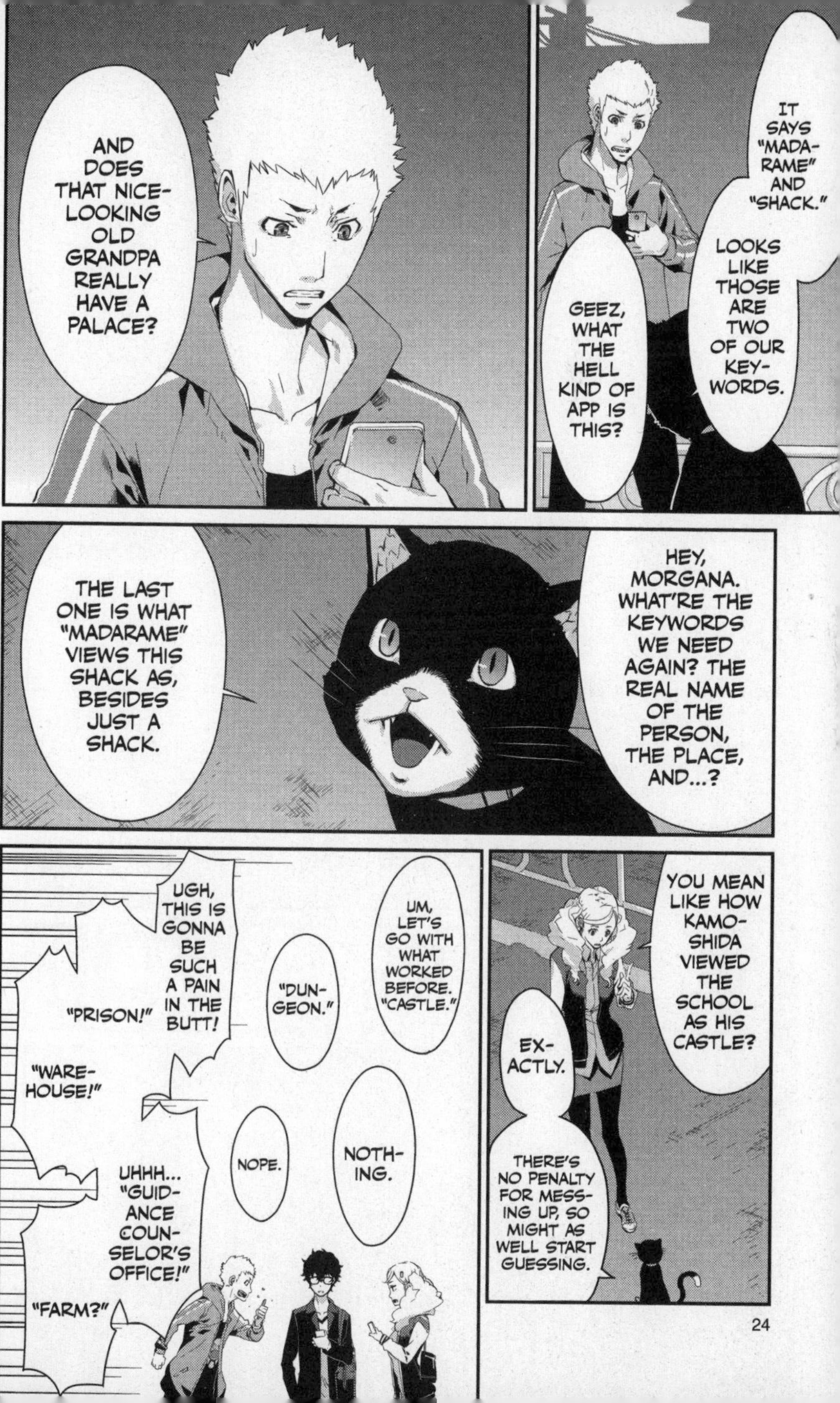
IT SAYS "MADARAME" AND "SHACK."
LOOKS LIKE THOSE ARE TWO OF OUR KEYWORDS.
GEEZ, WHAT THE HELL KIND OF APP IS THIS?
AND DOES THAT NICE-LOOKING OLD GRANDPA REALLY HAVE A PALACE?
HEY, MORGANA. WHAT'RE THE KEYWORDS WE NEED AGAIN? THE REAL NAME OF THE PERSON, THE PLACE, AND...?
THE LAST ONE IS WHAT "MADARAME" VIEWS THIS SHACK AS, BESIDES JUST A SHACK.
YOU MEAN LIKE HOW KAMOSHIDA VIEWED THE SCHOOL AS HIS CASTLE?
EXACTLY.
THERE'S NO PENALTY FOR MESSING UP, SO MIGHT AS WELL START GUESSING.
UM, LET'S GO WITH WHAT WORKED BEFORE. "CASTLE."
"DUNGEON."
UGH, THIS IS GONNA BE SUCH A PAIN IN THE BUTT!
"PRISON!"
"WAREHOUSE!"
NOTHING.
NOPE.
UHHH... "GUIDANCE COUNSELOR'S OFFICE!"
"FARM?"

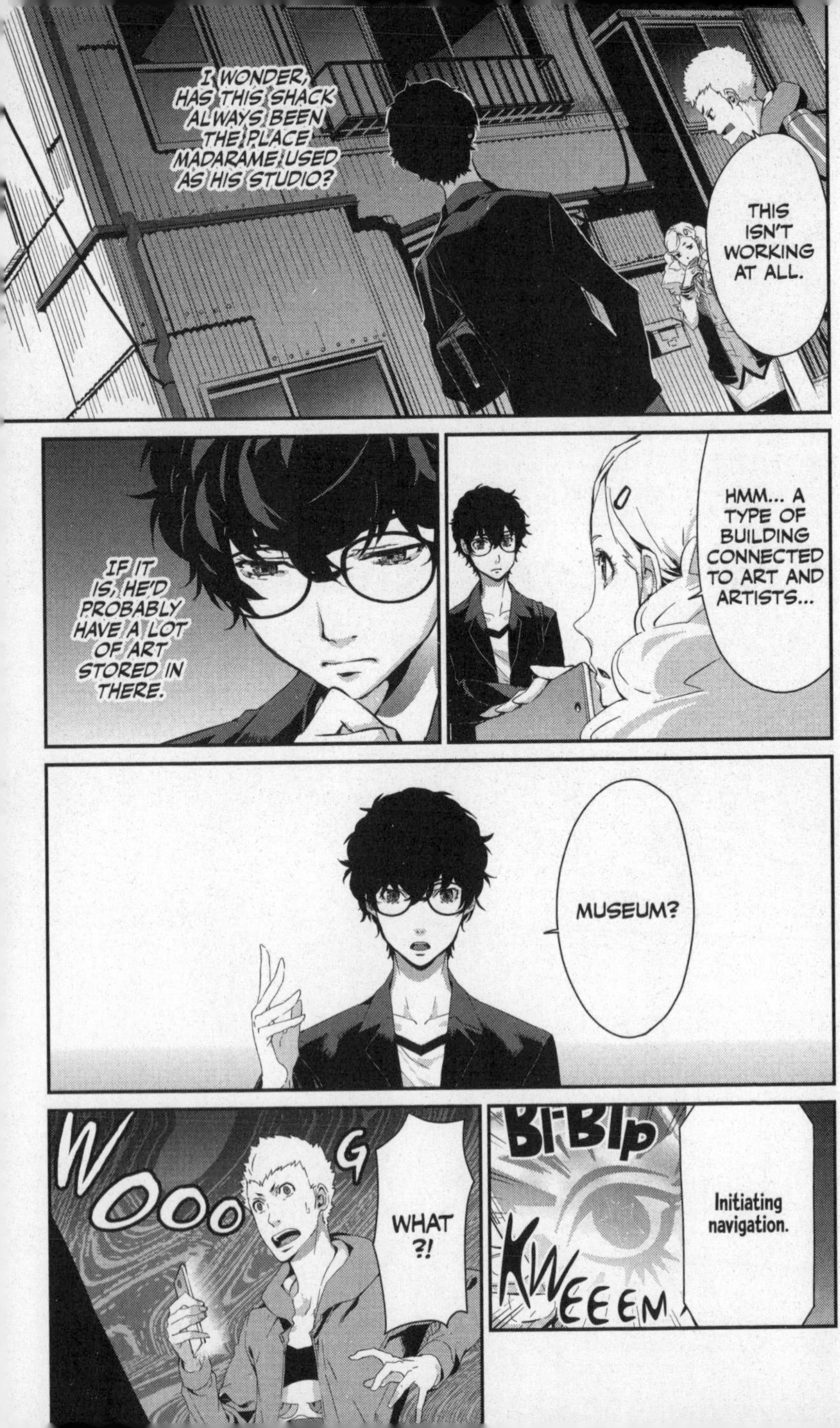

THIS ISN'T WORKING AT ALL.
I WONDER, HAS THIS SHACK ALWAYS BEEN THE PLACE MADARAME USED AS HIS STUDIO?
HMM... A TYPE OF BUILDING CONNECTED TO ART AND ARTISTS...
IF IT IS, HE'D PROBABLY HAVE A LOT OF ART STORED IN THERE.
MUSEUM?
BI-BIP
Initiating navigation.
KWEEEM
WOOOG
WHAT?!

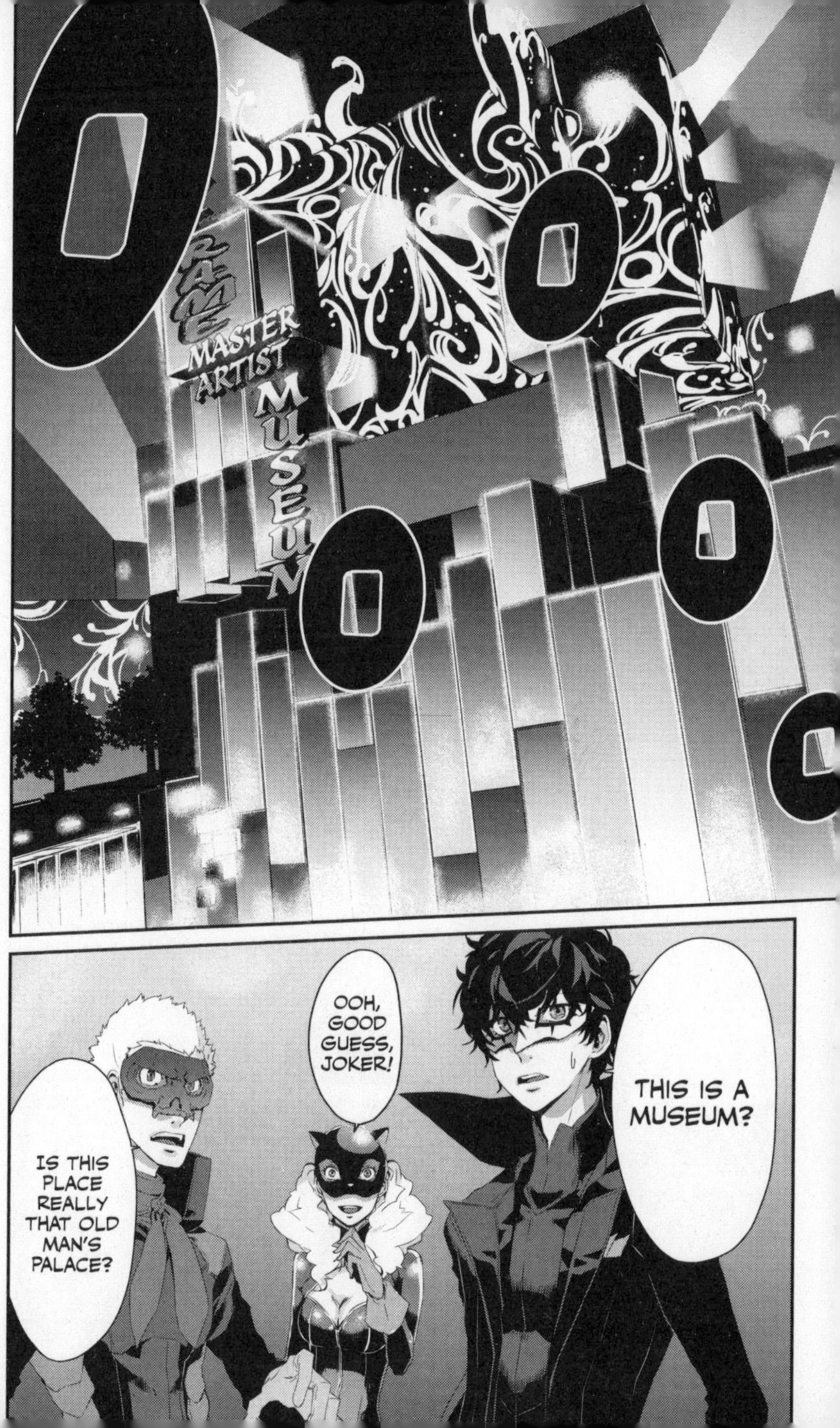
MASTER ARTIST MUSEUM
THIS IS A MUSEUM?
OOH, GOOD GUESS, JOKER!
IS THIS PLACE REALLY THAT OLD MAN'S PALACE?

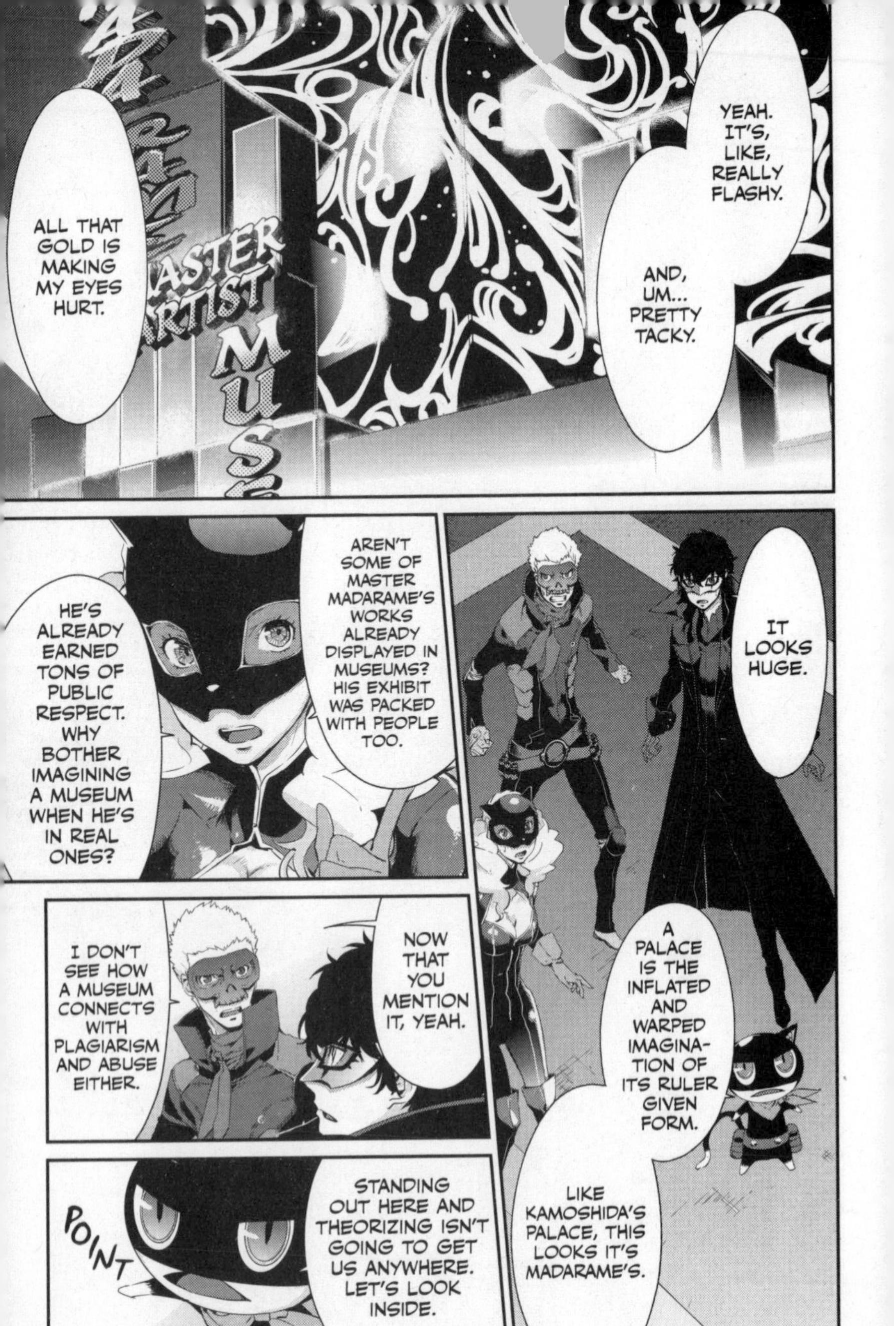
YEAH. IT'S, LIKE, REALLY FLASHY.
AND, UM... PRETTY TACKY.
ALL THAT GOLD IS MAKING MY EYES HURT.
IT LOOKS HUGE.
A PALACE IS THE INFLATED AND WARPED IMAGINATION OF ITS RULER GIVEN FORM.
LIKE KAMOSHIDA'S PALACE, THIS LOOKS IT'S MADARAME'S.
AREN'T SOME OF MASTER MADARAME'S WORKS ALREADY DISPLAYED IN MUSEUMS? HIS EXHIBIT WAS PACKED WITH PEOPLE TOO.
HE'S ALREADY EARNED TONS OF PUBLIC RESPECT. WHY BOTHER IMAGINING A MUSEUM WHEN HE'S IN REAL ONES?
NOW THAT YOU MENTION IT, YEAH.
I DON'T SEE HOW A MUSEUM CONNECTS WITH PLAGIARISM AND ABUSE EITHER.
STANDING OUT HERE AND THEORIZING ISN'T GOING TO GET US ANYWHERE. LET'S LOOK INSIDE.
POINT

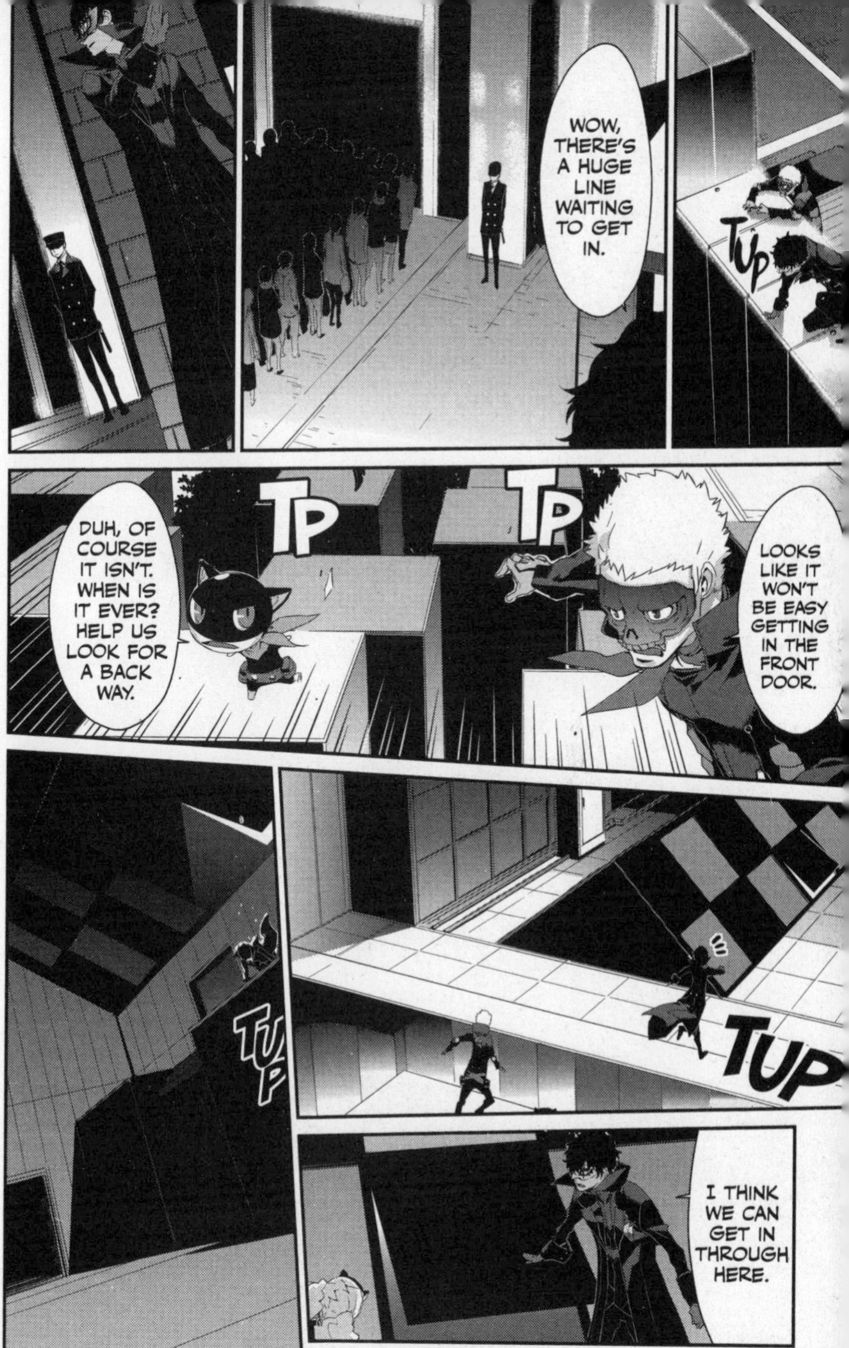
TUP
WOW, THERE'S A HUGE LINE WAITING TO GET IN.
LOOKS LIKE IT WON'T BE EASY GETTING IN THE FRONT DOOR.
TP
TP
DUH, OF COURSE IT ISN'T. WHEN IS IT EVER? HELP US LOOK FOR A BACK WAY.
TUP
I THINK WE CAN GET IN THROUGH HERE.
TUP

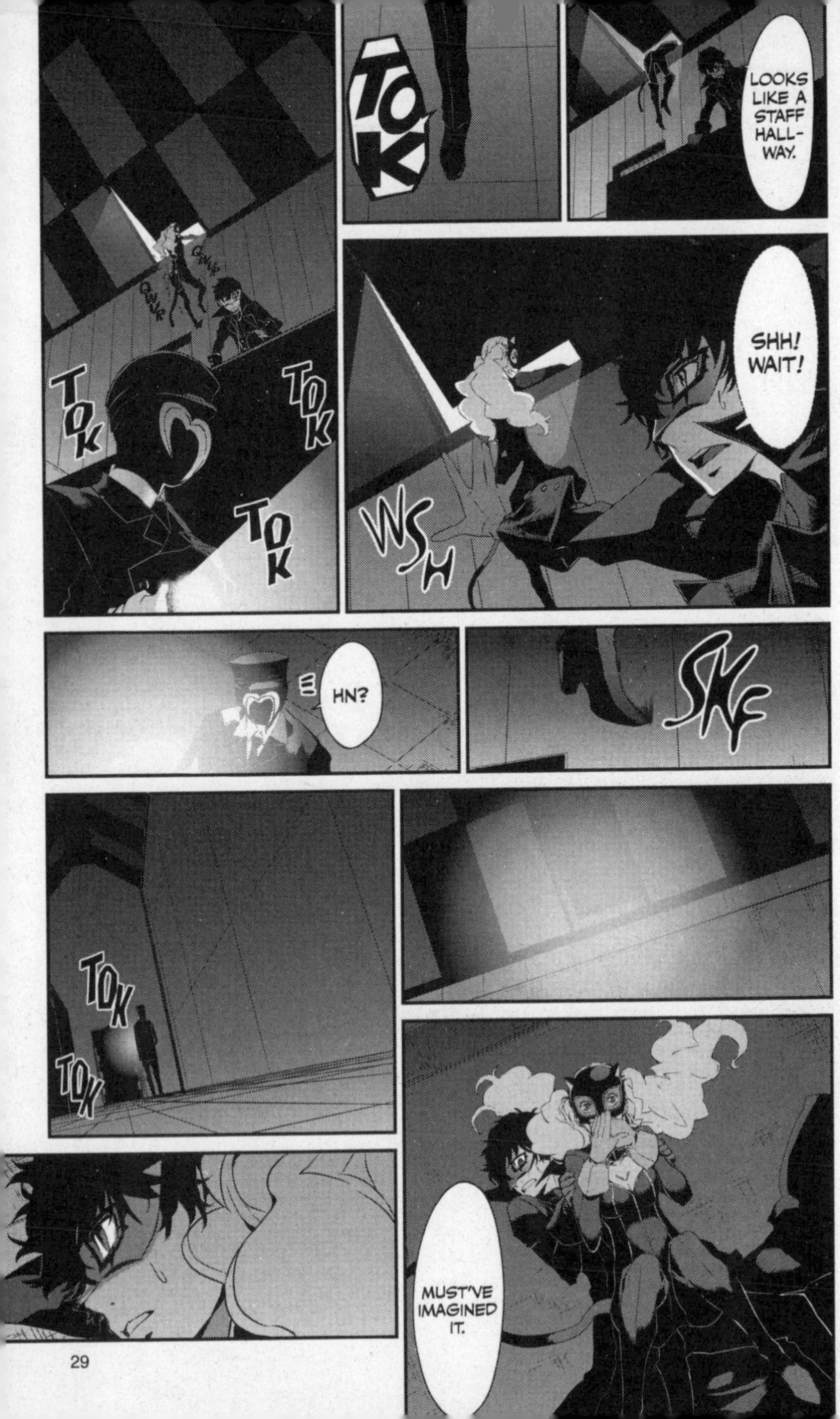
LOOKS LIKE A STAFF HALL-WAY.
TOK
SHH! WAIT!
WSH
TOK
TOK
TOK
SKF
HN?
TOK
TOK
MUST'VE IMAGINED IT.

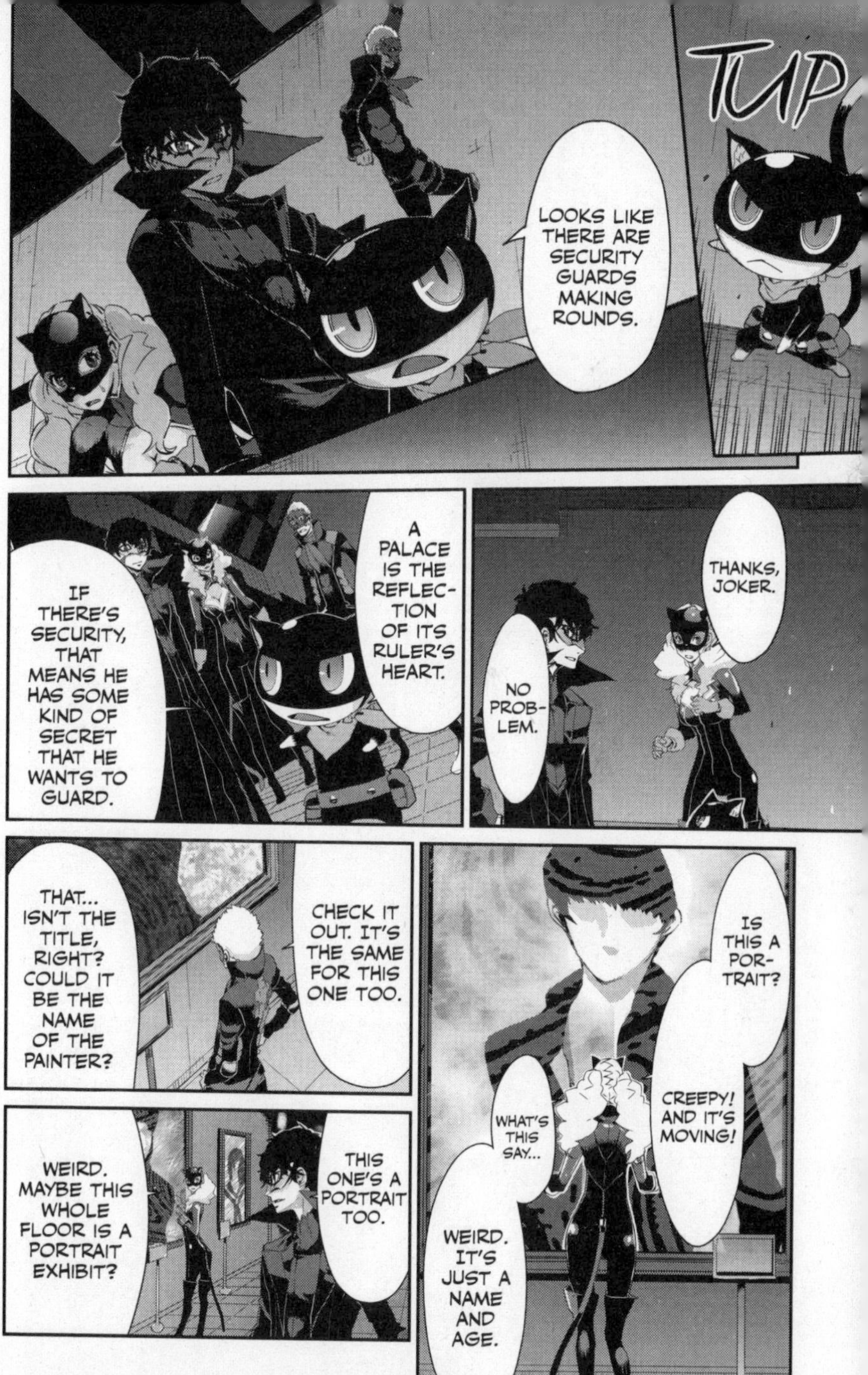
TUP
LOOKS LIKE THERE ARE SECURITY GUARDS MAKING ROUNDS.
THANKS, JOKER.
NO PROB-LEM.
A PALACE IS THE REFLEC-TION OF ITS RULER'S HEART.
IF THERE'S SECURITY, THAT MEANS HE HAS SOME KIND OF SECRET THAT HE WANTS TO GUARD.
IS THIS A POR-TRAIT?
CREEPY! AND IT'S MOVING!
WHAT'S THIS SAY...
WEIRD. IT'S JUST A NAME AND AGE.
CHECK IT OUT. IT'S THE SAME FOR THIS ONE TOO.
THAT... ISN'T THE TITLE, RIGHT? COULD IT BE THE NAME OF THE PAINTER?
THIS ONE'S A PORTRAIT TOO.
WEIRD. MAYBE THIS WHOLE FLOOR IS A PORTRAIT EXHIBIT?

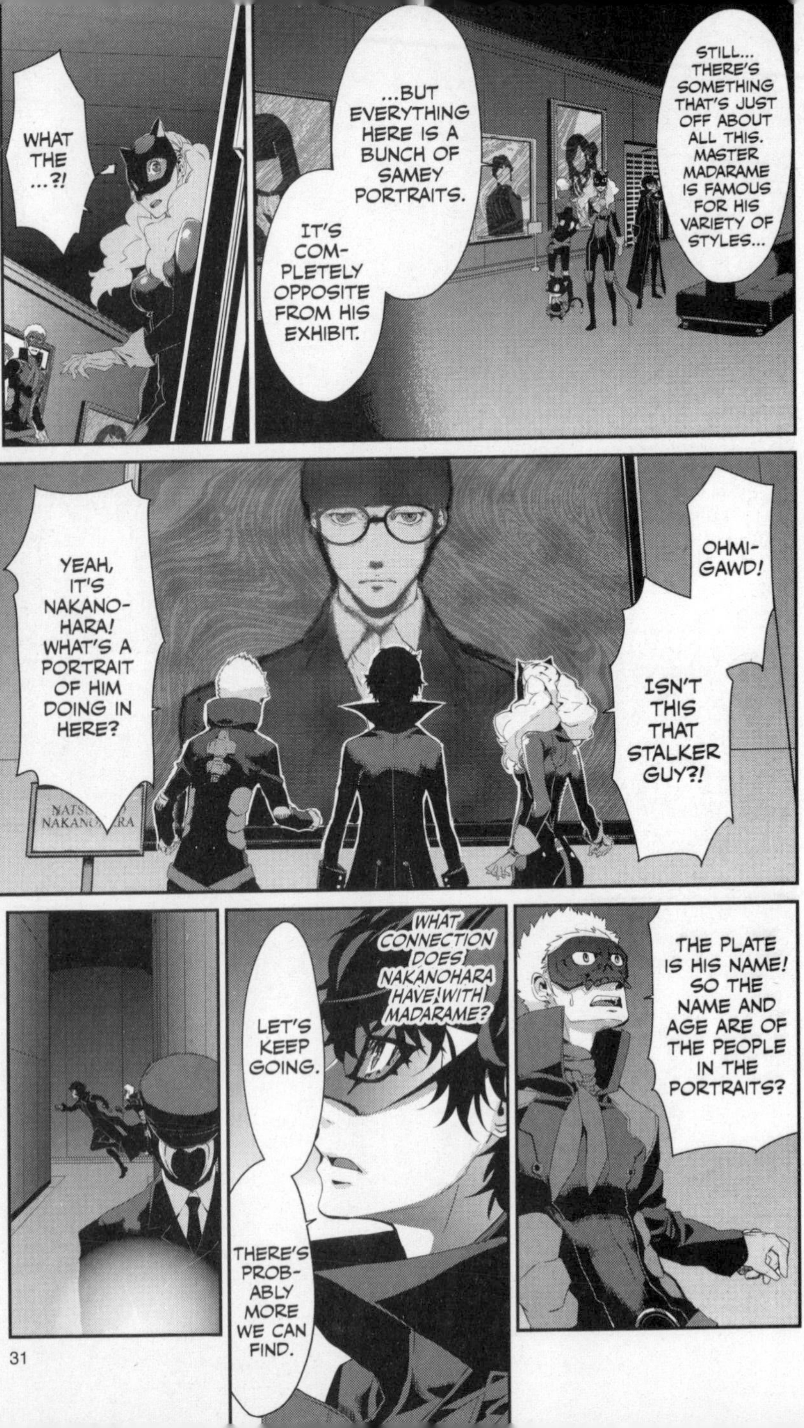

STILL... THERE'S SOMETHING THAT'S JUST OFF ABOUT ALL THIS. MASTER MADARAME IS FAMOUS FOR HIS VARIETY OF STYLES...
...BUT EVERYTHING HERE IS A BUNCH OF SAMEY PORTRAITS.
IT'S COM-PLETELY OPPOSITE FROM HIS EXHIBIT.
WHAT THE ...?!
OHMI-GAWD!
ISN'T THIS THAT STALKER GUY?!
YEAH, IT'S NAKANO-HARA! WHAT'S A PORTRAIT OF HIM DOING IN HERE?
THE PLATE IS HIS NAME! SO THE NAME AND AGE ARE OF THE PEOPLE IN THE PORTRAITS?
WHAT CONNECTION DOES NAKANOHARA HAVE WITH MADARAME?
LET'S KEEP GOING.
THERE'S PROB-ABLY MORE WE CAN FIND.

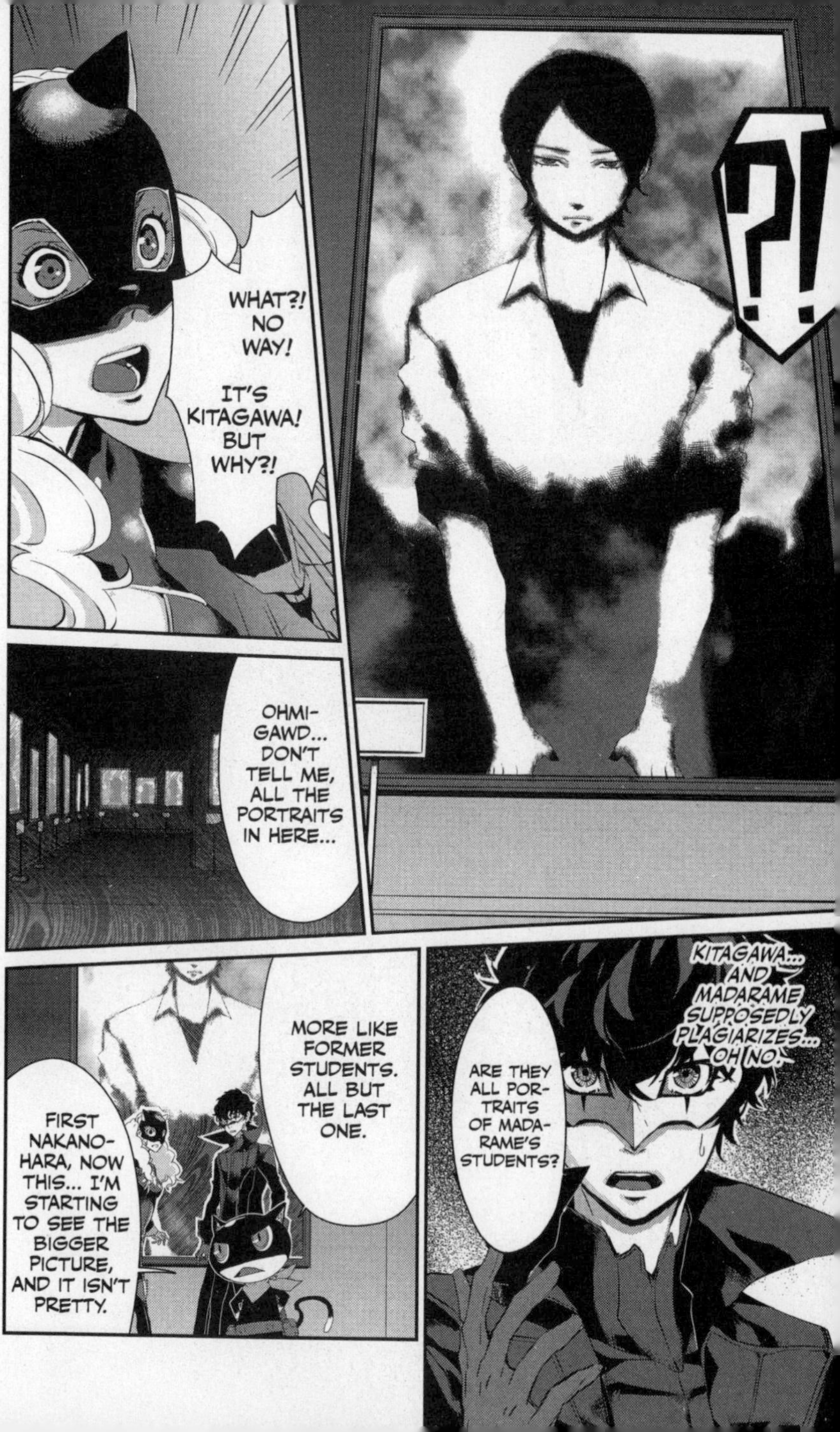
?!
WHAT?! NO WAY!
IT'S KITAGAWA! BUT WHY?!
OHMI-GAWD... DON'T TELL ME, ALL THE PORTRAITS IN HERE...
KITAGAWA... AND MADARAME SUPPOSEDLY PLAGIARIZES... OH NO.
ARE THEY ALL POR-TRAITS OF MADA-RAME'S STUDENTS?
MORE LIKE FORMER STUDENTS. ALL BUT THE LAST ONE.
FIRST NAKANO-HARA, NOW THIS... I'M STARTING TO SEE THE BIGGER PICTURE, AND IT ISN'T PRETTY.

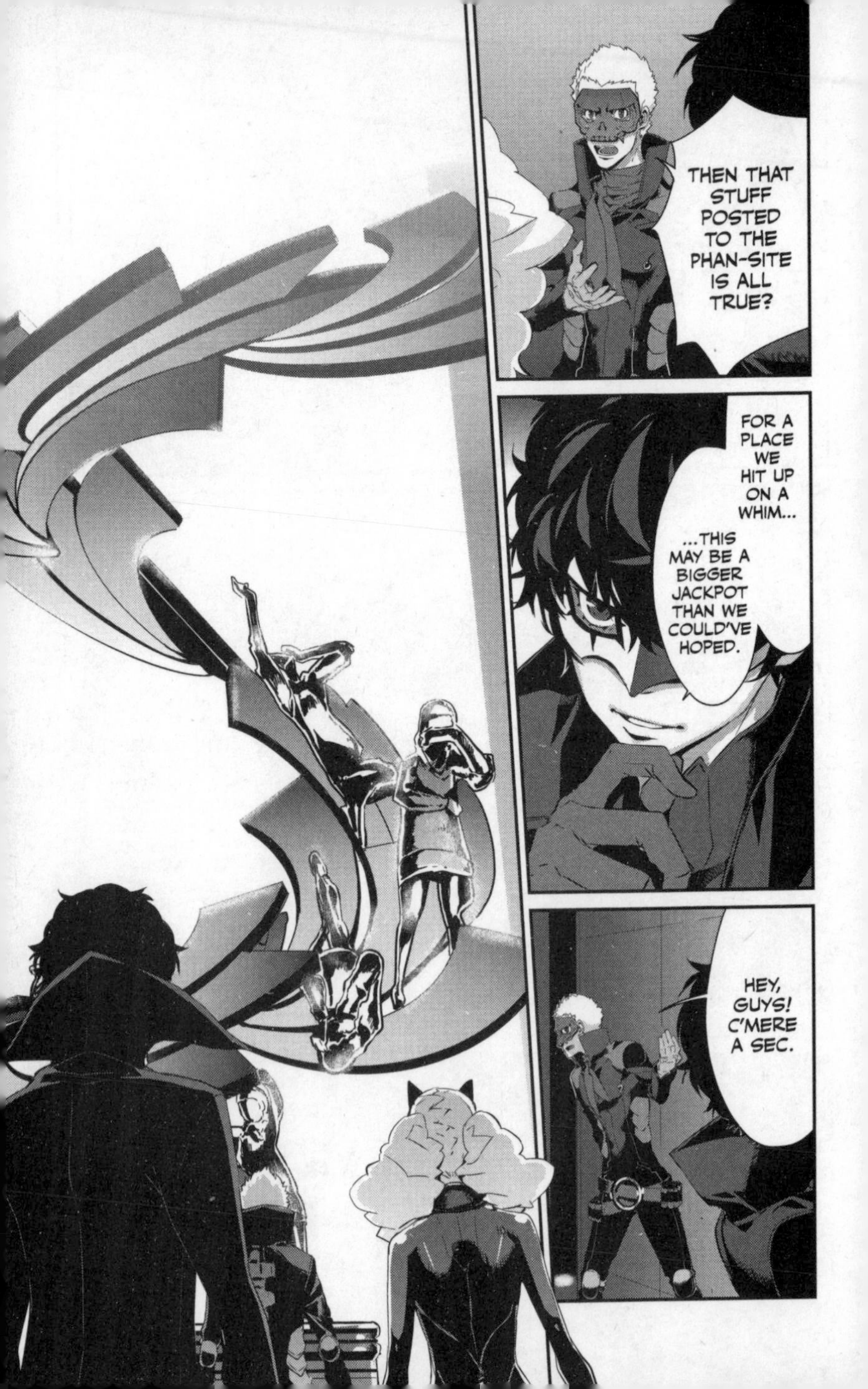
THEN THAT STUFF POSTED TO THE PHAN-SITE IS ALL TRUE?
FOR A PLACE WE HIT UP ON A WHIM...
...THIS MAY BE A BIGGER JACKPOT THAN WE COULD'VE HOPED.
HEY, GUYS! C'MERE A SEC.

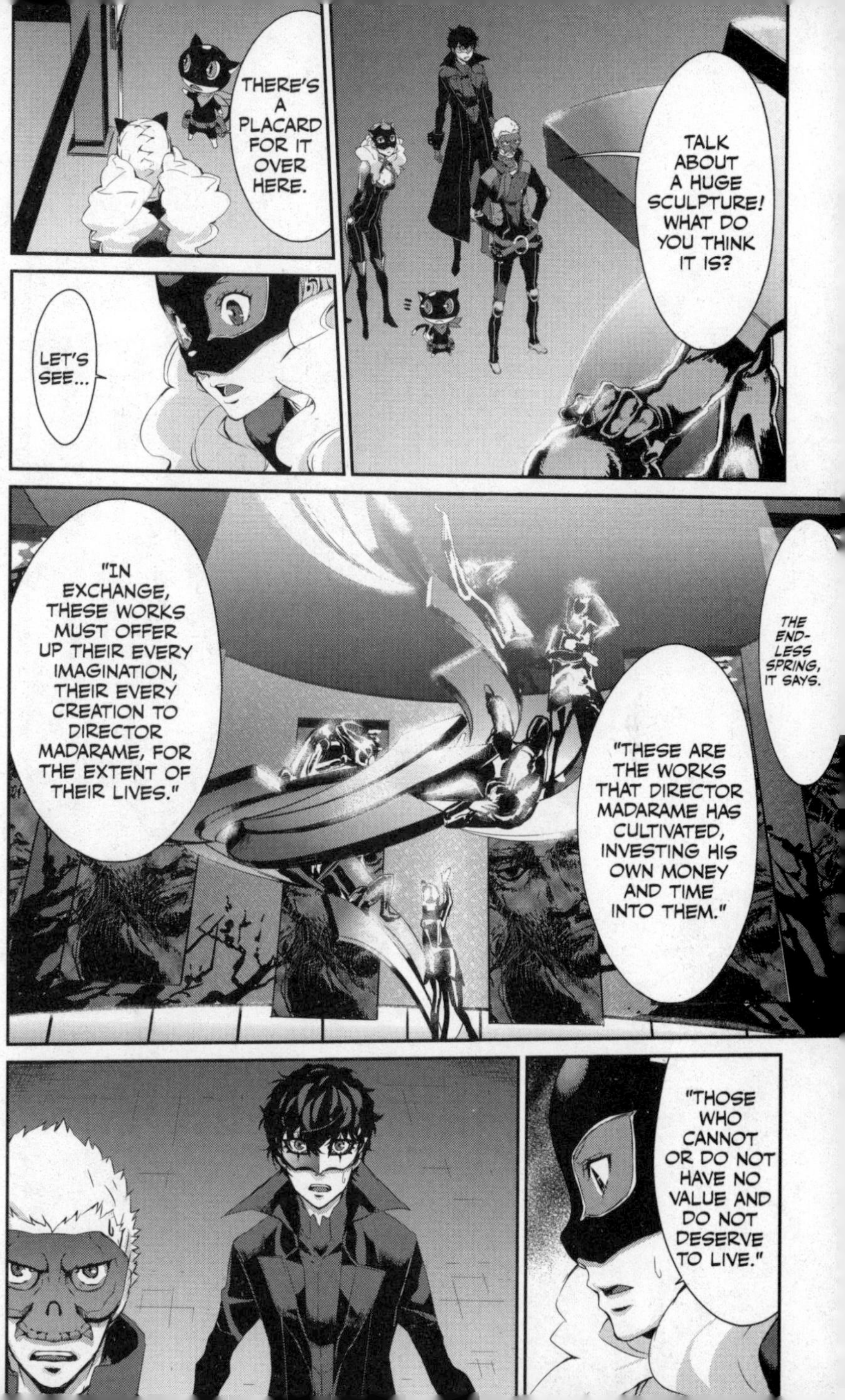
TALK ABOUT A HUGE SCULPTURE! WHAT DO YOU THINK IT IS?
THERE'S A PLACARD FOR IT OVER HERE.
LET'S SEE...
THE END-LESS SPRING, IT SAYS.
"THESE ARE THE WORKS THAT DIRECTOR MADARAME HAS CULTIVATED, INVESTING HIS OWN MONEY AND TIME INTO THEM."
"IN EXCHANGE, THESE WORKS MUST OFFER UP THEIR EVERY IMAGINATION, THEIR EVERY CREATION TO DIRECTOR MADARAME, FOR THE EXTENT OF THEIR LIVES."
"THOSE WHO CANNOT OR DO NOT HAVE NO VALUE AND DO NOT DESERVE TO LIVE."

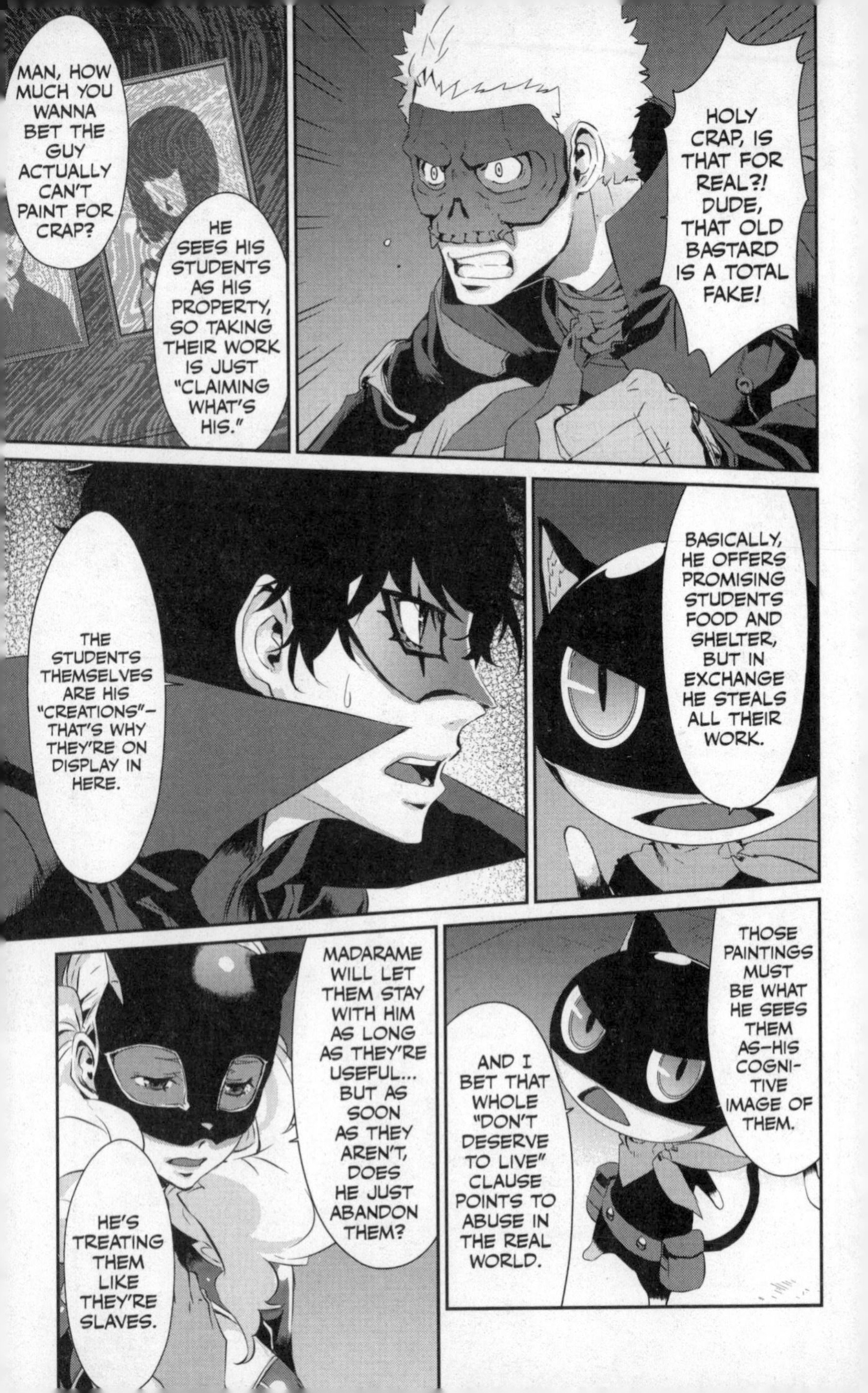
HOLY CRAP, IS THAT FOR REAL?! DUDE, THAT OLD BASTARD IS A TOTAL FAKE!
MAN, HOW MUCH YOU WANNA BET THE GUY ACTUALLY CAN'T PAINT FOR CRAP?
HE SEES HIS STUDENTS AS HIS PROPERTY, SO TAKING THEIR WORK IS JUST "CLAIMING WHAT'S HIS."
BASICALLY, HE OFFERS PROMISING STUDENTS FOOD AND SHELTER, BUT IN EXCHANGE HE STEALS ALL THEIR WORK.
THE STUDENTS THEMSELVES ARE HIS "CREATIONS"—THAT'S WHY THEY'RE ON DISPLAY IN HERE.
THOSE PAINTINGS MUST BE WHAT HE SEES THEM AS—HIS COGNI-TIVE IMAGE OF THEM.
AND I BET THAT WHOLE "DON'T DESERVE TO LIVE" CLAUSE POINTS TO ABUSE IN THE REAL WORLD.
MADARAME WILL LET THEM STAY WITH HIM AS LONG AS THEY'RE USEFUL... BUT AS SOON AS THEY AREN'T, DOES HE JUST ABANDON THEM?
HE'S TREATING THEM LIKE THEY'RE SLAVES.

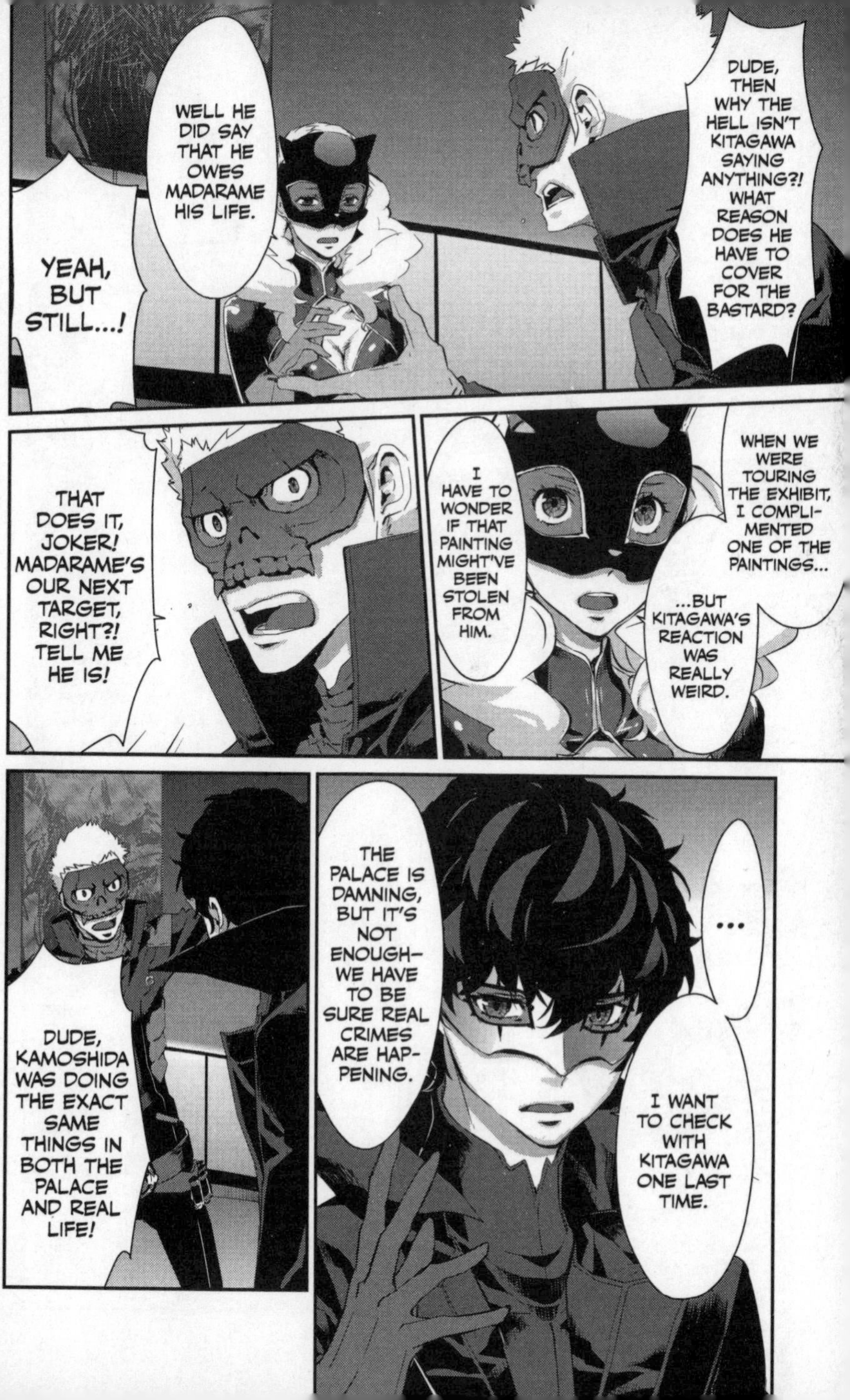
DUDE, THEN WHY THE HELL ISN'T KITAGAWA SAYING ANYTHING?! WHAT REASON DOES HE HAVE TO COVER FOR THE BASTARD?
WELL HE DID SAY THAT HE OWES MADARAME HIS LIFE.
YEAH, BUT STILL...!
WHEN WE WERE TOURING THE EXHIBIT, I COMPLI-MENTED ONE OF THE PAINTINGS...
...BUT KITAGAWA'S REACTION WAS REALLY WEIRD.
I HAVE TO WONDER IF THAT PAINTING MIGHT'VE BEEN STOLEN FROM HIM.
THAT DOES IT, JOKER! MADARAME'S OUR NEXT TARGET, RIGHT?! TELL ME HE IS!
...
THE PALACE IS DAMNING, BUT IT'S NOT ENOUGH— WE HAVE TO BE SURE REAL CRIMES ARE HAP-PENING.
I WANT TO CHECK WITH KITAGAWA ONE LAST TIME.
DUDE, KAMOSHIDA WAS DOING THE EXACT SAME THINGS IN BOTH THE PALACE AND REAL LIFE!

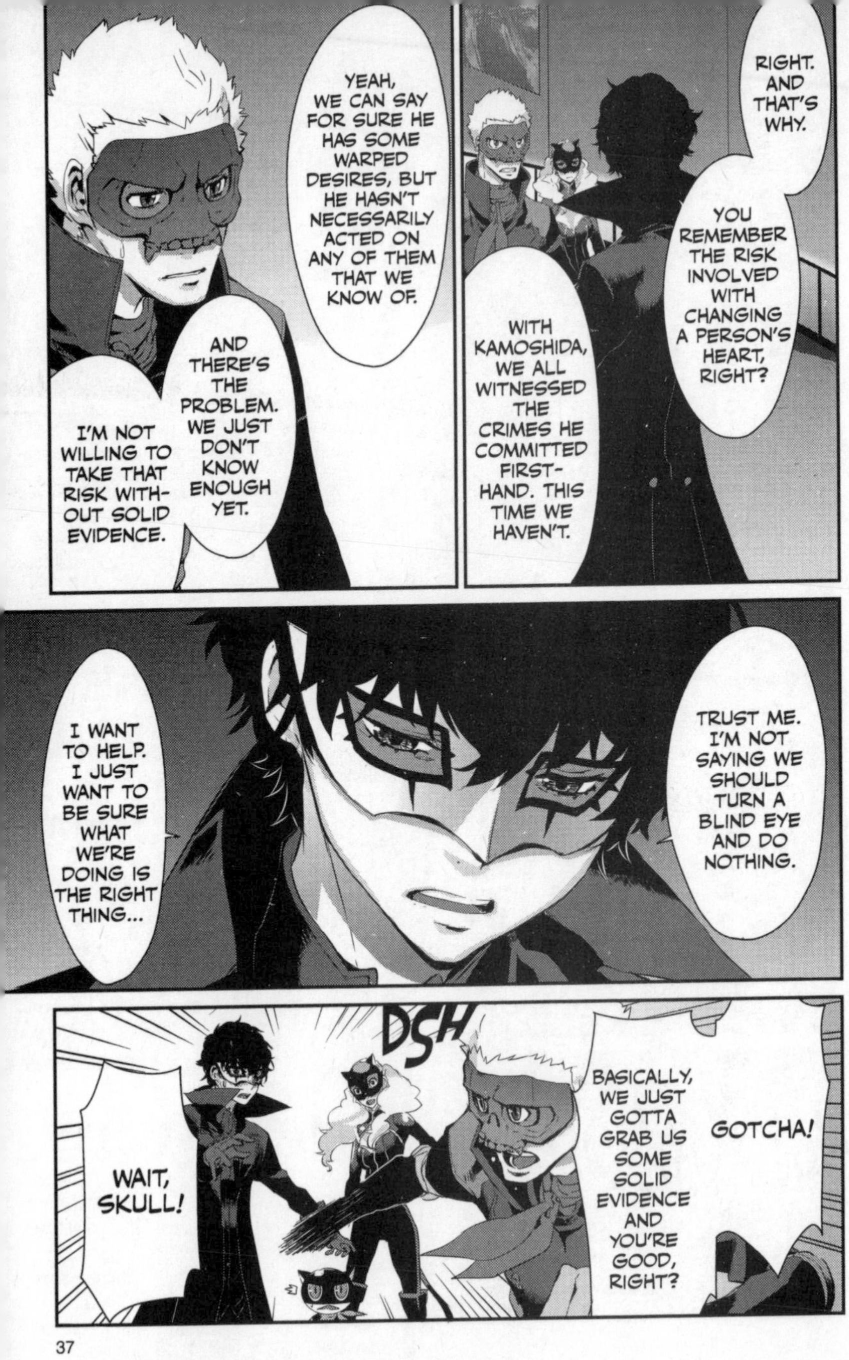
RIGHT. AND THAT'S WHY.
YOU REMEMBER THE RISK INVOLVED WITH CHANGING A PERSON'S HEART, RIGHT?
WITH KAMOSHIDA, WE ALL WITNESSED THE CRIMES HE COMMITTED FIRST-HAND. THIS TIME WE HAVEN'T.
YEAH, WE CAN SAY FOR SURE HE HAS SOME WARPED DESIRES, BUT HE HASN'T NECESSARILY ACTED ON ANY OF THEM THAT WE KNOW OF.
AND THERE'S THE PROBLEM. WE JUST DON'T KNOW ENOUGH YET.
I'M NOT WILLING TO TAKE THAT RISK WITH-OUT SOLID EVIDENCE.
TRUST ME. I'M NOT SAYING WE SHOULD TURN A BLIND EYE AND DO NOTHING.
I WANT TO HELP. I JUST WANT TO BE SURE WHAT WE'RE DOING IS THE RIGHT THING...
GOTCHA!
BASICALLY, WE JUST GOTTA GRAB US SOME SOLID EVIDENCE AND YOU'RE GOOD, RIGHT?
DSH
WAIT, SKULL!

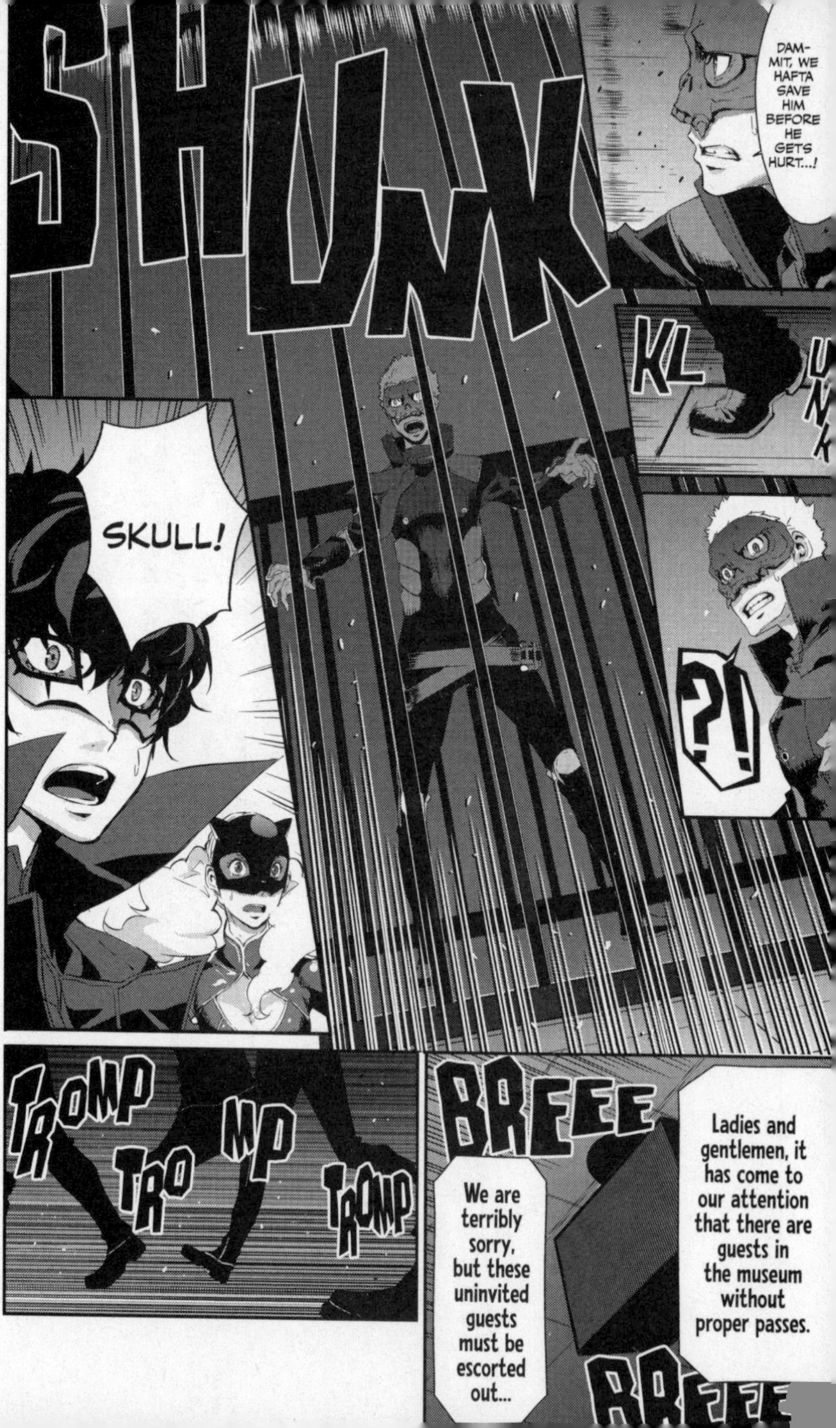
DAM-MIT, WE HAFTA SAVE HIM BEFORE HE GETS HURT...!
SHUNK
KLUNK
?!
SKULL!
BREEE
Ladies and gentlemen, it has come to our attention that there are guests in the museum without proper passes.
We are terribly sorry, but these uninvited guests must be escorted out...
BREEE
TROMP TROMP TROMP

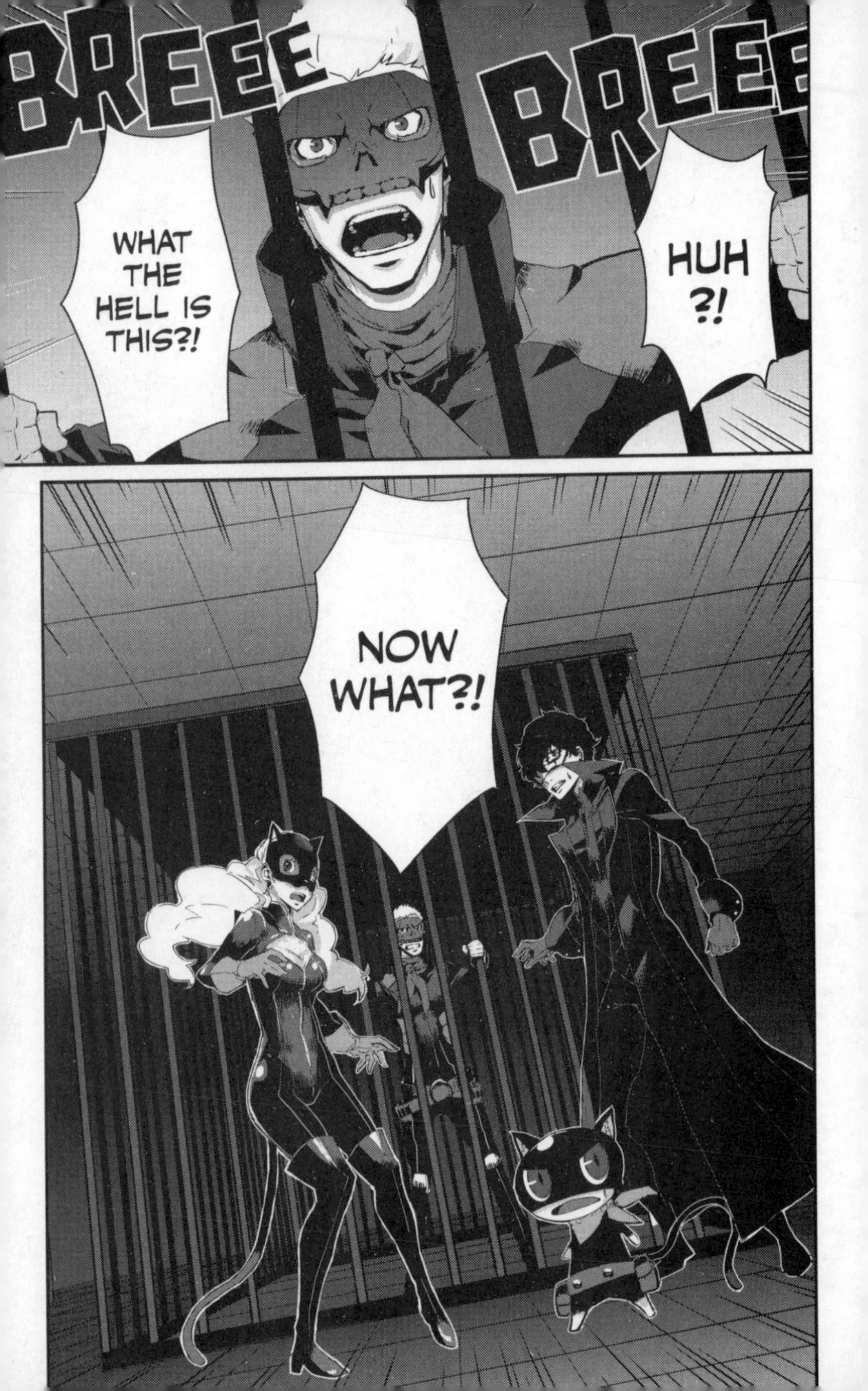
BREEE
HUH ?!
BREEE
WHAT THE HELL IS THIS?!
NOW WHAT?!

P5
PERSONA5

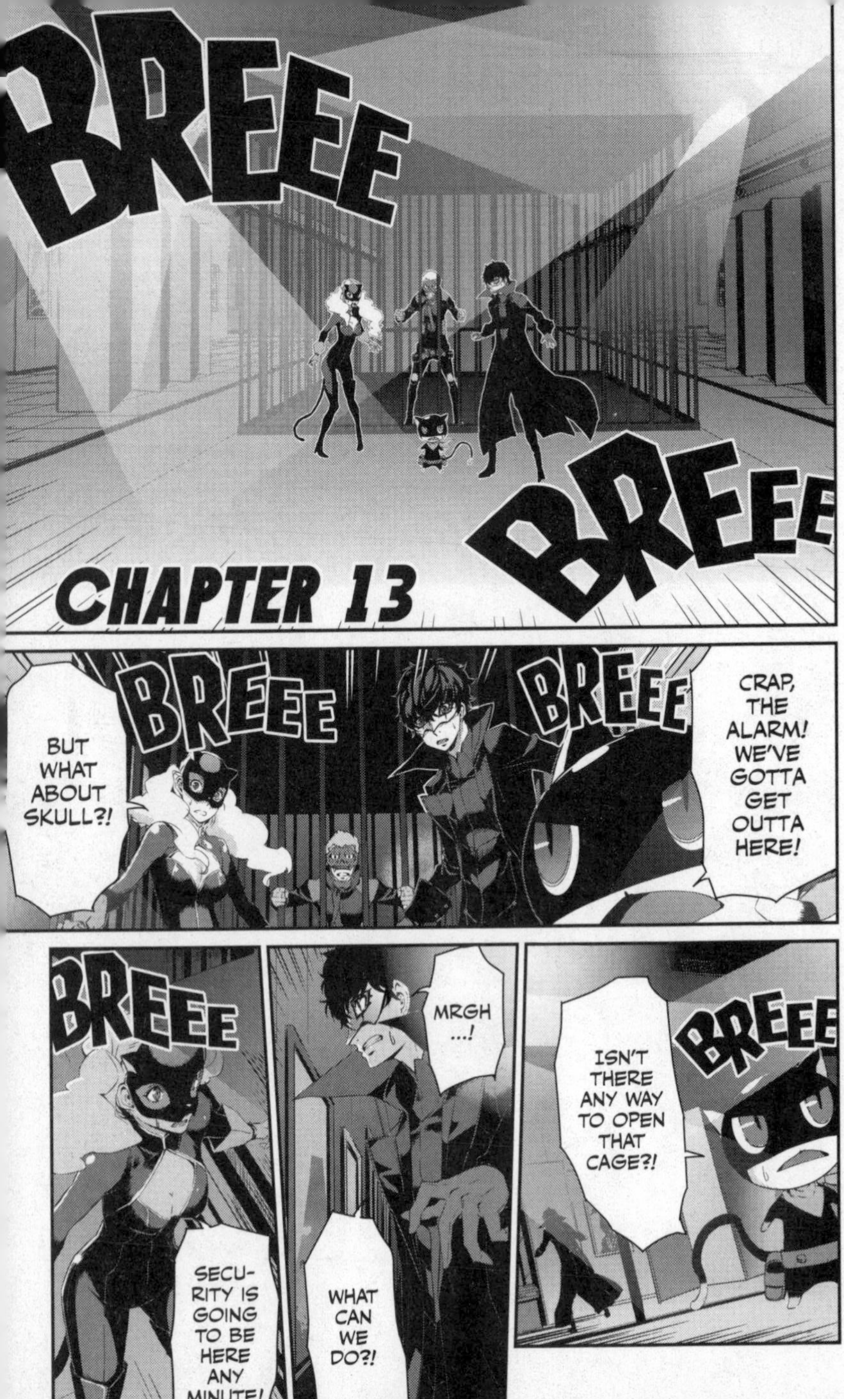
BREEE
BREEE
CHAPTER 13
CRAP, THE ALARM! WE'VE GOTTA GET OUTTA HERE!
BREEE
BREEE
BUT WHAT ABOUT SKULL?!
BREEE
ISN'T THERE ANY WAY TO OPEN THAT CAGE?!
MRGH ...!
WHAT CAN WE DO?!
BREEE
SECU-RITY IS GOING TO BE HERE ANY MINUTE!

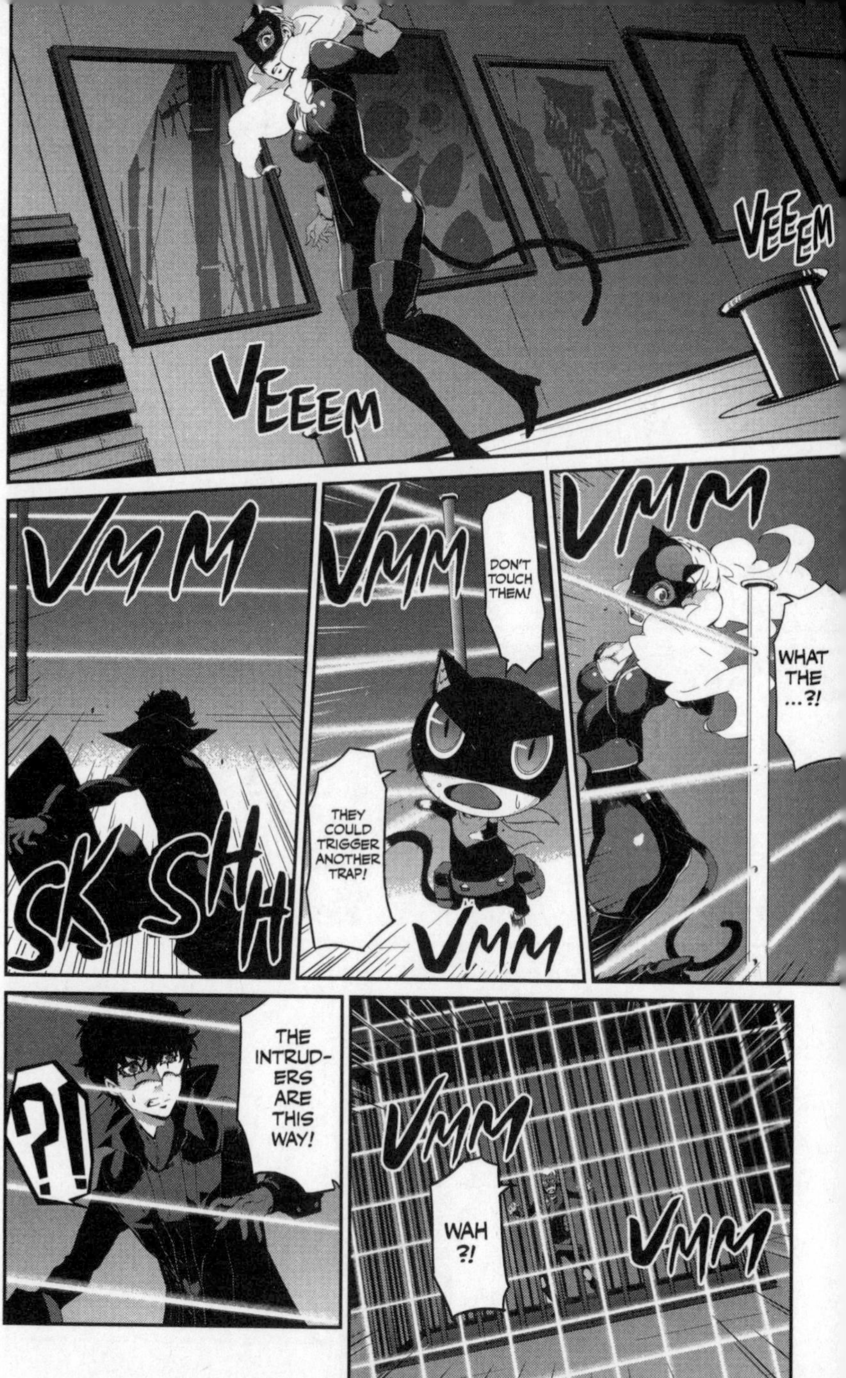

VEEEM
VEEEM
VMM
WHAT THE ...?!
VMM
DON'T TOUCH THEM!
THEY COULD TRIGGER ANOTHER TRAP!
VMM
VMM
SKSHH
VMM
WAH ?!
VMM
THE INTRUDERS ARE THIS WAY!
?!

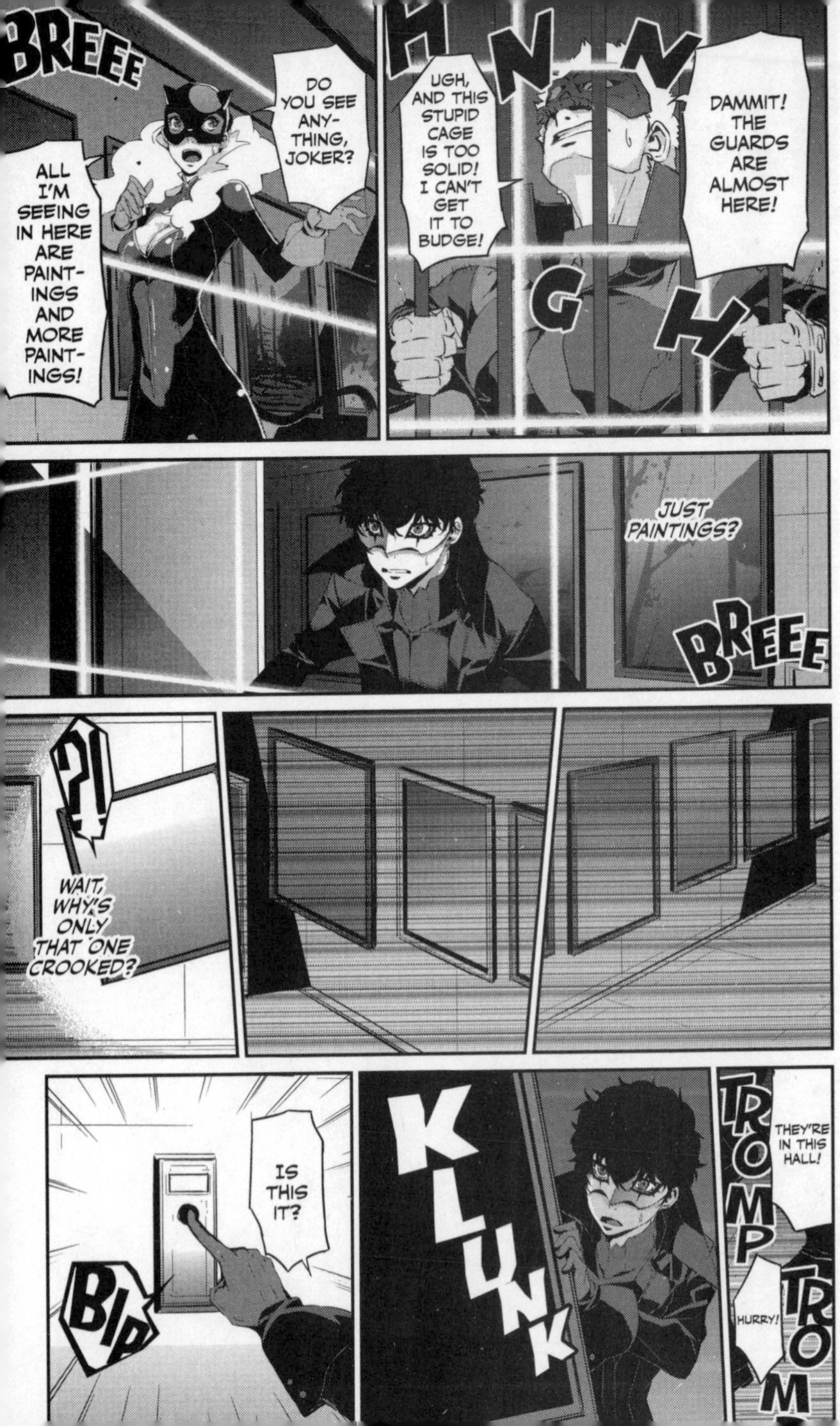
HNNGH
DAMMIT! THE GUARDS ARE ALMOST HERE!
UGH, AND THIS STUPID CAGE IS TOO SOLID! I CAN'T GET IT TO BUDGE!
BREEE
DO YOU SEE ANY-THING, JOKER?
ALL I'M SEEING IN HERE ARE PAINT-INGS AND MORE PAINT-INGS!
JUST PAINTINGS?
BREEE
?!
WAIT, WHY'S ONLY THAT ONE CROOKED?
TROMP
THEY'RE IN THIS HALL!
TROM
HURRY!
KLUNK
IS THIS IT?
BIP

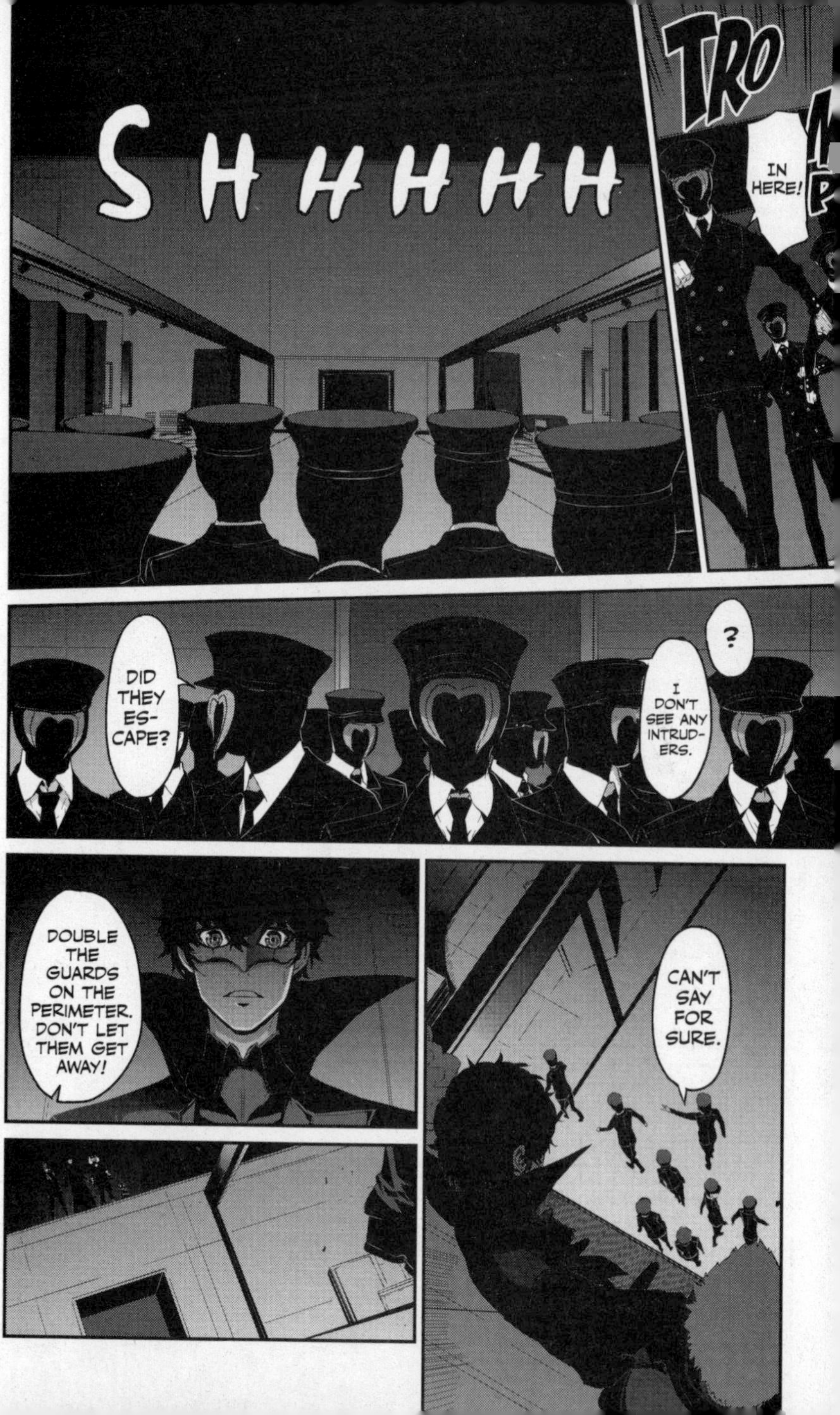
TRO
IN HERE!
SHHHHH
?
I DON'T SEE ANY INTRUDERS.
DID THEY ESCAPE?
CAN'T SAY FOR SURE.
DOUBLE THE GUARDS ON THE PERIMETER. DON'T LET THEM GET AWAY!

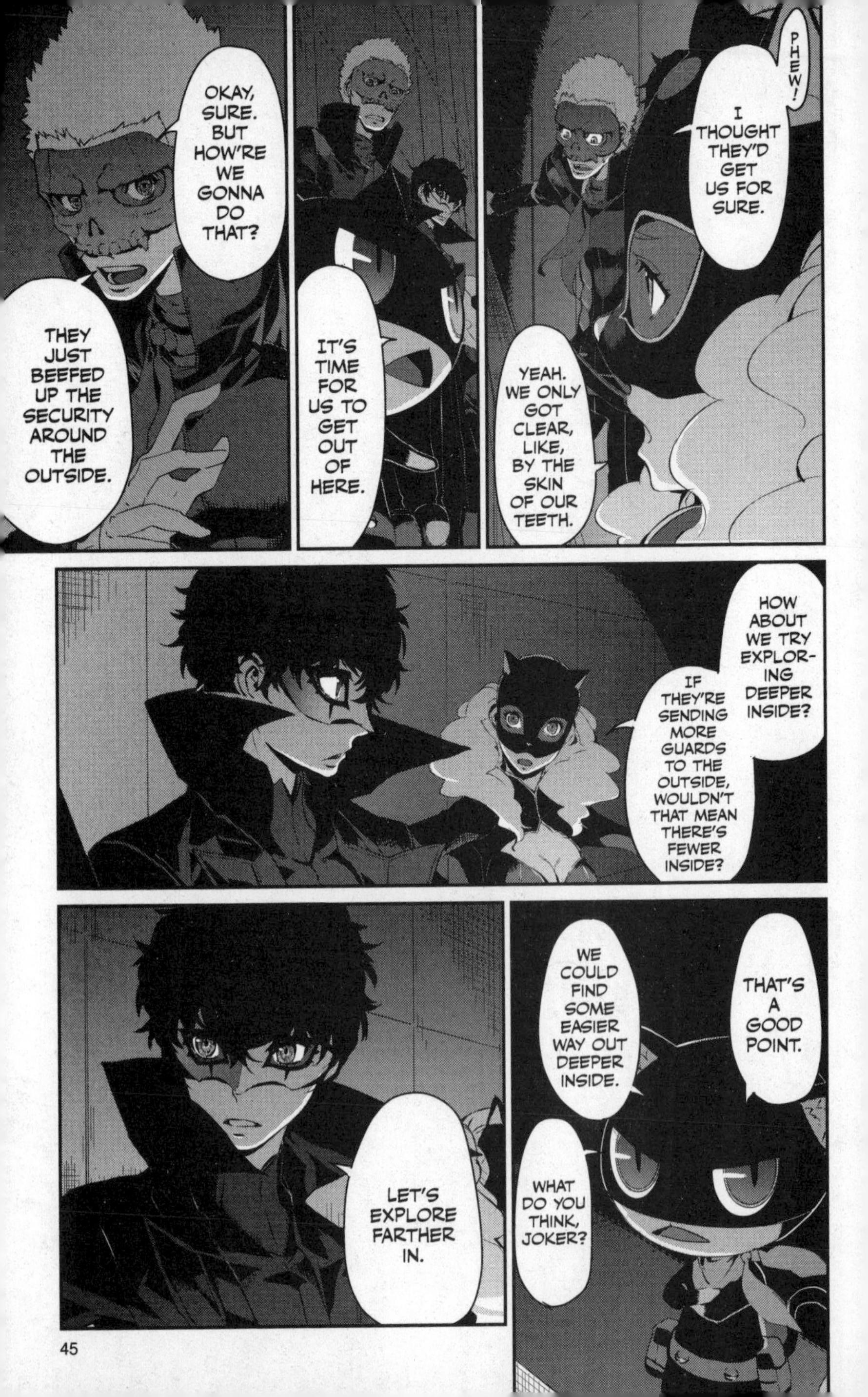
PHEW!
I THOUGHT THEY'D GET US FOR SURE.
YEAH. WE ONLY GOT CLEAR, LIKE, BY THE SKIN OF OUR TEETH.
IT'S TIME FOR US TO GET OUT OF HERE.
OKAY, SURE. BUT HOW'RE WE GONNA DO THAT?
THEY JUST BEEFED UP THE SECURITY AROUND THE OUTSIDE.
HOW ABOUT WE TRY EXPLOR-ING DEEPER INSIDE?
IF THEY'RE SENDING MORE GUARDS TO THE OUTSIDE, WOULDN'T THAT MEAN THERE'S FEWER INSIDE?
THAT'S A GOOD POINT.
WE COULD FIND SOME EASIER WAY OUT DEEPER INSIDE.
WHAT DO YOU THINK, JOKER?
LET'S EXPLORE FARTHER IN.

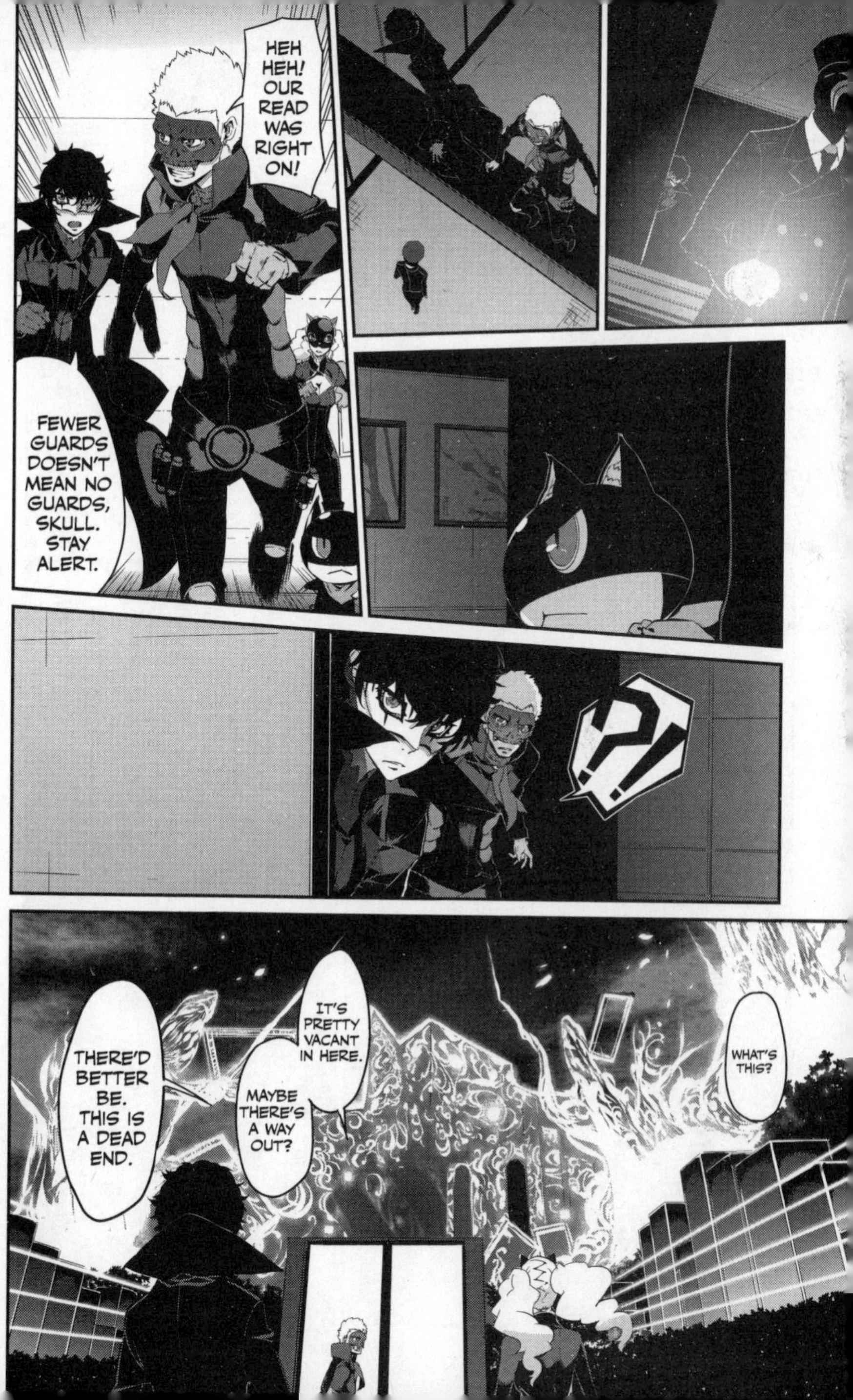
HEH HEH! OUR READ WAS RIGHT ON!
FEWER GUARDS DOESN'T MEAN NO GUARDS, SKULL. STAY ALERT.
?!
WHAT'S THIS?
IT'S PRETTY VACANT IN HERE.
MAYBE THERE'S A WAY OUT?
THERE'D BETTER BE. THIS IS A DEAD END.

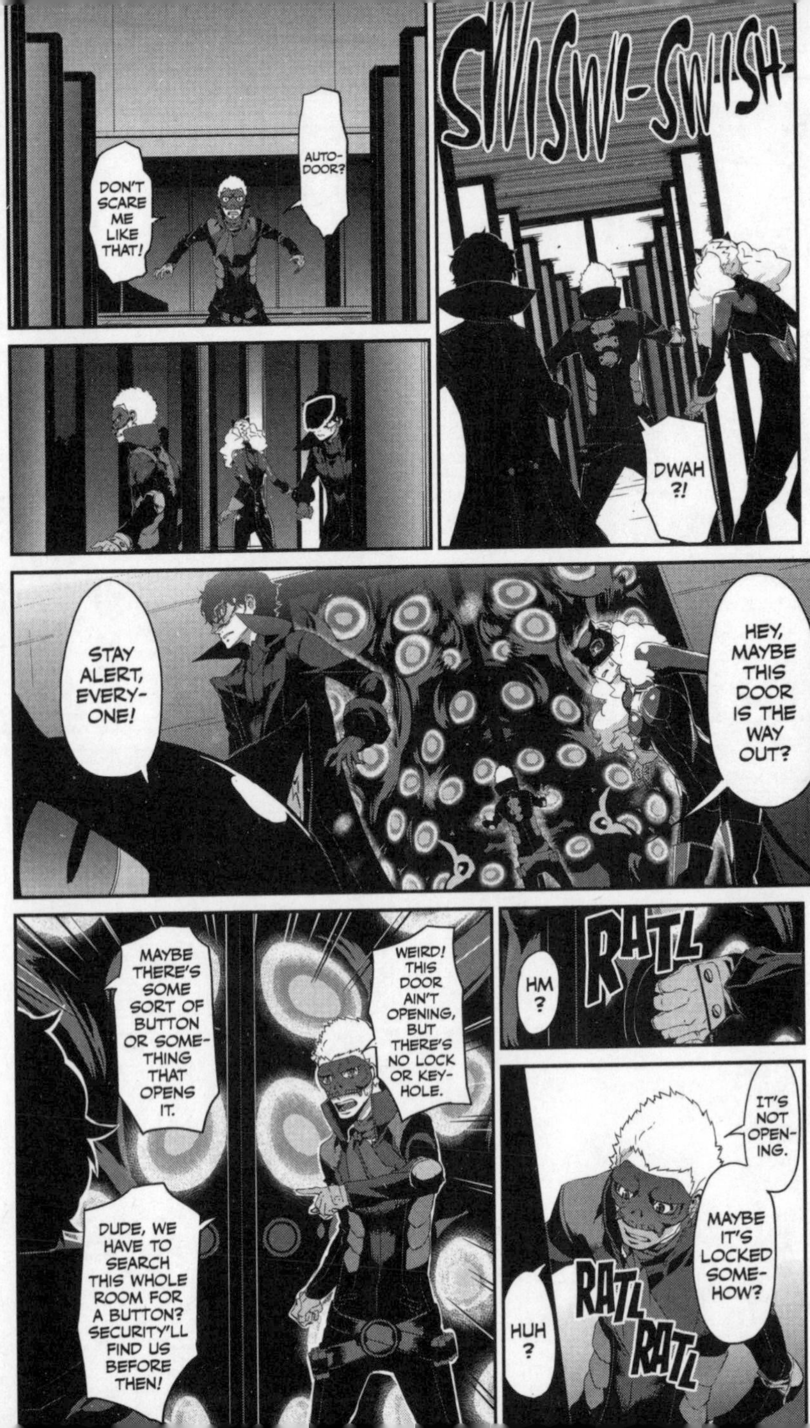
SWI SWI-SWISH
DWAH ?!
AUTO-DOOR?
DON'T SCARE ME LIKE THAT!
HEY, MAYBE THIS DOOR IS THE WAY OUT?
STAY ALERT, EVERY-ONE!
RATL
HM ?
IT'S NOT OPEN-ING.
MAYBE IT'S LOCKED SOME-HOW?
RATL RATL
HUH ?
WEIRD! THIS DOOR AIN'T OPENING, BUT THERE'S NO LOCK OR KEY-HOLE.
MAYBE THERE'S SOME SORT OF BUTTON OR SOME-THING THAT OPENS IT.
DUDE, WE HAVE TO SEARCH THIS WHOLE ROOM FOR A BUTTON? SECURITY'LL FIND US BEFORE THEN!

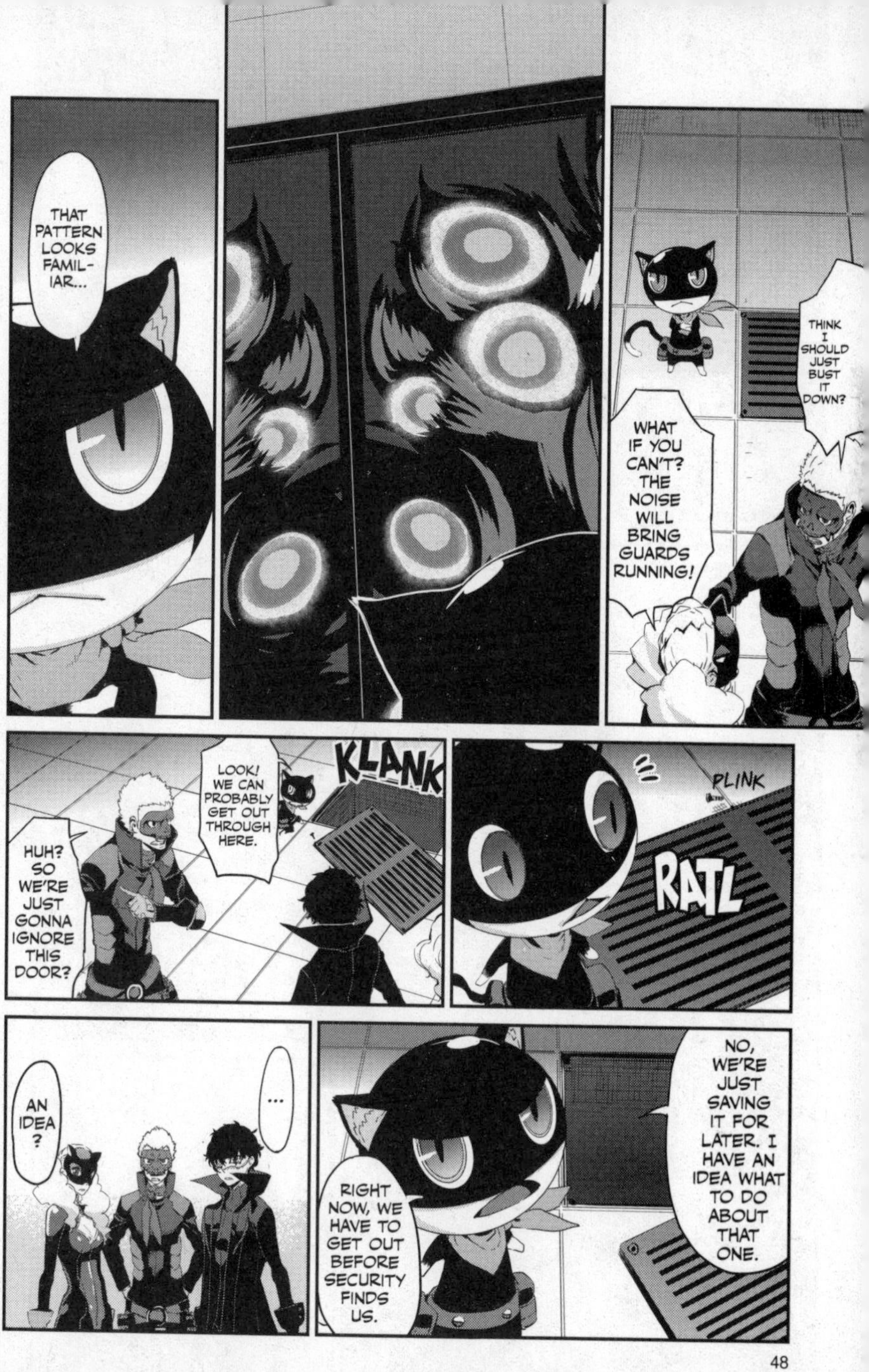
THINK I SHOULD JUST BUST IT DOWN?
WHAT IF YOU CAN'T? THE NOISE WILL BRING GUARDS RUNNING!
THAT PATTERN LOOKS FAMIL-IAR...
PLINK
RATL
KLANK
LOOK! WE CAN PROBABLY GET OUT THROUGH HERE.
HUH? SO WE'RE JUST GONNA IGNORE THIS DOOR?
NO, WE'RE JUST SAVING IT FOR LATER. I HAVE AN IDEA WHAT TO DO ABOUT THAT ONE.
RIGHT NOW, WE HAVE TO GET OUT BEFORE SECURITY FINDS US.
...
AN IDEA?

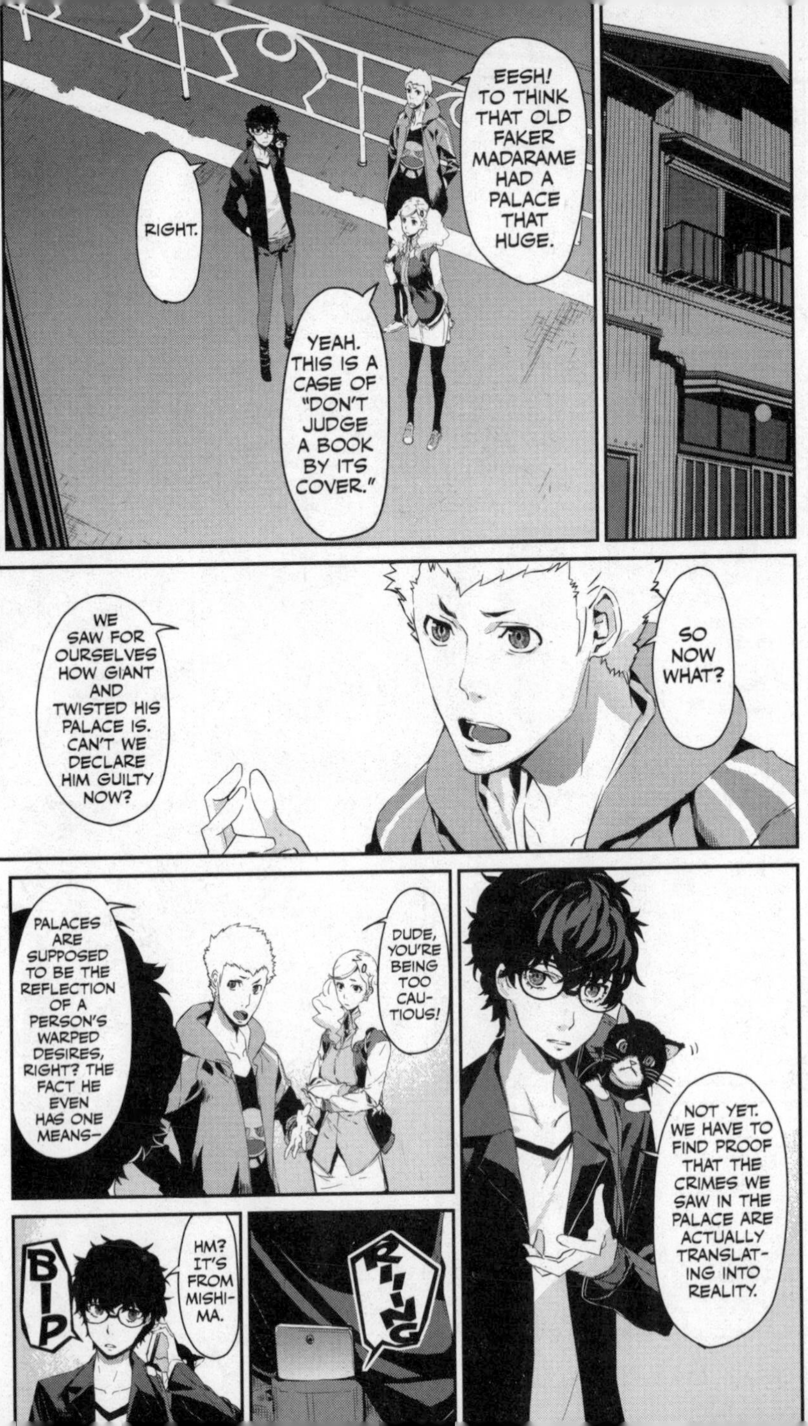
EESH! TO THINK THAT OLD FAKER MADARAME HAD A PALACE THAT HUGE.
RIGHT.
YEAH. THIS IS A CASE OF "DON'T JUDGE A BOOK BY ITS COVER."
SO NOW WHAT?
WE SAW FOR OURSELVES HOW GIANT AND TWISTED HIS PALACE IS. CAN'T WE DECLARE HIM GUILTY NOW?
NOT YET. WE HAVE TO FIND PROOF THAT THE CRIMES WE SAW IN THE PALACE ARE ACTUALLY TRANSLATING INTO REALITY.
DUDE, YOU'RE BEING TOO CAUTIOUS!
PALACES ARE SUPPOSED TO BE THE REFLECTION OF A PERSON'S WARPED DESIRES, RIGHT? THE FACT HE EVEN HAS ONE MEANS–
RIING
HM? IT'S FROM MISHIMA.
BIP

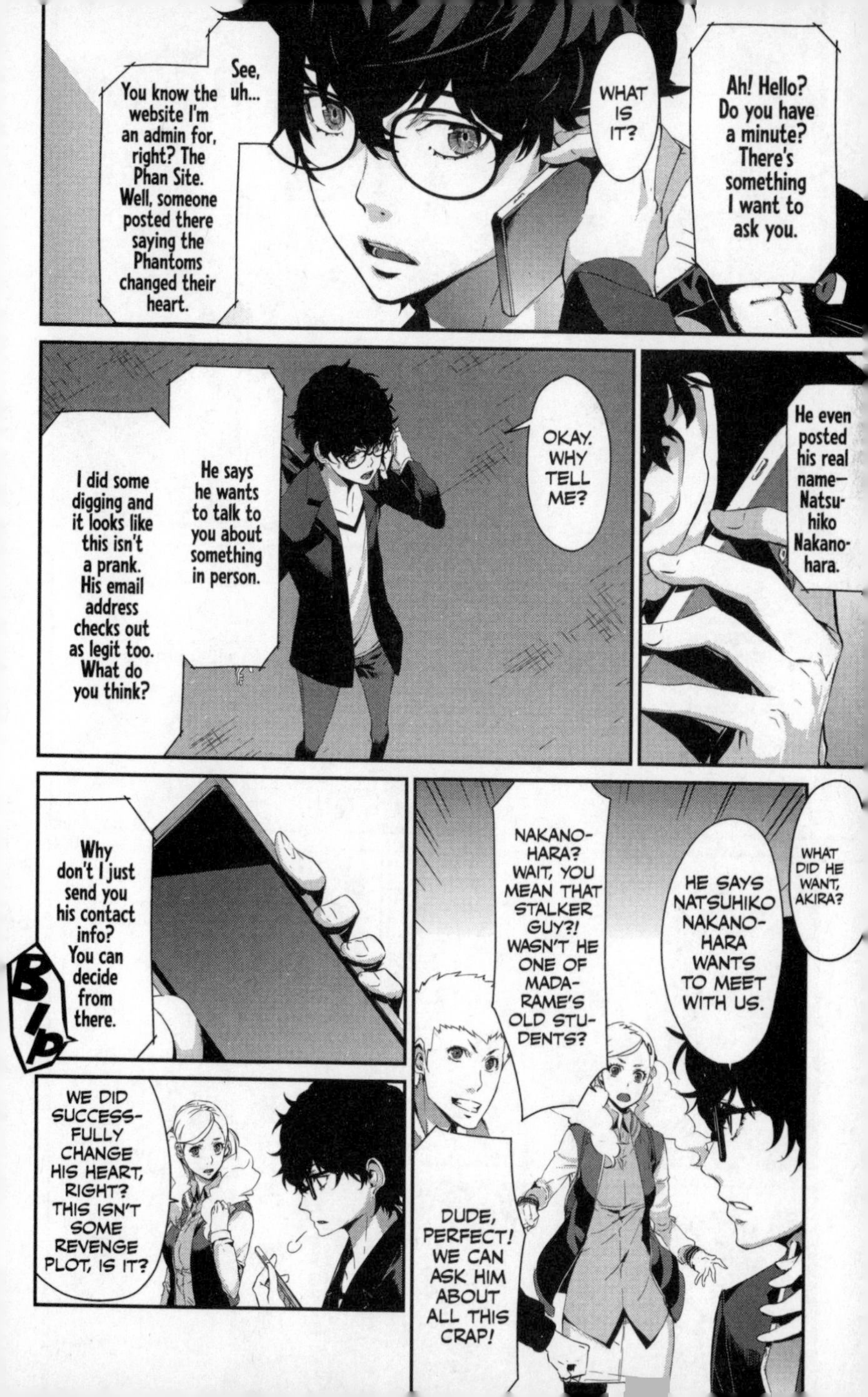
Ah! Hello? Do you have a minute? There's something I want to ask you.
WHAT IS IT?
See, uh...
You know the website I'm an admin for, right? The Phan Site. Well, someone posted there saying the Phantoms changed their heart.
He even posted his real name—Natsuhiko Nakanohara.
OKAY. WHY TELL ME?
He says he wants to talk to you about something in person.
I did some digging and it looks like this isn't a prank. His email address checks out as legit too. What do you think?
WHAT DID HE WANT, AKIRA?
HE SAYS NATSUHIKO NAKANOHARA WANTS TO MEET WITH US.
NAKANOHARA? WAIT, YOU MEAN THAT STALKER GUY?! WASN'T HE ONE OF MADARAME'S OLD STUDENTS?
DUDE, PERFECT! WE CAN ASK HIM ABOUT ALL THIS CRAP!
Why don't I just send you his contact info? You can decide from there.
BIP
WE DID SUCCESSFULLY CHANGE HIS HEART, RIGHT? THIS ISN'T SOME REVENGE PLOT, IS IT?

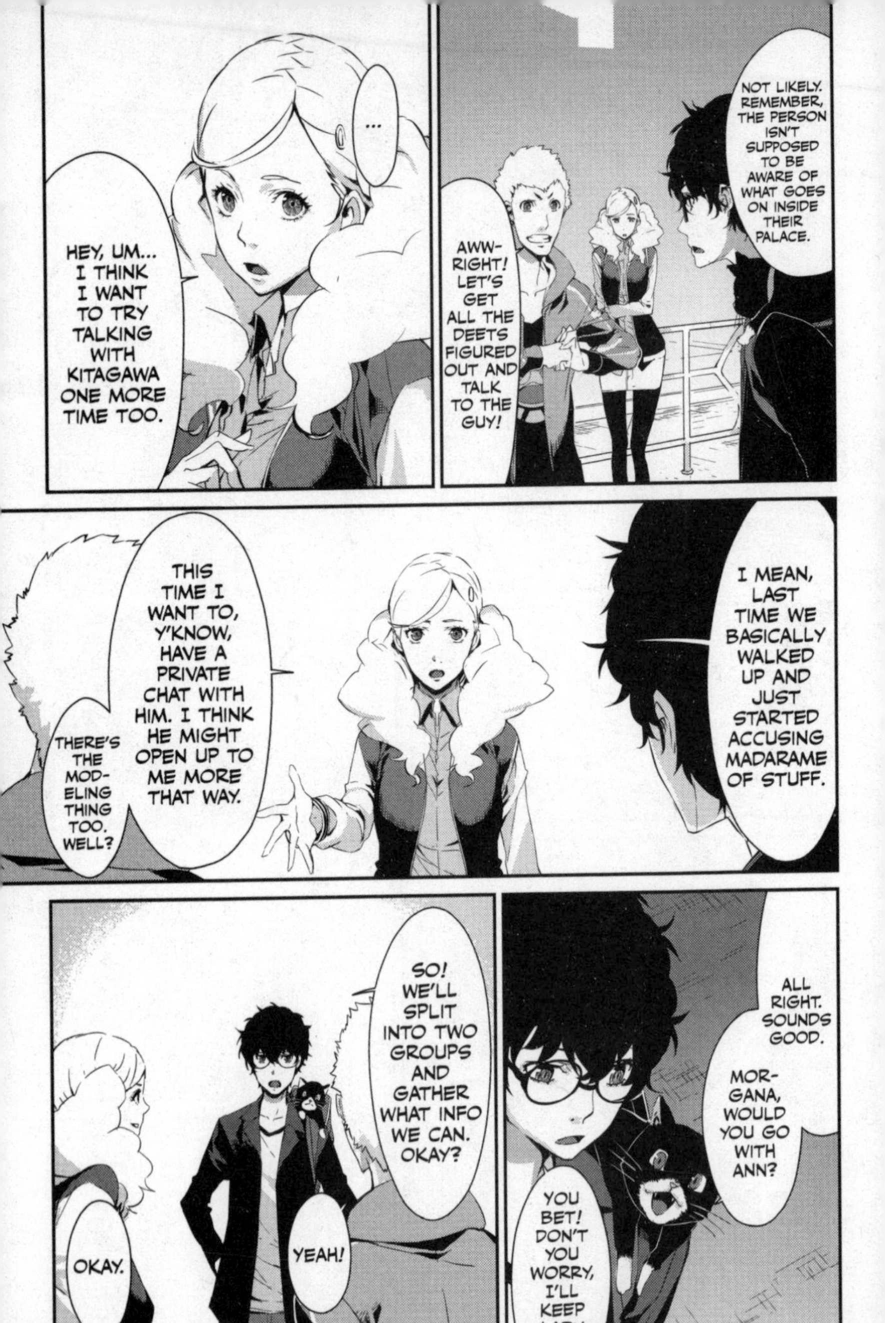
NOT LIKELY. REMEMBER, THE PERSON ISN'T SUPPOSED TO BE AWARE OF WHAT GOES ON INSIDE THEIR PALACE.
AWW-RIGHT! LET'S GET ALL THE DEETS FIGURED OUT AND TALK TO THE GUY!
...
HEY, UM... I THINK I WANT TO TRY TALKING WITH KITAGAWA ONE MORE TIME TOO.
I MEAN, LAST TIME WE BASICALLY WALKED UP AND JUST STARTED ACCUSING MADARAME OF STUFF.
THIS TIME I WANT TO, Y'KNOW, HAVE A PRIVATE CHAT WITH HIM. I THINK HE MIGHT OPEN UP TO ME MORE THAT WAY.
THERE'S THE MOD-ELING THING TOO. WELL?
ALL RIGHT. SOUNDS GOOD.
MOR-GANA, WOULD YOU GO WITH ANN?
YOU BET! DON'T YOU WORRY, I'LL KEEP LADY ANN SAFE!
SO! WE'LL SPLIT INTO TWO GROUPS AND GATHER WHAT INFO WE CAN. OKAY?
YEAH!
OKAY.

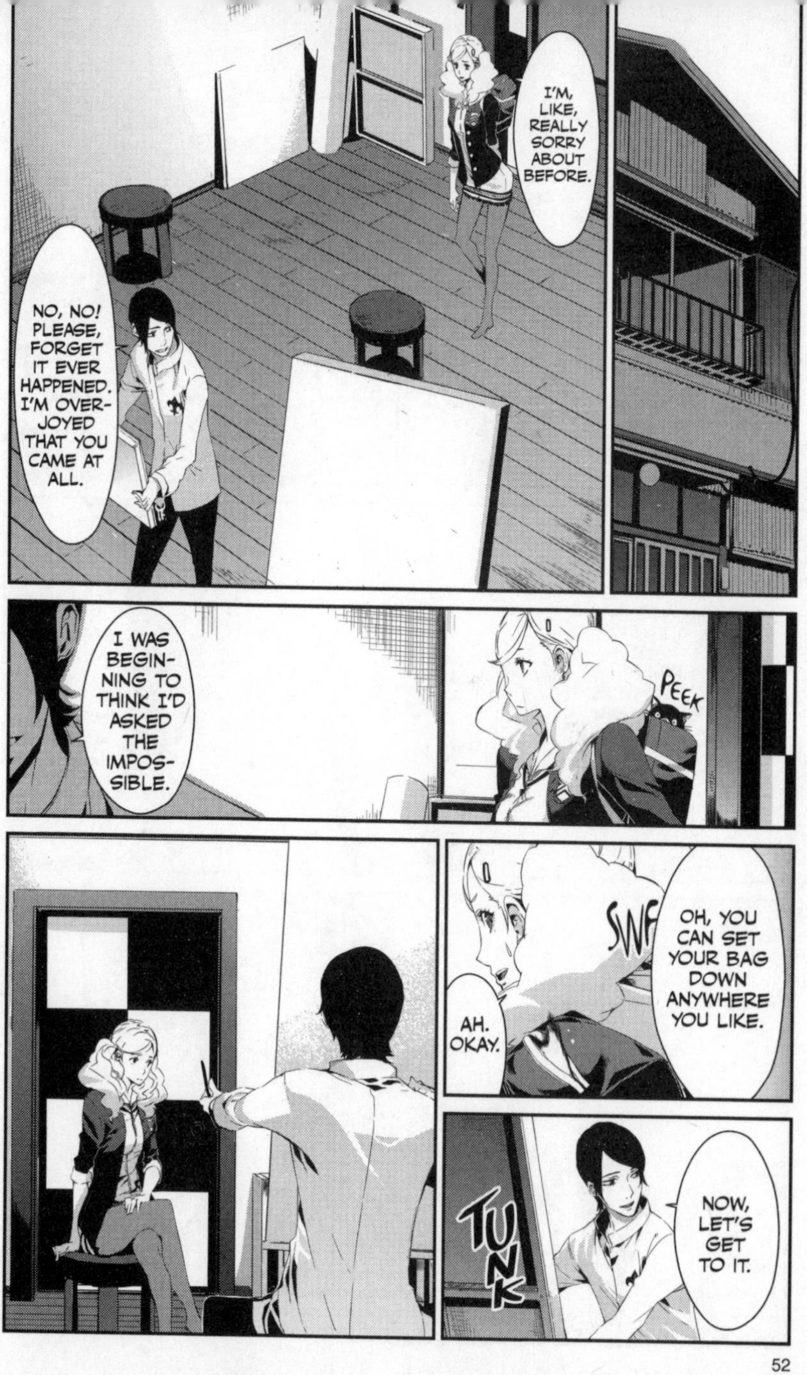
I'M, LIKE, REALLY SORRY ABOUT BEFORE.
NO, NO! PLEASE, FORGET IT EVER HAPPENED. I'M OVER-JOYED THAT YOU CAME AT ALL.
PEEK
I WAS BEGIN-NING TO THINK I'D ASKED THE IMPOS-SIBLE.
SWF
OH, YOU CAN SET YOUR BAG DOWN ANYWHERE YOU LIKE.
AH. OKAY.
NOW, LET'S GET TO IT.
TUNK

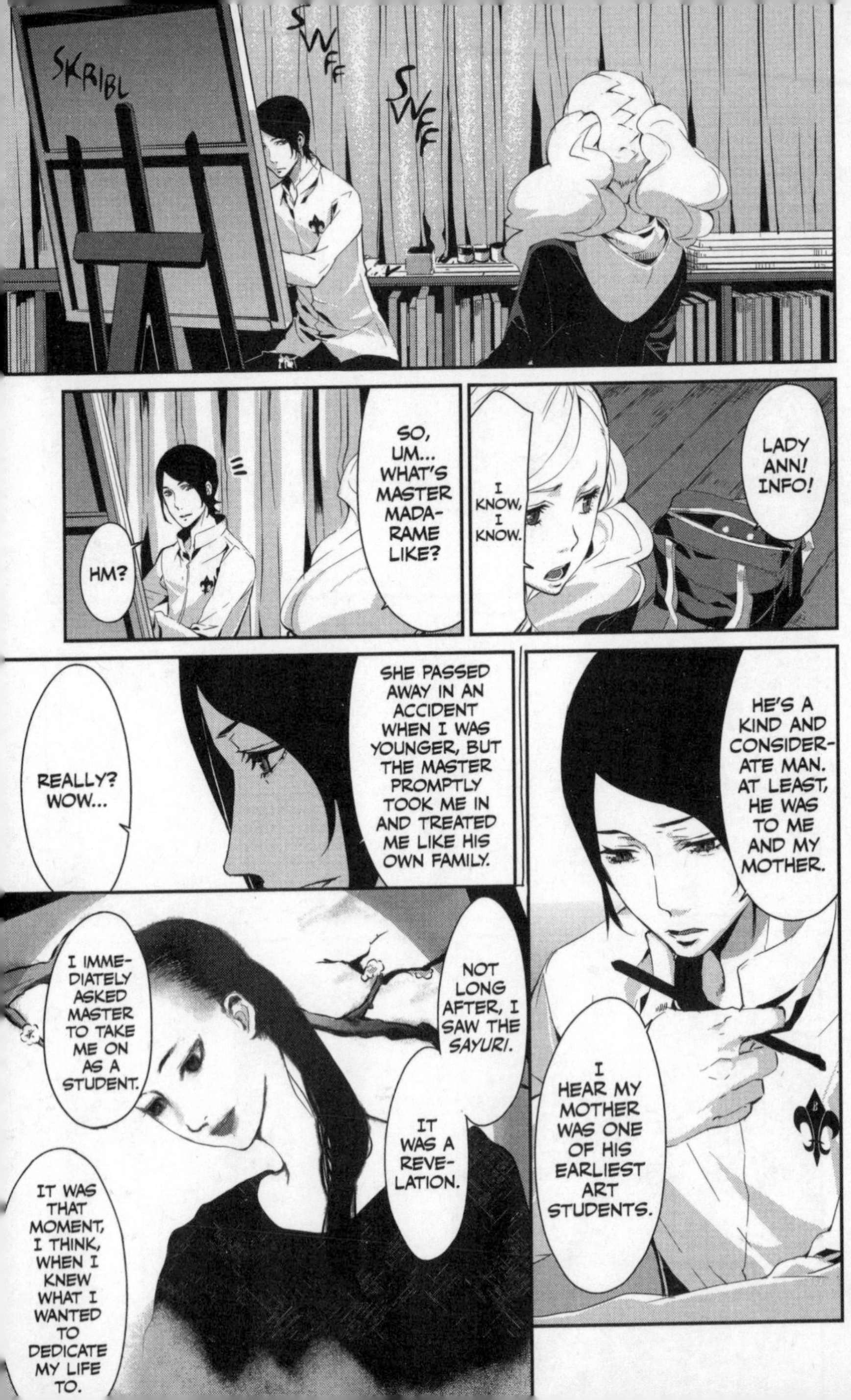
SNFF
SNFF
SKRIBL
LADY ANN! INFO!
I KNOW, I KNOW.
SO, UM... WHAT'S MASTER MADARAME LIKE?
HM?
HE'S A KIND AND CONSIDERATE MAN. AT LEAST, HE WAS TO ME AND MY MOTHER.
I HEAR MY MOTHER WAS ONE OF HIS EARLIEST ART STUDENTS.
SHE PASSED AWAY IN AN ACCIDENT WHEN I WAS YOUNGER, BUT THE MASTER PROMPTLY TOOK ME IN AND TREATED ME LIKE HIS OWN FAMILY.
REALLY? WOW...
NOT LONG AFTER, I SAW THE *SAYURI*.
IT WAS A REVELATION.
I IMMEDIATELY ASKED MASTER TO TAKE ME ON AS A STUDENT.
IT WAS THAT MOMENT, I THINK, WHEN I KNEW WHAT I WANTED TO DEDICATE MY LIFE TO.

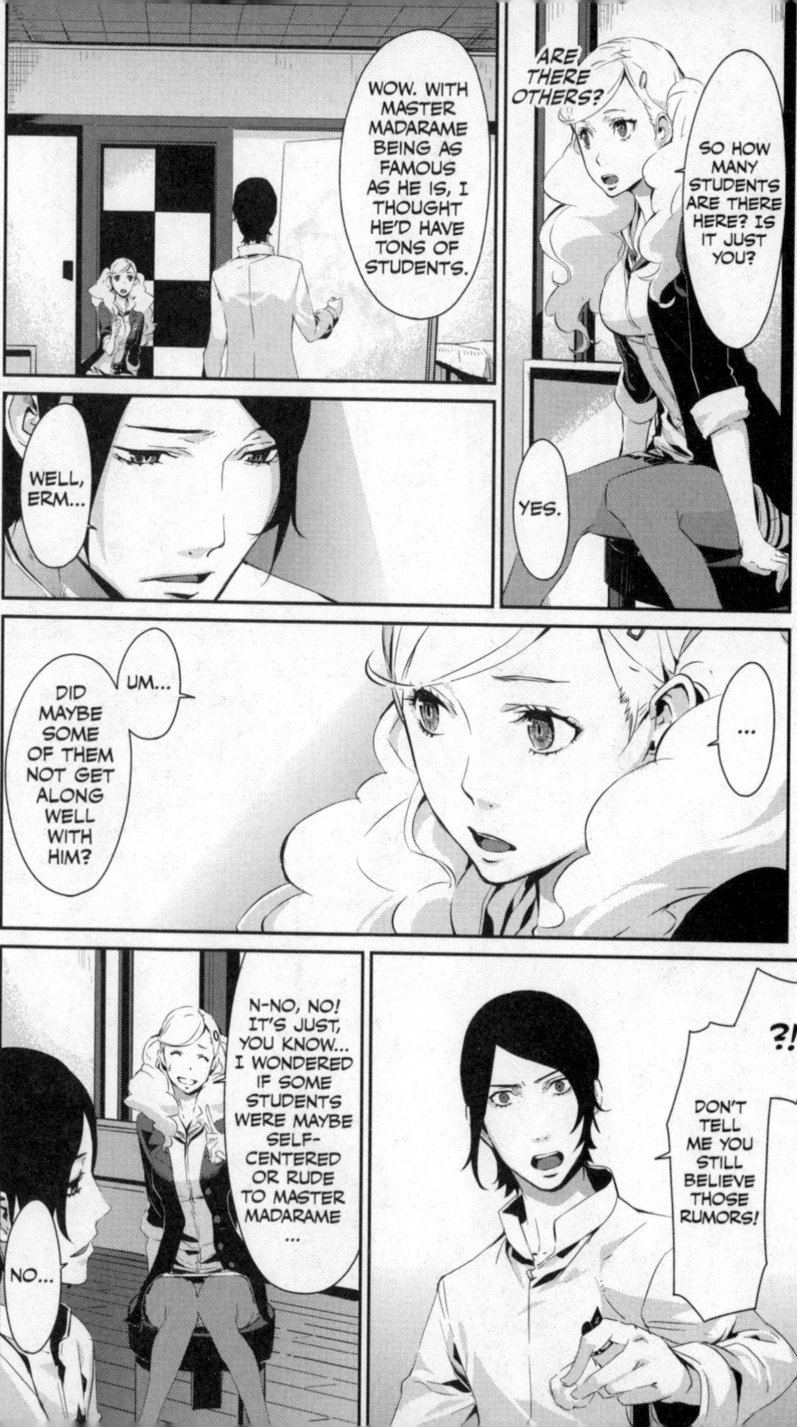
SO HOW MANY STUDENTS ARE THERE HERE? IS IT JUST YOU?
ARE THERE OTHERS?
YES.
WOW. WITH MASTER MADARAME BEING AS FAMOUS AS HE IS, I THOUGHT HE'D HAVE TONS OF STUDENTS.
WELL, ERM...
...
UM...
DID MAYBE SOME OF THEM NOT GET ALONG WELL WITH HIM?
?!
DON'T TELL ME YOU STILL BELIEVE THOSE RUMORS!
N-NO, NO! IT'S JUST, YOU KNOW... I WONDERED IF SOME STUDENTS WERE MAYBE SELF-CENTERED OR RUDE TO MASTER MADARAME ...
NO...

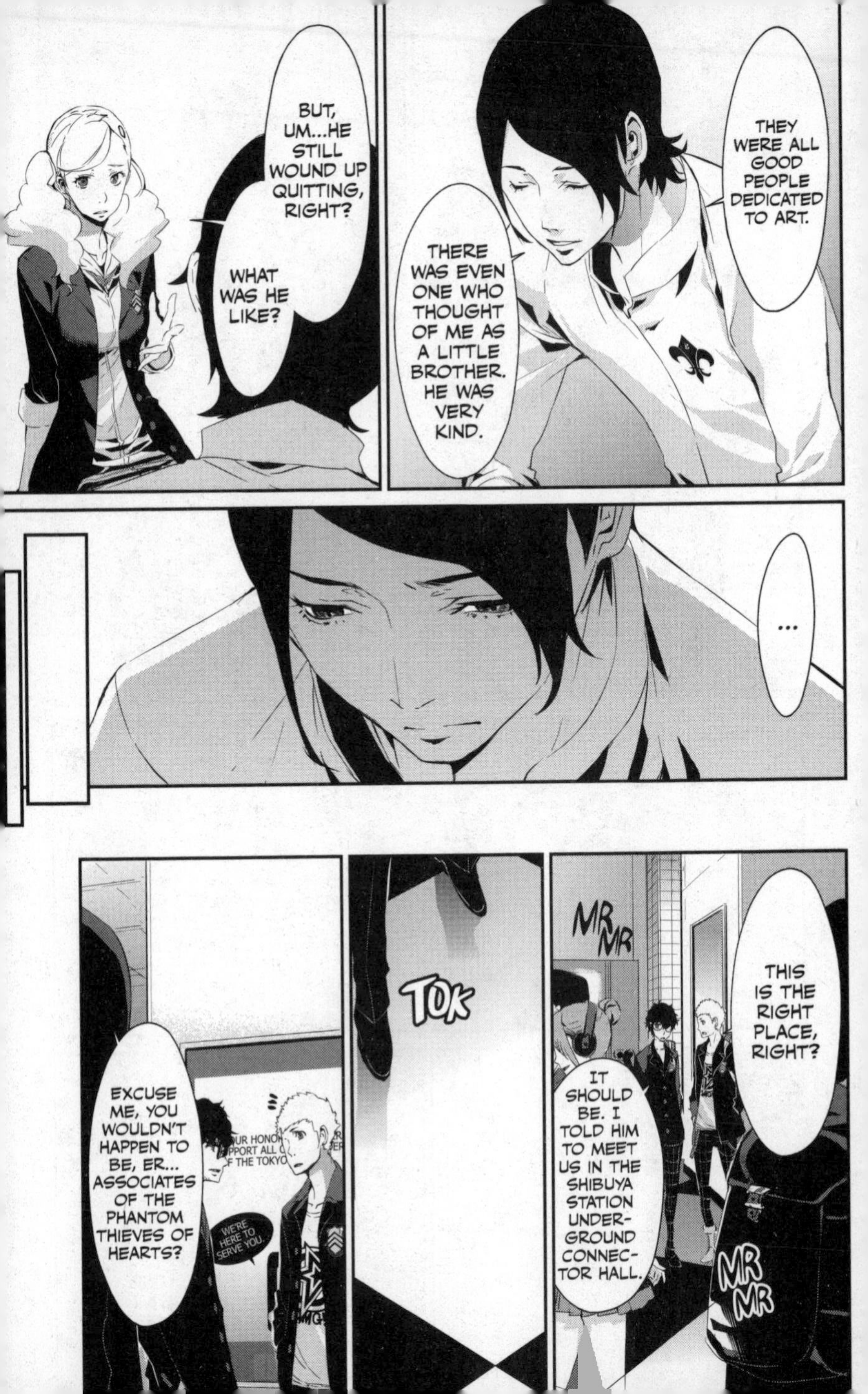
THEY WERE ALL GOOD PEOPLE DEDICATED TO ART.
THERE WAS EVEN ONE WHO THOUGHT OF ME AS A LITTLE BROTHER. HE WAS VERY KIND.
BUT, UM...HE STILL WOUND UP QUITTING, RIGHT?
WHAT WAS HE LIKE?
...
MR MR
THIS IS THE RIGHT PLACE, RIGHT?
IT SHOULD BE. I TOLD HIM TO MEET US IN THE SHIBUYA STATION UNDER-GROUND CONNEC-TOR HALL.
MR MR
TOK
EXCUSE ME, YOU WOULDN'T HAPPEN TO BE, ER... ASSOCIATES OF THE PHANTOM THIEVES OF HEARTS?
WE'RE HERE TO SERVE YOU.

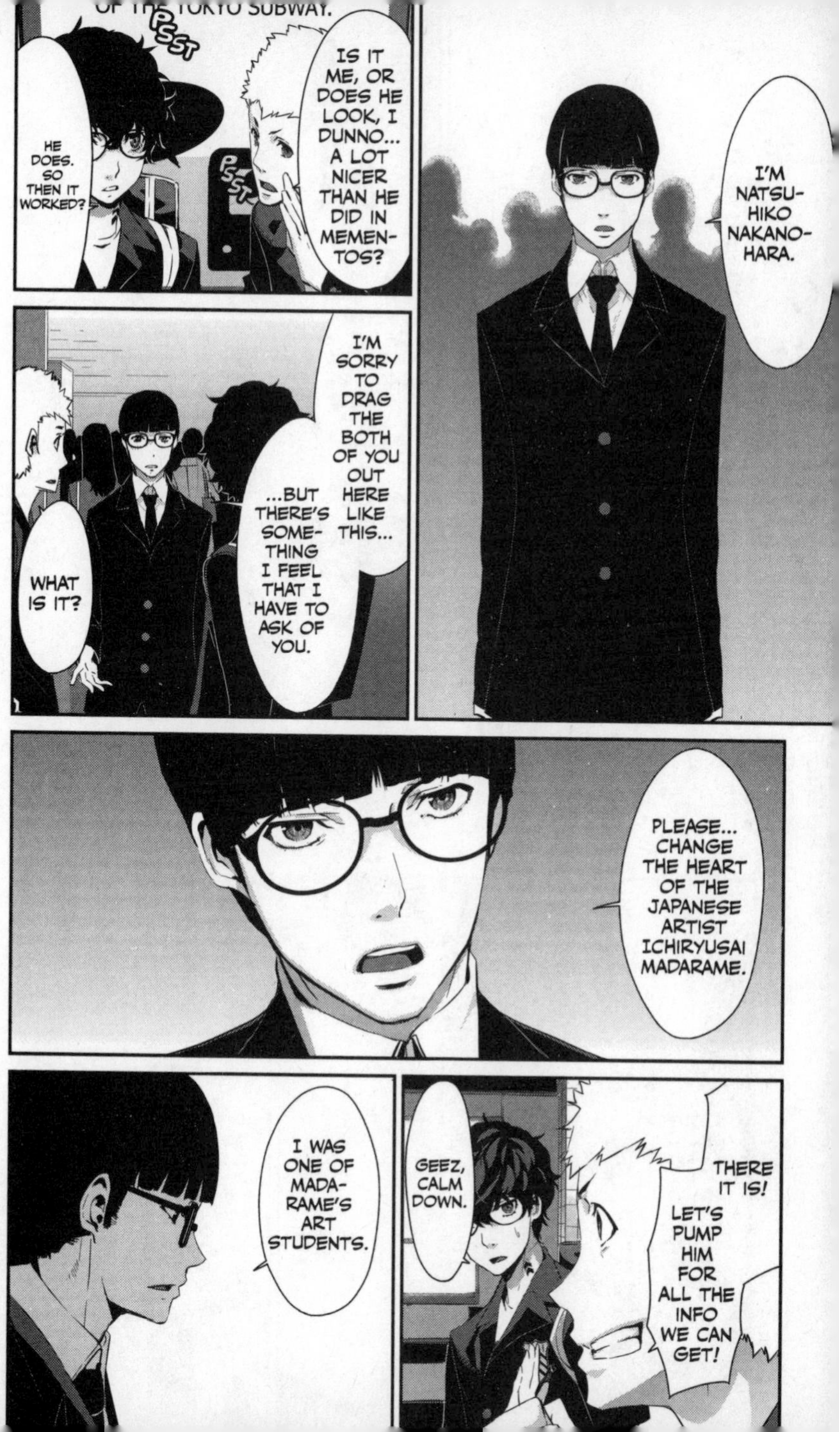
I'M NATSUHIKO NAKANOHARA.
OF THE TOKYO SUBWAY.
PSST
PSST
IS IT ME, OR DOES HE LOOK, I DUNNO... A LOT NICER THAN HE DID IN MEMENTOS?
HE DOES. SO THEN IT WORKED?
I'M SORRY TO DRAG THE BOTH OF YOU OUT HERE LIKE THIS...
...BUT THERE'S SOMETHING I FEEL THAT I HAVE TO ASK OF YOU.
WHAT IS IT?
PLEASE... CHANGE THE HEART OF THE JAPANESE ARTIST ICHIRYUSAI MADARAME.
THERE IT IS!
LET'S PUMP HIM FOR ALL THE INFO WE CAN GET!
GEEZ, CALM DOWN.
I WAS ONE OF MADARAME'S ART STUDENTS.

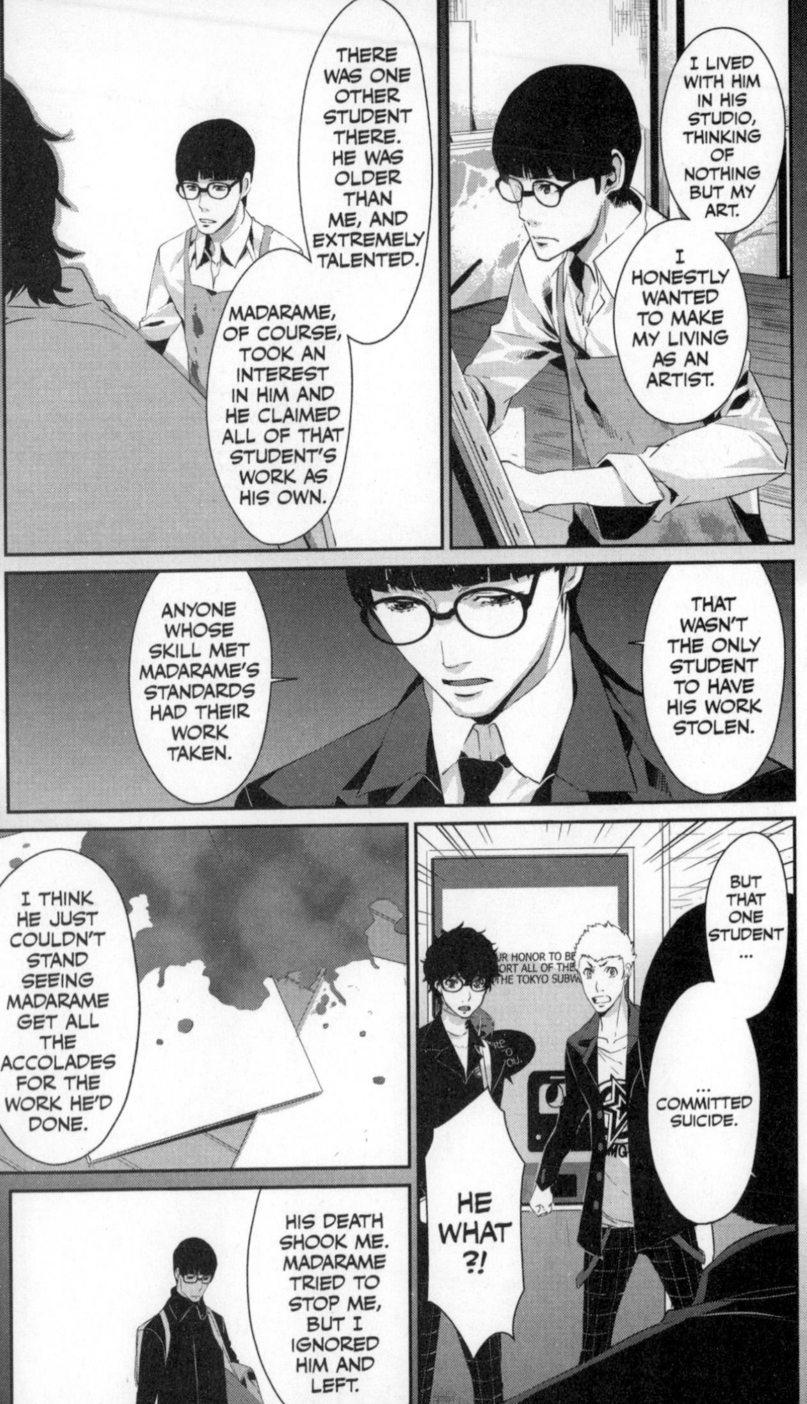
I LIVED WITH HIM IN HIS STUDIO, THINKING OF NOTHING BUT MY ART.
I HONESTLY WANTED TO MAKE MY LIVING AS AN ARTIST.
THERE WAS ONE OTHER STUDENT THERE. HE WAS OLDER THAN ME, AND EXTREMELY TALENTED.
MADARAME, OF COURSE, TOOK AN INTEREST IN HIM AND HE CLAIMED ALL OF THAT STUDENT'S WORK AS HIS OWN.
THAT WASN'T THE ONLY STUDENT TO HAVE HIS WORK STOLEN.
ANYONE WHOSE SKILL MET MADARAME'S STANDARDS HAD THEIR WORK TAKEN.
BUT THAT ONE STUDENT ...
... COMMITTED SUICIDE.
HE WHAT ?!
I THINK HE JUST COULDN'T STAND SEEING MADARAME GET ALL THE ACCOLADES FOR THE WORK HE'D DONE.
HIS DEATH SHOOK ME. MADARAME TRIED TO STOP ME, BUT I IGNORED HIM AND LEFT.

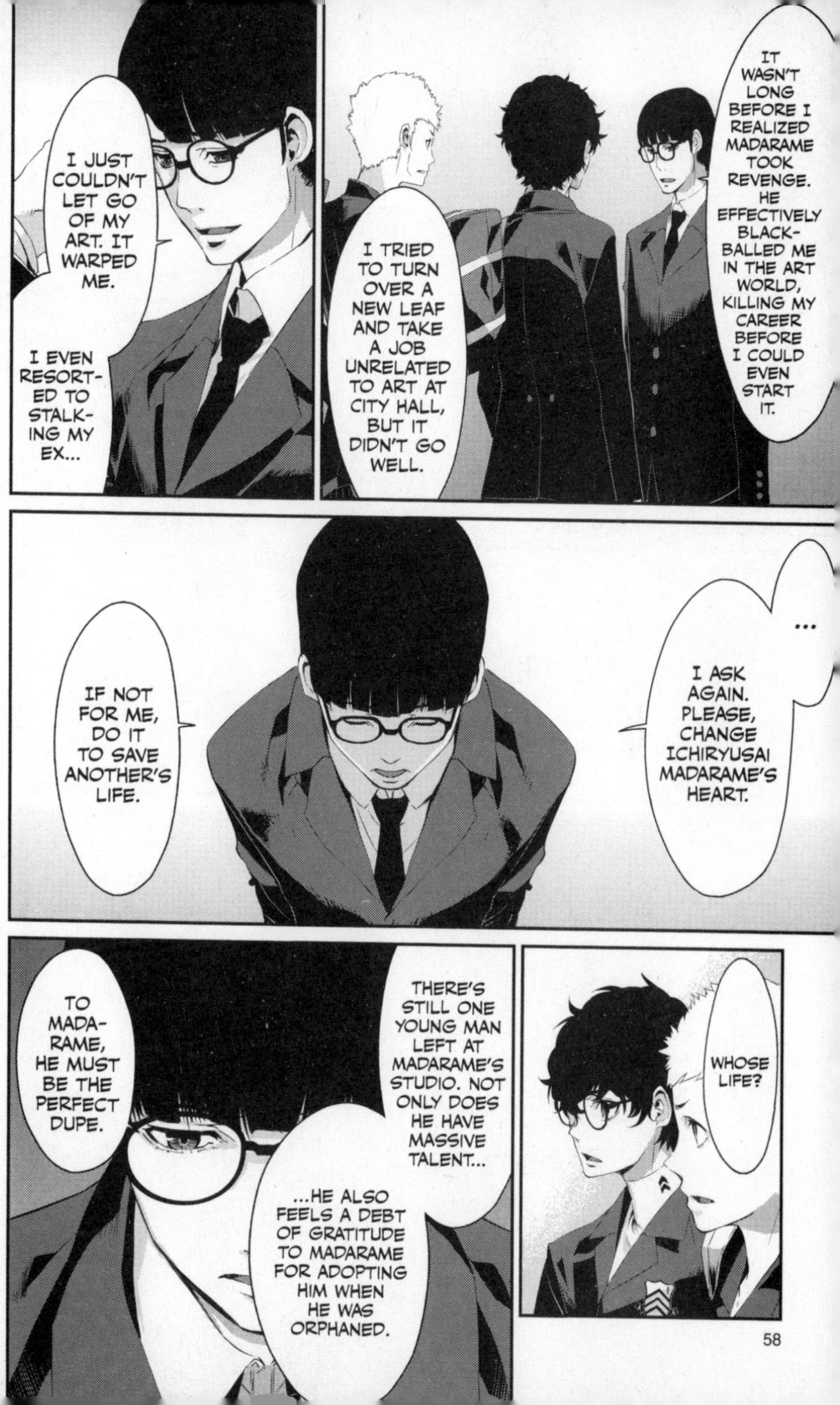
IT WASN'T LONG BEFORE I REALIZED MADARAME TOOK REVENGE. HE EFFECTIVELY BLACK-BALLED ME IN THE ART WORLD, KILLING MY CAREER BEFORE I COULD EVEN START IT.
I TRIED TO TURN OVER A NEW LEAF AND TAKE A JOB UNRELATED TO ART AT CITY HALL, BUT IT DIDN'T GO WELL.
I JUST COULDN'T LET GO OF MY ART. IT WARPED ME.
I EVEN RESORTED TO STALKING MY EX...
...
I ASK AGAIN. PLEASE, CHANGE ICHIRYUSAI MADARAME'S HEART.
IF NOT FOR ME, DO IT TO SAVE ANOTHER'S LIFE.
WHOSE LIFE?
THERE'S STILL ONE YOUNG MAN LEFT AT MADARAME'S STUDIO. NOT ONLY DOES HE HAVE MASSIVE TALENT...
...HE ALSO FEELS A DEBT OF GRATITUDE TO MADARAME FOR ADOPTING HIM WHEN HE WAS ORPHANED.
TO MADARAME, HE MUST BE THE PERFECT DUPE.

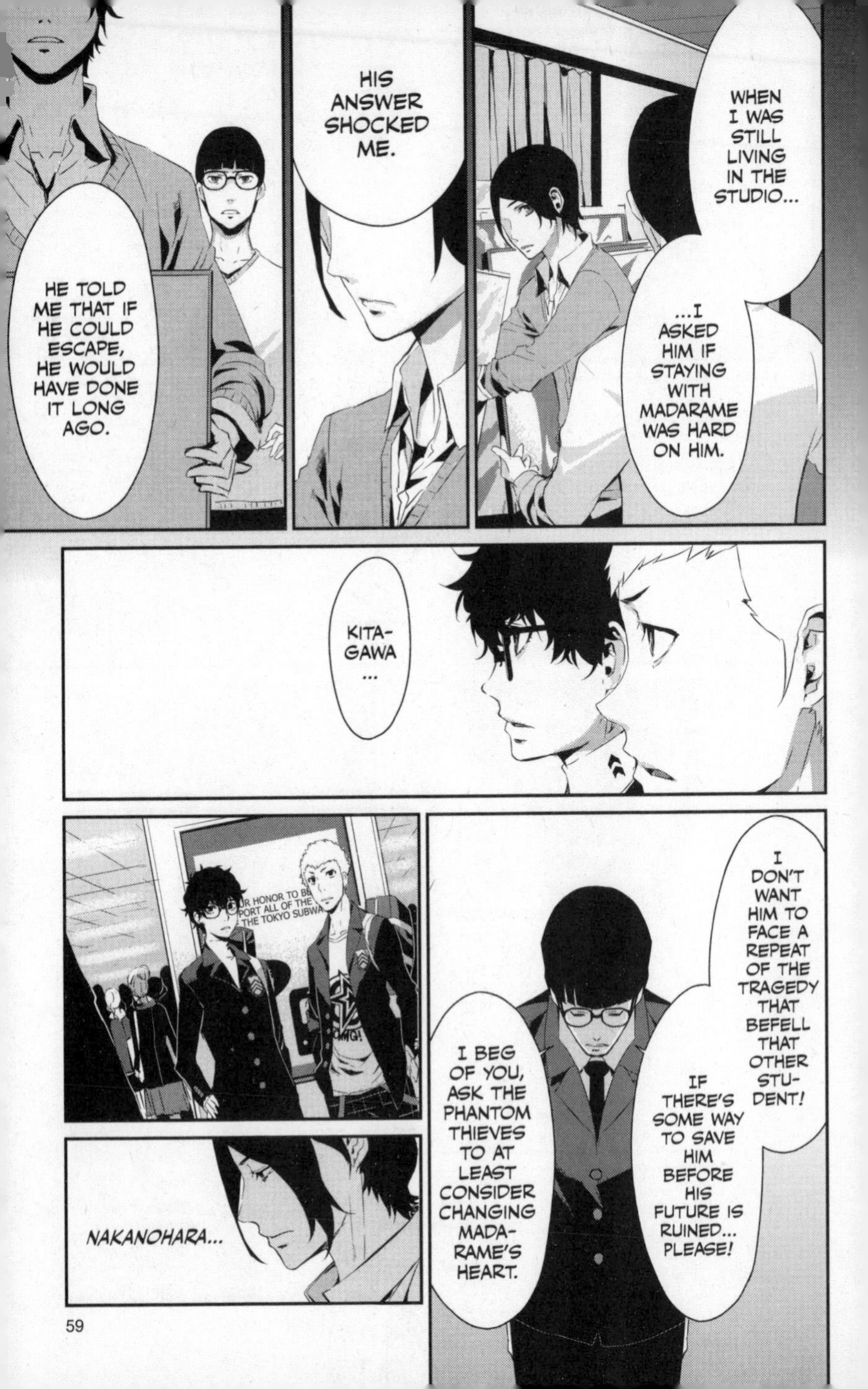
WHEN I WAS STILL LIVING IN THE STUDIO...
...I ASKED HIM IF STAYING WITH MADARAME WAS HARD ON HIM.
HIS ANSWER SHOCKED ME.
HE TOLD ME THAT IF HE COULD ESCAPE, HE WOULD HAVE DONE IT LONG AGO.
KITA-GAWA ...
I DON'T WANT HIM TO FACE A REPEAT OF THE TRAGEDY THAT BEFELL THAT OTHER STU-DENT!
IF THERE'S SOME WAY TO SAVE HIM BEFORE HIS FUTURE IS RUINED... PLEASE!
I BEG OF YOU, ASK THE PHANTOM THIEVES TO AT LEAST CONSIDER CHANGING MADA-RAME'S HEART.
NAKANOHARA...

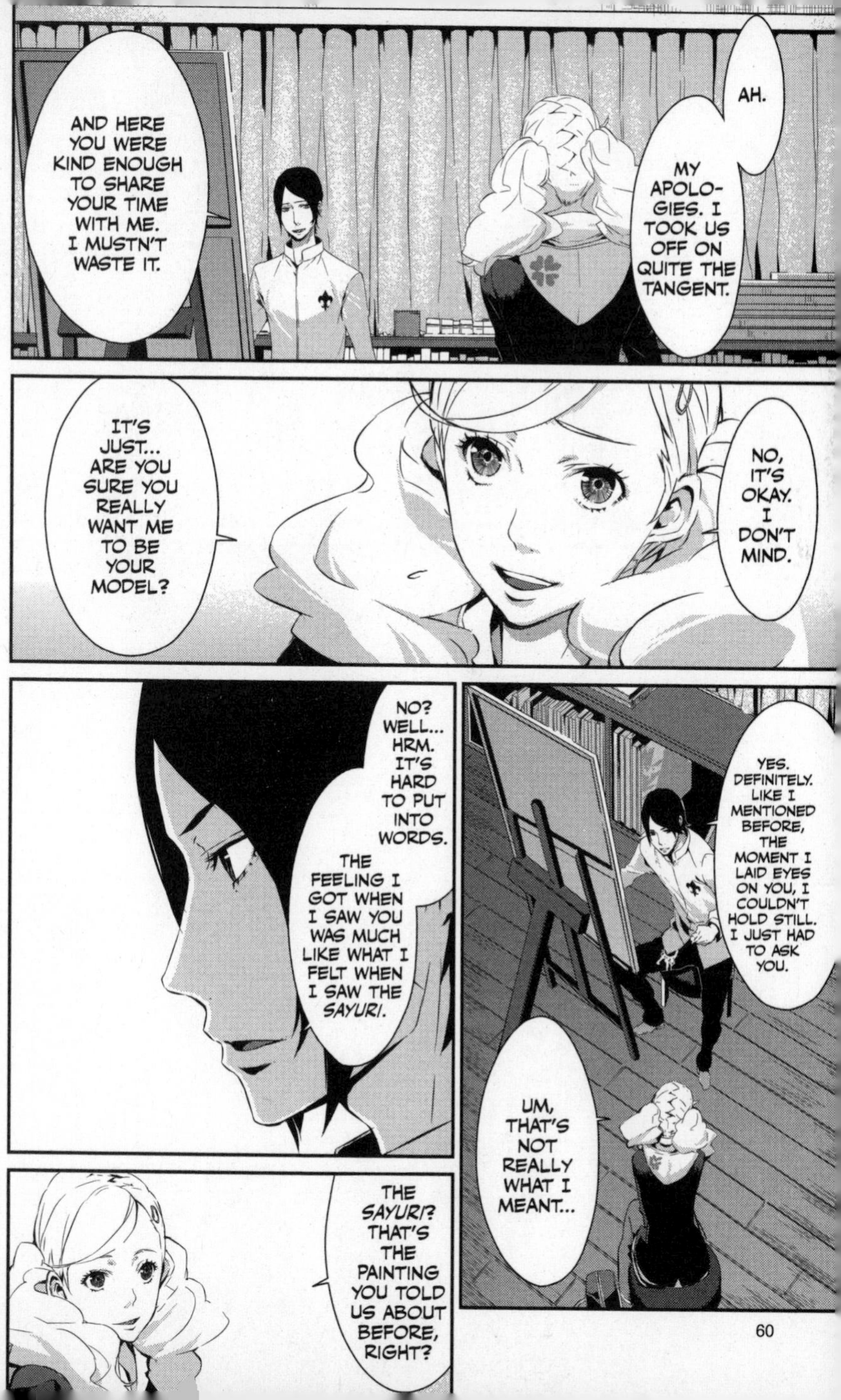
AH.
MY APOLOGIES. I TOOK US OFF ON QUITE THE TANGENT.
AND HERE YOU WERE KIND ENOUGH TO SHARE YOUR TIME WITH ME. I MUSTN'T WASTE IT.
NO, IT'S OKAY. I DON'T MIND.
IT'S JUST... ARE YOU SURE YOU REALLY WANT ME TO BE YOUR MODEL?
YES. DEFINITELY. LIKE I MENTIONED BEFORE, THE MOMENT I LAID EYES ON YOU, I COULDN'T HOLD STILL. I JUST HAD TO ASK YOU.
UM, THAT'S NOT REALLY WHAT I MEANT...
NO? WELL... HRM. IT'S HARD TO PUT INTO WORDS.
THE FEELING I GOT WHEN I SAW YOU WAS MUCH LIKE WHAT I FELT WHEN I SAW THE *SAYURI*.
THE *SAYURI*? THAT'S THE PAINTING YOU TOLD US ABOUT BEFORE, RIGHT?

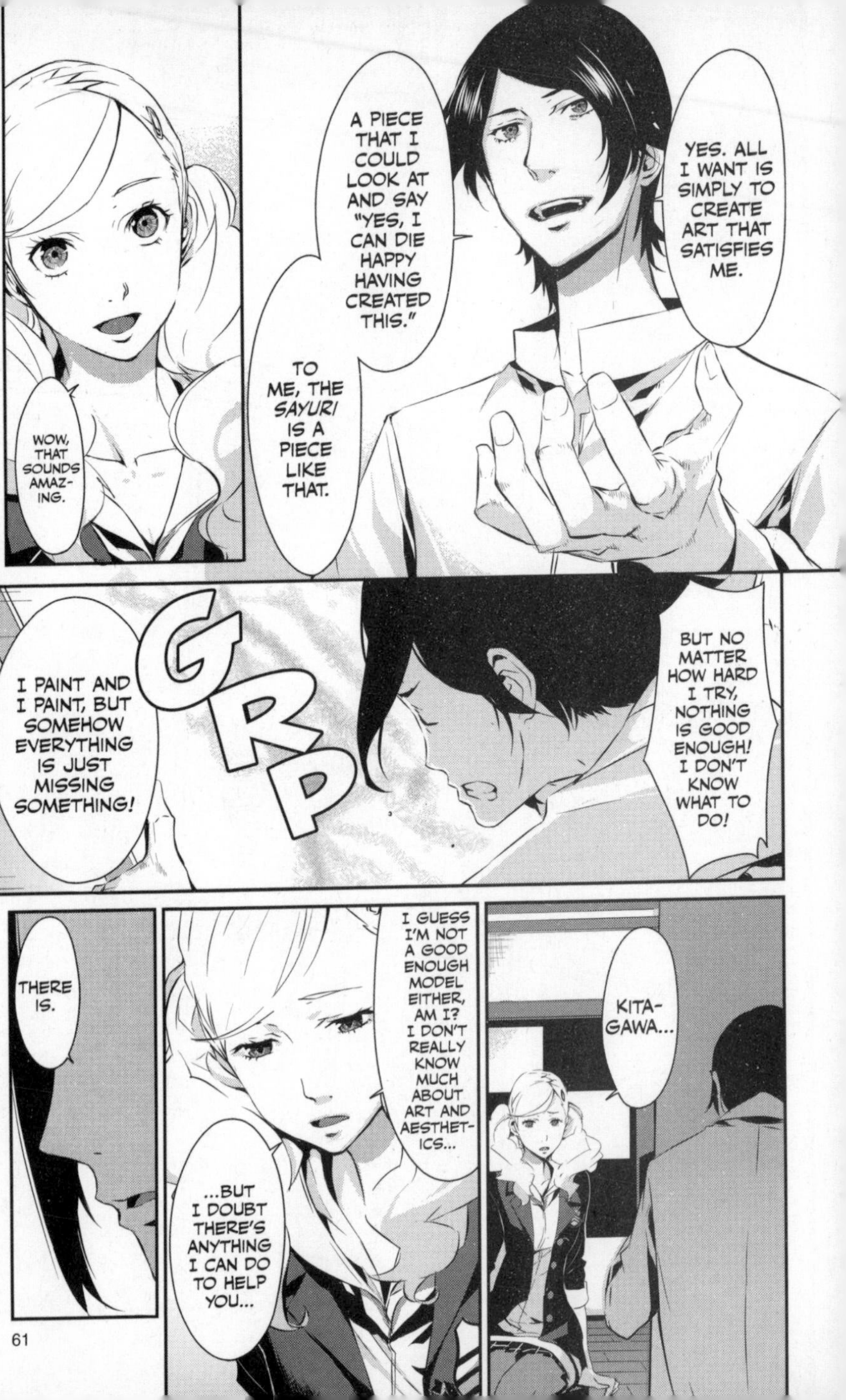
YES. ALL I WANT IS SIMPLY TO CREATE ART THAT SATISFIES ME.
A PIECE THAT I COULD LOOK AT AND SAY "YES, I CAN DIE HAPPY HAVING CREATED THIS."
TO ME, THE *SAYURI* IS A PIECE LIKE THAT.
WOW, THAT SOUNDS AMAZ-ING.
BUT NO MATTER HOW HARD I TRY, NOTHING IS GOOD ENOUGH! I DON'T KNOW WHAT TO DO!
GRP
I PAINT AND I PAINT, BUT SOMEHOW EVERYTHING IS JUST MISSING SOMETHING!
KITA-GAWA...
I GUESS I'M NOT A GOOD ENOUGH MODEL EITHER, AM I? I DON'T REALLY KNOW MUCH ABOUT ART AND AESTHET-ICS...
...BUT I DOUBT THERE'S ANYTHING I CAN DO TO HELP YOU...
THERE IS.

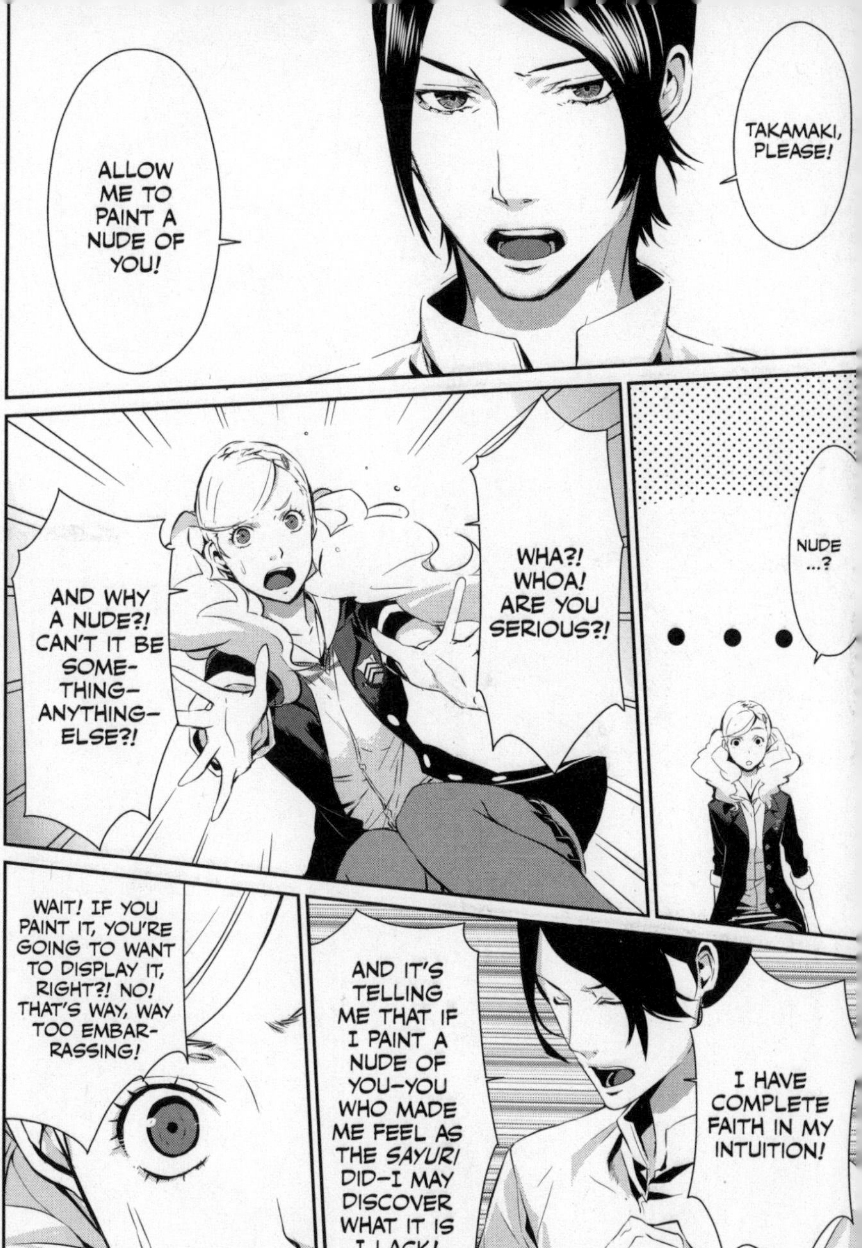
TAKAMAKI, PLEASE!
ALLOW ME TO PAINT A NUDE OF YOU!
NUDE ...?
• • •
WHA?! WHOA! ARE YOU SERIOUS?!
AND WHY A NUDE?! CAN'T IT BE SOME-THING—ANYTHING—ELSE?!
I HAVE COMPLETE FAITH IN MY INTUITION!
AND IT'S TELLING ME THAT IF I PAINT A NUDE OF YOU—YOU WHO MADE ME FEEL AS THE *SAYURI* DID—I MAY DISCOVER WHAT IT IS I LACK!
WAIT! IF YOU PAINT IT, YOU'RE GOING TO WANT TO DISPLAY IT, RIGHT?! NO! THAT'S WAY, WAY TOO EMBAR-RASSING!

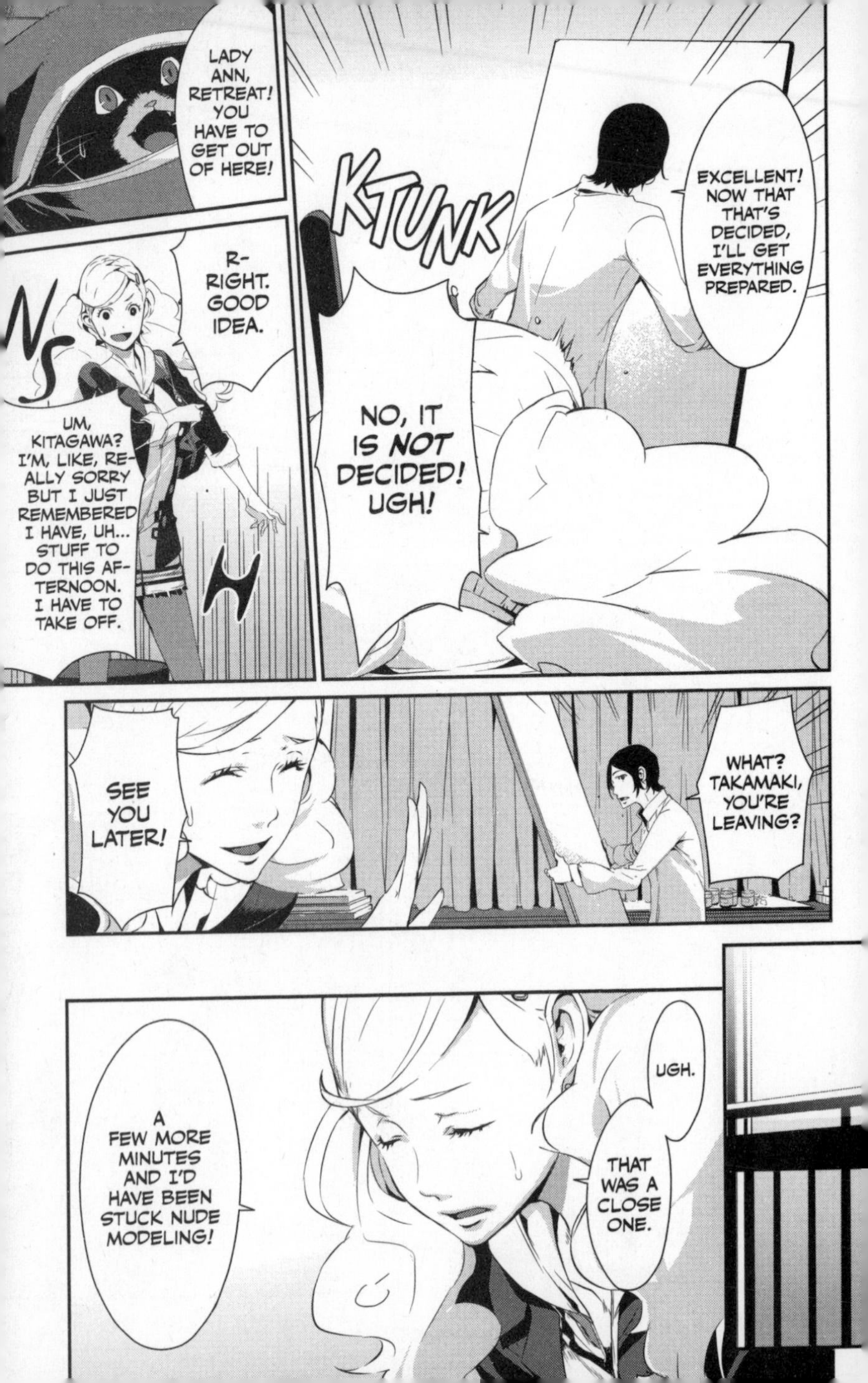
EXCELLENT! NOW THAT THAT'S DECIDED, I'LL GET EVERYTHING PREPARED.
KTUNK
NO, IT IS NOT DECIDED! UGH!
LADY ANN, RETREAT! YOU HAVE TO GET OUT OF HERE!
R-RIGHT. GOOD IDEA.
UM, KITAGAWA? I'M, LIKE, RE-ALLY SORRY BUT I JUST REMEMBERED I HAVE, UH... STUFF TO DO THIS AF-TERNOON. I HAVE TO TAKE OFF.
WHAT? TAKAMAKI, YOU'RE LEAVING?
SEE YOU LATER!
UGH.
THAT WAS A CLOSE ONE.
A FEW MORE MINUTES AND I'D HAVE BEEN STUCK NUDE MODELING!

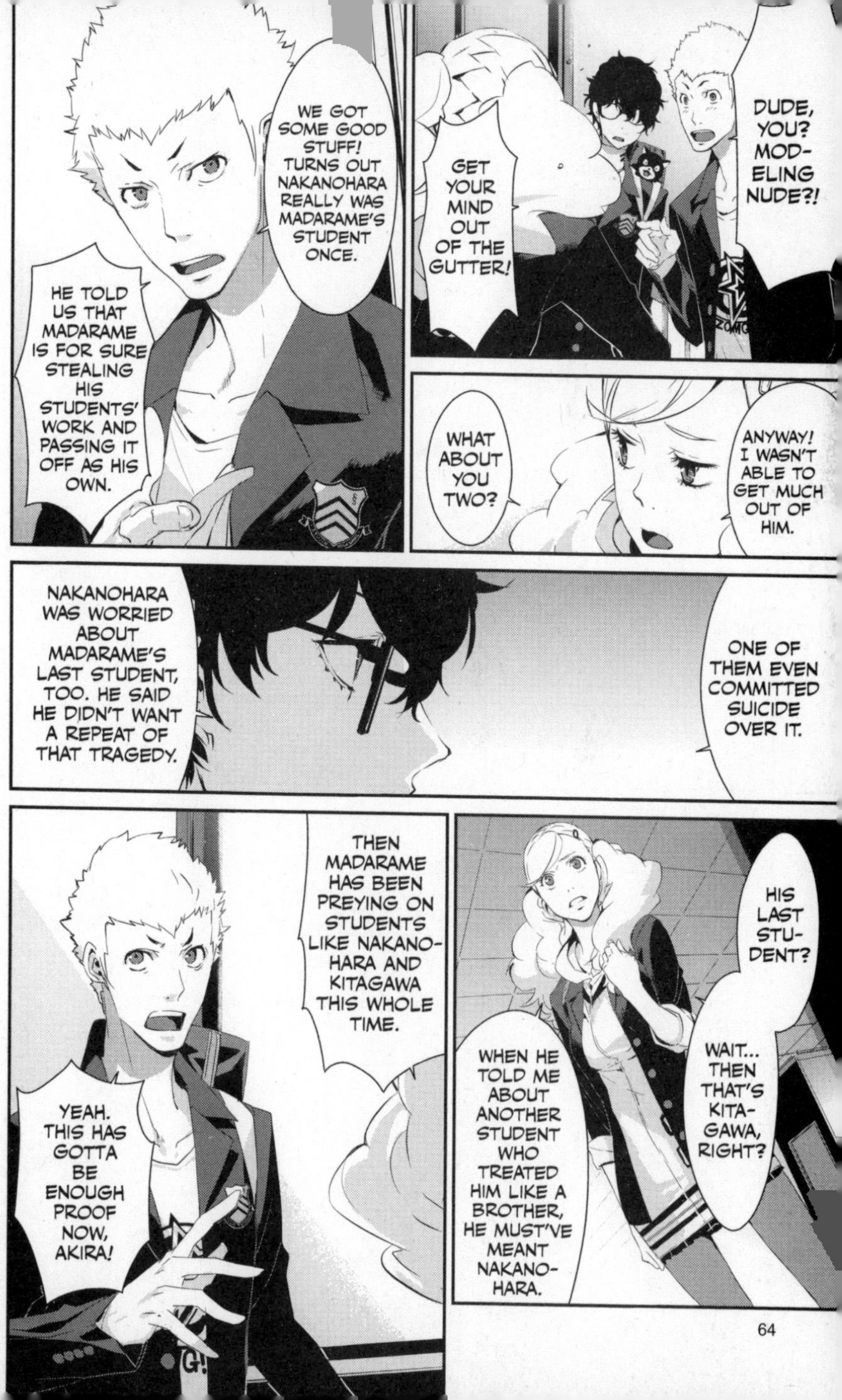
DUDE, YOU? MODELING NUDE?!
GET YOUR MIND OUT OF THE GUTTER!
ANYWAY! I WASN'T ABLE TO GET MUCH OUT OF HIM.
WHAT ABOUT YOU TWO?
WE GOT SOME GOOD STUFF! TURNS OUT NAKANOHARA REALLY WAS MADARAME'S STUDENT ONCE.
HE TOLD US THAT MADARAME IS FOR SURE STEALING HIS STUDENTS' WORK AND PASSING IT OFF AS HIS OWN.
ONE OF THEM EVEN COMMITTED SUICIDE OVER IT.
NAKANOHARA WAS WORRIED ABOUT MADARAME'S LAST STUDENT, TOO. HE SAID HE DIDN'T WANT A REPEAT OF THAT TRAGEDY.
HIS LAST STUDENT?
WAIT... THEN THAT'S KITAGAWA, RIGHT?
WHEN HE TOLD ME ABOUT ANOTHER STUDENT WHO TREATED HIM LIKE A BROTHER, HE MUST'VE MEANT NAKANOHARA.
THEN MADARAME HAS BEEN PREYING ON STUDENTS LIKE NAKANOHARA AND KITAGAWA THIS WHOLE TIME.
YEAH. THIS HAS GOTTA BE ENOUGH PROOF NOW, AKIRA!

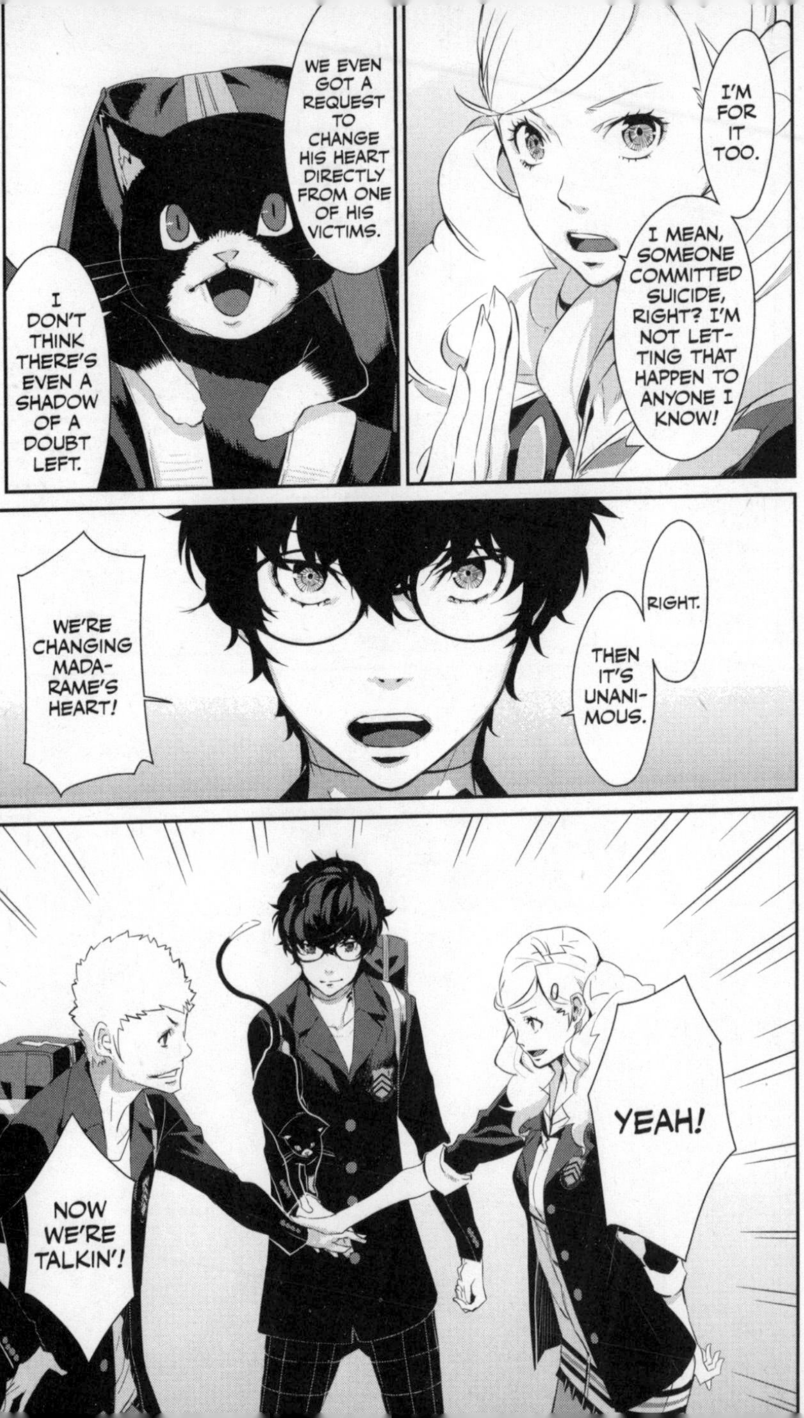
I'M FOR IT TOO.
I MEAN, SOMEONE COMMITTED SUICIDE, RIGHT? I'M NOT LET-TING THAT HAPPEN TO ANYONE I KNOW!
WE EVEN GOT A REQUEST TO CHANGE HIS HEART DIRECTLY FROM ONE OF HIS VICTIMS.
I DON'T THINK THERE'S EVEN A SHADOW OF A DOUBT LEFT.
RIGHT.
THEN IT'S UNANI-MOUS.
WE'RE CHANGING MADA-RAME'S HEART!
YEAH!
NOW WE'RE TALKIN'!

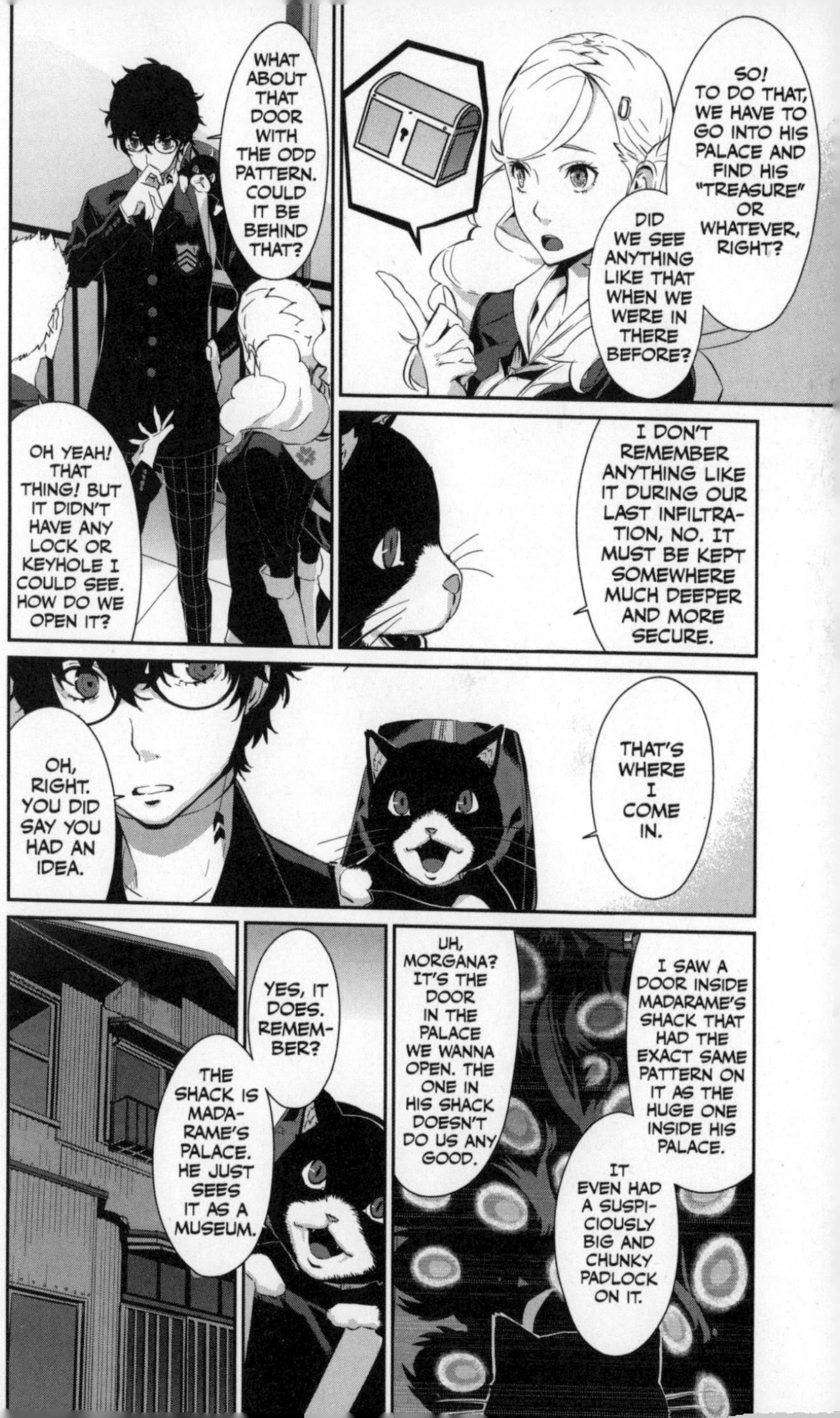

SO! TO DO THAT, WE HAVE TO GO INTO HIS PALACE AND FIND HIS "TREASURE" OR WHATEVER, RIGHT?
DID WE SEE ANYTHING LIKE THAT WHEN WE WERE IN THERE BEFORE?
I DON'T REMEMBER ANYTHING LIKE IT DURING OUR LAST INFILTRATION, NO. IT MUST BE KEPT SOMEWHERE MUCH DEEPER AND MORE SECURE.
WHAT ABOUT THAT DOOR WITH THE ODD PATTERN. COULD IT BE BEHIND THAT?
OH YEAH! THAT THING! BUT IT DIDN'T HAVE ANY LOCK OR KEYHOLE I COULD SEE. HOW DO WE OPEN IT?
THAT'S WHERE I COME IN.
OH, RIGHT. YOU DID SAY YOU HAD AN IDEA.
I SAW A DOOR INSIDE MADARAME'S SHACK THAT HAD THE EXACT SAME PATTERN ON IT AS THE HUGE ONE INSIDE HIS PALACE.
IT EVEN HAD A SUSPICIOUSLY BIG AND CHUNKY PADLOCK ON IT.
UH, MORGANA? IT'S THE DOOR IN THE PALACE WE WANNA OPEN. THE ONE IN HIS SHACK DOESN'T DO US ANY GOOD.
YES, IT DOES. REMEMBER?
THE SHACK IS MADA-RAME'S PALACE. HE JUST SEES IT AS A MUSEUM.

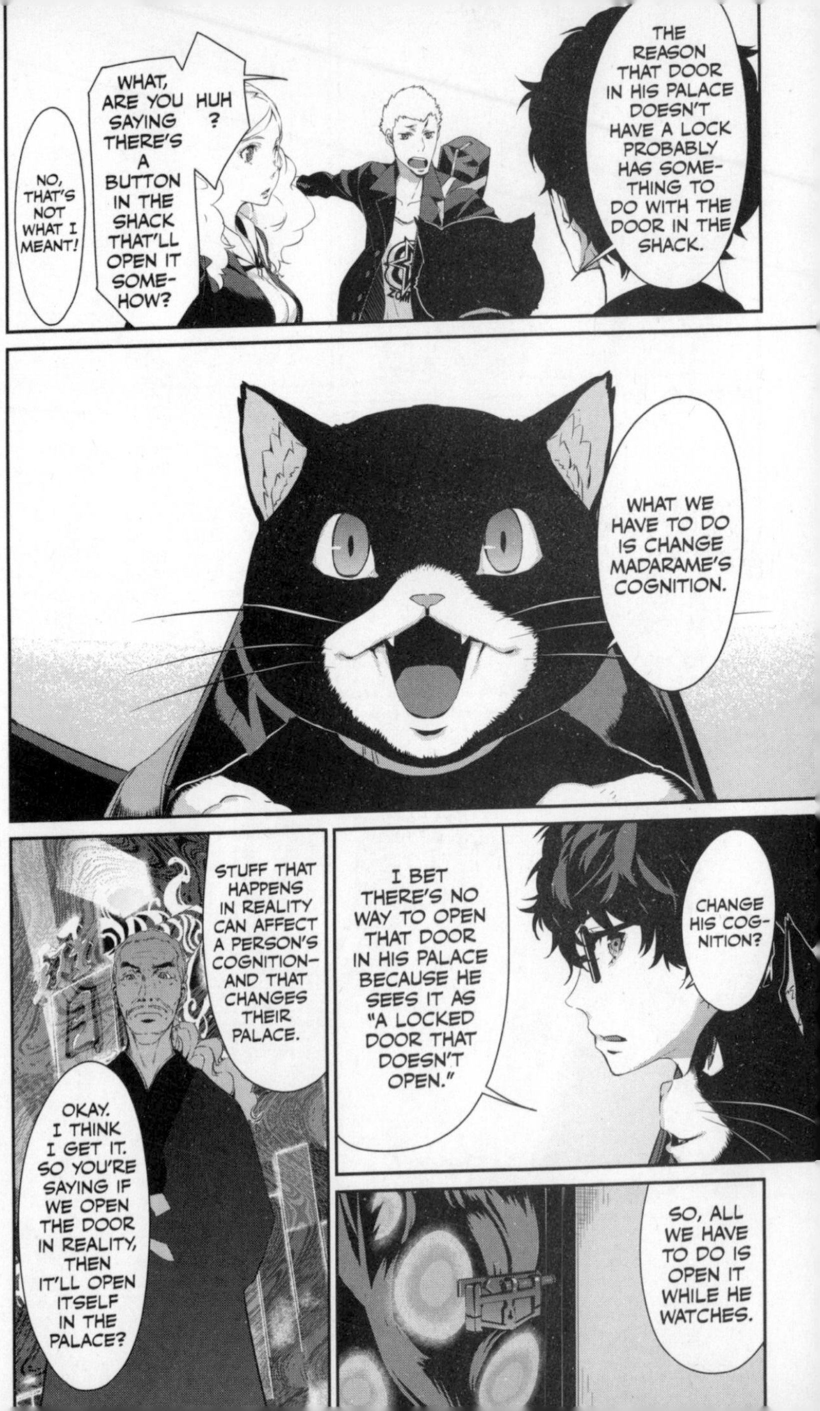
THE REASON THAT DOOR IN HIS PALACE DOESN'T HAVE A LOCK PROBABLY HAS SOME-THING TO DO WITH THE DOOR IN THE SHACK.
HUH?
WHAT, ARE YOU SAYING THERE'S A BUTTON IN THE SHACK THAT'LL OPEN IT SOME-HOW?
NO, THAT'S NOT WHAT I MEANT!
WHAT WE HAVE TO DO IS CHANGE MADARAME'S COGNITION.
CHANGE HIS COG-NITION?
I BET THERE'S NO WAY TO OPEN THAT DOOR IN HIS PALACE BECAUSE HE SEES IT AS "A LOCKED DOOR THAT DOESN'T OPEN."
SO, ALL WE HAVE TO DO IS OPEN IT WHILE HE WATCHES.
STUFF THAT HAPPENS IN REALITY CAN AFFECT A PERSON'S COGNITION—AND THAT CHANGES THEIR PALACE.
OKAY. I THINK I GET IT. SO YOU'RE SAYING IF WE OPEN THE DOOR IN REALITY, THEN IT'LL OPEN ITSELF IN THE PALACE?

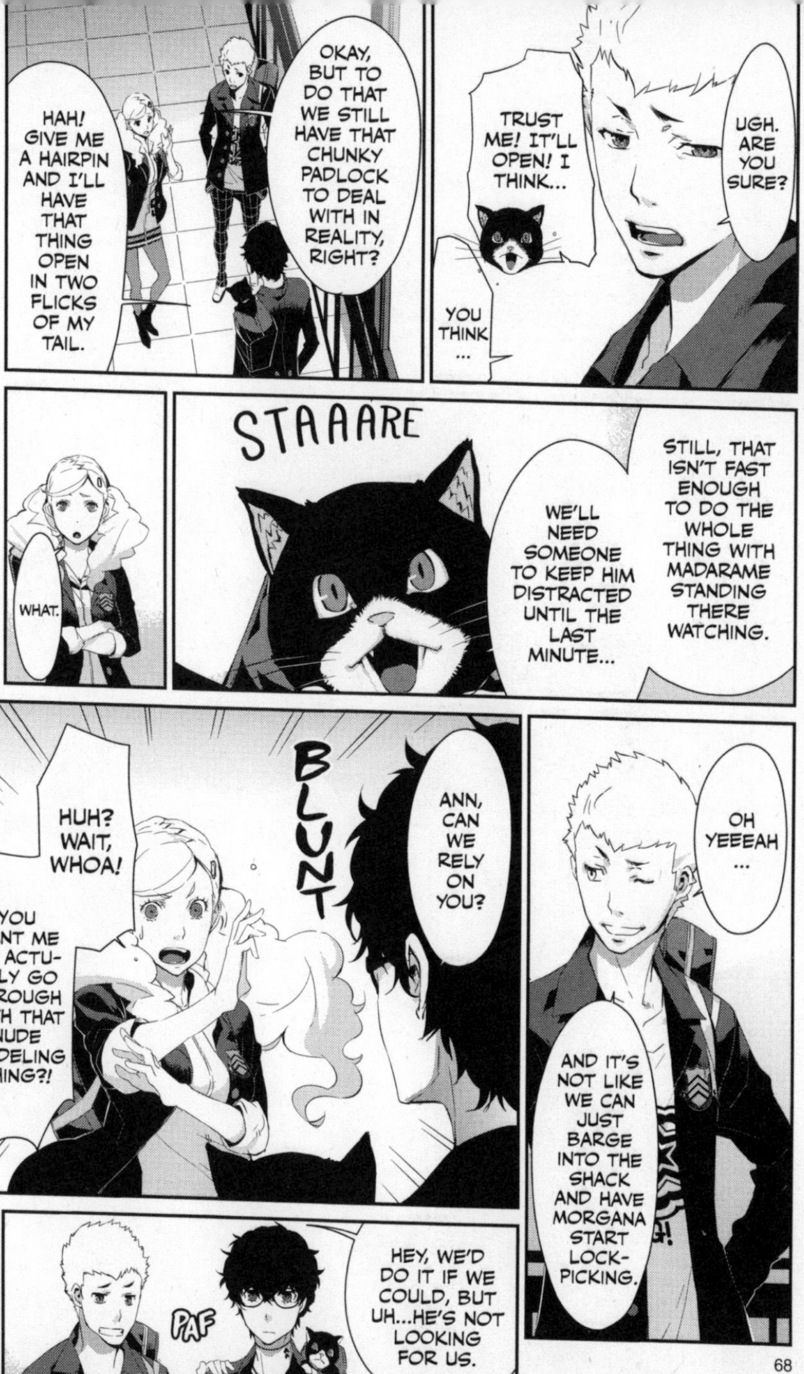

UGH. ARE YOU SURE?
TRUST ME! IT'LL OPEN! I THINK...
YOU THINK ...
OKAY, BUT TO DO THAT WE STILL HAVE THAT CHUNKY PADLOCK TO DEAL WITH IN REALITY, RIGHT?
HAH! GIVE ME A HAIRPIN AND I'LL HAVE THAT THING OPEN IN TWO FLICKS OF MY TAIL.
STILL, THAT ISN'T FAST ENOUGH TO DO THE WHOLE THING WITH MADARAME STANDING THERE WATCHING.
WE'LL NEED SOMEONE TO KEEP HIM DISTRACTED UNTIL THE LAST MINUTE...
STAAARE
WHAT.
OH YEEEAH ...
AND IT'S NOT LIKE WE CAN JUST BARGE INTO THE SHACK AND HAVE MORGANA START LOCK-PICKING.
ANN, CAN WE RELY ON YOU?
BLUNT
HUH? WAIT, WHOA!
YOU WANT ME TO ACTU-ALLY GO THROUGH WITH THAT NUDE MODELING THING?!
HEY, WE'D DO IT IF WE COULD, BUT UH...HE'S NOT LOOKING FOR US.
PAF

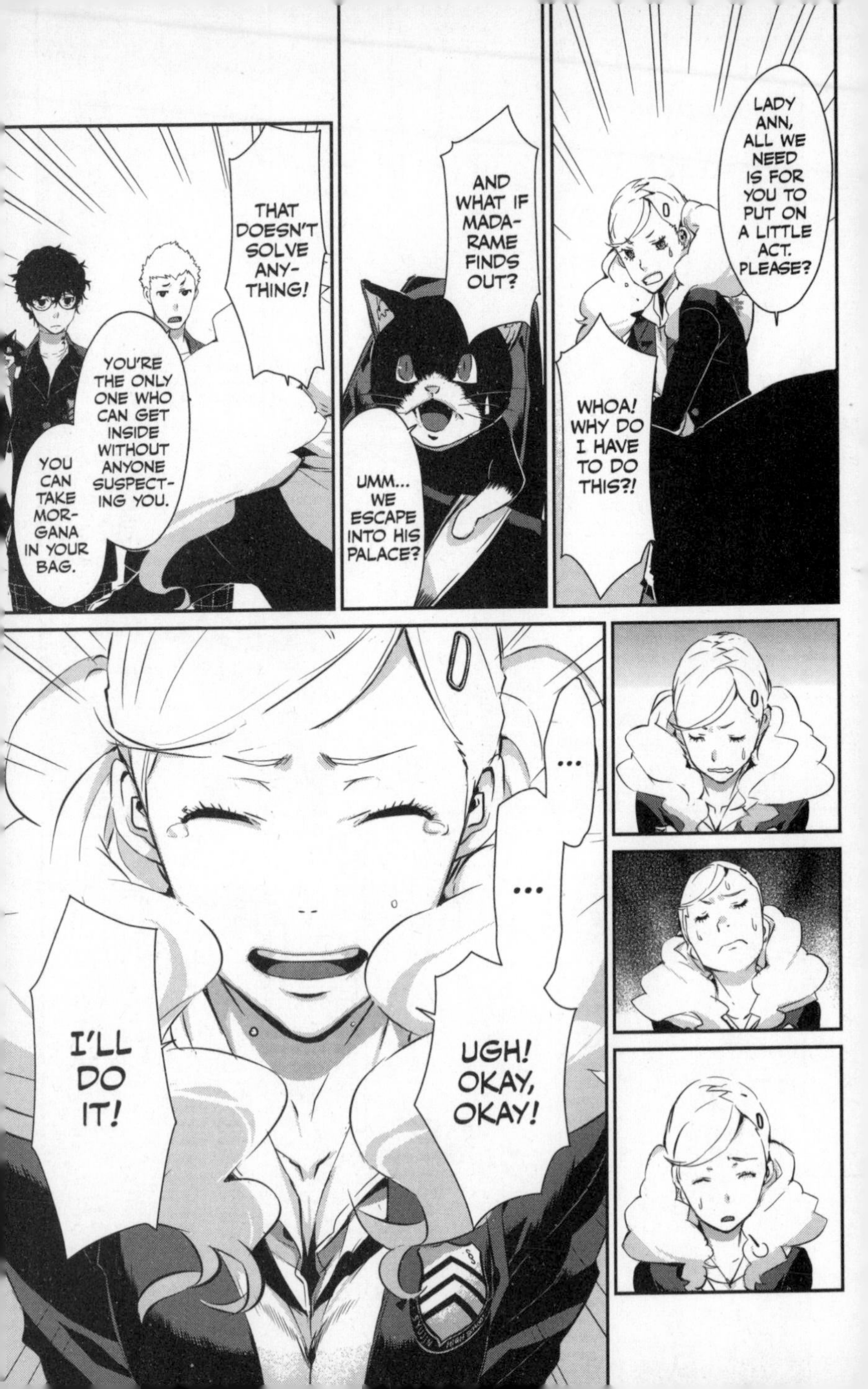
LADY ANN, ALL WE NEED IS FOR YOU TO PUT ON A LITTLE ACT. PLEASE?
WHOA! WHY DO I HAVE TO DO THIS?!
AND WHAT IF MADA-RAME FINDS OUT?
UMM... WE ESCAPE INTO HIS PALACE?
THAT DOESN'T SOLVE ANY-THING!
YOU'RE THE ONLY ONE WHO CAN GET INSIDE WITHOUT ANYONE SUSPECT-ING YOU.
YOU CAN TAKE MOR-GANA IN YOUR BAG.
...
...
UGH! OKAY, OKAY!
I'LL DO IT!

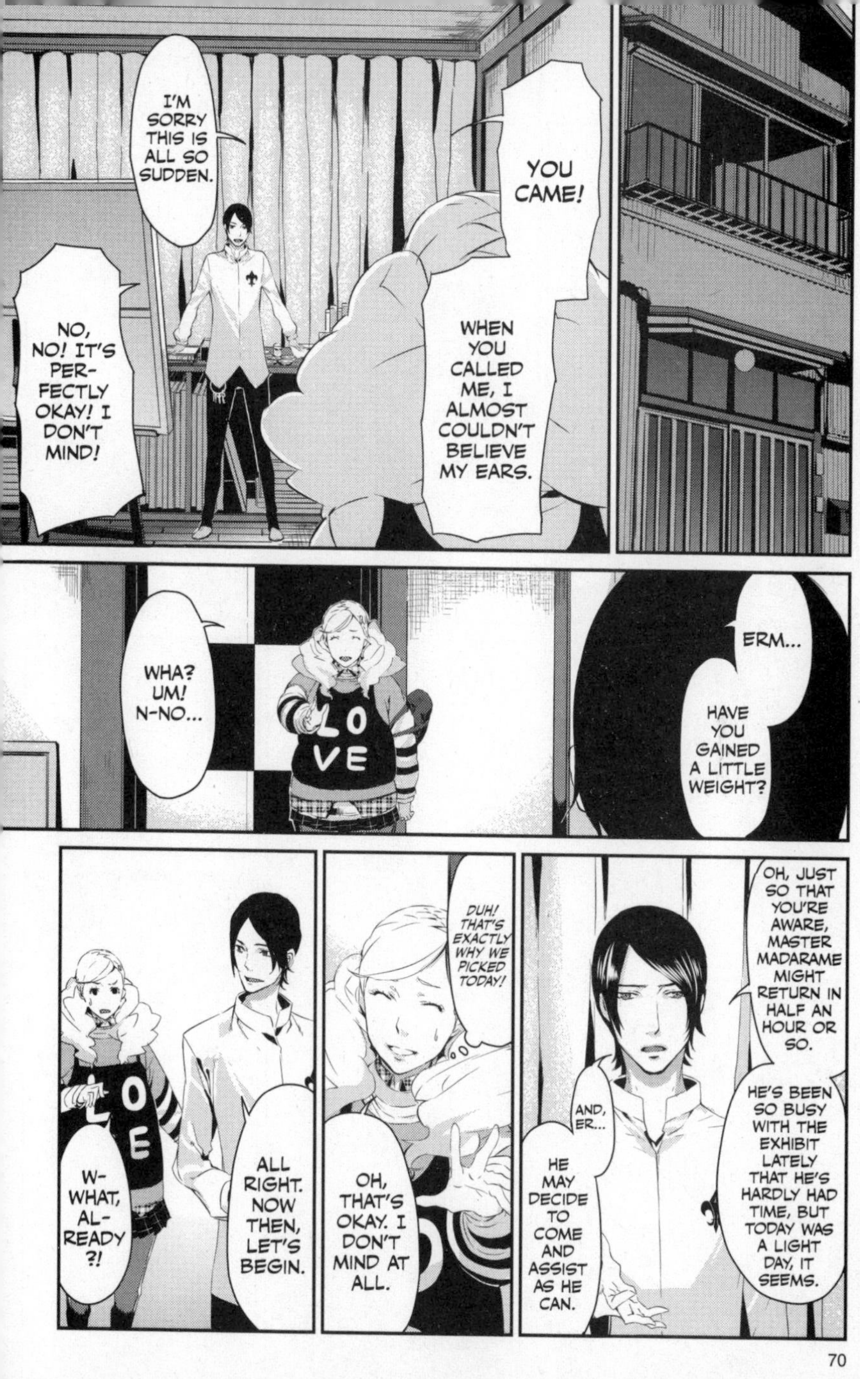
YOU CAME!
WHEN YOU CALLED ME, I ALMOST COULDN'T BELIEVE MY EARS.
I'M SORRY THIS IS ALL SO SUDDEN.
NO, NO! IT'S PER-FECTLY OKAY! I DON'T MIND!
ERM...
HAVE YOU GAINED A LITTLE WEIGHT?
WHA? UM! N-NO...
LO VE
OH, JUST SO THAT YOU'RE AWARE, MASTER MADARAME MIGHT RETURN IN HALF AN HOUR OR SO.
HE'S BEEN SO BUSY WITH THE EXHIBIT LATELY THAT HE'S HARDLY HAD TIME, BUT TODAY WAS A LIGHT DAY, IT SEEMS.
AND, ER...
HE MAY DECIDE TO COME AND ASSIST AS HE CAN.
DUH! THAT'S EXACTLY WHY WE PICKED TODAY!
OH, THAT'S OKAY. I DON'T MIND AT ALL.
ALL RIGHT. NOW THEN, LET'S BEGIN.
W-WHAT, AL-READY?!

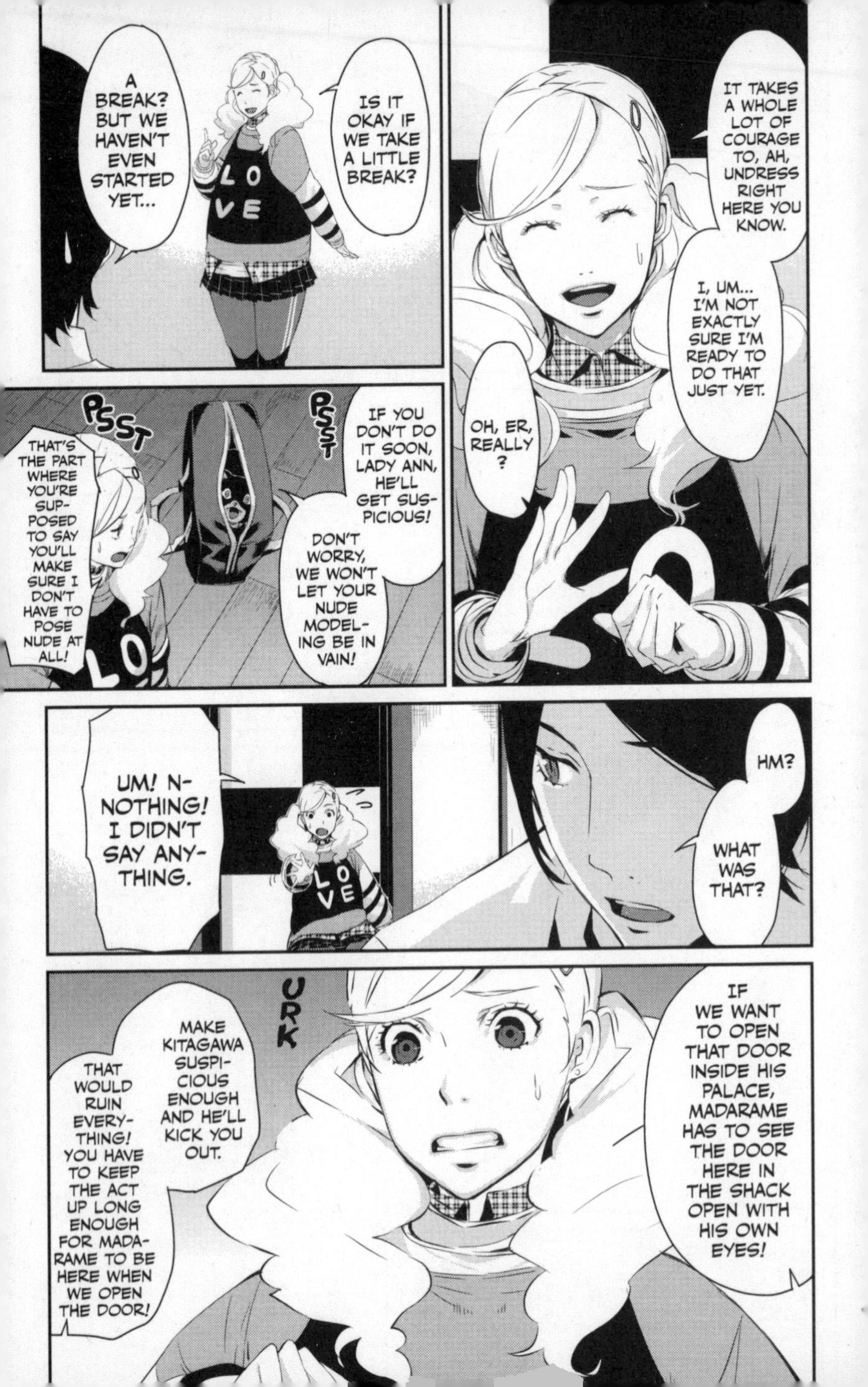
IT TAKES A WHOLE LOT OF COURAGE TO, AH, UNDRESS RIGHT HERE YOU KNOW.
I, UM... I'M NOT EXACTLY SURE I'M READY TO DO THAT JUST YET.
OH, ER, REALLY?
IS IT OKAY IF WE TAKE A LITTLE BREAK?
A BREAK? BUT WE HAVEN'T EVEN STARTED YET...
PSST
IF YOU DON'T DO IT SOON, LADY ANN, HE'LL GET SUSPICIOUS!
DON'T WORRY, WE WON'T LET YOUR NUDE MODELING BE IN VAIN!
PSST
THAT'S THE PART WHERE YOU'RE SUPPOSED TO SAY YOU'LL MAKE SURE I DON'T HAVE TO POSE NUDE AT ALL!
HM?
WHAT WAS THAT?
UM! N-NOTHING! I DIDN'T SAY ANYTHING.
IF WE WANT TO OPEN THAT DOOR INSIDE HIS PALACE, MADARAME HAS TO SEE THE DOOR HERE IN THE SHACK OPEN WITH HIS OWN EYES!
URK
MAKE KITAGAWA SUSPICIOUS ENOUGH AND HE'LL KICK YOU OUT.
THAT WOULD RUIN EVERYTHING! YOU HAVE TO KEEP THE ACT UP LONG ENOUGH FOR MADARAME TO BE HERE WHEN WE OPEN THE DOOR!

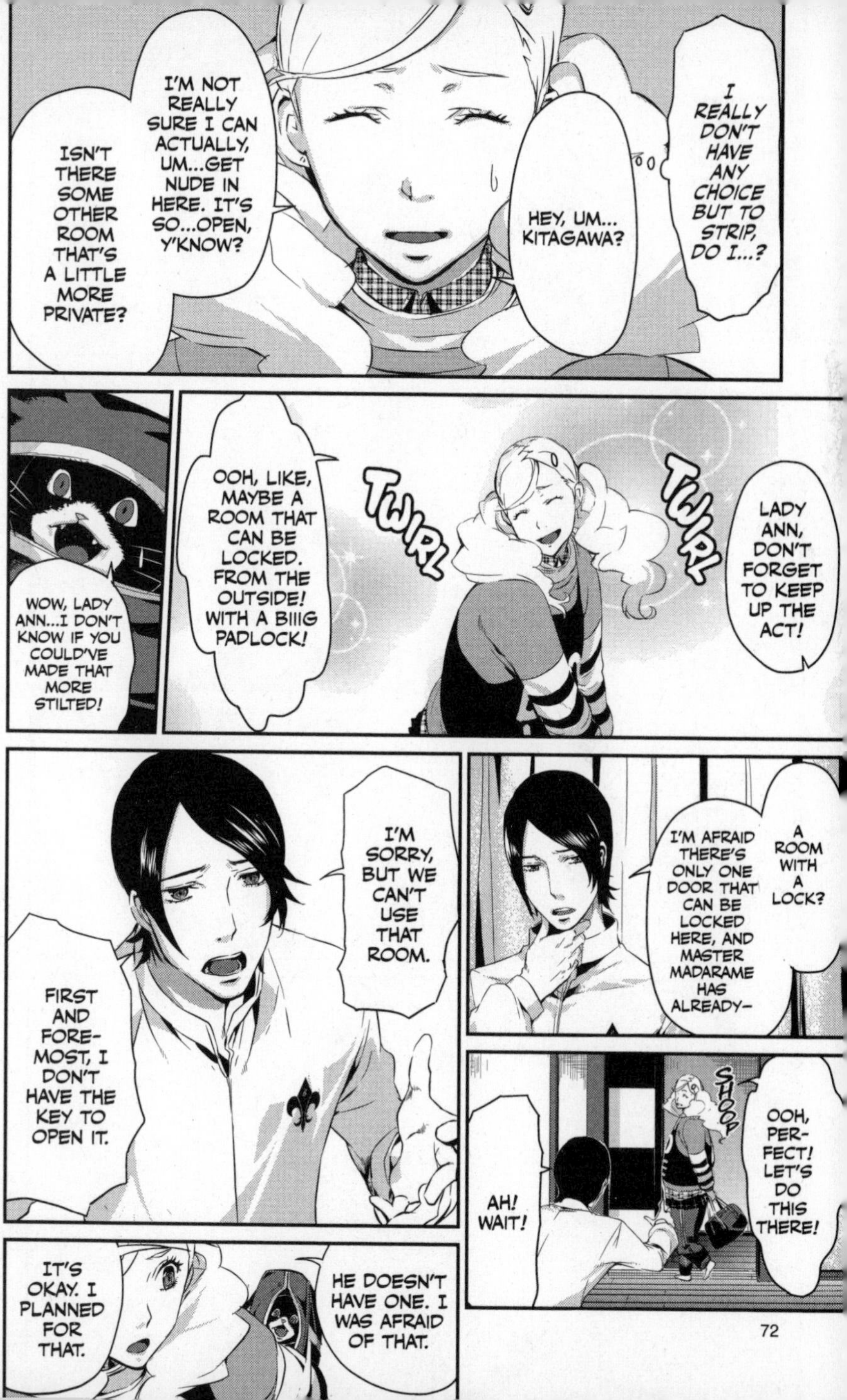
I REALLY DON'T HAVE ANY CHOICE BUT TO STRIP, DO I...?
HEY, UM... KITAGAWA?
I'M NOT REALLY SURE I CAN ACTUALLY, UM...GET NUDE IN HERE. IT'S SO...OPEN, Y'KNOW?
ISN'T THERE SOME OTHER ROOM THAT'S A LITTLE MORE PRIVATE?
LADY ANN, DON'T FORGET TO KEEP UP THE ACT!
TWIRL
TWIRL
OOH, LIKE, MAYBE A ROOM THAT CAN BE LOCKED. FROM THE OUTSIDE! WITH A BIIIG PADLOCK!
WOW, LADY ANN...I DON'T KNOW IF YOU COULD'VE MADE THAT MORE STILTED!
A ROOM WITH A LOCK?
I'M AFRAID THERE'S ONLY ONE DOOR THAT CAN BE LOCKED HERE, AND MASTER MADARAME HAS ALREADY-
OOH, PER-FECT! LET'S DO THIS THERE!
SHOOP
AH! WAIT!
I'M SORRY, BUT WE CAN'T USE THAT ROOM.
FIRST AND FORE-MOST, I DON'T HAVE THE KEY TO OPEN IT.
HE DOESN'T HAVE ONE. I WAS AFRAID OF THAT.
IT'S OKAY. I PLANNED FOR THAT.

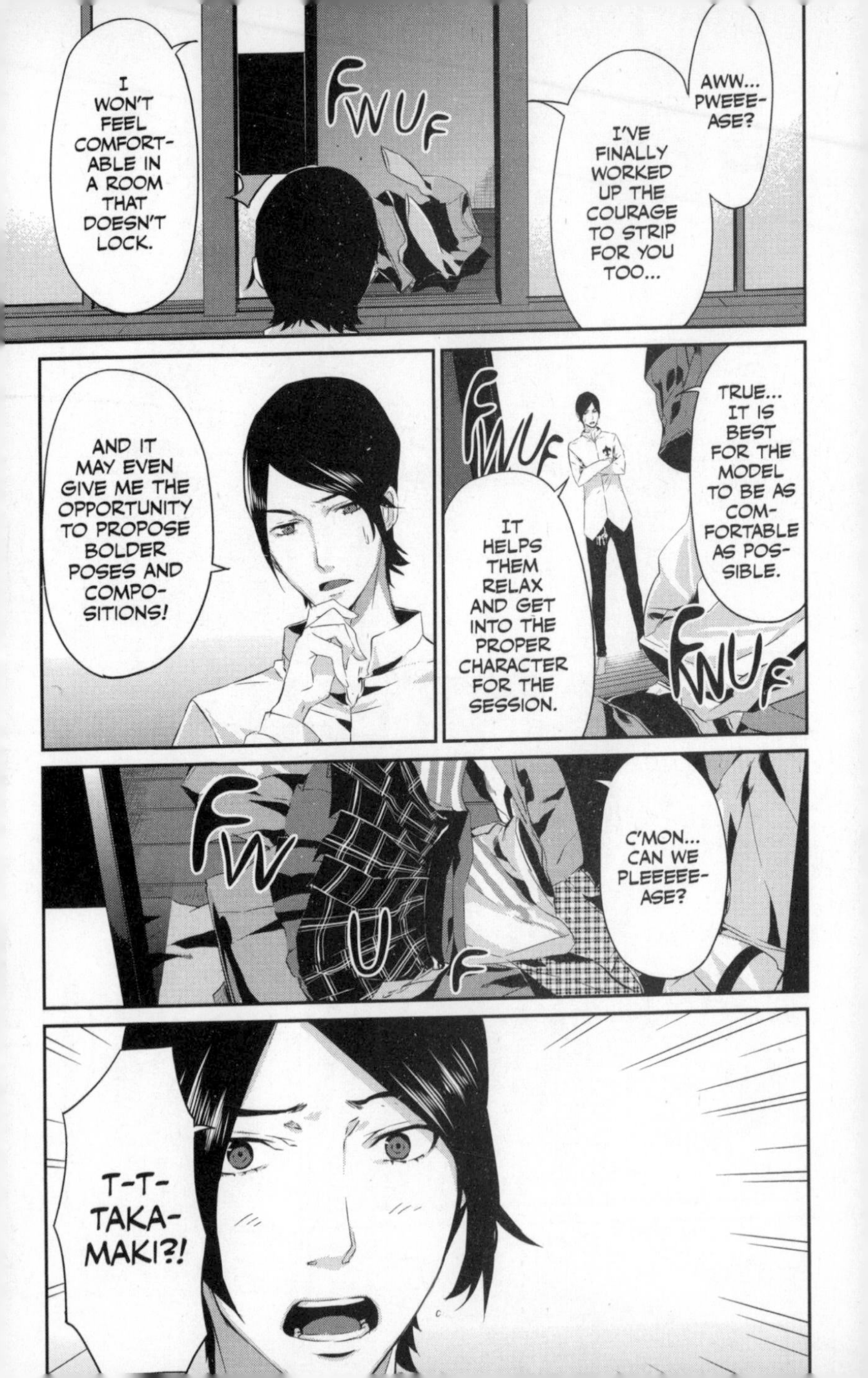
AWW... PWEEEE-ASE?
I'VE FINALLY WORKED UP THE COURAGE TO STRIP FOR YOU TOO...
FWUF
I WON'T FEEL COMFORT-ABLE IN A ROOM THAT DOESN'T LOCK.
TRUE... IT IS BEST FOR THE MODEL TO BE AS COM-FORTABLE AS POS-SIBLE.
FWUF
FWUF
IT HELPS THEM RELAX AND GET INTO THE PROPER CHARACTER FOR THE SESSION.
AND IT MAY EVEN GIVE ME THE OPPORTUNITY TO PROPOSE BOLDER POSES AND COMPO-SITIONS!
C'MON... CAN WE PLEEEEEE-ASE?
FWUF
T-T-TAKA-MAKI?!

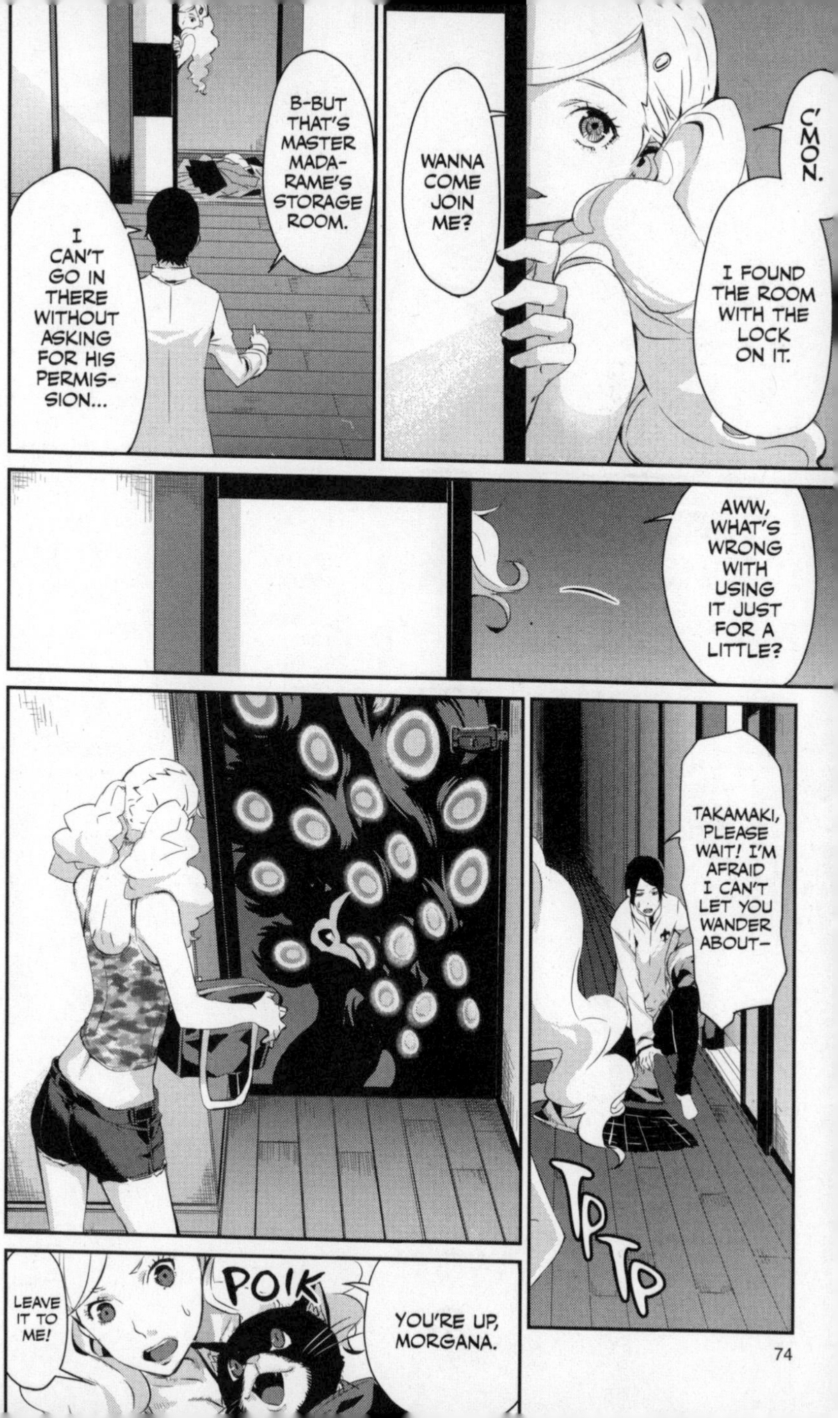
C'MON.
I FOUND THE ROOM WITH THE LOCK ON IT.
WANNA COME JOIN ME?
B-BUT THAT'S MASTER MADARAME'S STORAGE ROOM.
I CAN'T GO IN THERE WITHOUT ASKING FOR HIS PERMISSION...
AWW, WHAT'S WRONG WITH USING IT JUST FOR A LITTLE?
TAKAMAKI, PLEASE WAIT! I'M AFRAID I CAN'T LET YOU WANDER ABOUT-
TP TP
YOU'RE UP, MORGANA.
POIK
LEAVE IT TO ME!

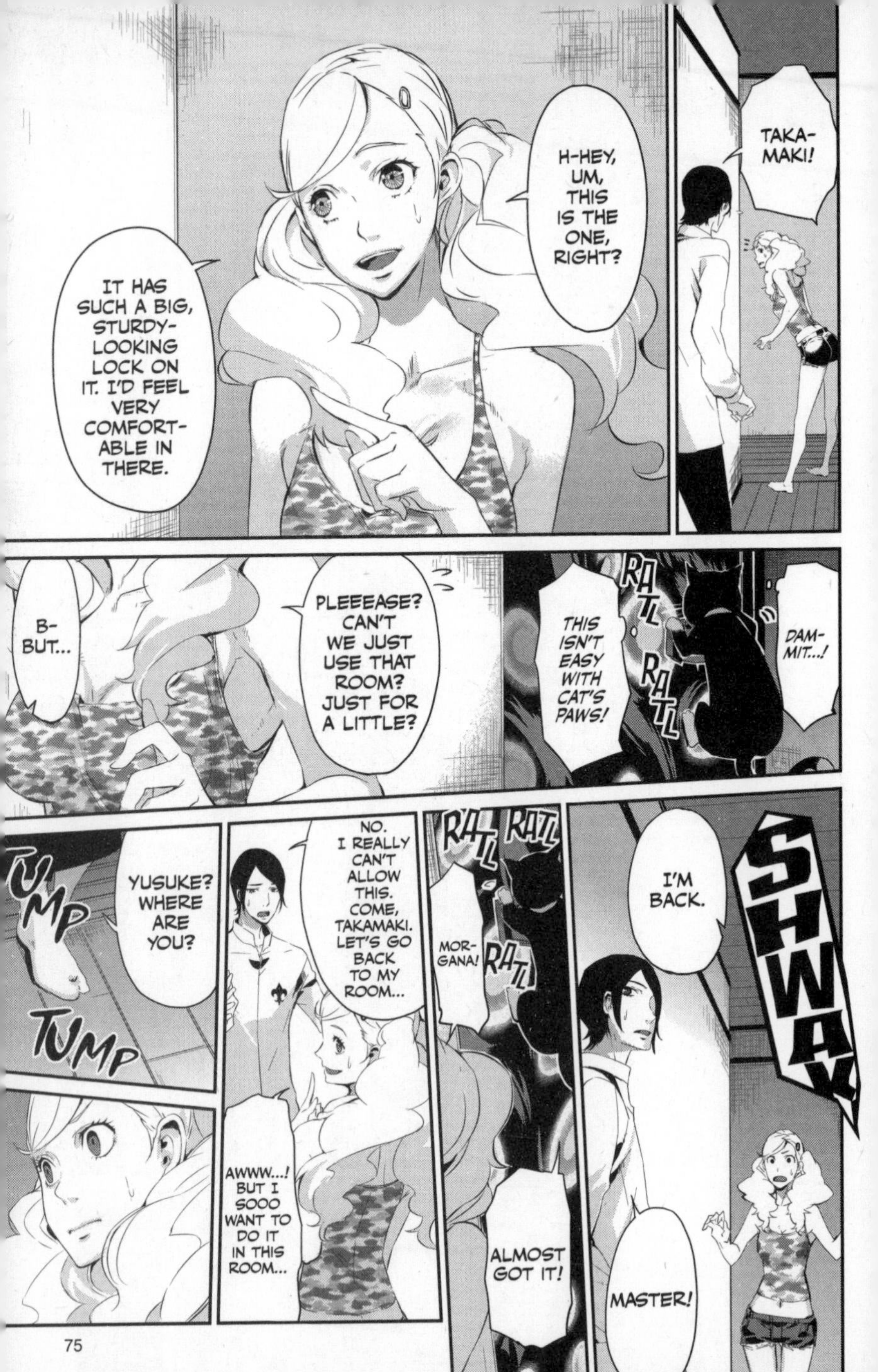
TAKA-MAKI!
H-HEY, UM, THIS IS THE ONE, RIGHT?
IT HAS SUCH A BIG, STURDY-LOOKING LOCK ON IT. I'D FEEL VERY COMFORT-ABLE IN THERE.
DAM-MIT...!
RATTL
THIS ISN'T EASY WITH CAT'S PAWS!
RATTL
PLEEEASE? CAN'T WE JUST USE THAT ROOM? JUST FOR A LITTLE?
B-BUT...
SHWAY
I'M BACK.
MASTER!
RATTL RATTL
MORGANA!
RATTL
ALMOST GOT IT!
NO. I REALLY CAN'T ALLOW THIS. COME, TAKAMAKI. LET'S GO BACK TO MY ROOM...
AWWW...! BUT I SOOO WANT TO DO IT IN THIS ROOM...
YUSUKE? WHERE ARE YOU?
TUMP
TUMP

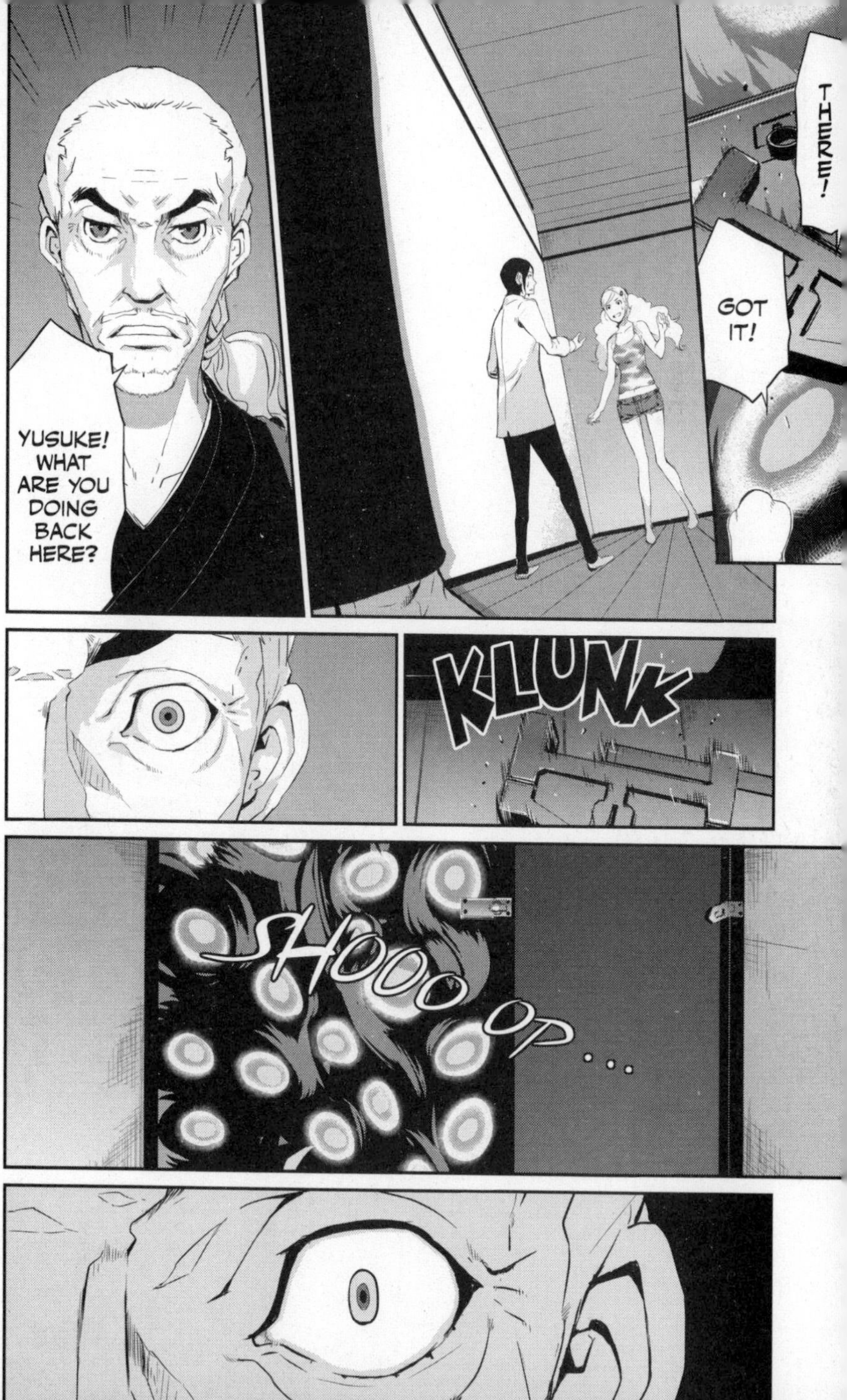
THERE!
GOT IT!
YUSUKE! WHAT ARE YOU DOING BACK HERE?
KLUNK
SHOOOOP...

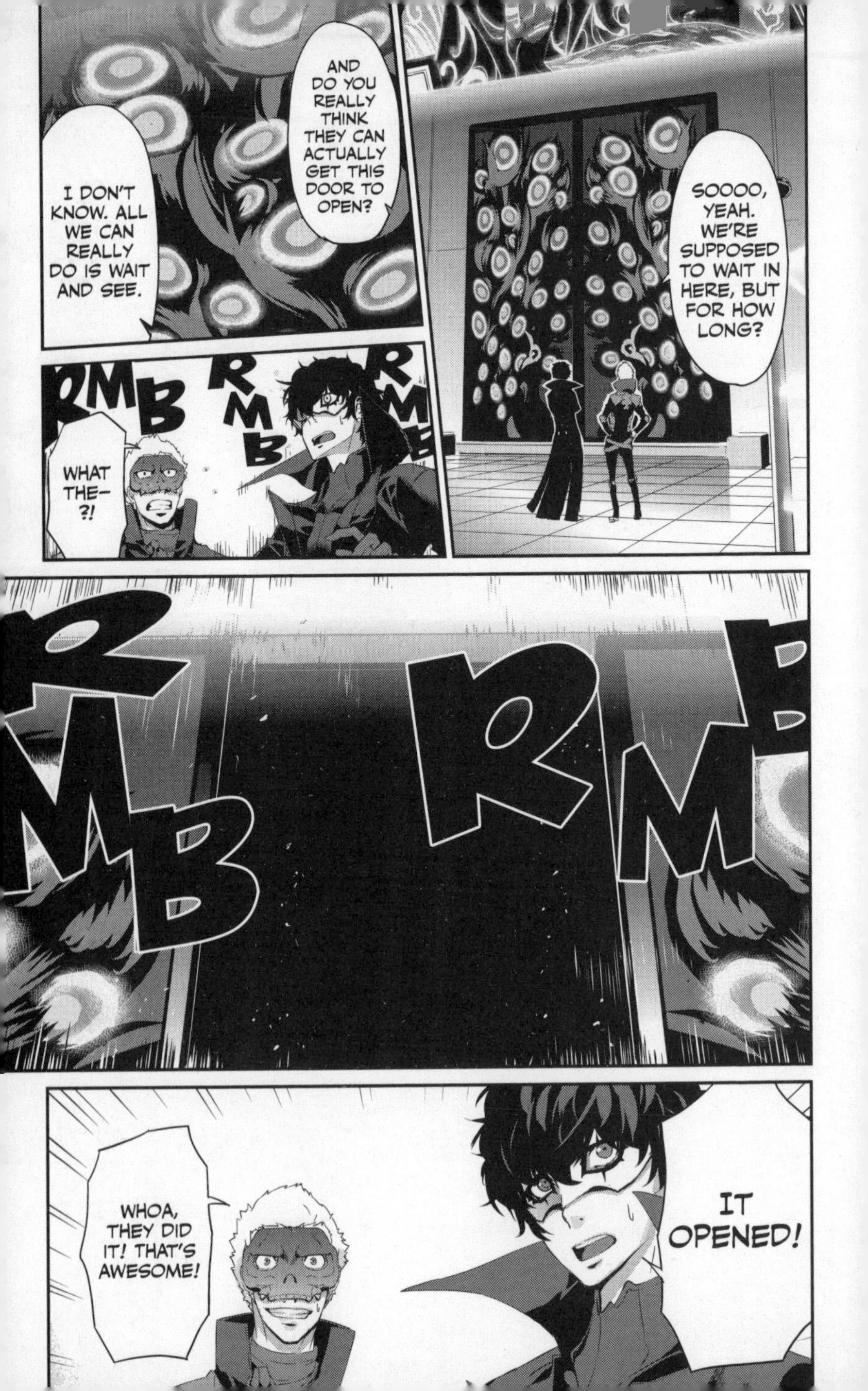
SOOOO, YEAH. WE'RE SUPPOSED TO WAIT IN HERE, BUT FOR HOW LONG?
AND DO YOU REALLY THINK THEY CAN ACTUALLY GET THIS DOOR TO OPEN?
I DON'T KNOW. ALL WE CAN REALLY DO IS WAIT AND SEE.
RMB
RMB
RMB
WHAT THE—?!
RMB
RMB
RMB
IT OPENED!
WHOA, THEY DID IT! THAT'S AWESOME!

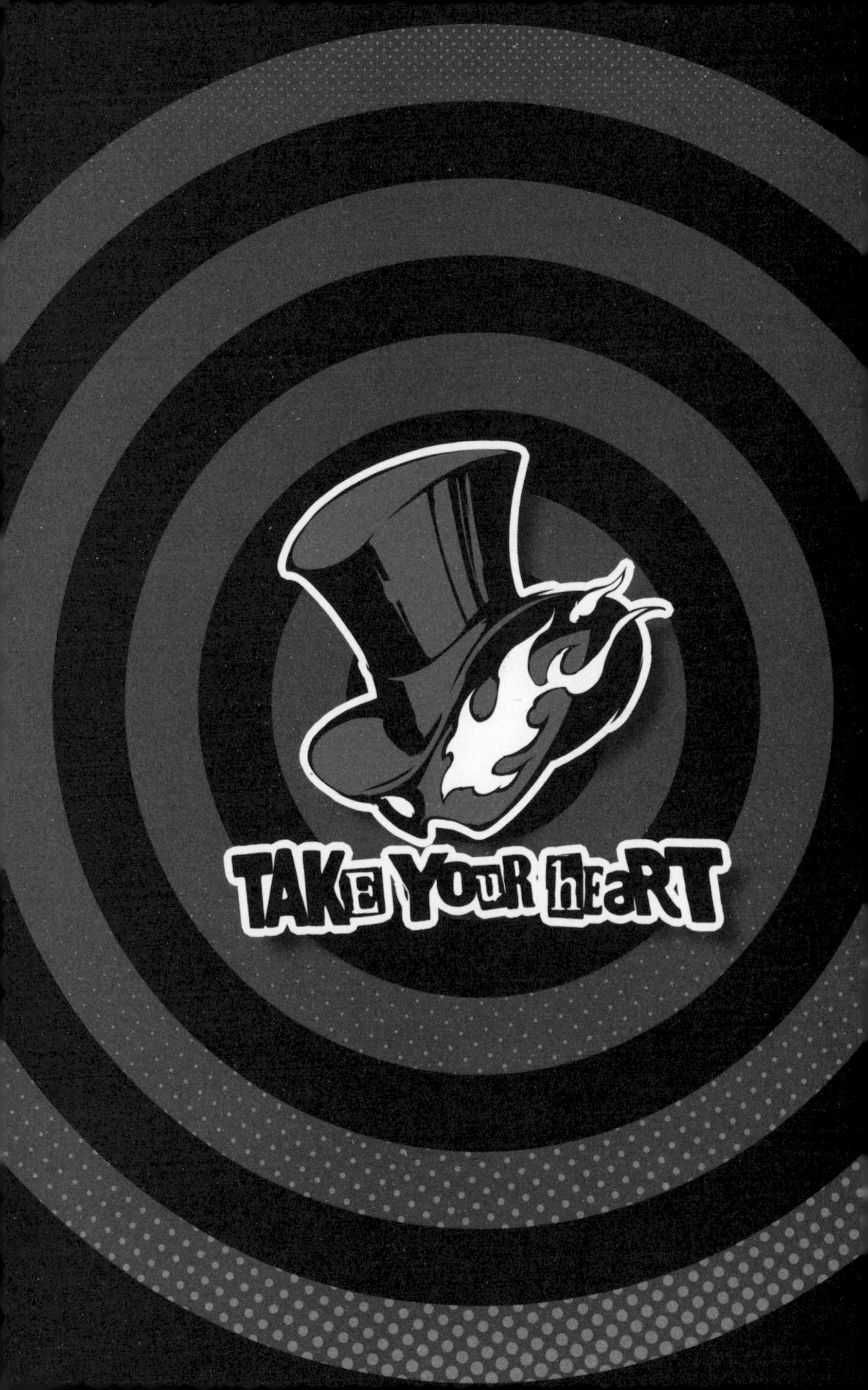
TAKE YOUR HEART

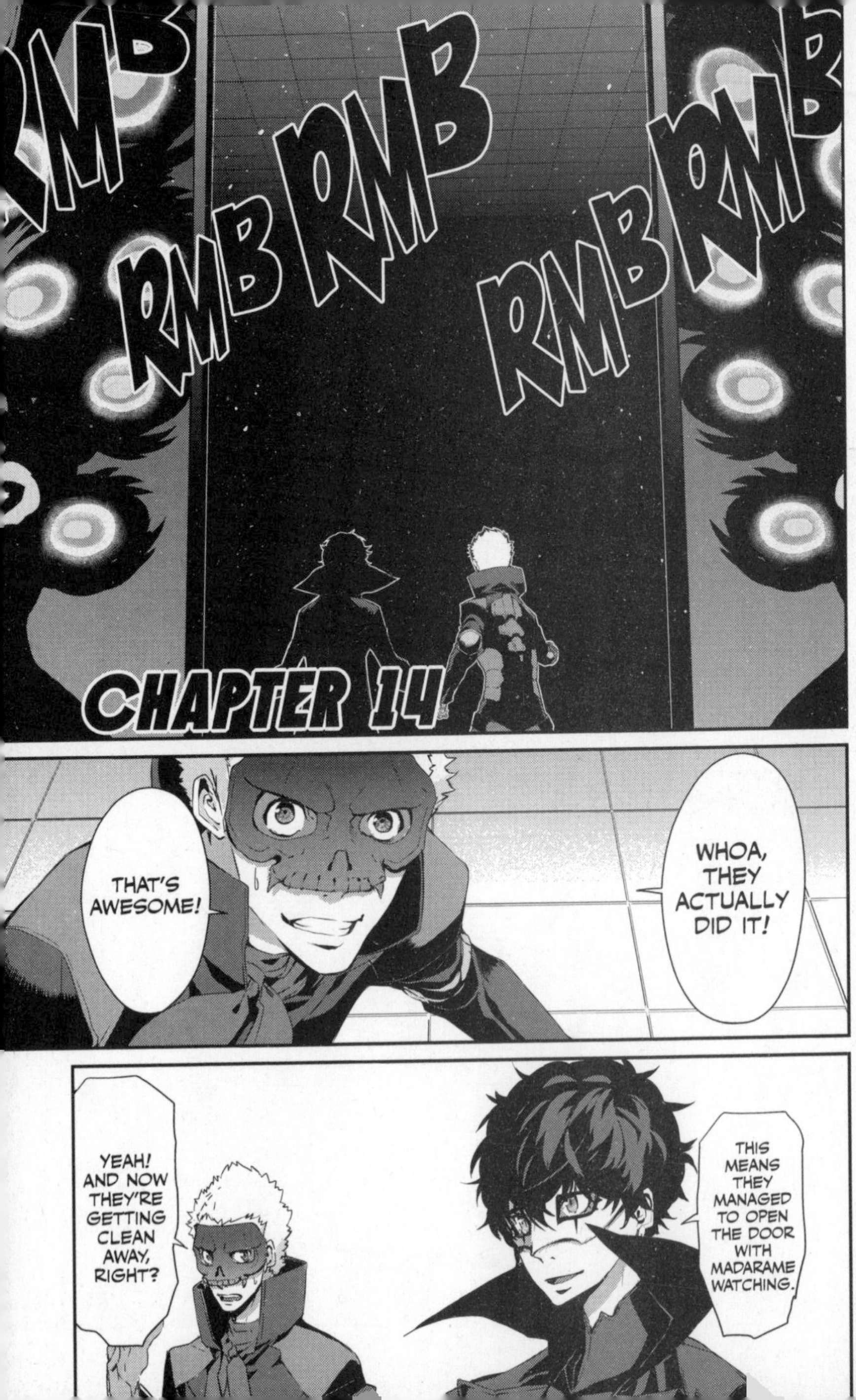
RMB RMB RMB RMB RMB RMB RMB
CHAPTER 14
WHOA, THEY ACTUALLY DID IT!
THAT'S AWESOME!
THIS MEANS THEY MANAGED TO OPEN THE DOOR WITH MADARAME WATCHING.
YEAH! AND NOW THEY'RE GETTING CLEAN AWAY, RIGHT?

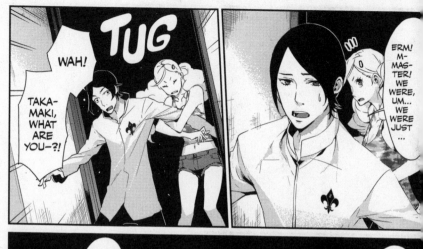

ERM! M-MASTER! WE WERE, UM... WE WERE JUST ...
TUG
WAH!
TAKAMAKI, WHAT ARE YOU—?!
THIS IS REALLY BAD...!
LIGHTS... LIGHTS...
IS THIS IT?
WHAT ON EARTH ...?

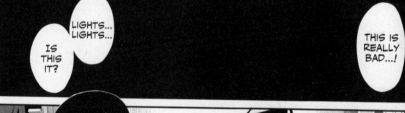

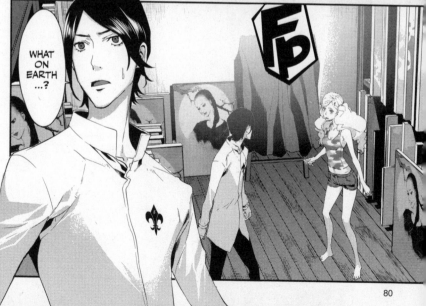

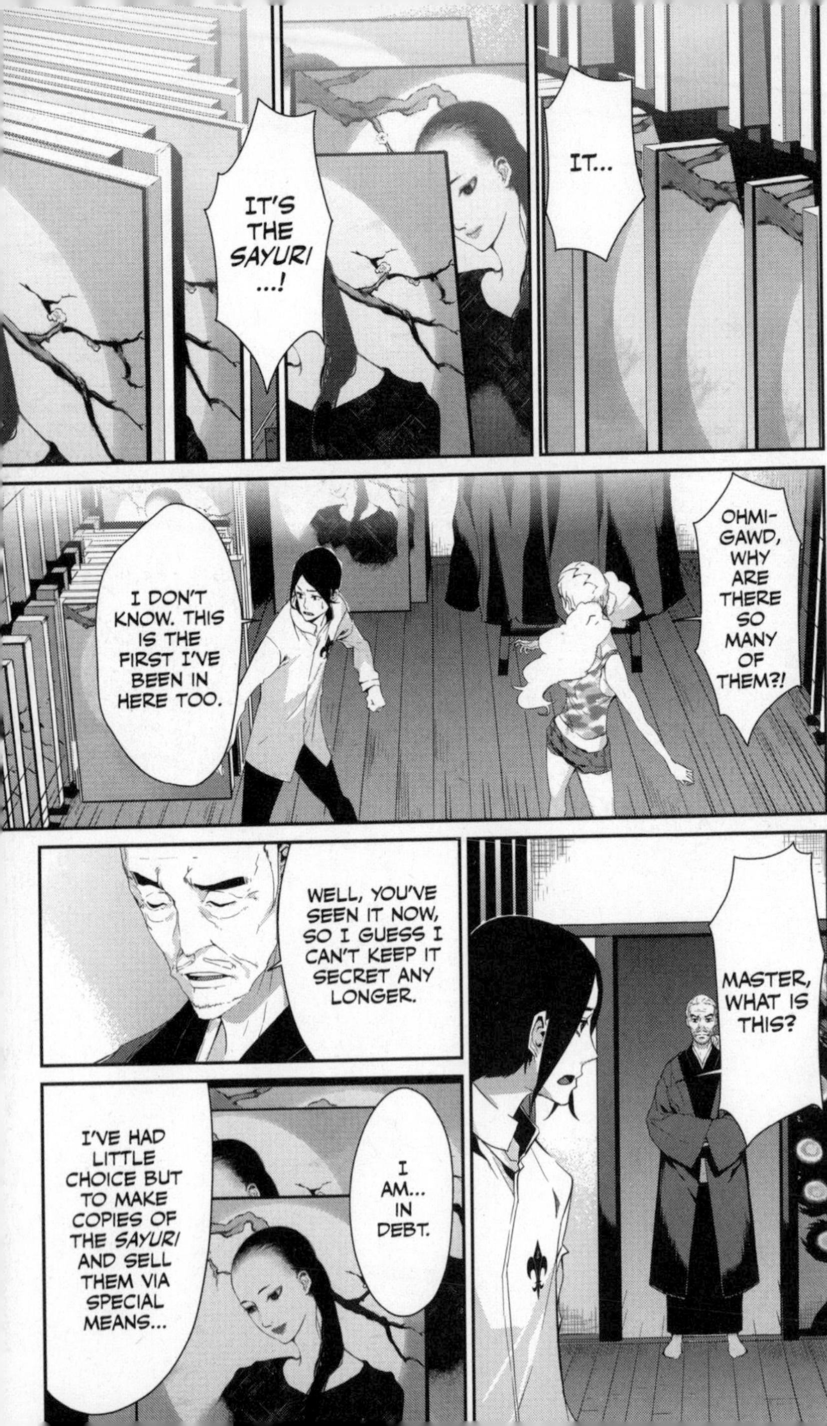
IT...
IT'S THE SAYURI...!
OHMI-GAWD, WHY ARE THERE SO MANY OF THEM?!
I DON'T KNOW. THIS IS THE FIRST I'VE BEEN IN HERE TOO.
MASTER, WHAT IS THIS?
WELL, YOU'VE SEEN IT NOW, SO I GUESS I CAN'T KEEP IT SECRET ANY LONGER.
I AM... IN DEBT.
I'VE HAD LITTLE CHOICE BUT TO MAKE COPIES OF THE SAYURI AND SELL THEM VIA SPECIAL MEANS...

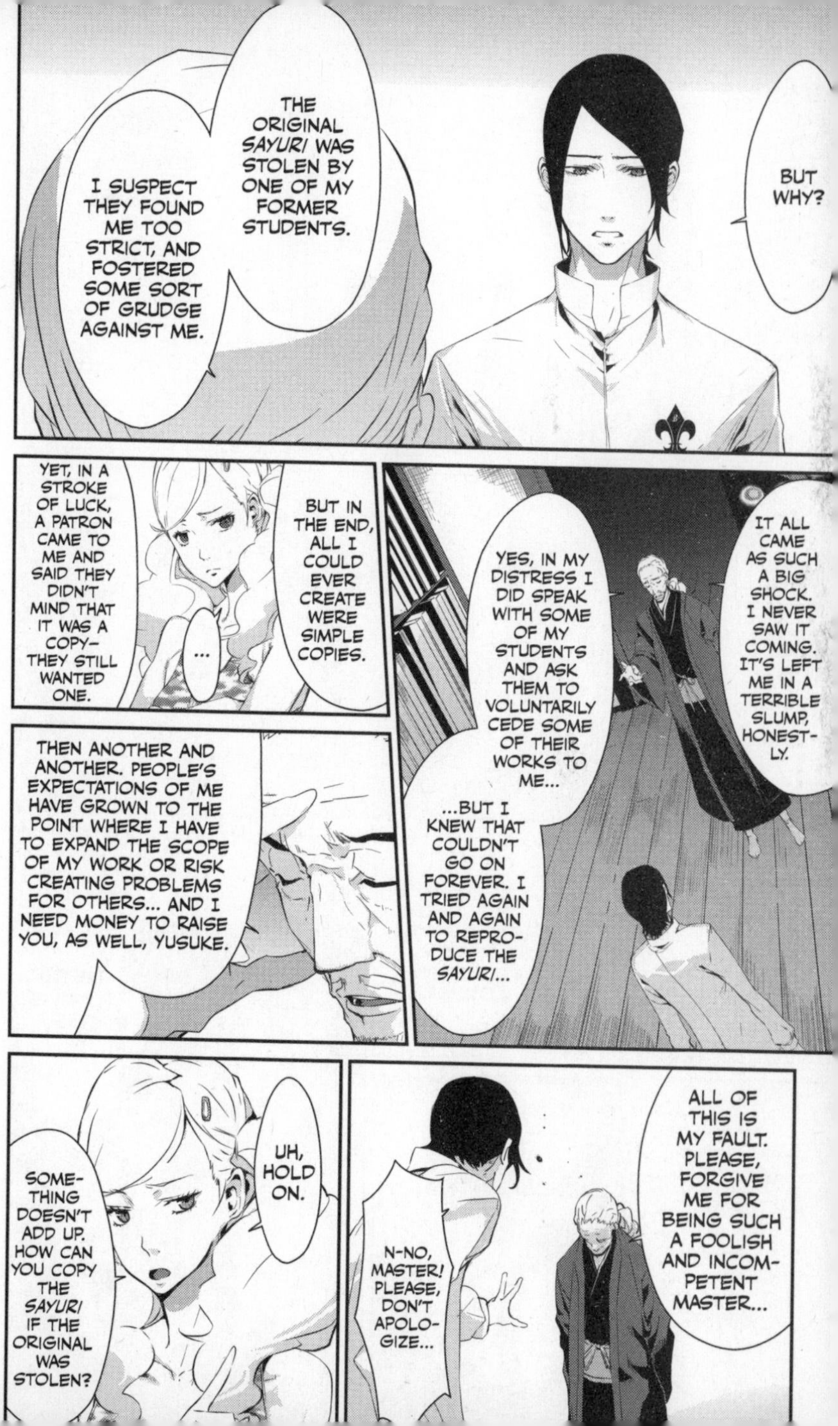
BUT WHY?
THE ORIGINAL SAYURI WAS STOLEN BY ONE OF MY FORMER STUDENTS.
I SUSPECT THEY FOUND ME TOO STRICT, AND FOSTERED SOME SORT OF GRUDGE AGAINST ME.
IT ALL CAME AS SUCH A BIG SHOCK. I NEVER SAW IT COMING. IT'S LEFT ME IN A TERRIBLE SLUMP, HONESTLY.
YES, IN MY DISTRESS I DID SPEAK WITH SOME OF MY STUDENTS AND ASK THEM TO VOLUNTARILY CEDE SOME OF THEIR WORKS TO ME...
...BUT I KNEW THAT COULDN'T GO ON FOREVER. I TRIED AGAIN AND AGAIN TO REPRODUCE THE SAYURI...
BUT IN THE END, ALL I COULD EVER CREATE WERE SIMPLE COPIES.
...
YET, IN A STROKE OF LUCK, A PATRON CAME TO ME AND SAID THEY DIDN'T MIND THAT IT WAS A COPY—THEY STILL WANTED ONE.
THEN ANOTHER AND ANOTHER. PEOPLE'S EXPECTATIONS OF ME HAVE GROWN TO THE POINT WHERE I HAVE TO EXPAND THE SCOPE OF MY WORK OR RISK CREATING PROBLEMS FOR OTHERS... AND I NEED MONEY TO RAISE YOU, AS WELL, YUSUKE.
ALL OF THIS IS MY FAULT. PLEASE, FORGIVE ME FOR BEING SUCH A FOOLISH AND INCOMPETENT MASTER...
N-NO, MASTER! PLEASE, DON'T APOLOGIZE...
UH, HOLD ON.
SOMETHING DOESN'T ADD UP. HOW CAN YOU COPY THE SAYURI IF THE ORIGINAL WAS STOLEN?

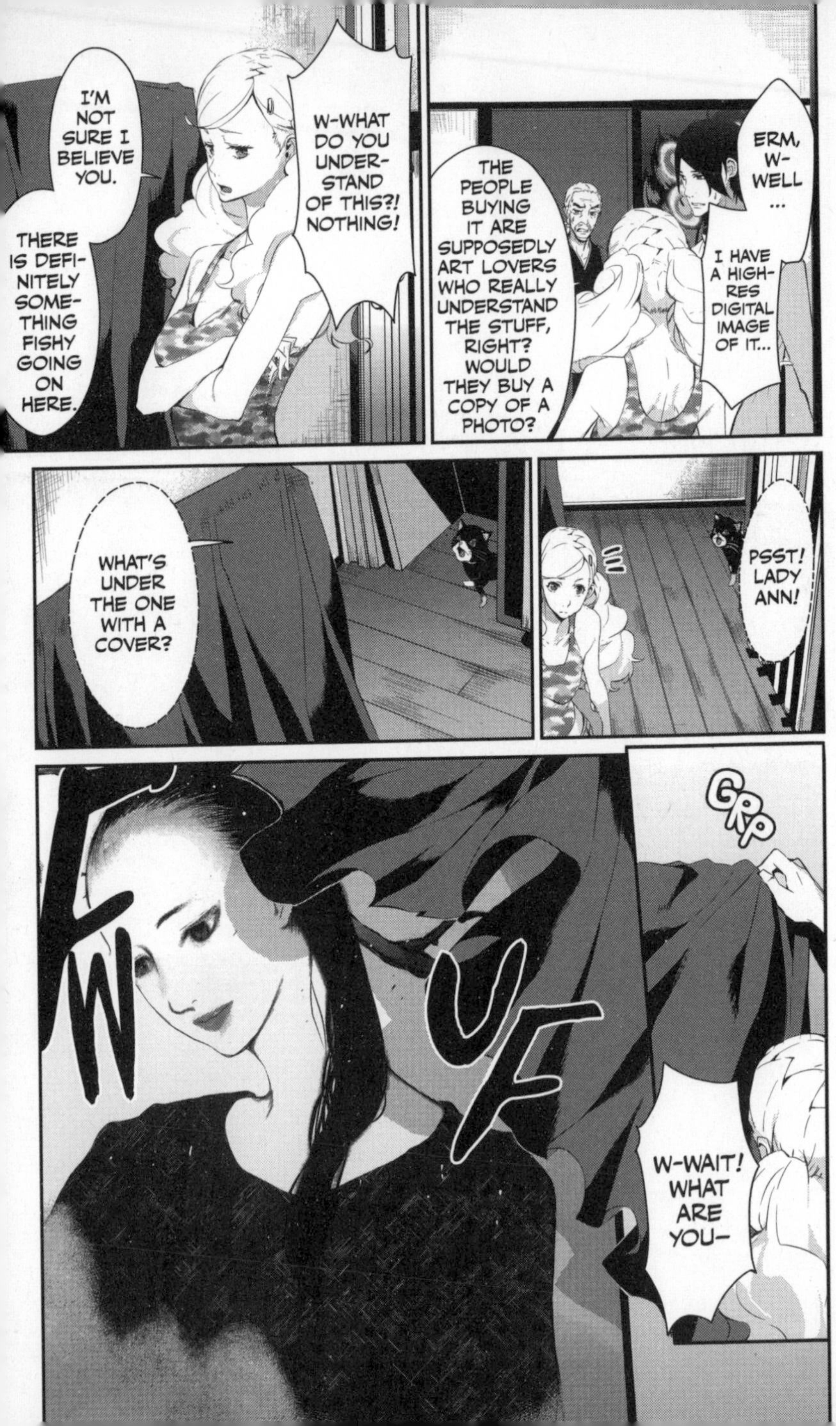
ERM, W-WELL ...
I HAVE A HIGH-RES DIGITAL IMAGE OF IT...
THE PEOPLE BUYING IT ARE SUPPOSEDLY ART LOVERS WHO REALLY UNDERSTAND THE STUFF, RIGHT? WOULD THEY BUY A COPY OF A PHOTO?
W-WHAT DO YOU UNDERSTAND OF THIS?! NOTHING!
I'M NOT SURE I BELIEVE YOU.
THERE IS DEFINITELY SOMETHING FISHY GOING ON HERE.
PSST! LADY ANN!
WHAT'S UNDER THE ONE WITH A COVER?
GRP
W-WAIT! WHAT ARE YOU-
WUF

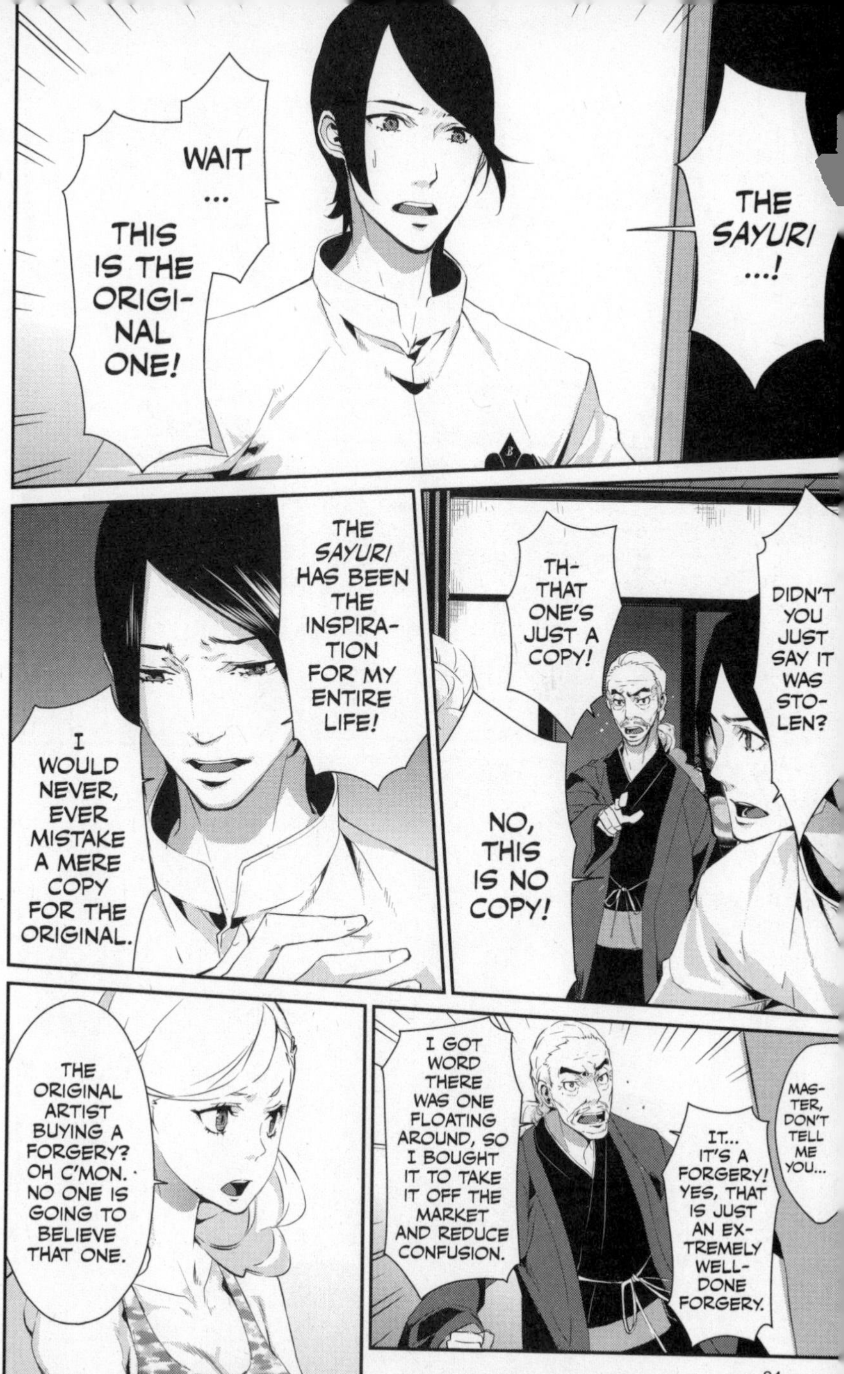
THE SAYURI ...!
WAIT ... THIS IS THE ORIGINAL ONE!
DIDN'T YOU JUST SAY IT WAS STOLEN?
TH-THAT ONE'S JUST A COPY!
NO, THIS IS NO COPY!
THE SAYURI HAS BEEN THE INSPIRATION FOR MY ENTIRE LIFE!
I WOULD NEVER, EVER MISTAKE A MERE COPY FOR THE ORIGINAL.
MASTER, DON'T TELL ME YOU...
IT... IT'S A FORGERY! YES, THAT IS JUST AN EXTREMELY WELL-DONE FORGERY.
I GOT WORD THERE WAS ONE FLOATING AROUND, SO I BOUGHT IT TO TAKE IT OFF THE MARKET AND REDUCE CONFUSION.
THE ORIGINAL ARTIST BUYING A FORGERY? OH C'MON. NO ONE IS GOING TO BELIEVE THAT ONE.

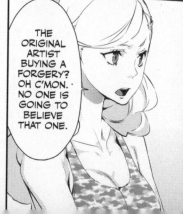

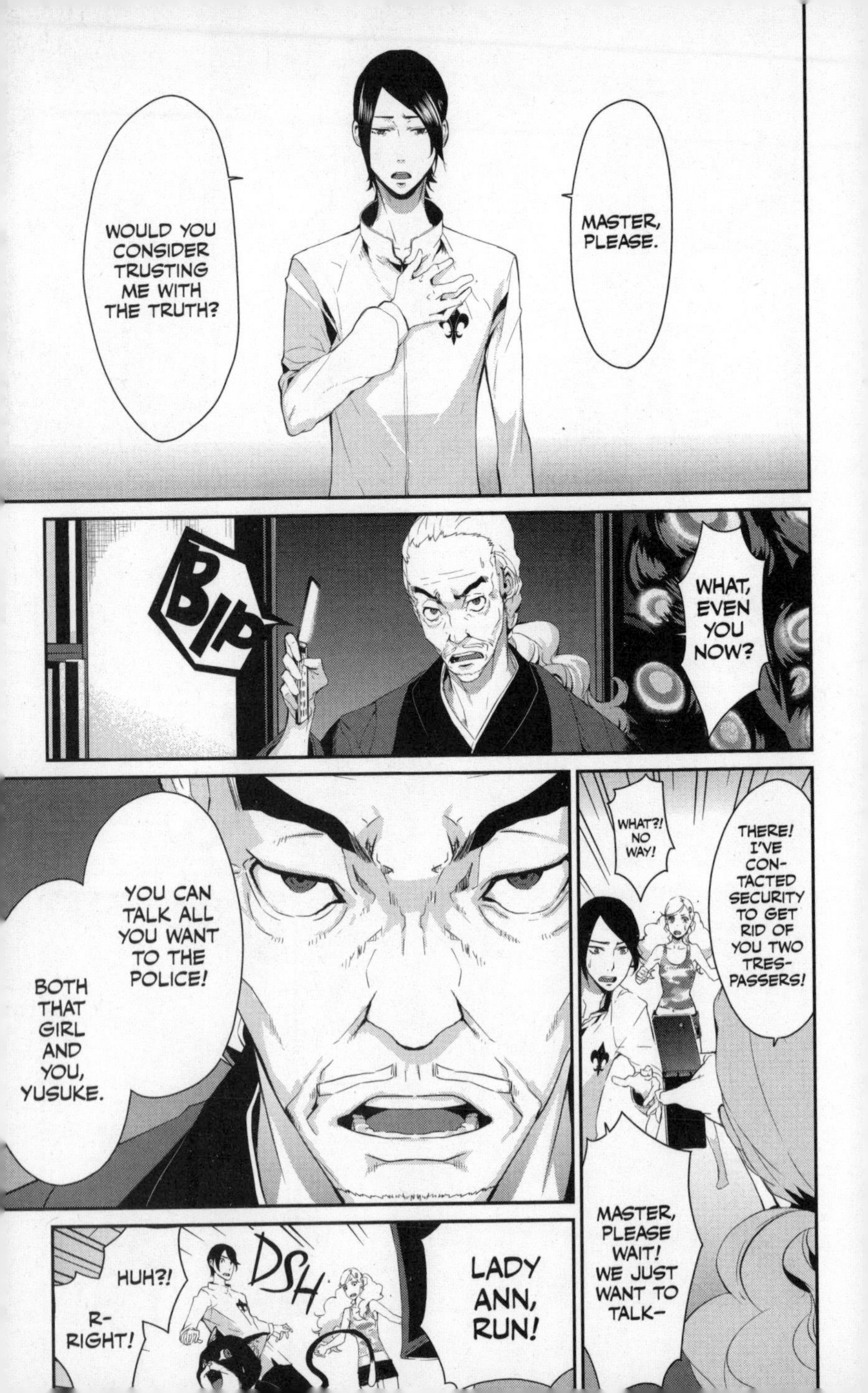
MASTER, PLEASE.
WOULD YOU CONSIDER TRUSTING ME WITH THE TRUTH?
WHAT, EVEN YOU NOW?
BIP
THERE! I'VE CON-TACTED SECURITY TO GET RID OF YOU TWO TRES-PASSERS!
WHAT?! NO WAY!
YOU CAN TALK ALL YOU WANT TO THE POLICE!
BOTH THAT GIRL AND YOU, YUSUKE.
MASTER, PLEASE WAIT! WE JUST WANT TO TALK–
LADY ANN, RUN!
DSH
HUH?!
R-RIGHT!

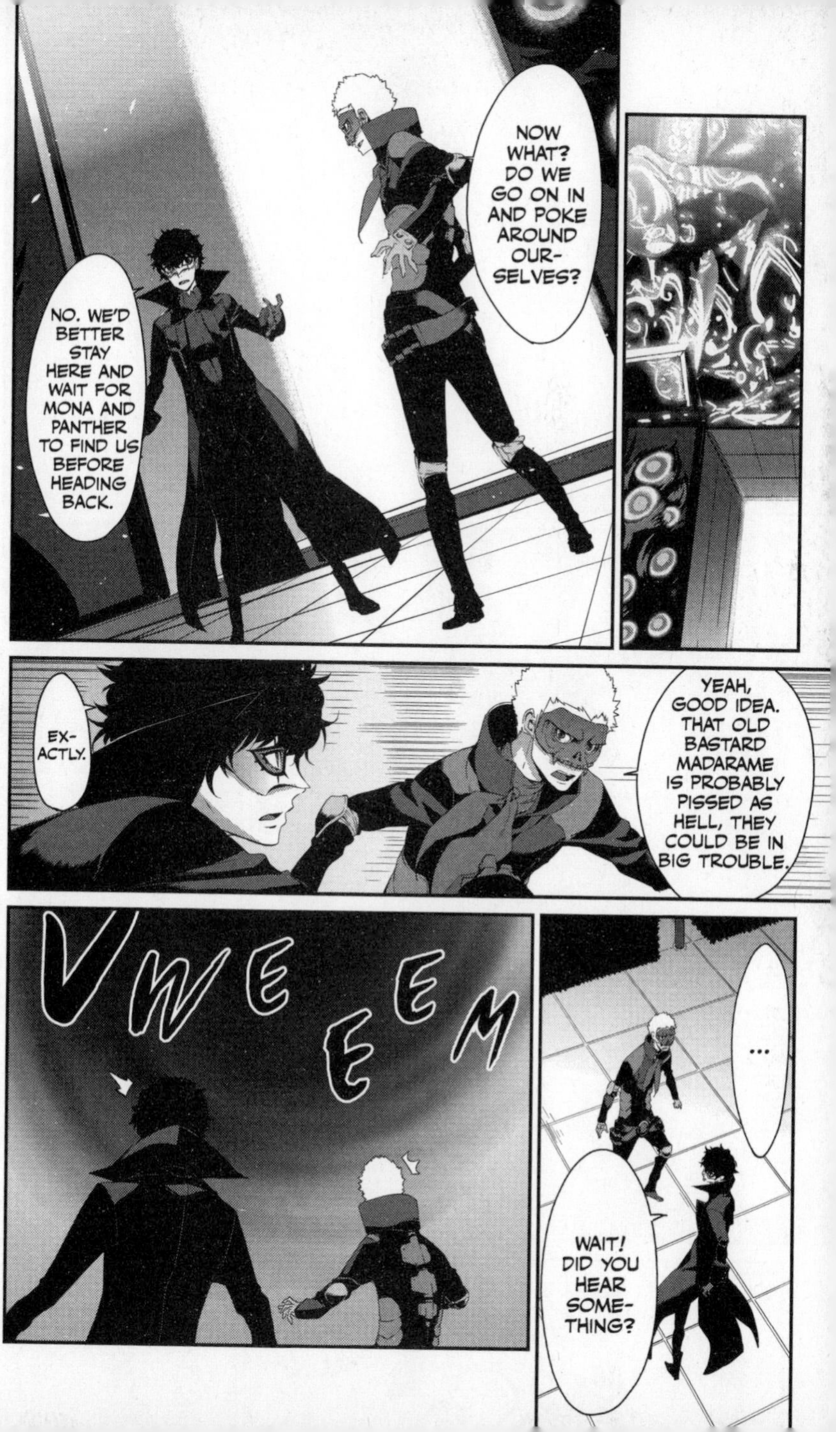
NOW WHAT? DO WE GO ON IN AND POKE AROUND OUR-SELVES?
NO. WE'D BETTER STAY HERE AND WAIT FOR MONA AND PANTHER TO FIND US BEFORE HEADING BACK.
YEAH, GOOD IDEA. THAT OLD BASTARD MADARAME IS PROBABLY PISSED AS HELL, THEY COULD BE IN BIG TROUBLE.
EX-ACTLY.
...
WAIT! DID YOU HEAR SOME-THING?
VWEEEM

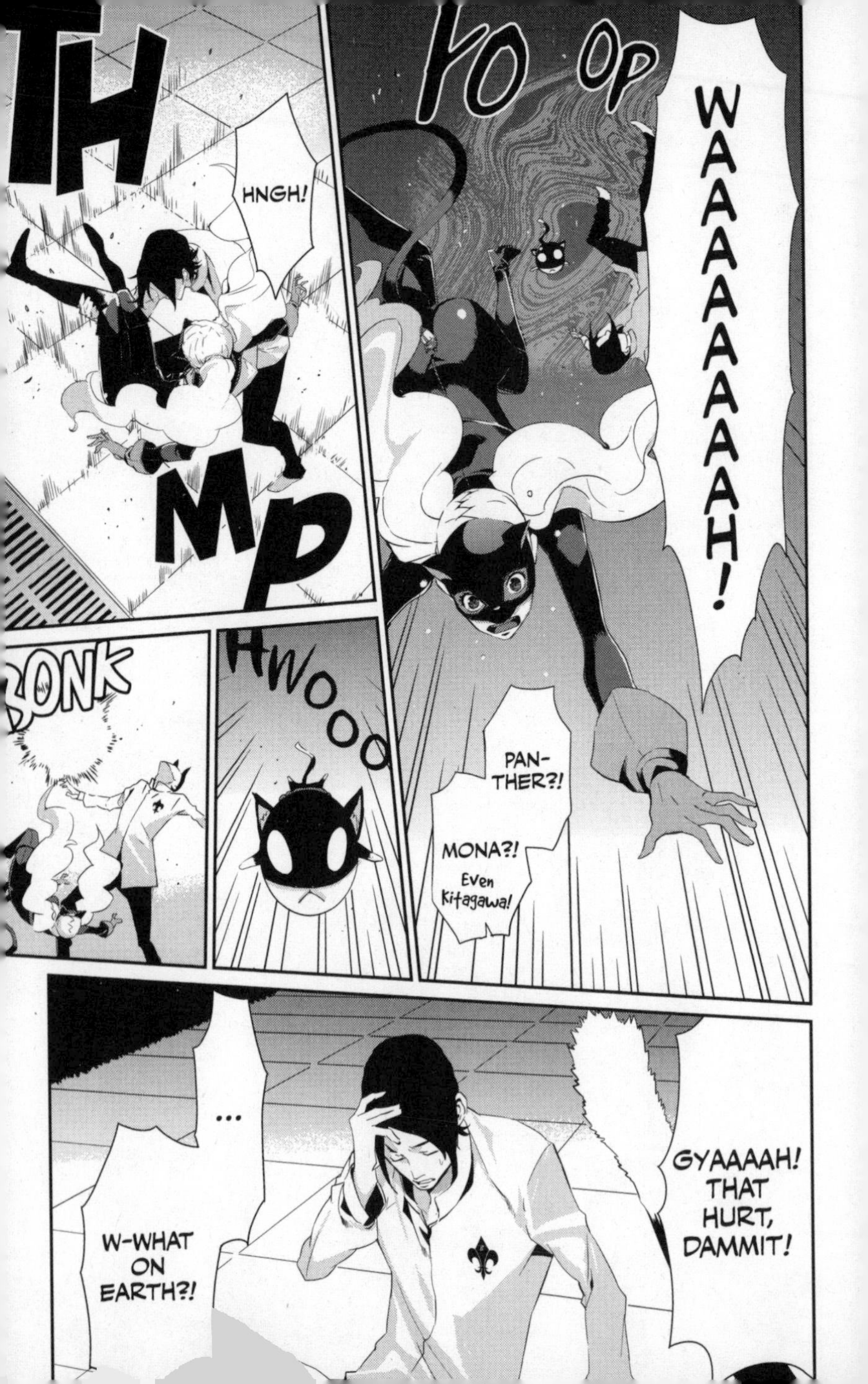
YOOP
WAAAAAAAAH!
PAN-THER?!
MONA?!
Even Kitagawa!
HNGH!
THMP
HWOOOO
BONK
GYAAAAH! THAT HURT, DAMMIT!
...
W-WHAT ON EARTH?!

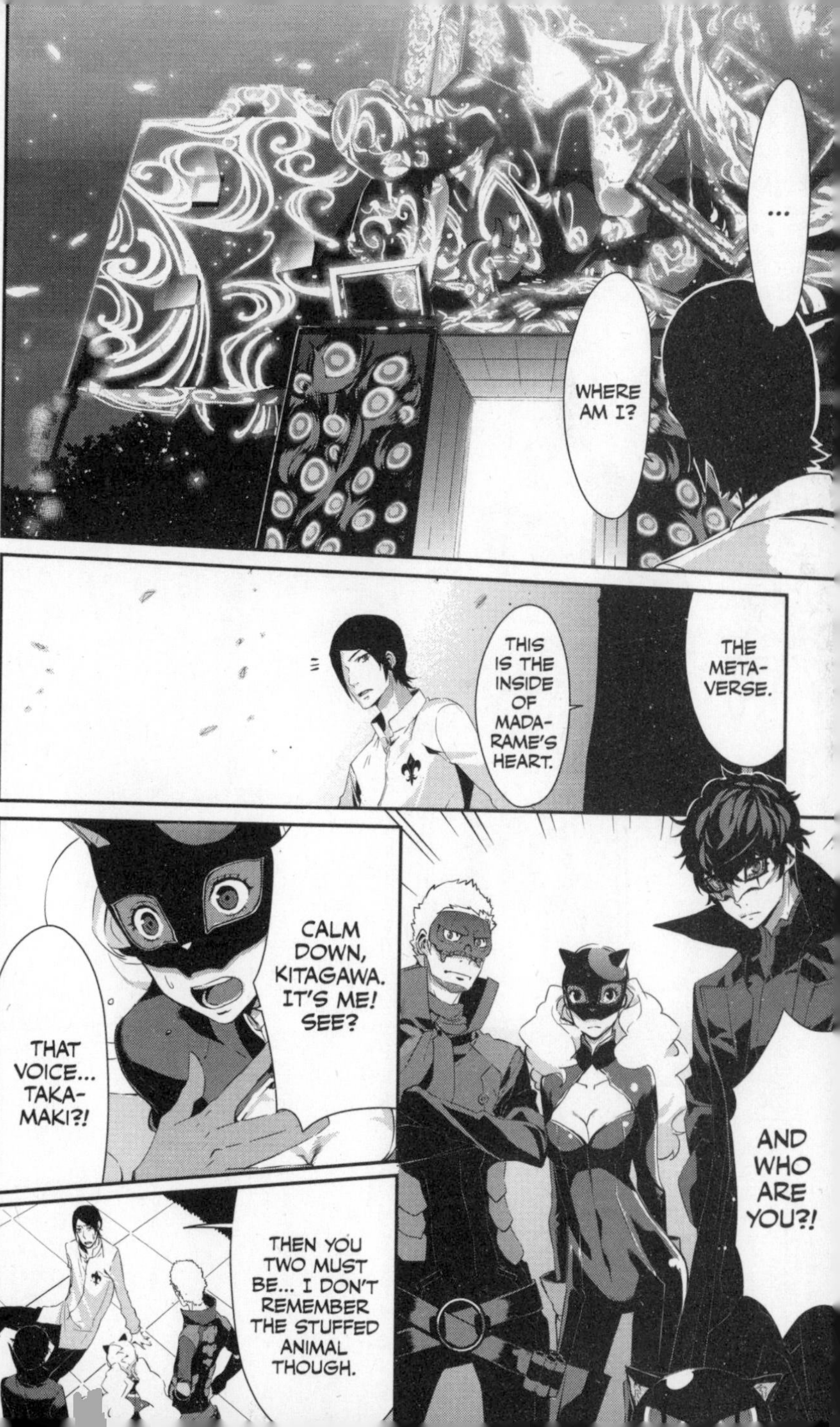
...
WHERE AM I?
THE META-VERSE.
THIS IS THE INSIDE OF MADA-RAME'S HEART.
AND WHO ARE YOU?!
CALM DOWN, KITAGAWA. IT'S ME! SEE?
THAT VOICE... TAKA-MAKI?!
THEN YOU TWO MUST BE... I DON'T REMEMBER THE STUFFED ANIMAL THOUGH.

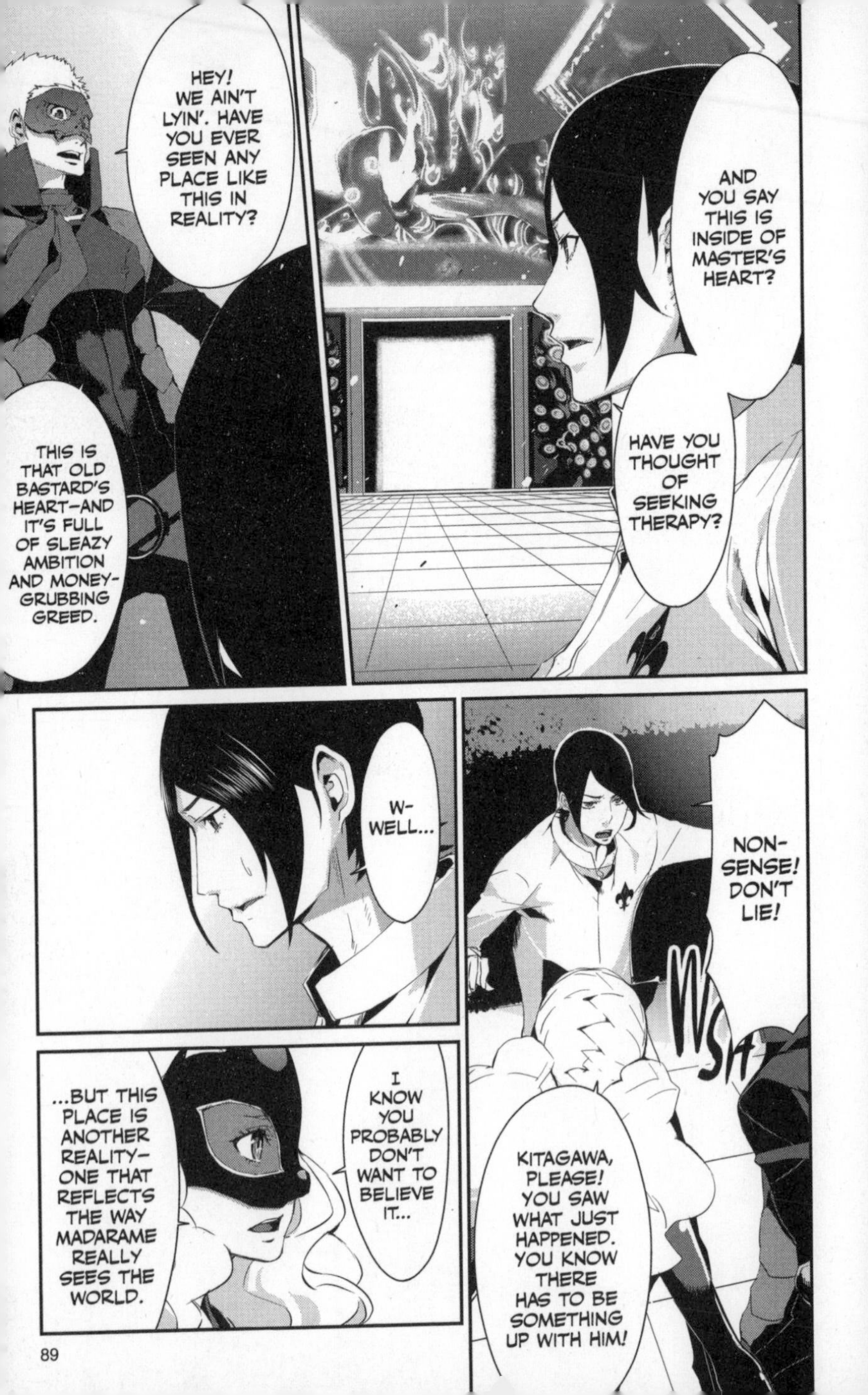
AND YOU SAY THIS IS INSIDE OF MASTER'S HEART?
HAVE YOU THOUGHT OF SEEKING THERAPY?
HEY! WE AIN'T LYIN'. HAVE YOU EVER SEEN ANY PLACE LIKE THIS IN REALITY?
THIS IS THAT OLD BASTARD'S HEART—AND IT'S FULL OF SLEAZY AMBITION AND MONEY-GRUBBING GREED.
NON-SENSE! DON'T LIE!
WSH
KITAGAWA, PLEASE! YOU SAW WHAT JUST HAPPENED. YOU KNOW THERE HAS TO BE SOMETHING UP WITH HIM!
W-WELL...
I KNOW YOU PROBABLY DON'T WANT TO BELIEVE IT...
...BUT THIS PLACE IS ANOTHER REALITY—ONE THAT REFLECTS THE WAY MADARAME REALLY SEES THE WORLD.

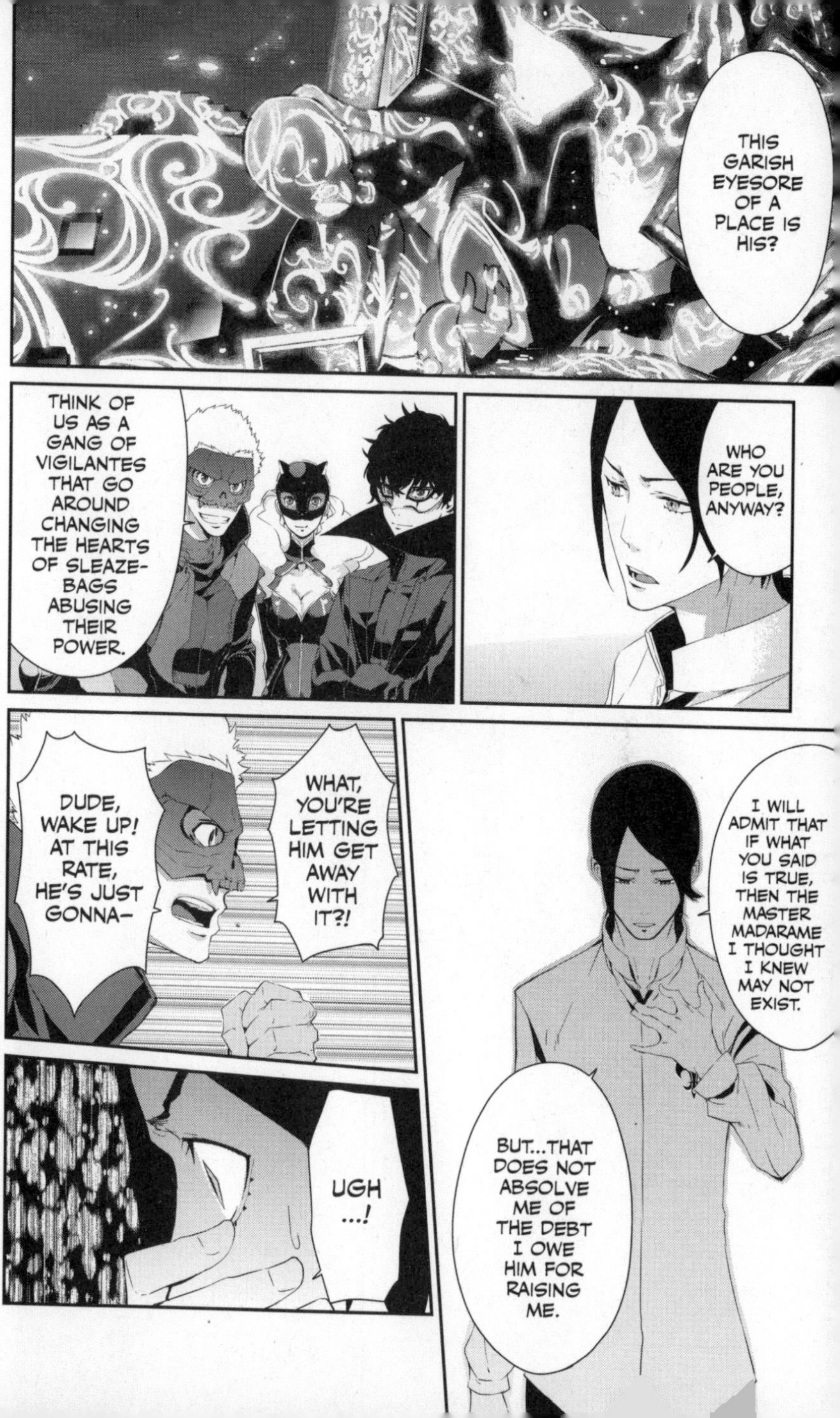
THIS GARISH EYESORE OF A PLACE IS HIS?
WHO ARE YOU PEOPLE, ANYWAY?
THINK OF US AS A GANG OF VIGILANTES THAT GO AROUND CHANGING THE HEARTS OF SLEAZE-BAGS ABUSING THEIR POWER.
I WILL ADMIT THAT IF WHAT YOU SAID IS TRUE, THEN THE MASTER MADARAME I THOUGHT I KNEW MAY NOT EXIST.
BUT...THAT DOES NOT ABSOLVE ME OF THE DEBT I OWE HIM FOR RAISING ME.
WHAT, YOU'RE LETTING HIM GET AWAY WITH IT?!
DUDE, WAKE UP! AT THIS RATE, HE'S JUST GONNA–
UGH ...!

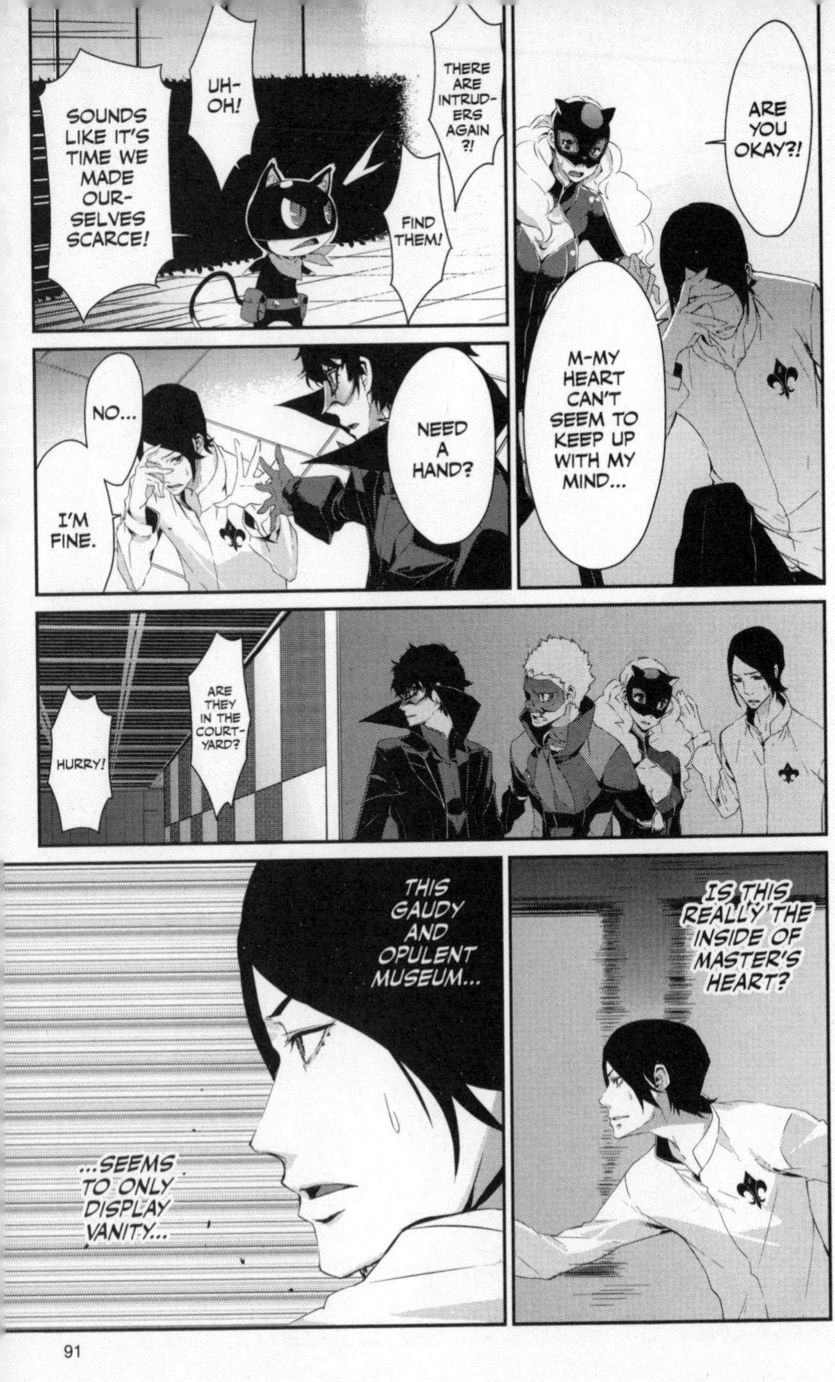
ARE YOU OKAY?!
M-MY HEART CAN'T SEEM TO KEEP UP WITH MY MIND...
THERE ARE INTRUDERS AGAIN?!
FIND THEM!
UH-OH!
SOUNDS LIKE IT'S TIME WE MADE OURSELVES SCARCE!
NEED A HAND?
NO...
I'M FINE.
ARE THEY IN THE COURTYARD?
HURRY!
IS THIS REALLY THE INSIDE OF MASTER'S HEART?
THIS GAUDY AND OPULENT MUSEUM...
...SEEMS TO ONLY DISPLAY VANITY...

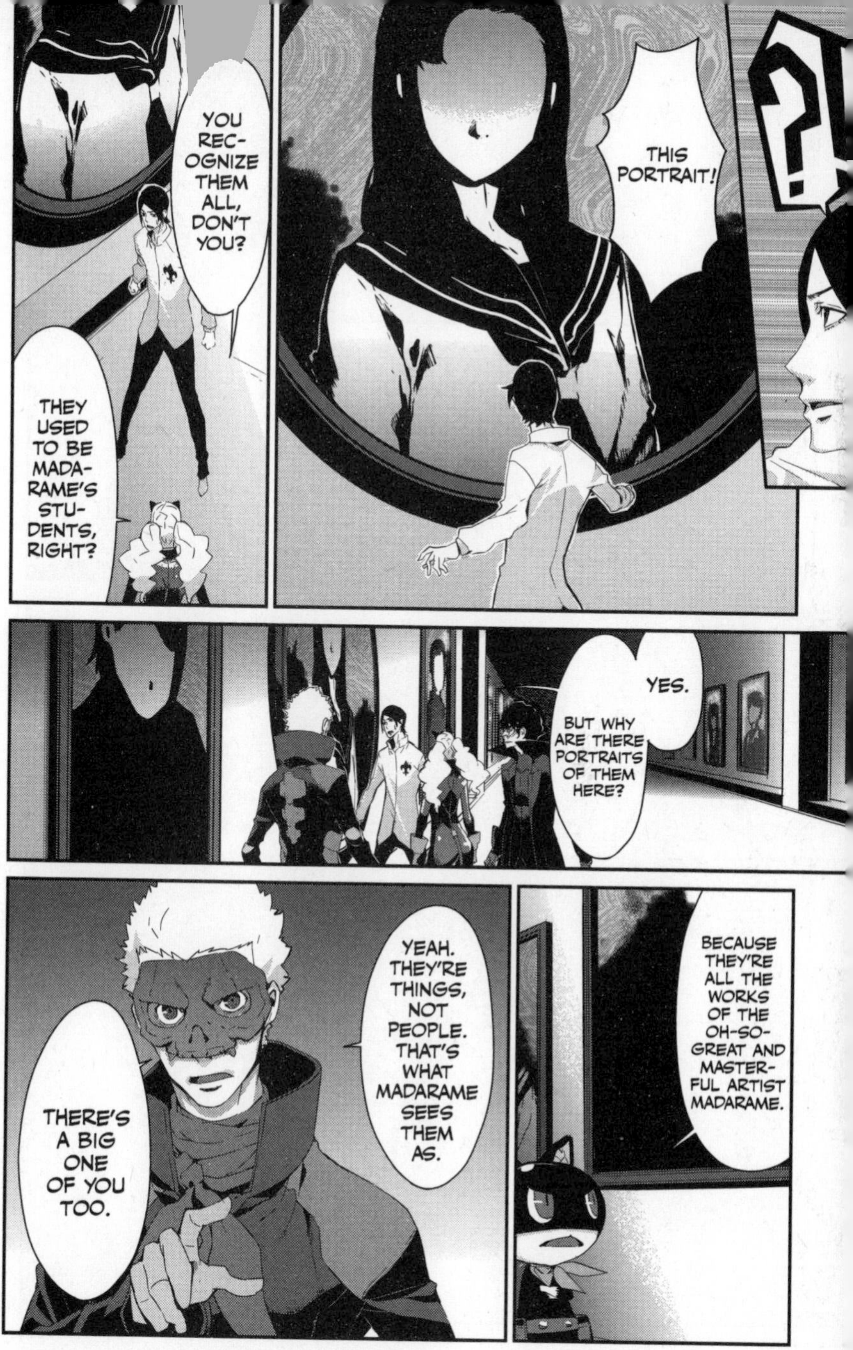
?!
THIS PORTRAIT!
YOU RECOGNIZE THEM ALL, DON'T YOU?
THEY USED TO BE MADARAME'S STUDENTS, RIGHT?
YES.
BUT WHY ARE THERE PORTRAITS OF THEM HERE?
BECAUSE THEY'RE ALL THE WORKS OF THE OH-SO-GREAT AND MASTERFUL ARTIST MADARAME.
YEAH. THEY'RE THINGS, NOT PEOPLE. THAT'S WHAT MADARAME SEES THEM AS.
THERE'S A BIG ONE OF YOU TOO.

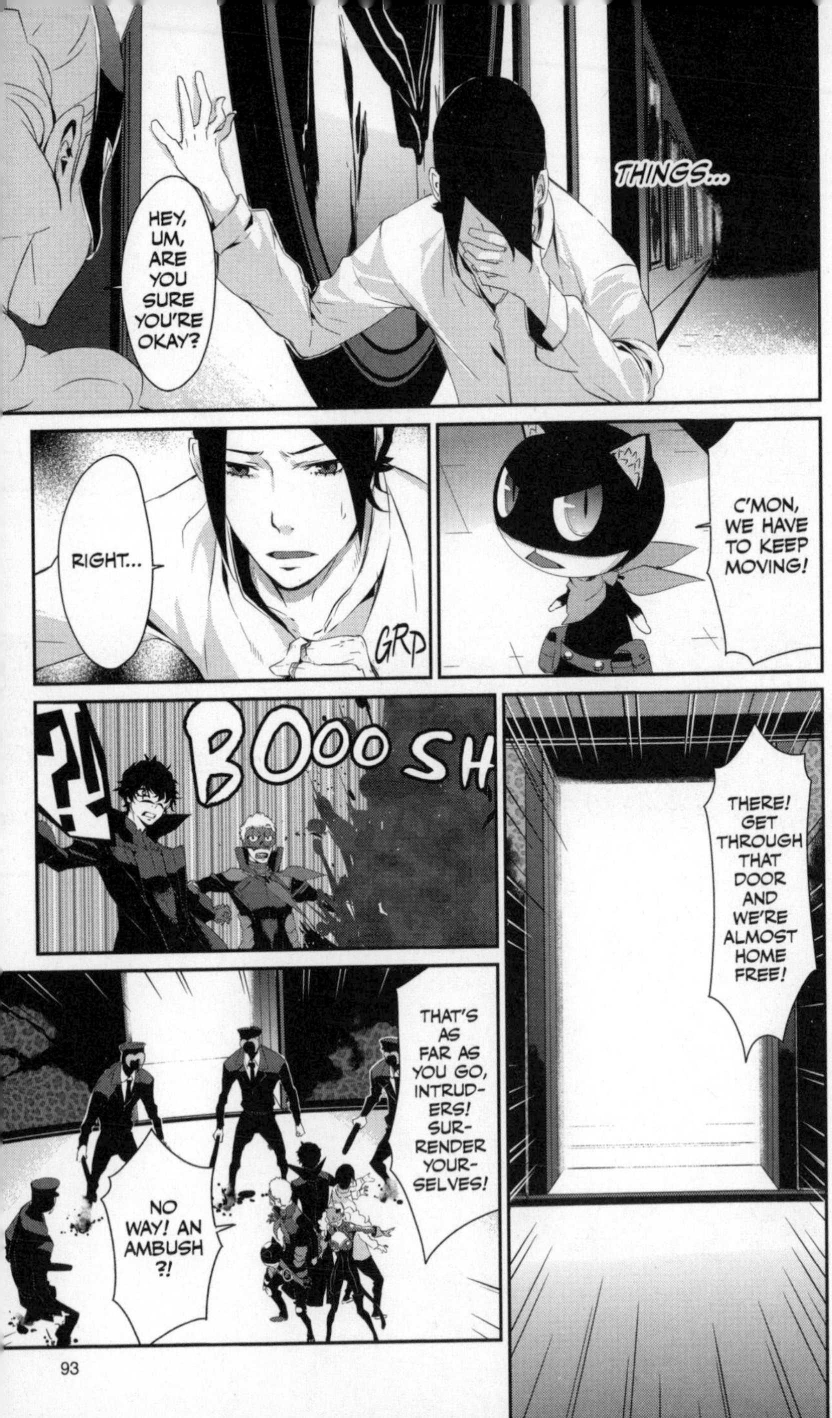
THINGS...
HEY, UM, ARE YOU SURE YOU'RE OKAY?
C'MON, WE HAVE TO KEEP MOVING!
RIGHT...
GRP
THERE! GET THROUGH THAT DOOR AND WE'RE ALMOST HOME FREE!
?!
BOOOSH
THAT'S AS FAR AS YOU GO, INTRUD-ERS! SUR-RENDER YOUR-SELVES!
NO WAY! AN AMBUSH ?!

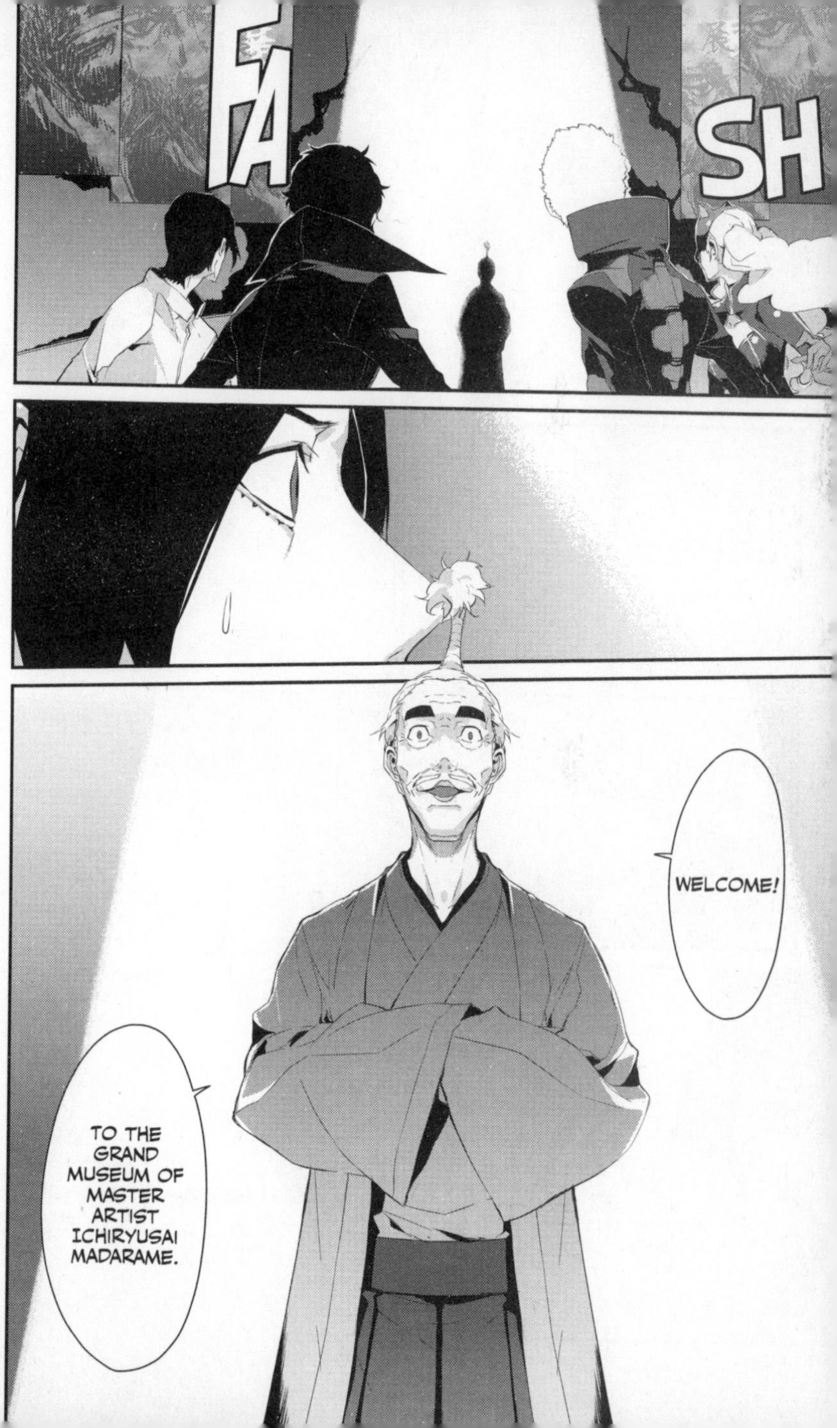
FASH
WELCOME!
TO THE GRAND MUSEUM OF MASTER ARTIST ICHIRYUSAI MADARAME.

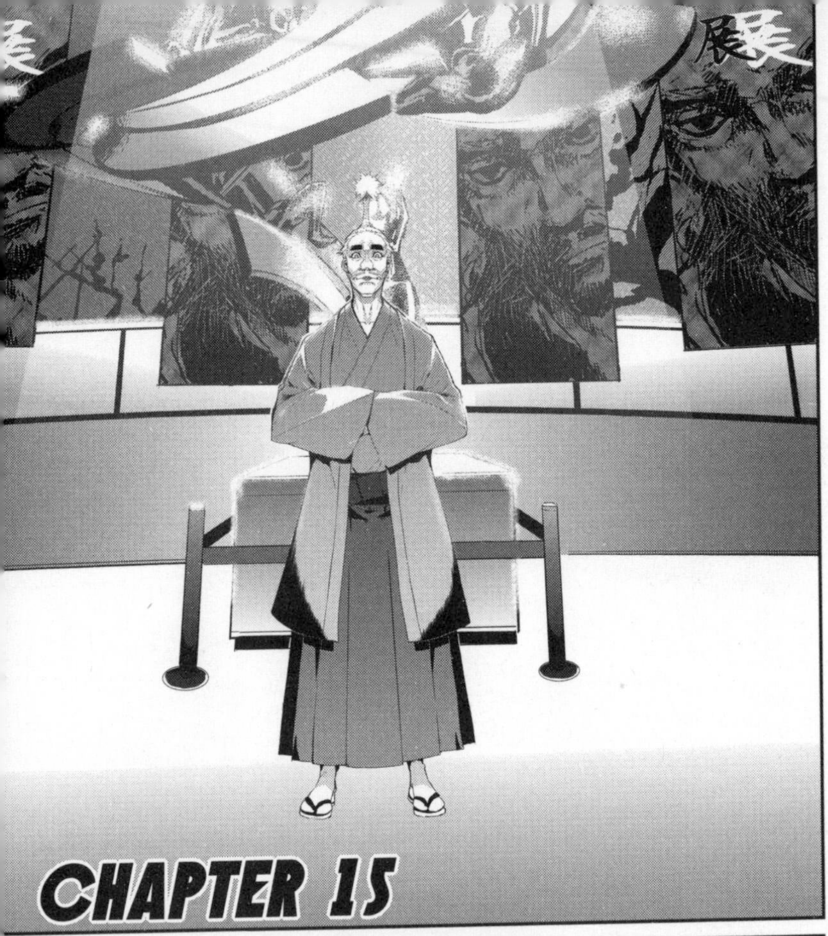
CHAPTER 15

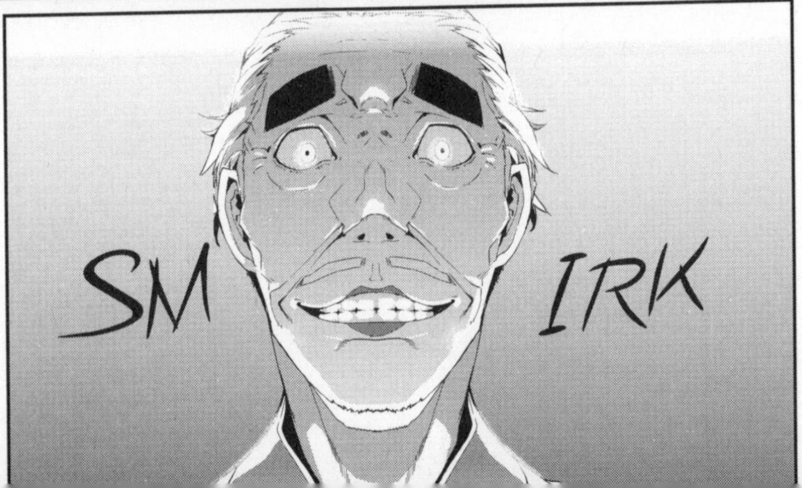
SMIRK

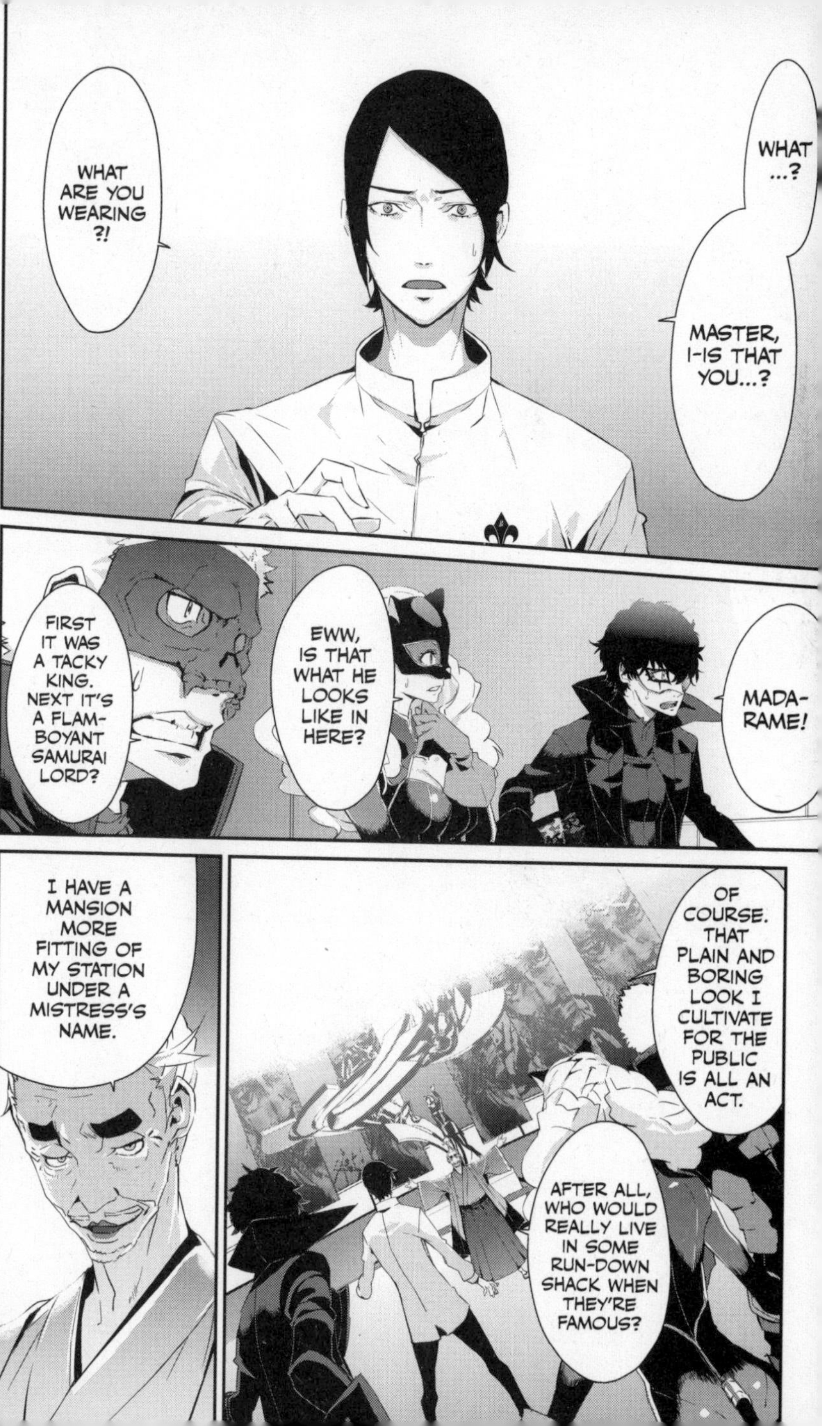
WHAT ...?
MASTER, I-IS THAT YOU...?
WHAT ARE YOU WEARING ?!
MADA-RAME!
EWW, IS THAT WHAT HE LOOKS LIKE IN HERE?
FIRST IT WAS A TACKY KING. NEXT IT'S A FLAM-BOYANT SAMURAI LORD?
OF COURSE. THAT PLAIN AND BORING LOOK I CULTIVATE FOR THE PUBLIC IS ALL AN ACT.
AFTER ALL, WHO WOULD REALLY LIVE IN SOME RUN-DOWN SHACK WHEN THEY'RE FAMOUS?
I HAVE A MANSION MORE FITTING OF MY STATION UNDER A MISTRESS'S NAME.

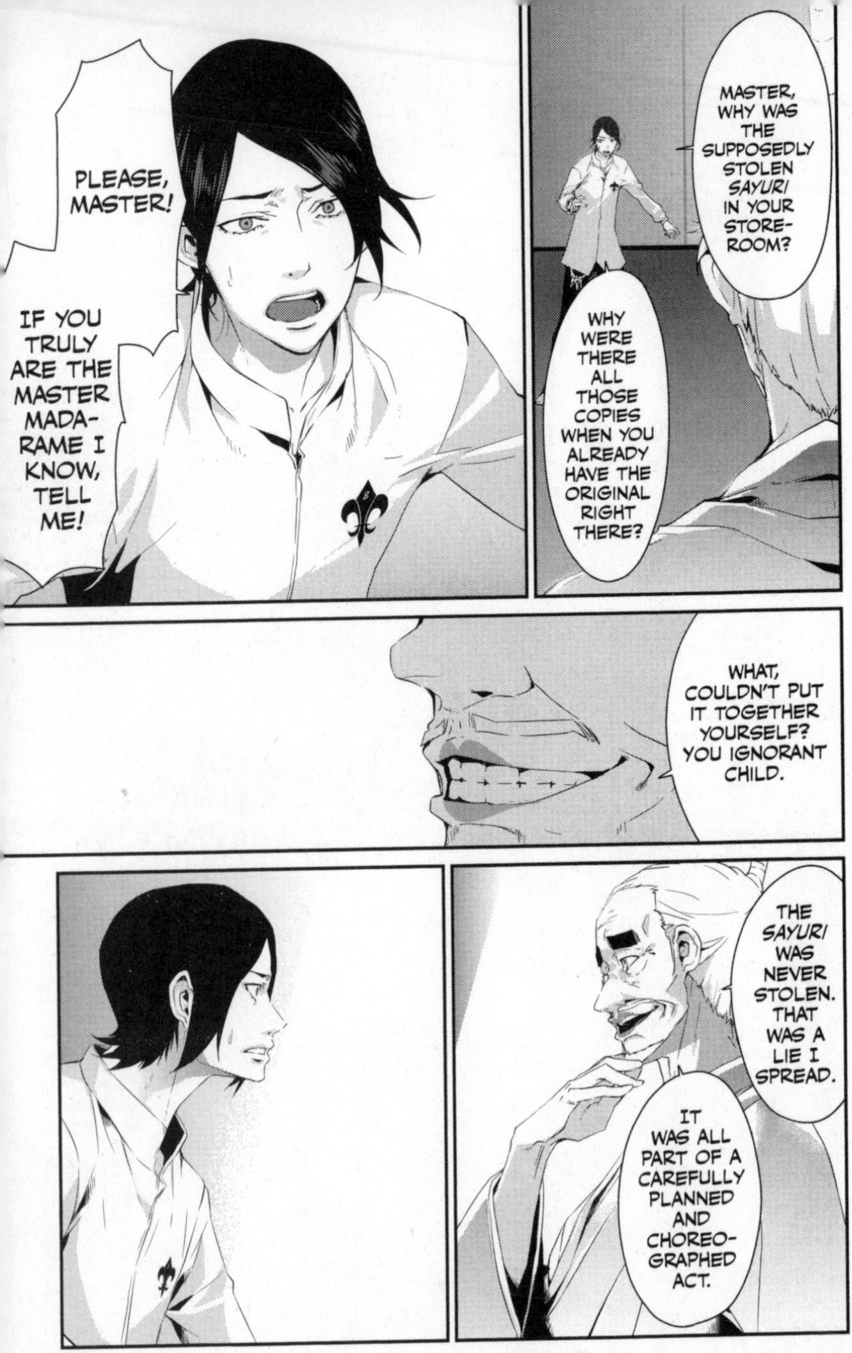
MASTER, WHY WAS THE SUPPOSEDLY STOLEN *SAYURI* IN YOUR STORE-ROOM?
WHY WERE THERE ALL THOSE COPIES WHEN YOU ALREADY HAVE THE ORIGINAL RIGHT THERE?
PLEASE, MASTER!
IF YOU TRULY ARE THE MASTER MADA-RAME I KNOW, TELL ME!
WHAT, COULDN'T PUT IT TOGETHER YOURSELF? YOU IGNORANT CHILD.
THE *SAYURI* WAS NEVER STOLEN. THAT WAS A LIE I SPREAD.
IT WAS ALL PART OF A CAREFULLY PLANNED AND CHOREO-GRAPHED ACT.

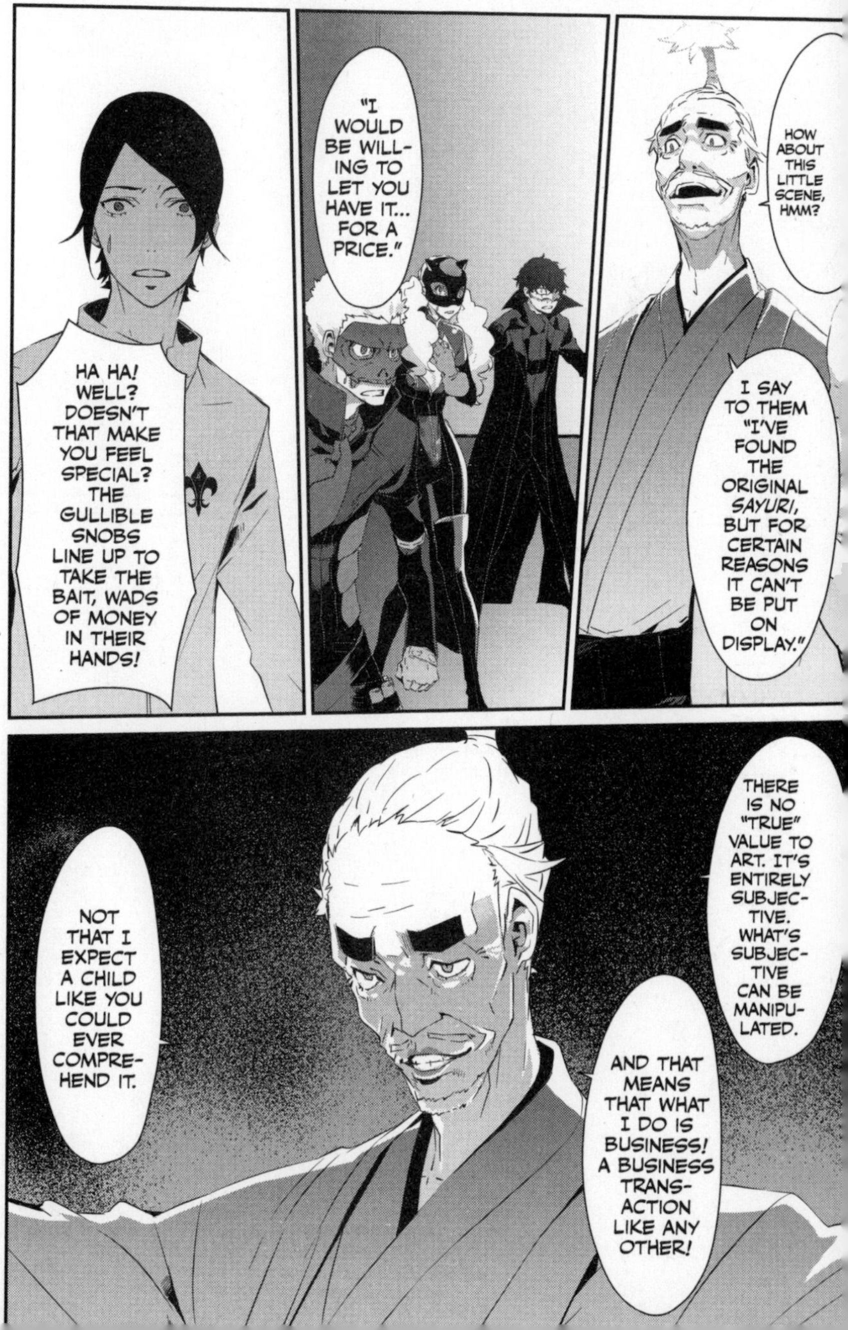
HOW ABOUT THIS LITTLE SCENE, HMM?
I SAY TO THEM "I'VE FOUND THE ORIGINAL *SAYURI*, BUT FOR CERTAIN REASONS IT CAN'T BE PUT ON DISPLAY."
"I WOULD BE WILL-ING TO LET YOU HAVE IT... FOR A PRICE."
HA HA! WELL? DOESN'T THAT MAKE YOU FEEL SPECIAL? THE GULLIBLE SNOBS LINE UP TO TAKE THE BAIT, WADS OF MONEY IN THEIR HANDS!
THERE IS NO "TRUE" VALUE TO ART. IT'S ENTIRELY SUBJEC-TIVE. WHAT'S SUBJEC-TIVE CAN BE MANIPU-LATED.
AND THAT MEANS THAT WHAT I DO IS BUSINESS! A BUSINESS TRANS-ACTION LIKE ANY OTHER!
NOT THAT I EXPECT A CHILD LIKE YOU COULD EVER COMPRE-HEND IT.

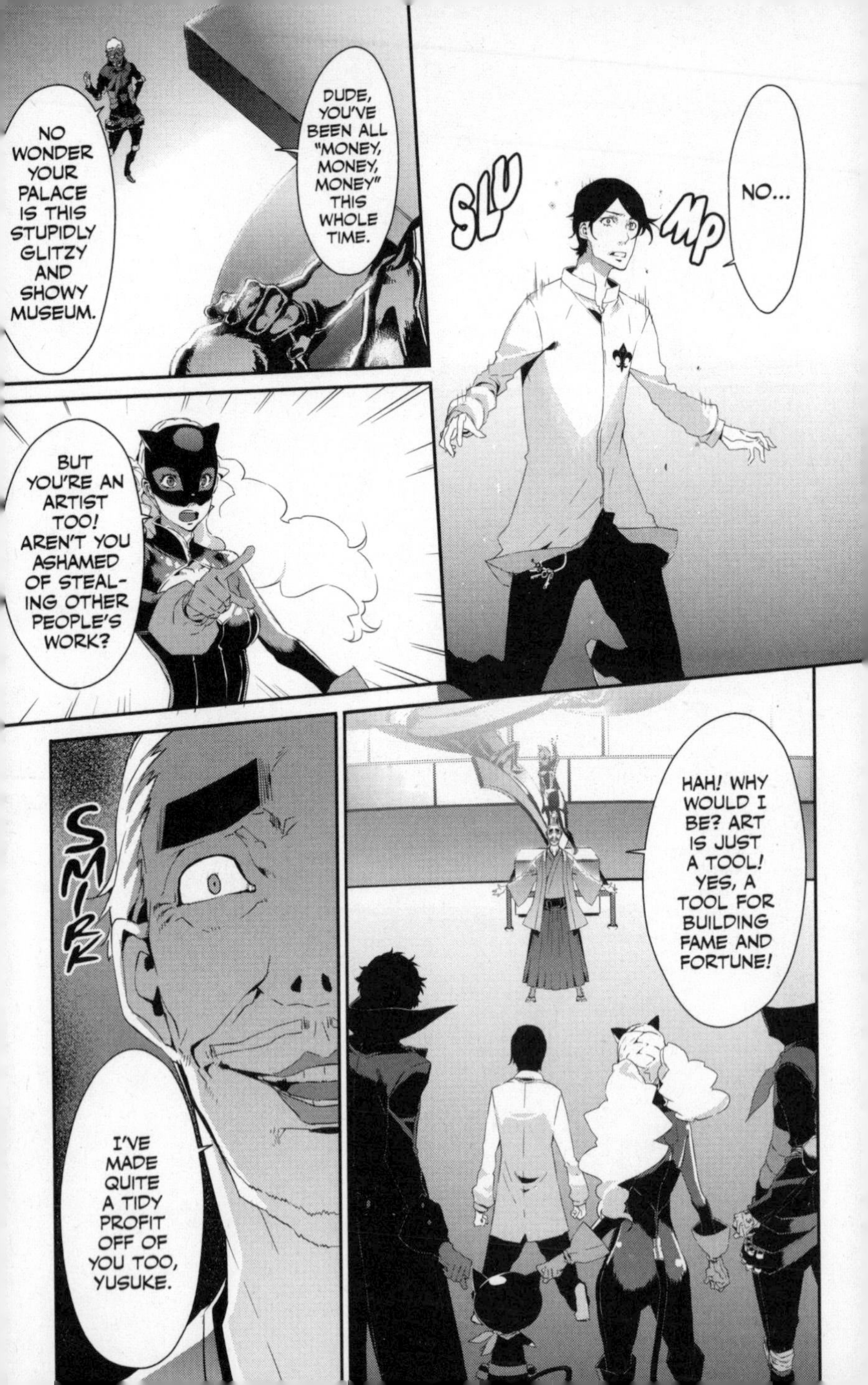
NO...
SLUMP
DUDE, YOU'VE BEEN ALL "MONEY, MONEY, MONEY" THIS WHOLE TIME.
NO WONDER YOUR PALACE IS THIS STUPIDLY GLITZY AND SHOWY MUSEUM.
BUT YOU'RE AN ARTIST TOO! AREN'T YOU ASHAMED OF STEAL-ING OTHER PEOPLE'S WORK?
HAH! WHY WOULD I BE? ART IS JUST A TOOL! YES, A TOOL FOR BUILDING FAME AND FORTUNE!
SMIRK
I'VE MADE QUITE A TIDY PROFIT OFF OF YOU TOO, YUSUKE.

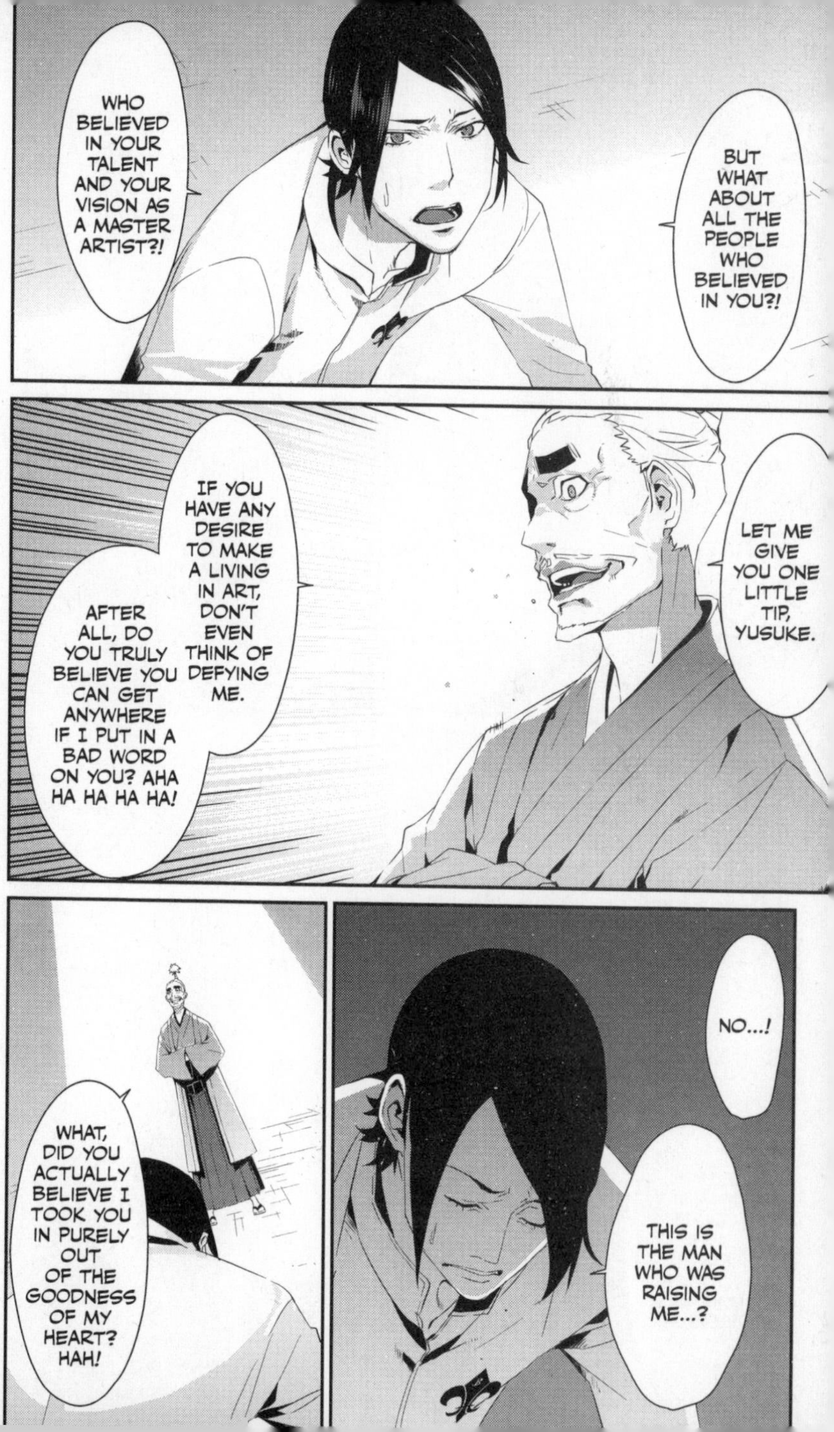
BUT WHAT ABOUT ALL THE PEOPLE WHO BELIEVED IN YOU?!
WHO BELIEVED IN YOUR TALENT AND YOUR VISION AS A MASTER ARTIST?!
LET ME GIVE YOU ONE LITTLE TIP, YUSUKE.
IF YOU HAVE ANY DESIRE TO MAKE A LIVING IN ART, DON'T EVEN THINK OF DEFYING ME.
AFTER ALL, DO YOU TRULY BELIEVE YOU CAN GET ANYWHERE IF I PUT IN A BAD WORD ON YOU? AHA HA HA HA HA!
NO...!
THIS IS THE MAN WHO WAS RAISING ME...?
WHAT, DID YOU ACTUALLY BELIEVE I TOOK YOU IN PURELY OUT OF THE GOODNESS OF MY HEART? HAH!

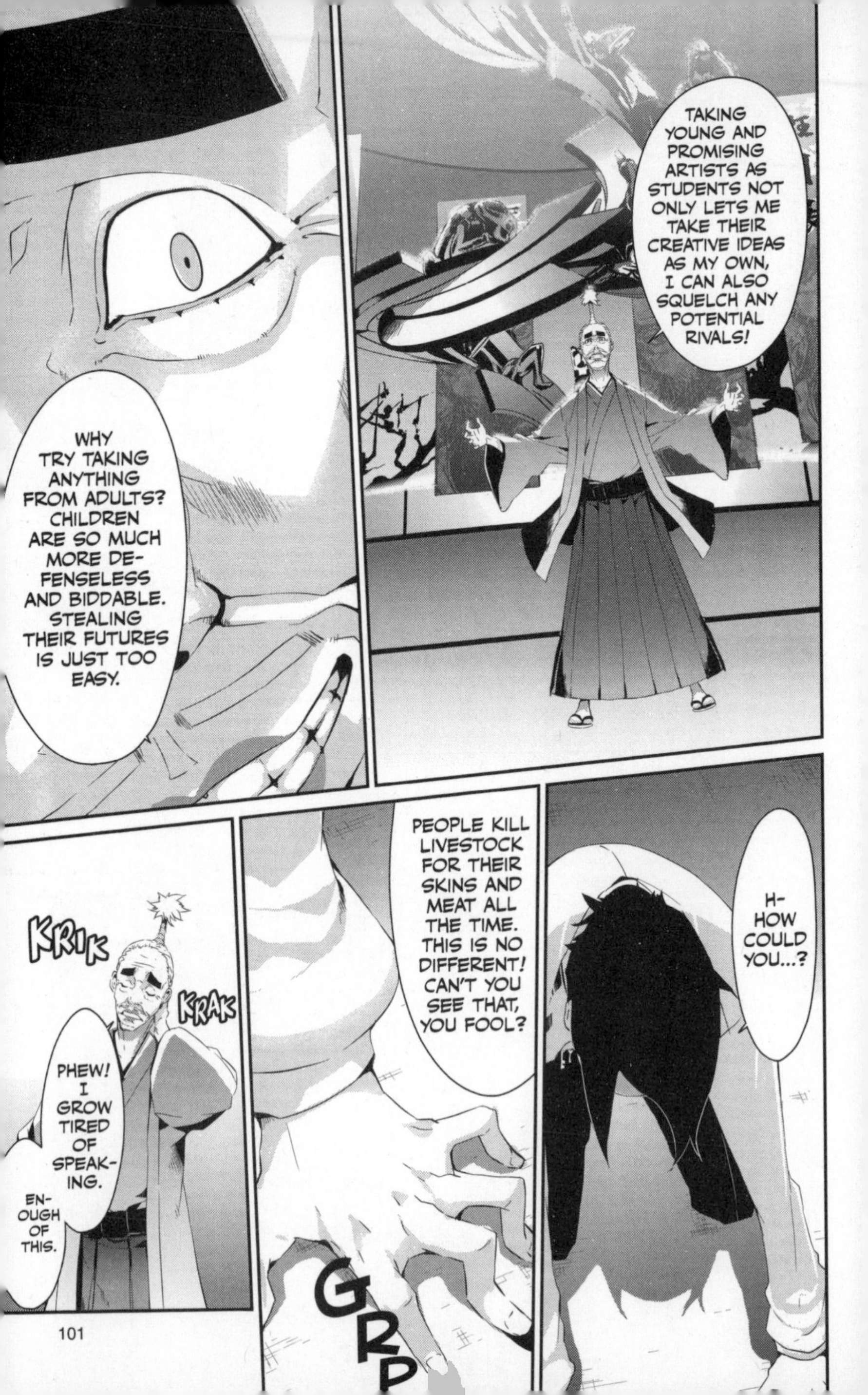

TAKING YOUNG AND PROMISING ARTISTS AS STUDENTS NOT ONLY LETS ME TAKE THEIR CREATIVE IDEAS AS MY OWN, I CAN ALSO SQUELCH ANY POTENTIAL RIVALS!
WHY TRY TAKING ANYTHING FROM ADULTS? CHILDREN ARE SO MUCH MORE DE-FENSELESS AND BIDDABLE. STEALING THEIR FUTURES IS JUST TOO EASY.
H-HOW COULD YOU...?
PEOPLE KILL LIVESTOCK FOR THEIR SKINS AND MEAT ALL THE TIME. THIS IS NO DIFFERENT! CAN'T YOU SEE THAT, YOU FOOL?
GRP
KRIK
KRAK
PHEW! I GROW TIRED OF SPEAK-ING.
EN-OUGH OF THIS.

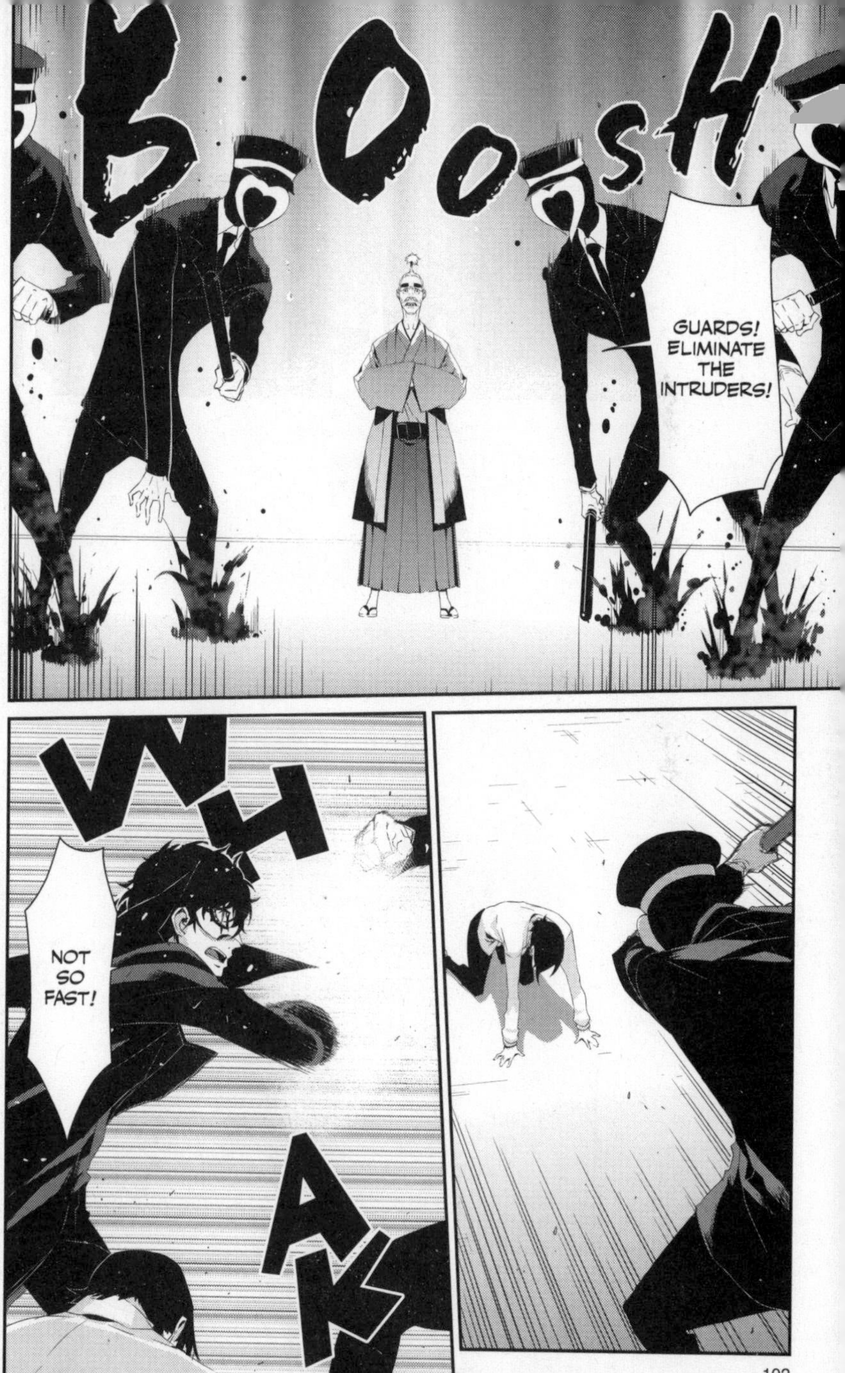
BOOSH
GUARDS! ELIMINATE THE INTRUDERS!
NOT SO FAST!

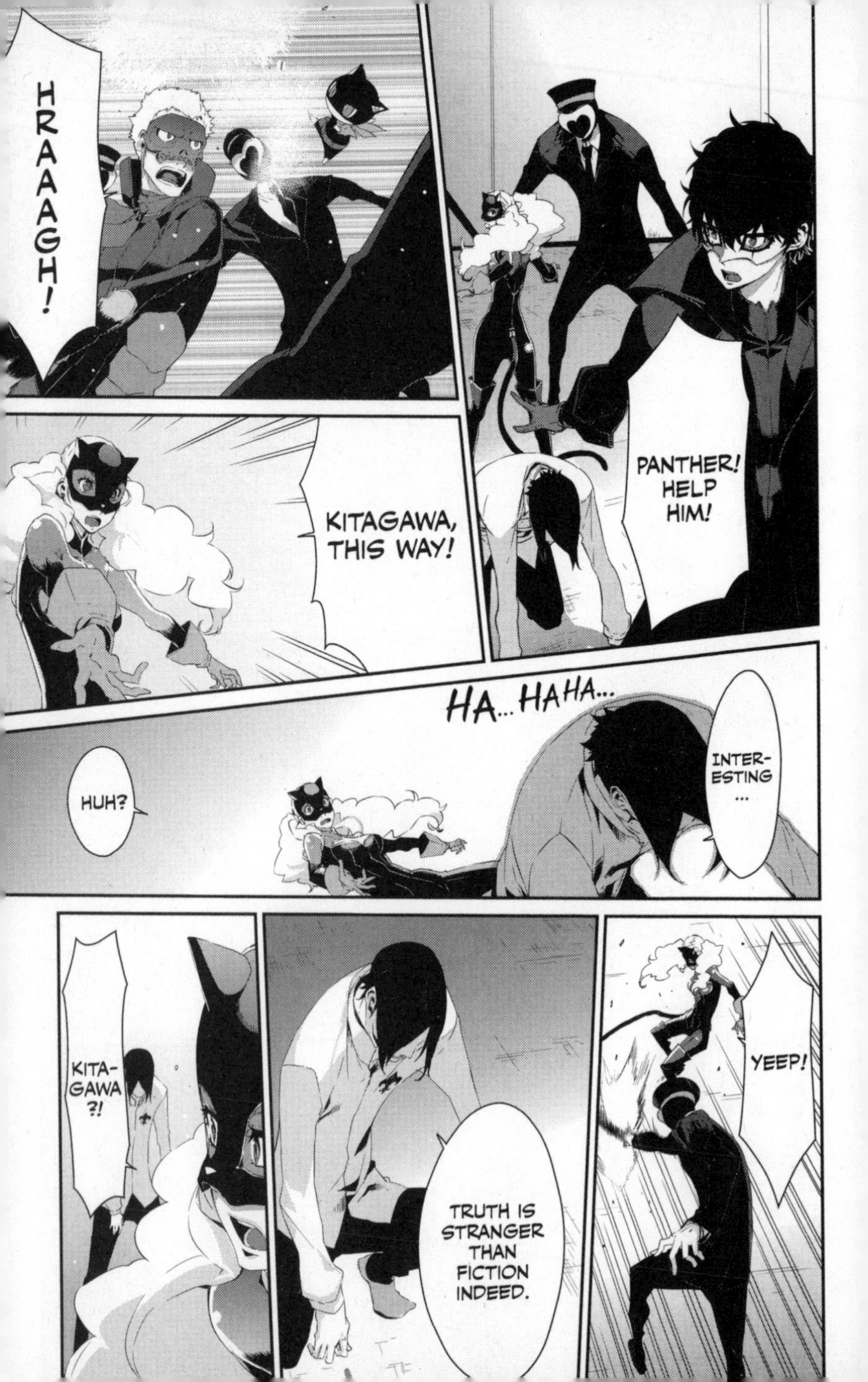
PANTHER! HELP HIM!
HRAAAGH!
KITAGAWA, THIS WAY!
HA... HAHA...
INTER-ESTING...
HUH?
YEEP!
TRUTH IS STRANGER THAN FICTION INDEED.
KITA-GAWA?!

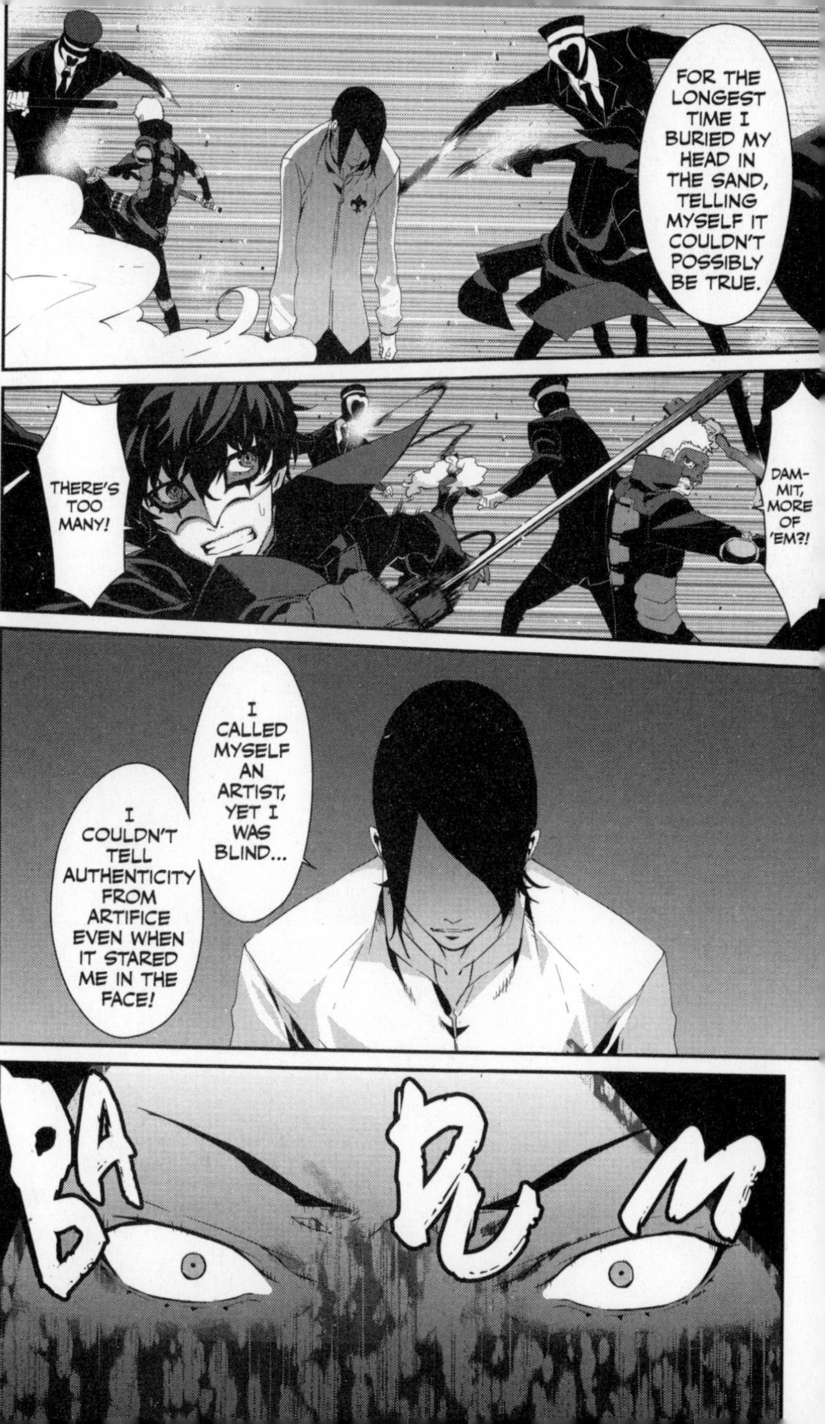
FOR THE LONGEST TIME I BURIED MY HEAD IN THE SAND, TELLING MYSELF IT COULDN'T POSSIBLY BE TRUE.
DAM-MIT, MORE OF 'EM?!
THERE'S TOO MANY!
I CALLED MYSELF AN ARTIST, YET I WAS BLIND...
I COULDN'T TELL AUTHENTICITY FROM ARTIFICE EVEN WHEN IT STARED ME IN THE FACE!
BA DUM

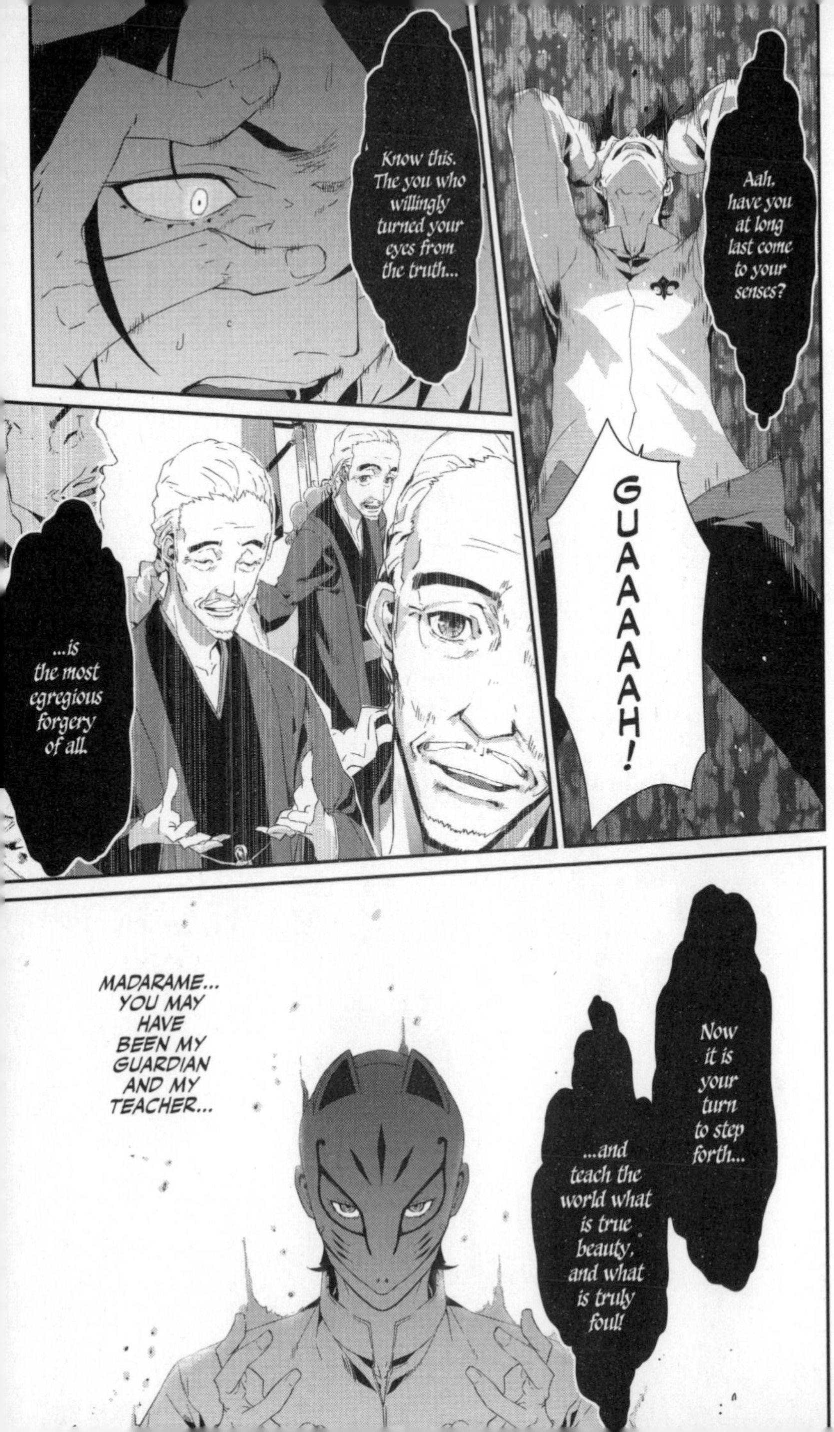
Aah, have you at long last come to your senses?
GUAAAAAAH!
Know this. The you who willingly turned your eyes from the truth...
...is the most egregious forgery of all.
Now it is your turn to step forth...
...and teach the world what is true beauty, and what is truly foul!
MADARAME... YOU MAY HAVE BEEN MY GUARDIAN AND MY TEACHER...

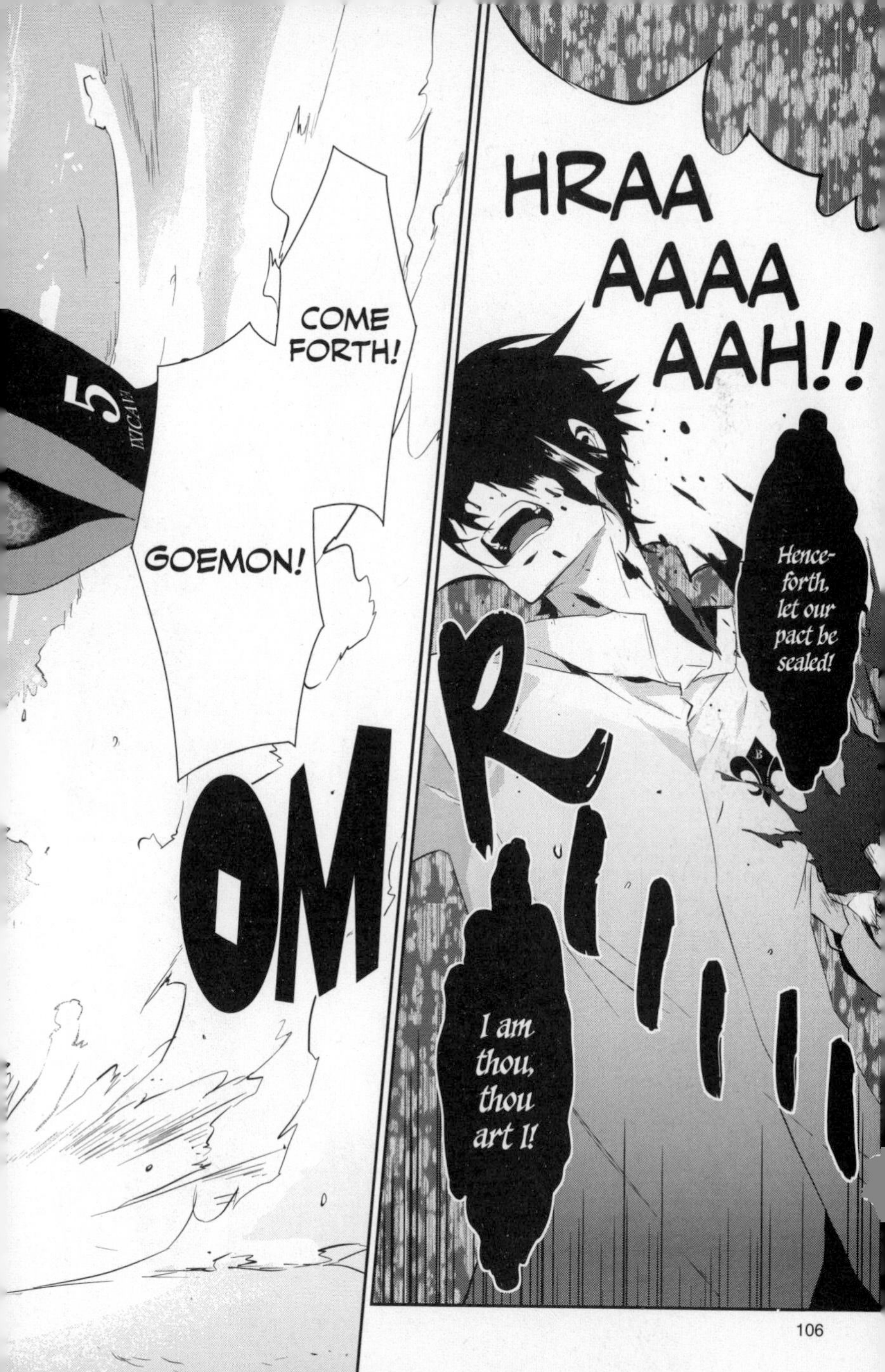
HRAA AAAA AAH!!
Henceforth, let our pact be sealed!
R
I am thou, thou art I!
COME FORTH!
GOEMON!
OM

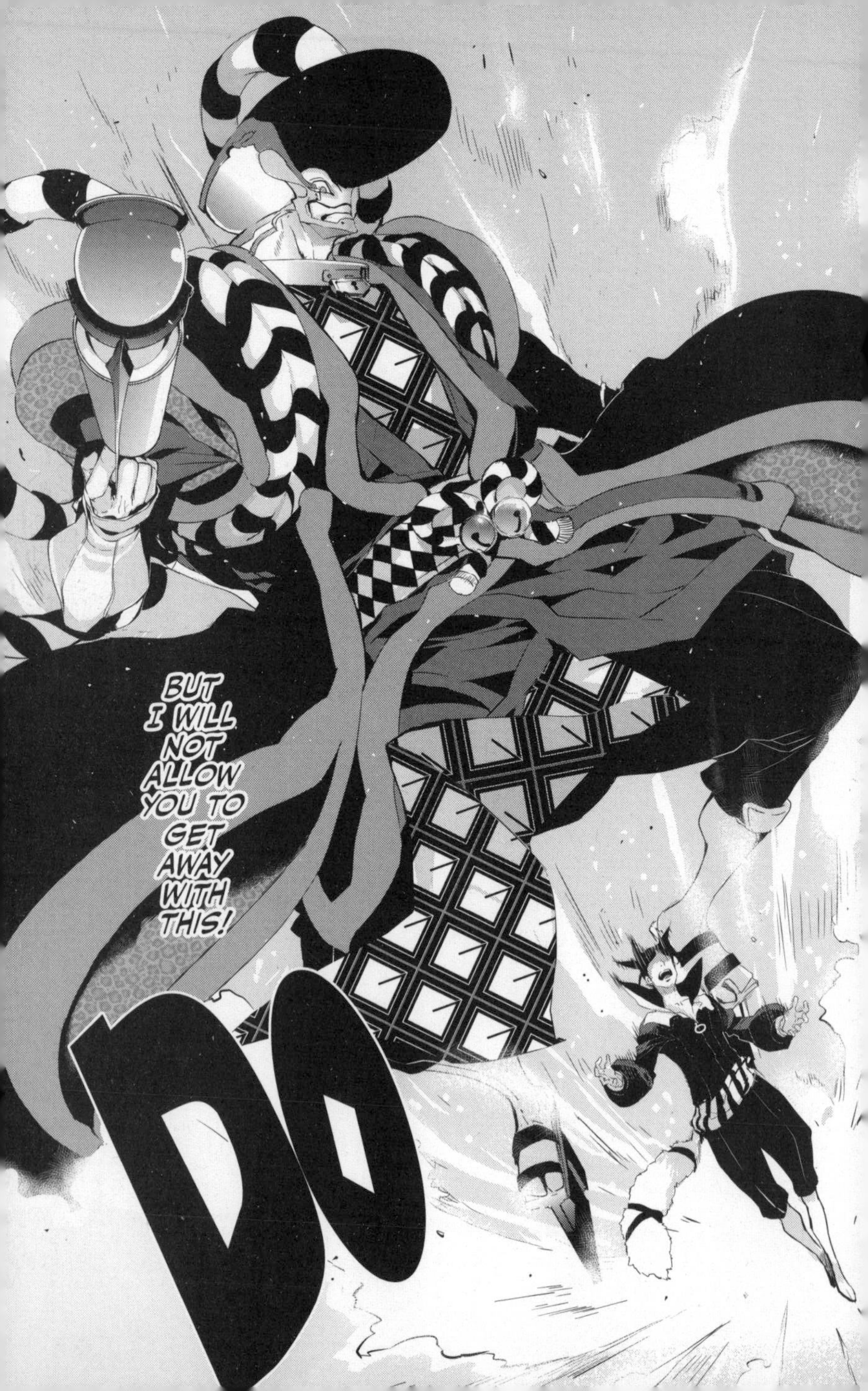
BUT I WILL NOT ALLOW YOU TO GET AWAY WITH THIS!
DO

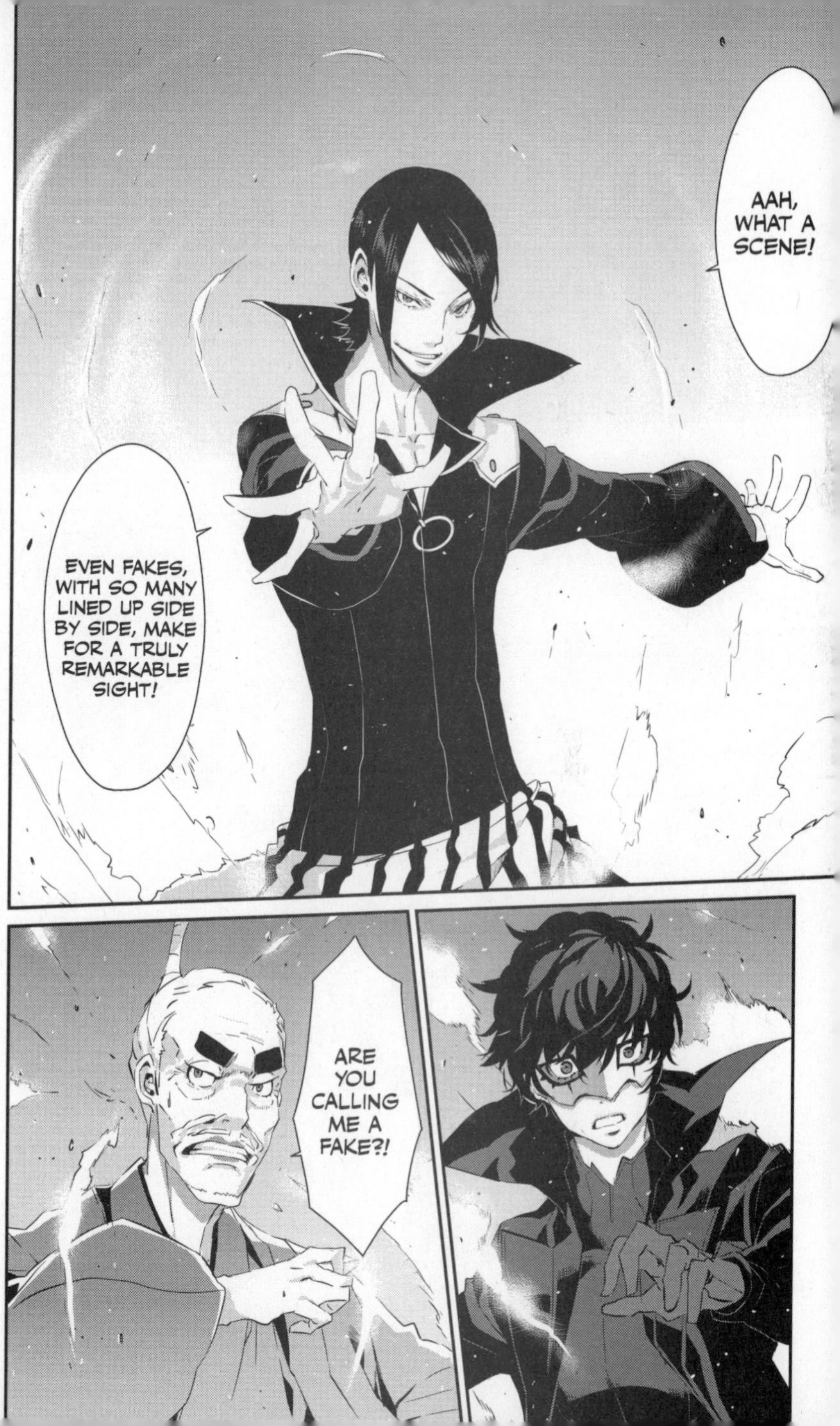
AAH, WHAT A SCENE!
EVEN FAKES, WITH SO MANY LINED UP SIDE BY SIDE, MAKE FOR A TRULY REMARKABLE SIGHT!
ARE YOU CALLING ME A FAKE?!

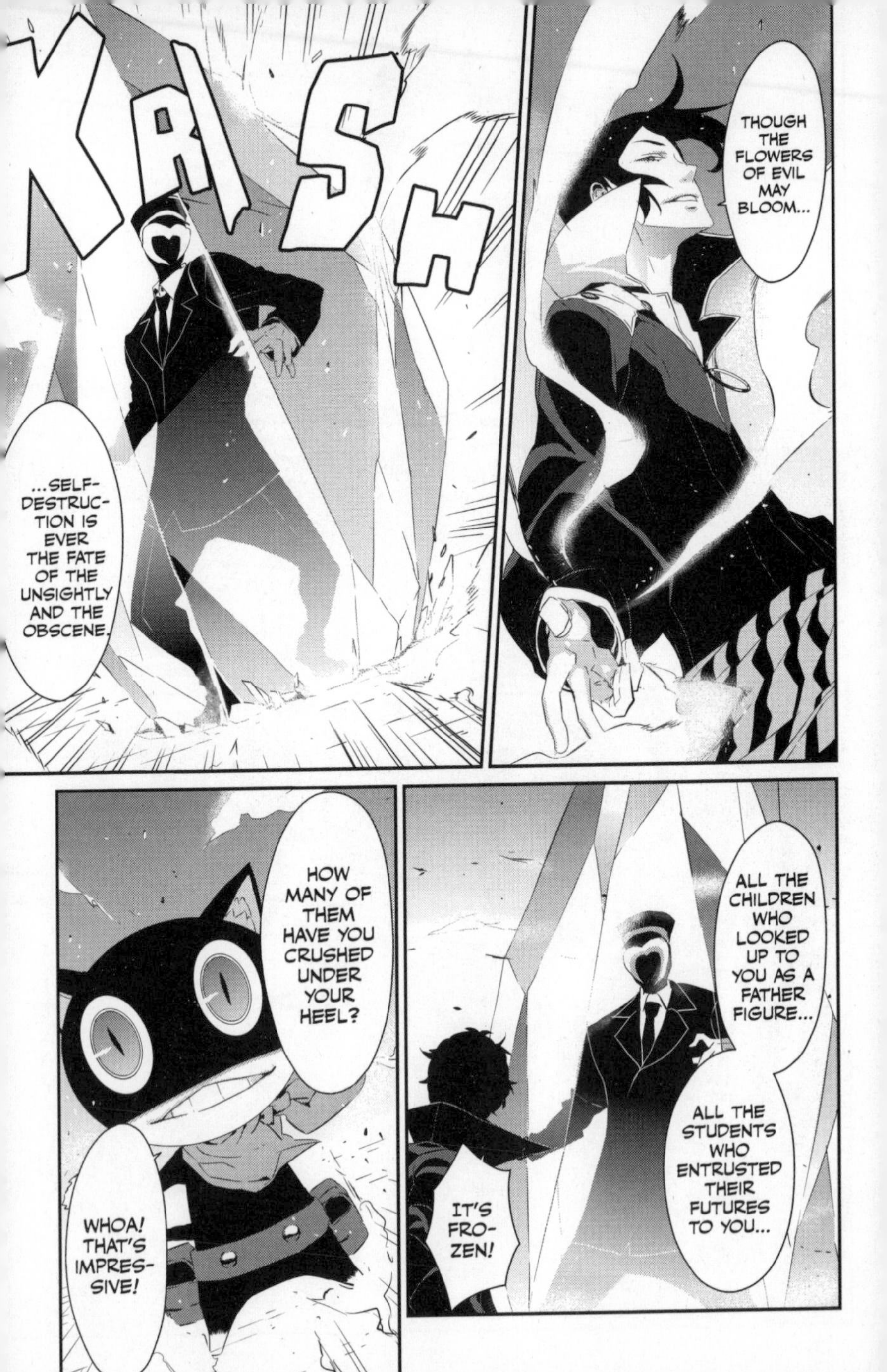
THOUGH THE FLOWERS OF EVIL MAY BLOOM...
KRASH
...SELF-DESTRUCTION IS EVER THE FATE OF THE UNSIGHTLY AND THE OBSCENE.
ALL THE CHILDREN WHO LOOKED UP TO YOU AS A FATHER FIGURE...
ALL THE STUDENTS WHO ENTRUSTED THEIR FUTURES TO YOU...
IT'S FROZEN!
HOW MANY OF THEM HAVE YOU CRUSHED UNDER YOUR HEEL?
WHOA! THAT'S IMPRESSIVE!

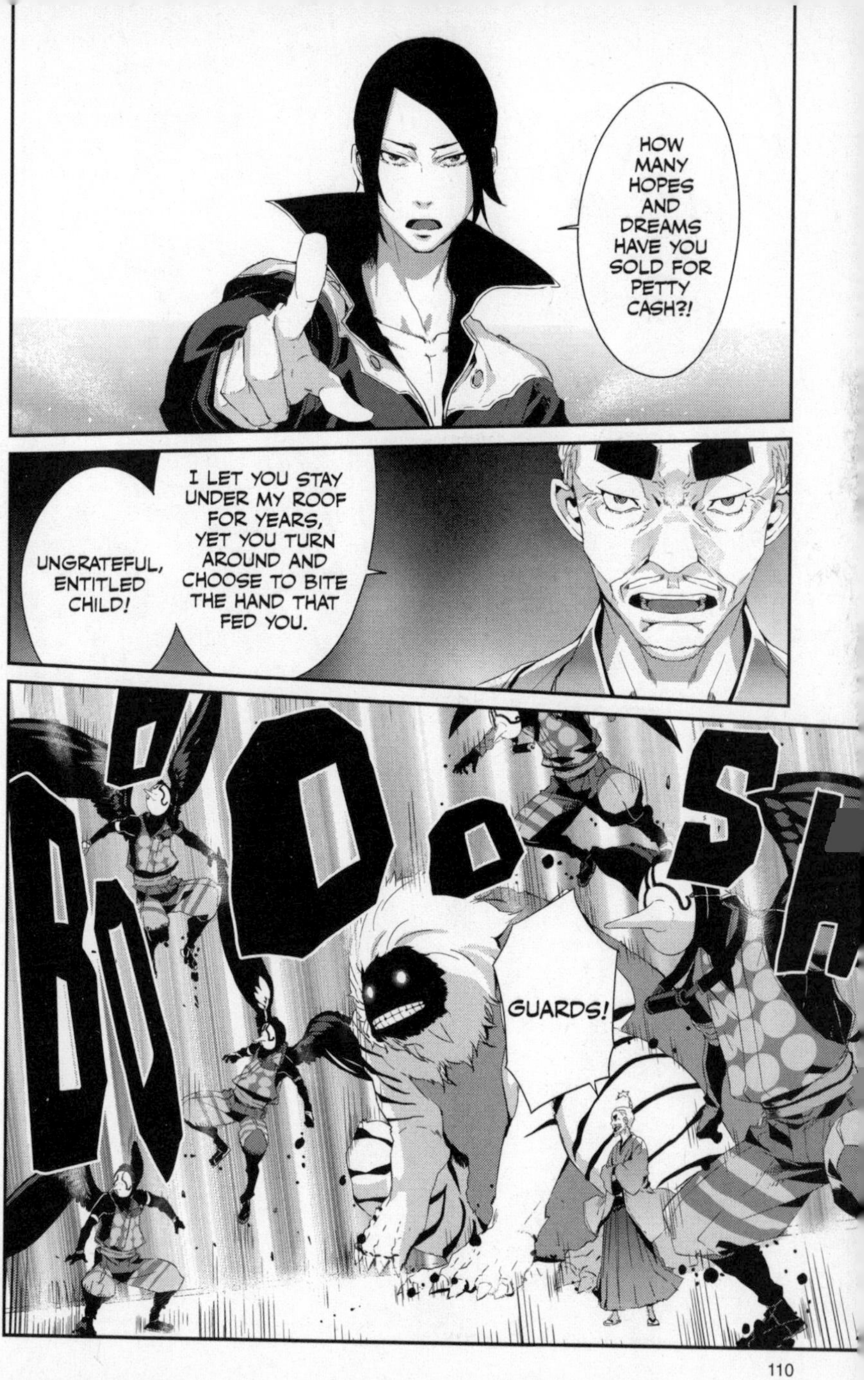
HOW MANY HOPES AND DREAMS HAVE YOU SOLD FOR PETTY CASH?!
I LET YOU STAY UNDER MY ROOF FOR YEARS, YET YOU TURN AROUND AND CHOOSE TO BITE THE HAND THAT FED YOU.
UNGRATEFUL, ENTITLED CHILD!
GUARDS!

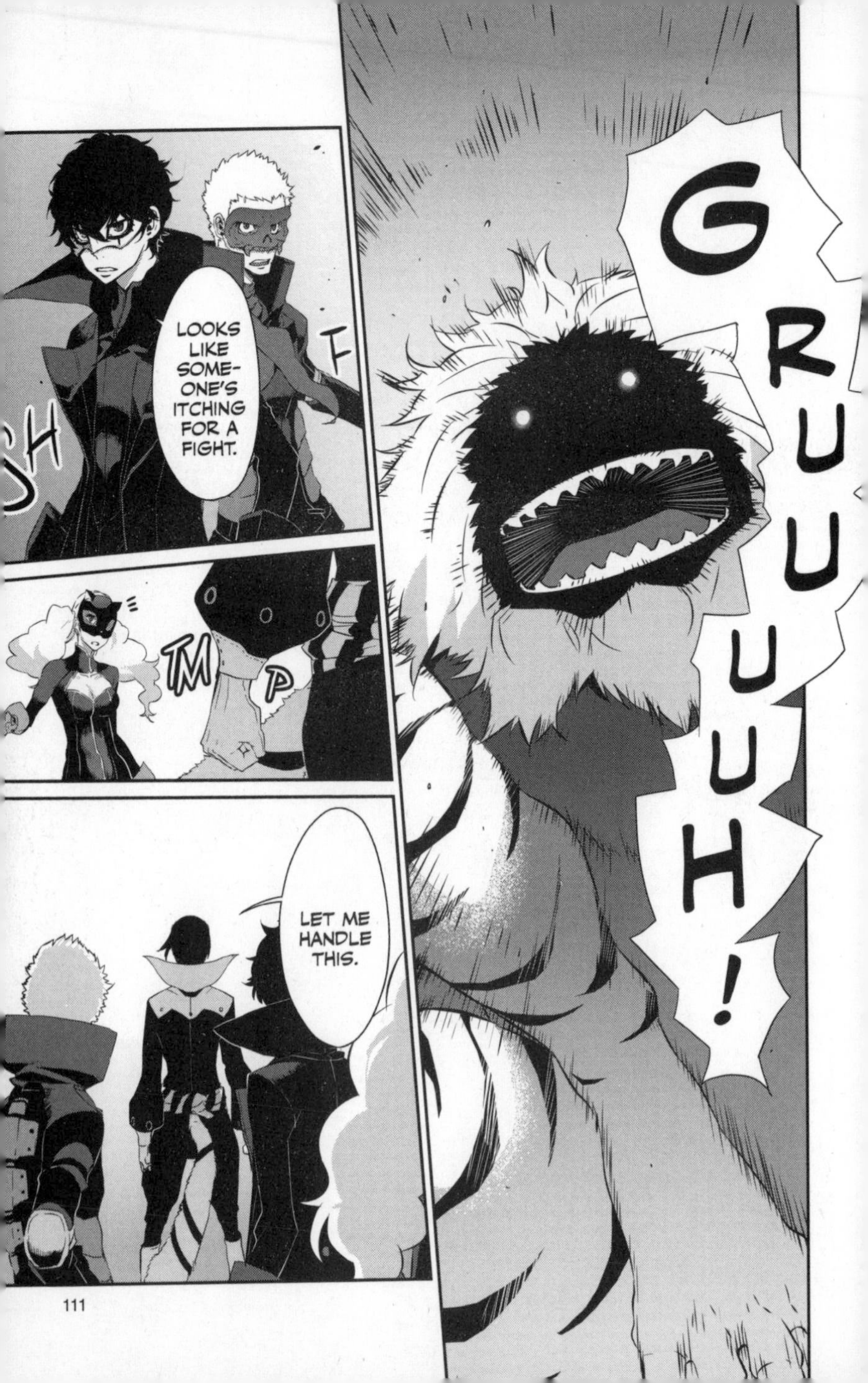
GRUUUUH!
F
SH
LOOKS LIKE SOME-ONE'S ITCHING FOR A FIGHT.
TM
P
LET ME HANDLE THIS.

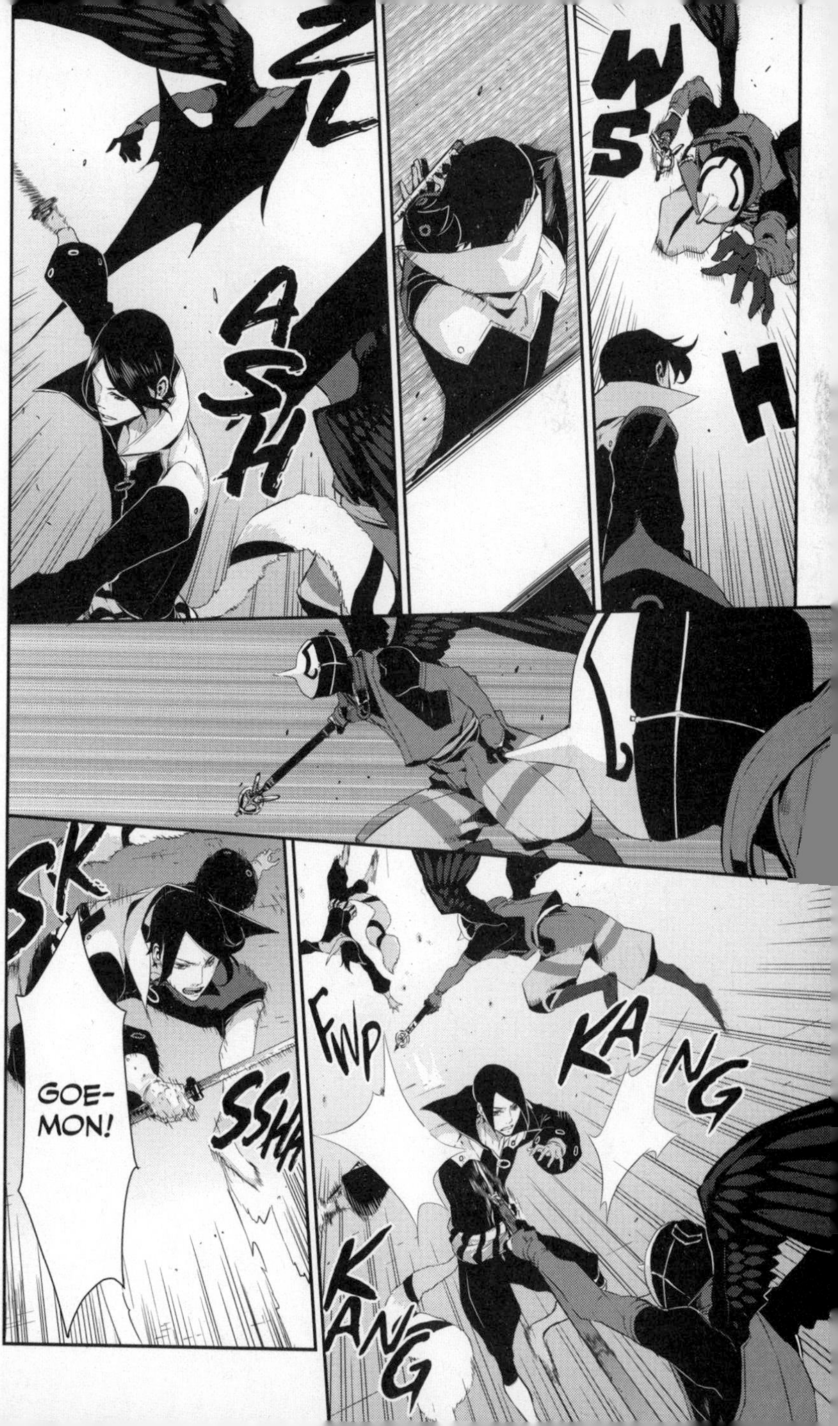
WSH
KANG
FWP
KANG
GOE-MON!

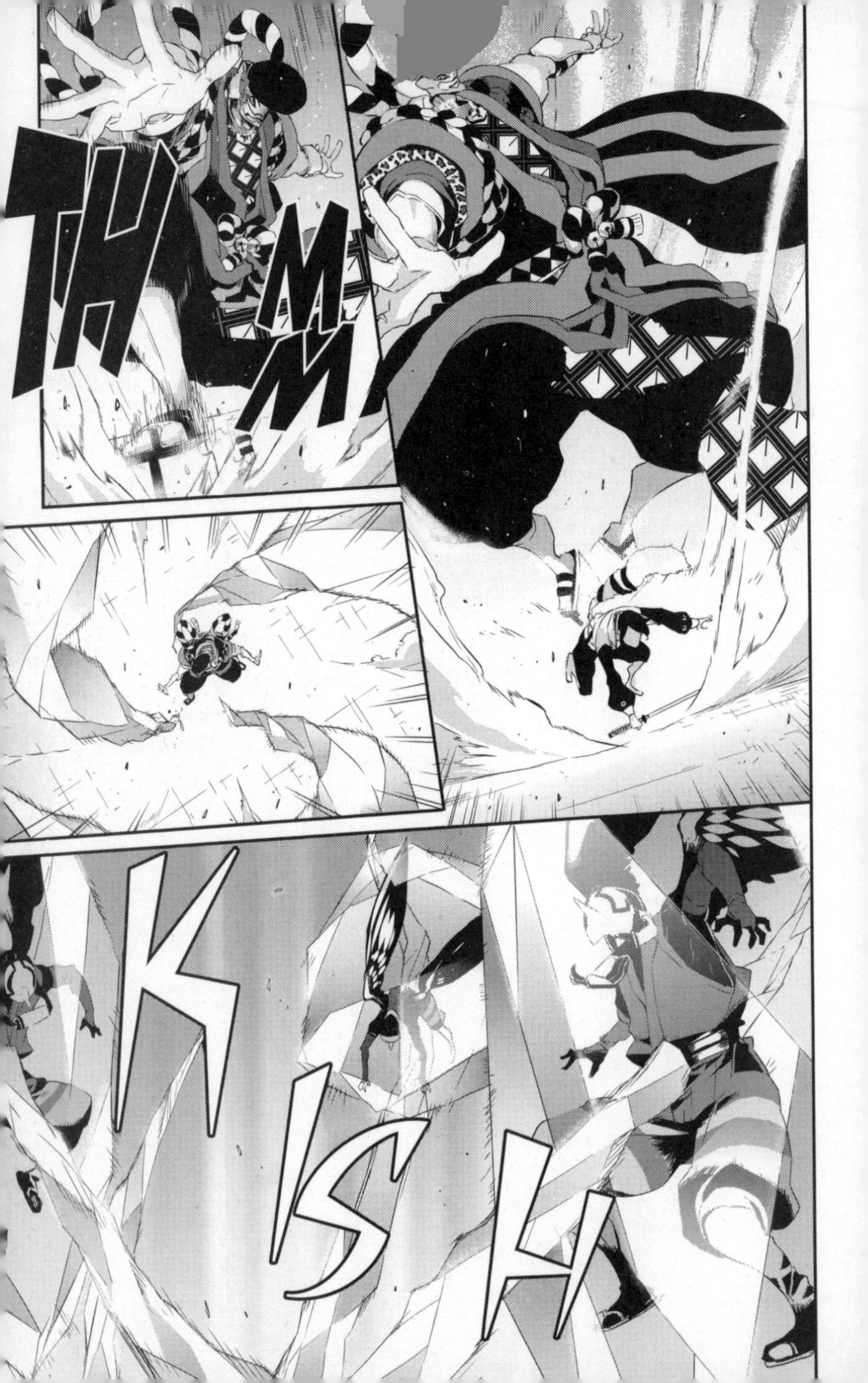
THMMM
KSSH

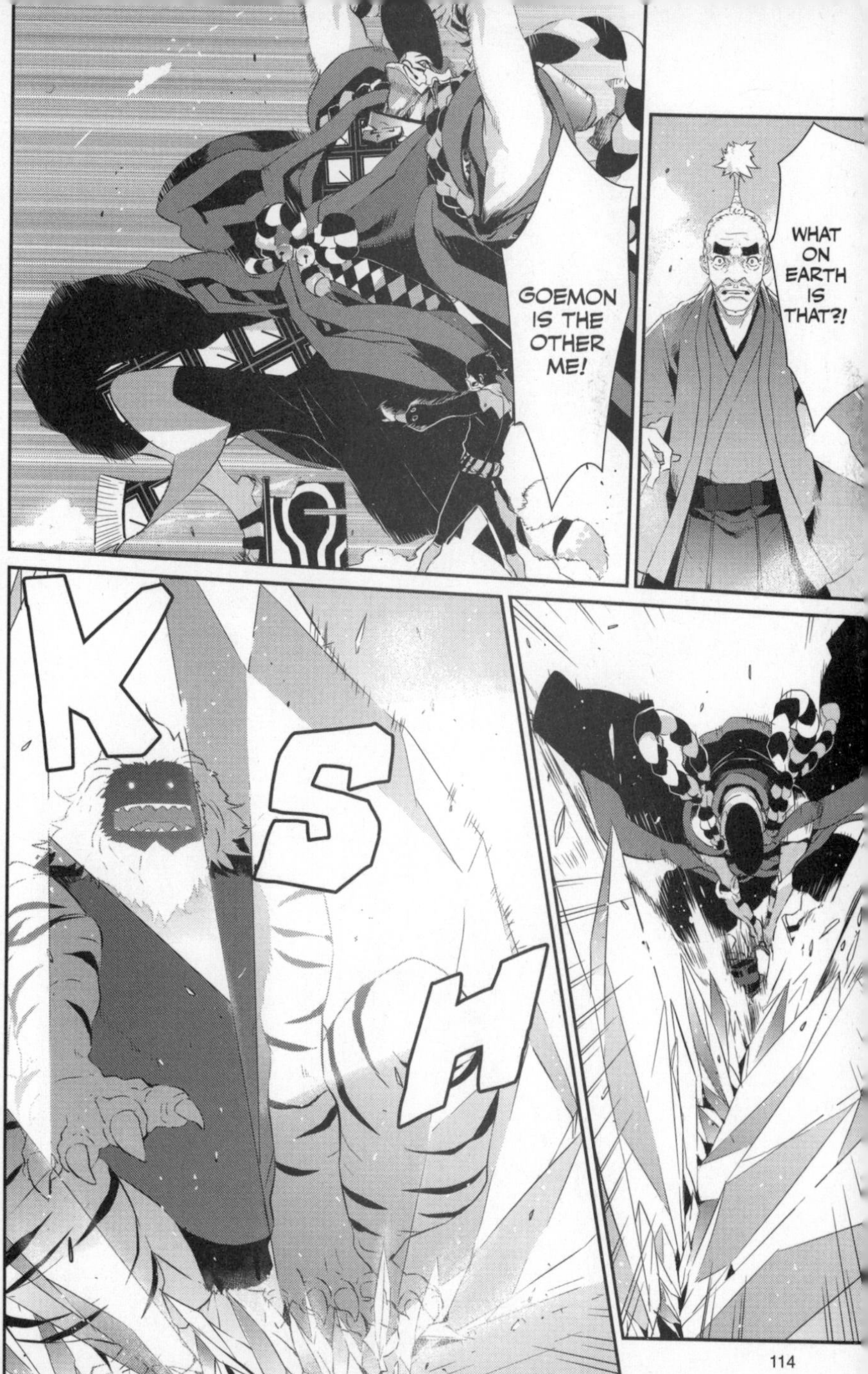
WHAT ON EARTH IS THAT?!
GOEMON IS THE OTHER ME!
KSH

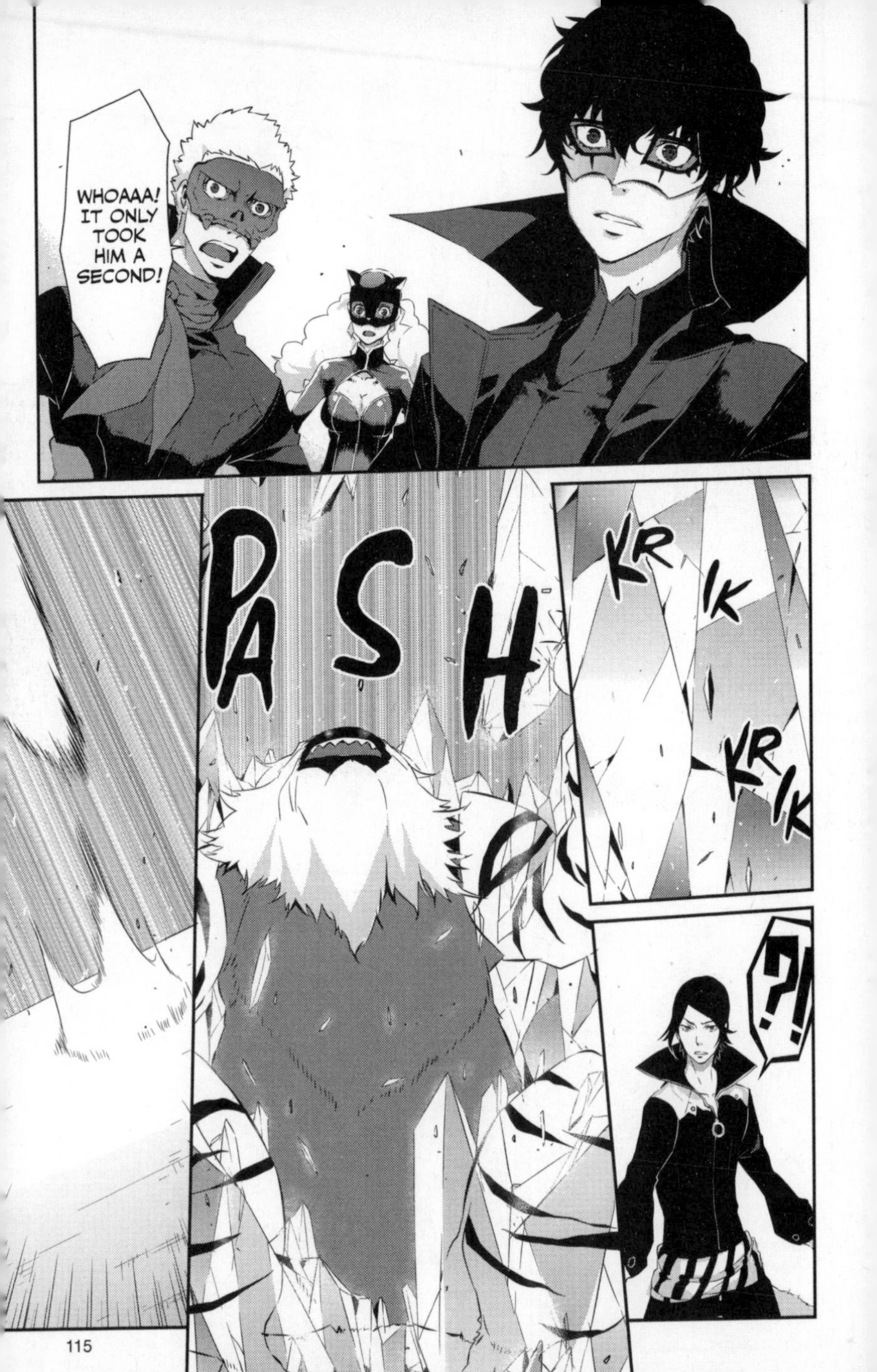
WHOAAA! IT ONLY TOOK HIM A SECOND!
KRIK
KRIK
PASH
?!

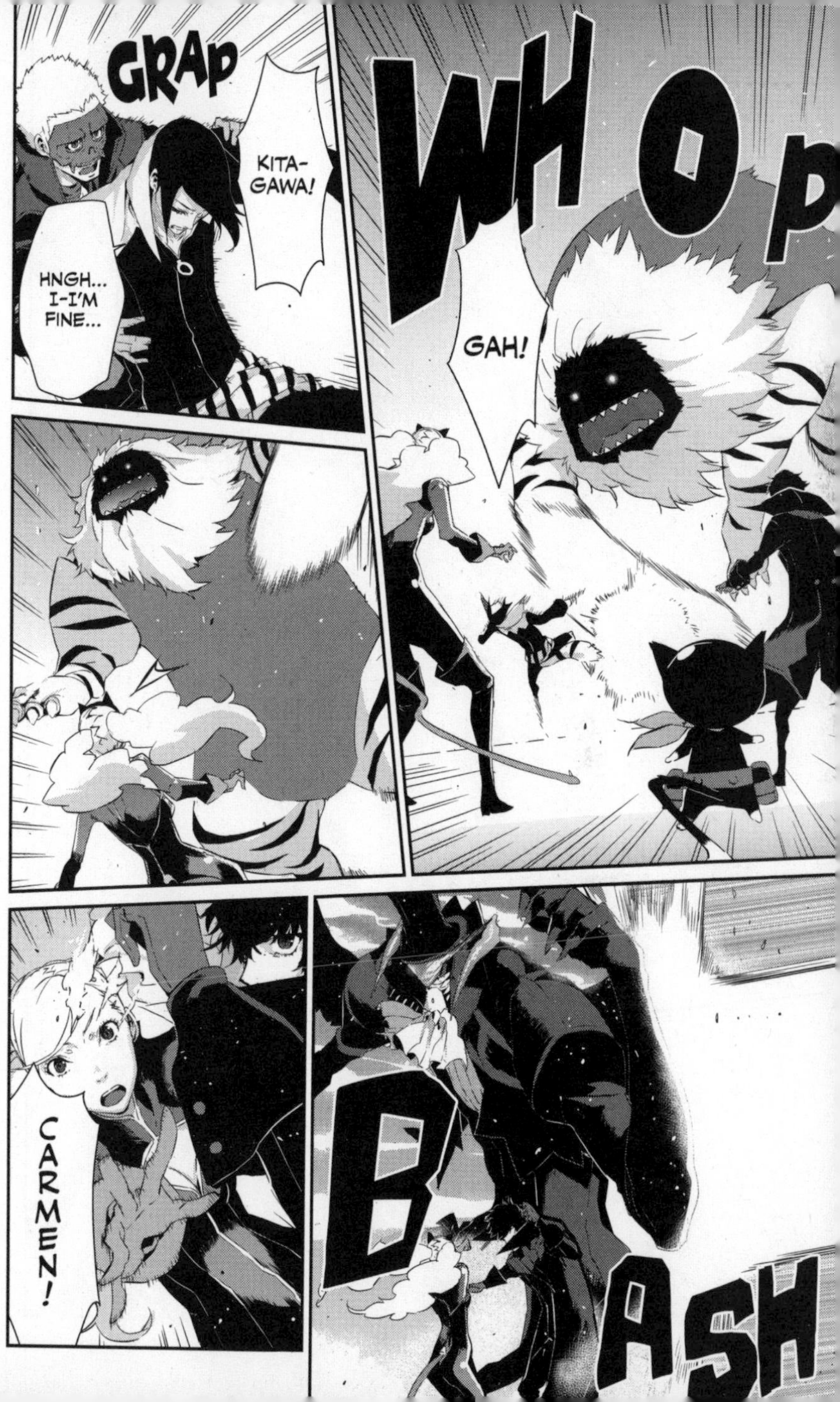
WHOP
GAH!
GRAP
KITA-GAWA!
HNGH... I-I'M FINE...
BASH
CARMEN!

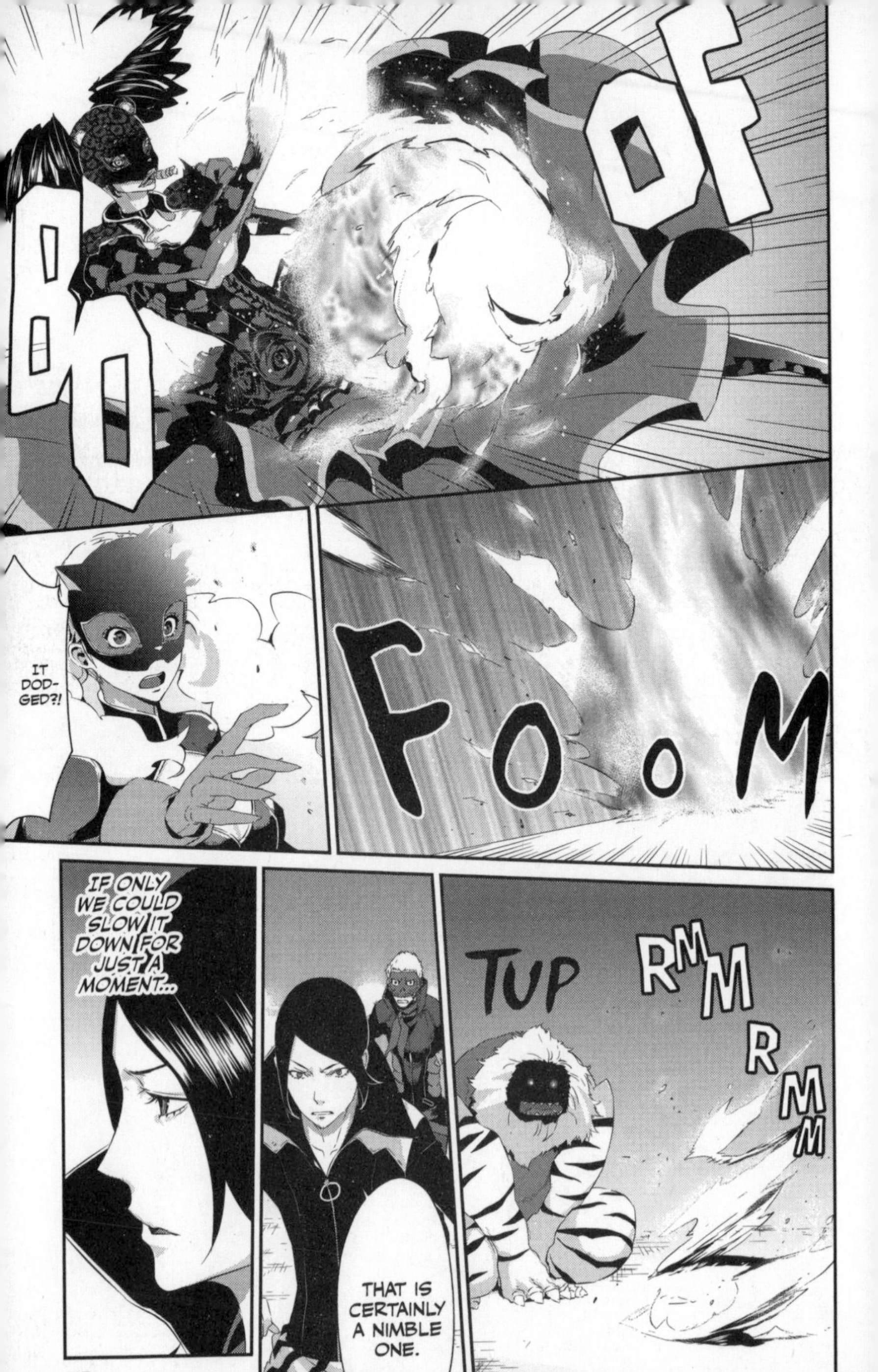
BOOF
FOOM
IT DODGED?!
RMMM
RMMM
TUP
THAT IS CERTAINLY A NIMBLE ONE.
IF ONLY WE COULD SLOW IT DOWN FOR JUST A MOMENT...

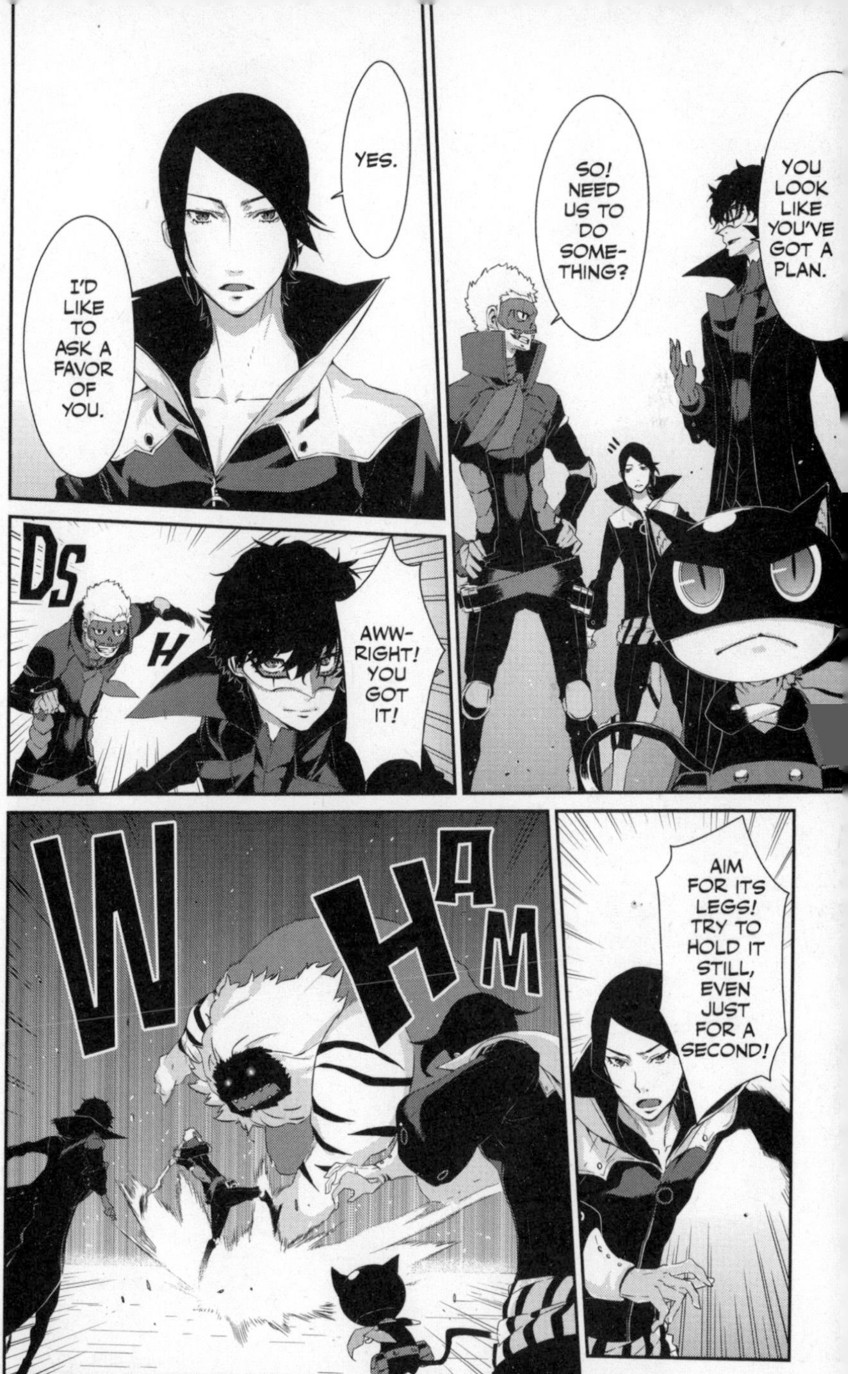
YOU LOOK LIKE YOU'VE GOT A PLAN.
SO! NEED US TO DO SOME-THING?
YES.
I'D LIKE TO ASK A FAVOR OF YOU.
AWW-RIGHT! YOU GOT IT!
DSH
AIM FOR ITS LEGS! TRY TO HOLD IT STILL, EVEN JUST FOR A SECOND!
WHAM

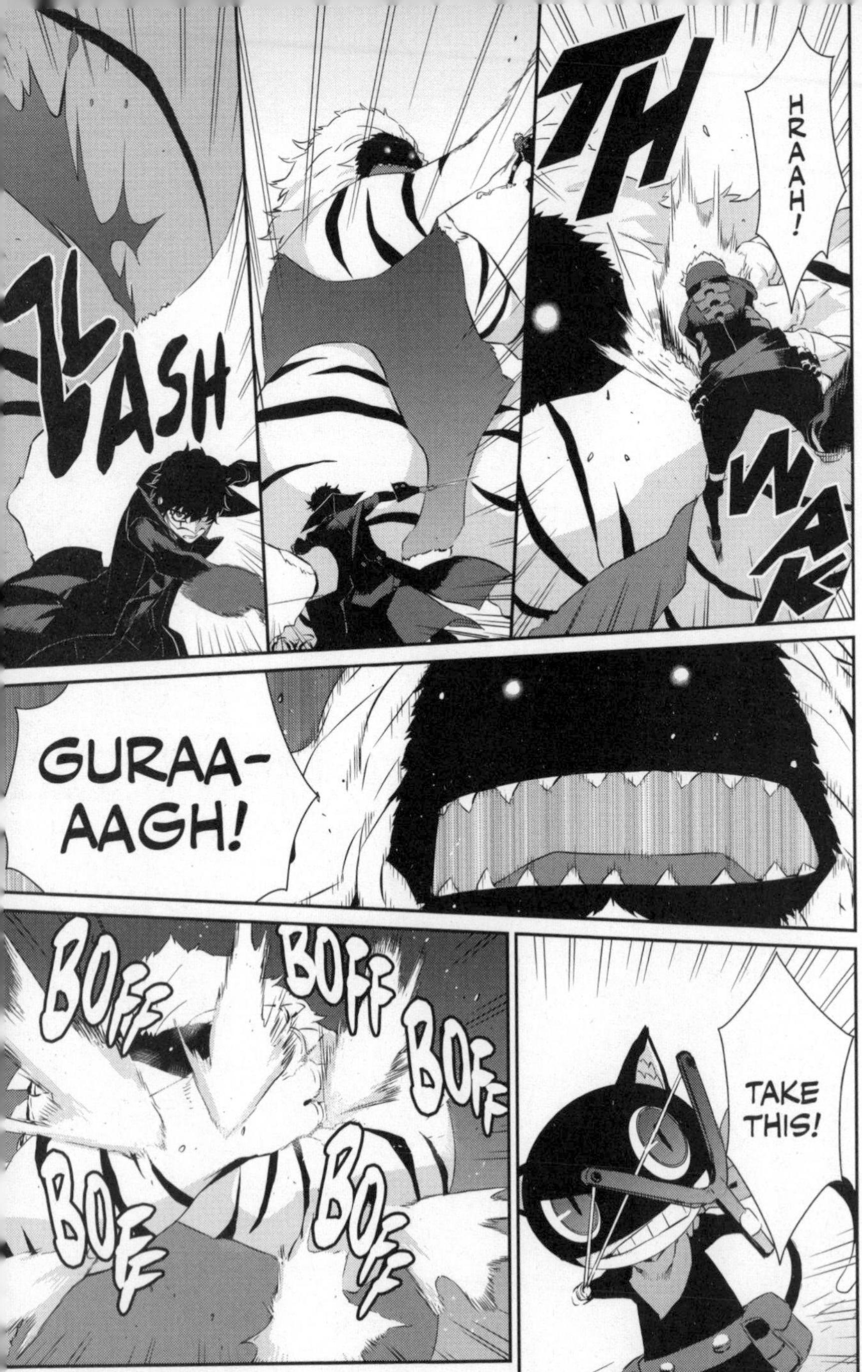
HRAAAH!
TH
WAK
ZASH
GURAA-
AAGH!
TAKE
THIS!
BOFF
BOFF
BOFF
BOFF
BOFF

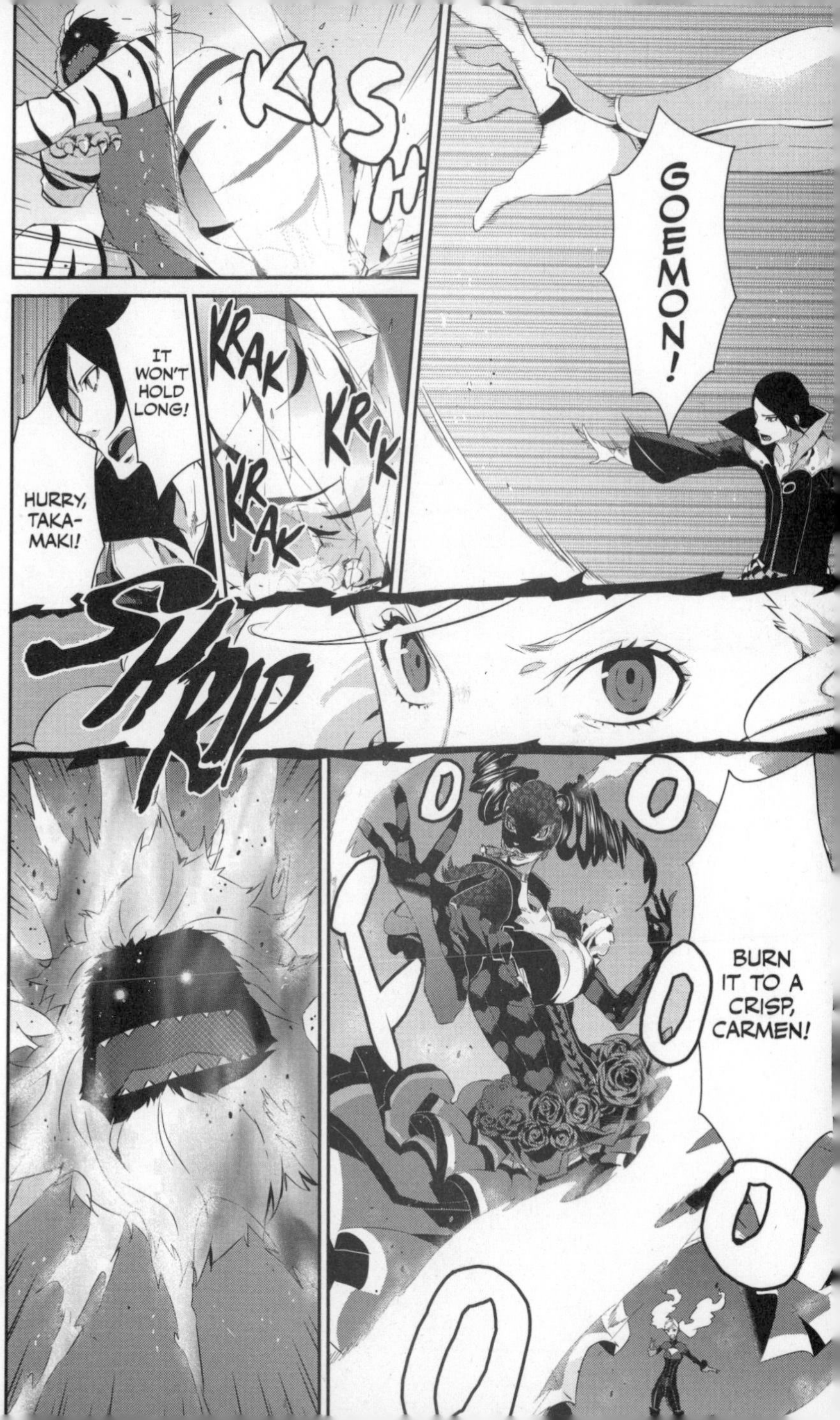
GOEMON!
KISHH
KRAK KRIK KRAK
IT WON'T HOLD LONG!
HURRY, TAKA-MAKI!
SHRIP
OOOOO
BURN IT TO A CRISP, CARMEN!

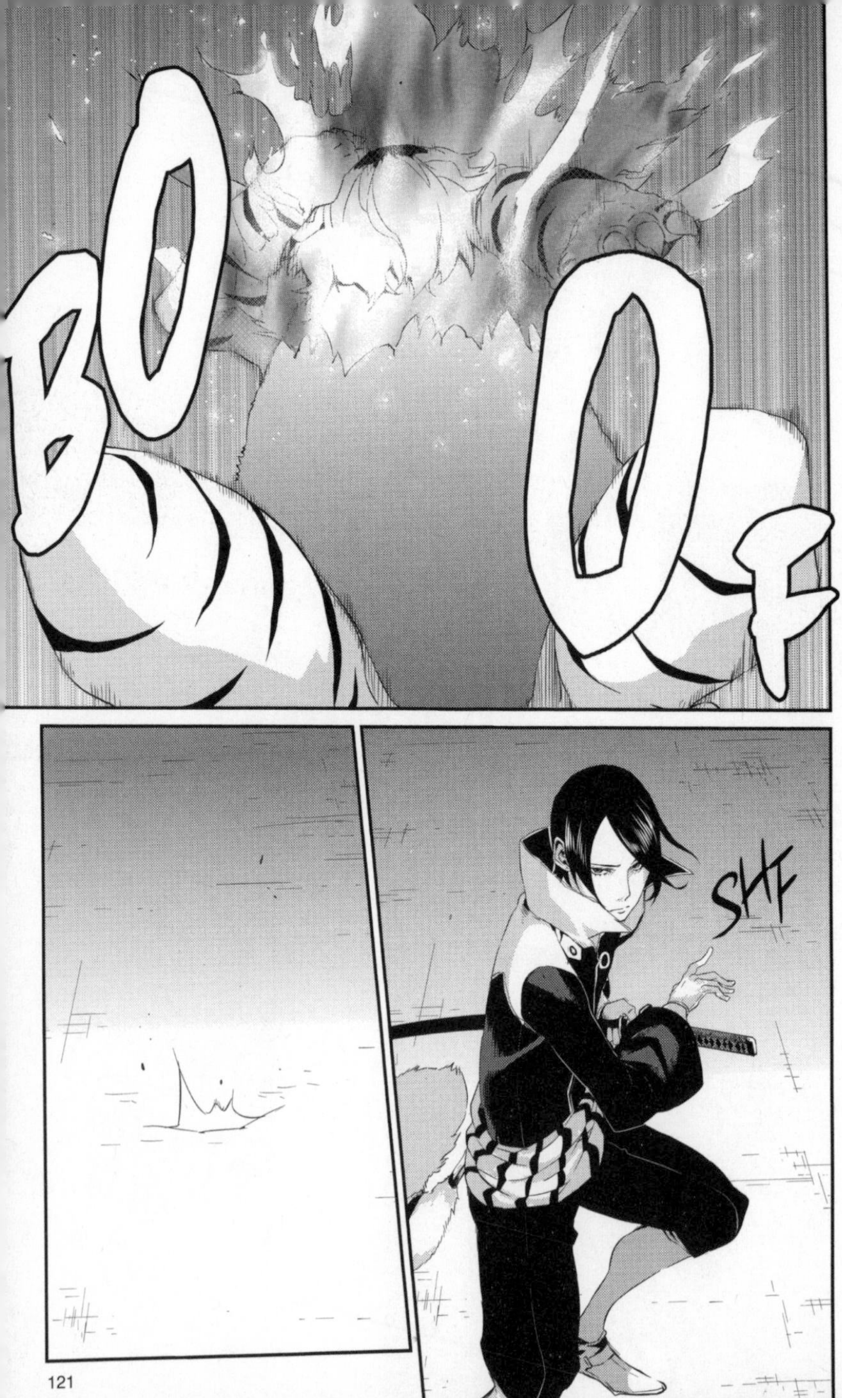
BOOOF
SHF

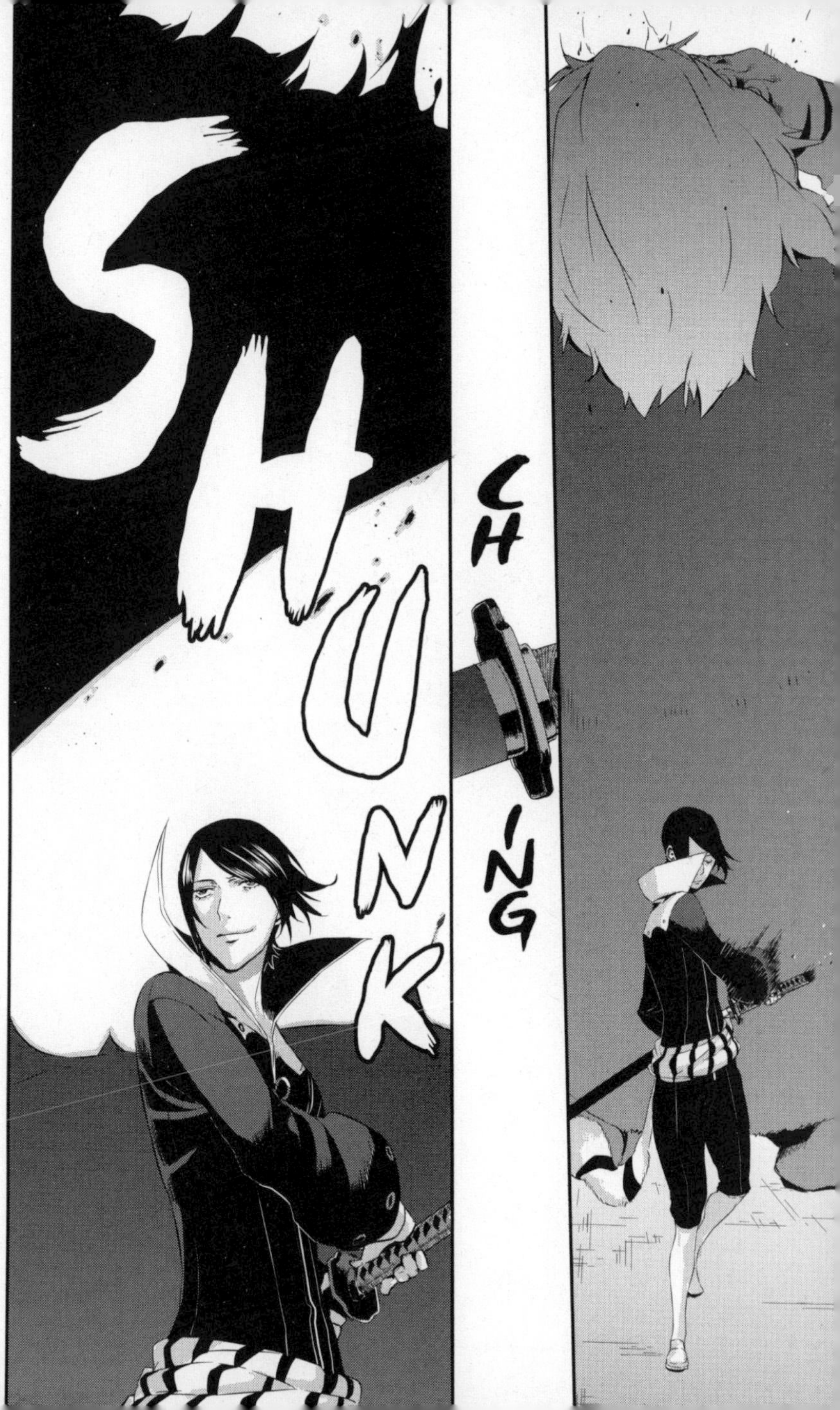
CHING
SHUNK

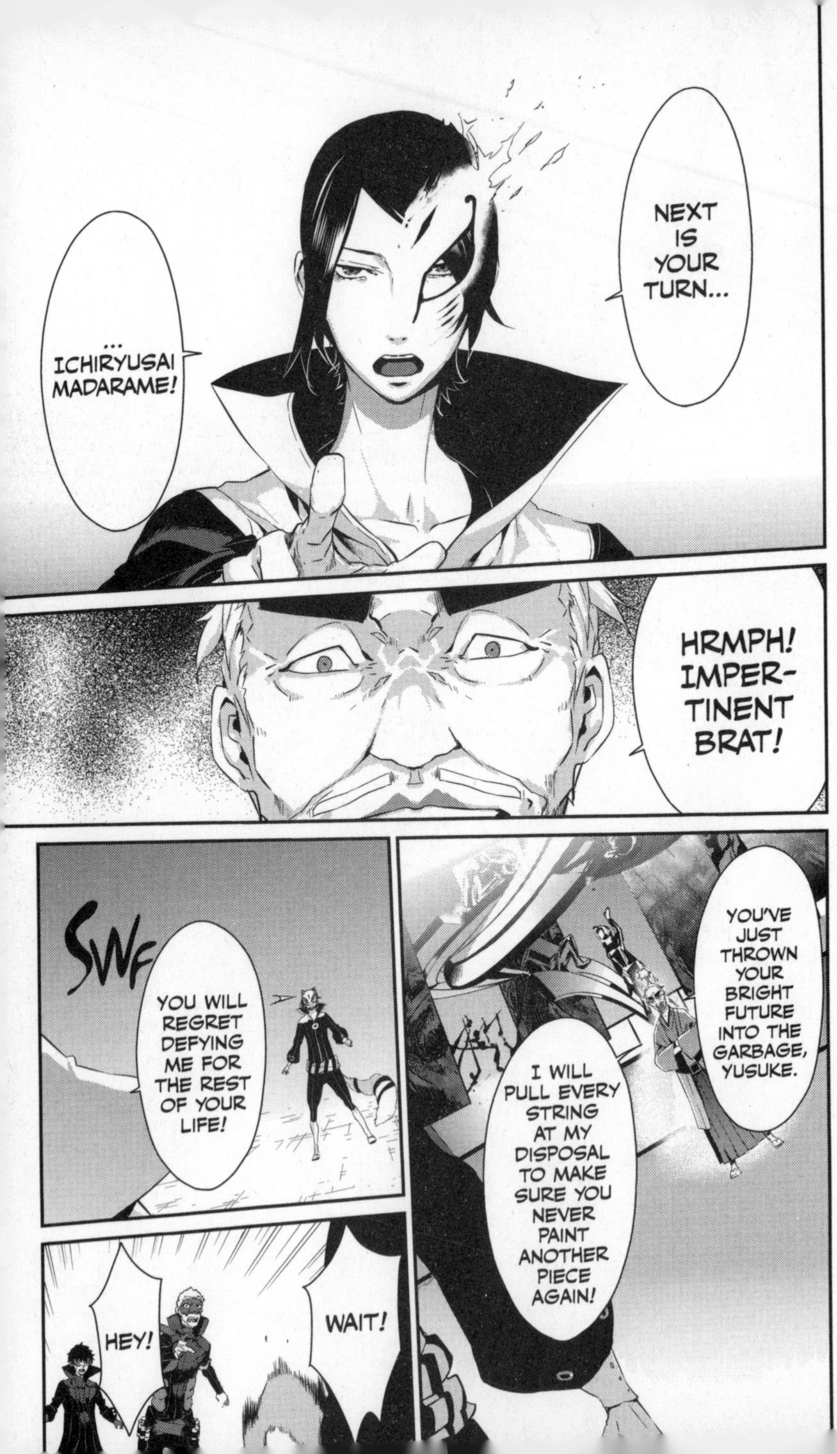
NEXT IS YOUR TURN...
... ICHIRYUSAI MADARAME!
HRMPH! IMPER-TINENT BRAT!
YOU'VE JUST THROWN YOUR BRIGHT FUTURE INTO THE GARBAGE, YUSUKE.
I WILL PULL EVERY STRING AT MY DISPOSAL TO MAKE SURE YOU NEVER PAINT ANOTHER PIECE AGAIN!
SWF
YOU WILL REGRET DEFYING ME FOR THE REST OF YOUR LIFE!
WAIT!
HEY!

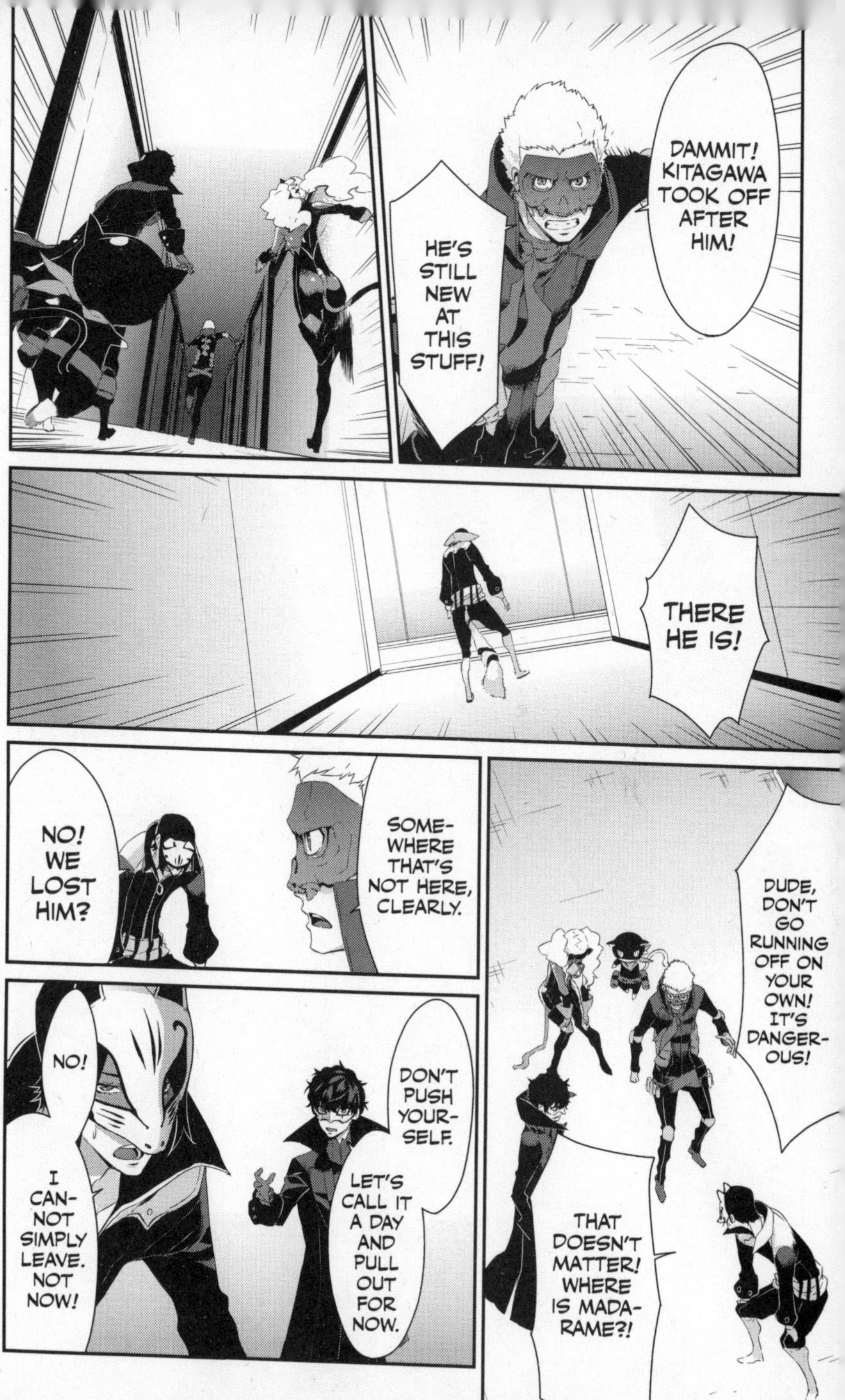
DAMMIT! KITAGAWA TOOK OFF AFTER HIM!
HE'S STILL NEW AT THIS STUFF!
THERE HE IS!
DUDE, DON'T GO RUNNING OFF ON YOUR OWN! IT'S DANGER-OUS!
THAT DOESN'T MATTER! WHERE IS MADA-RAME?!
SOME-WHERE THAT'S NOT HERE, CLEARLY.
NO! WE LOST HIM?
DON'T PUSH YOUR-SELF.
LET'S CALL IT A DAY AND PULL OUT FOR NOW.
NO!
I CAN-NOT SIMPLY LEAVE. NOT NOW!

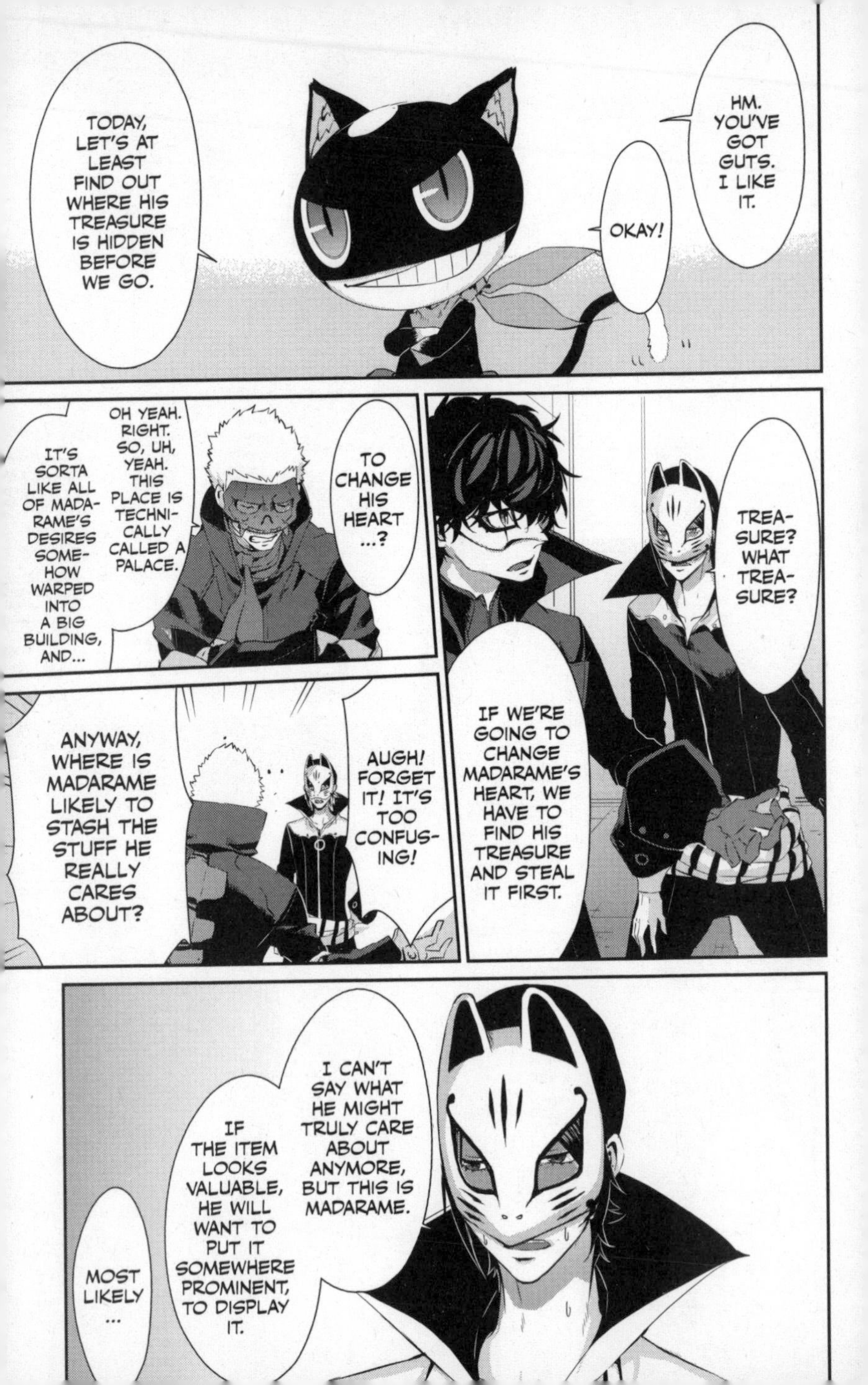
HM. YOU'VE GOT GUTS. I LIKE IT.
OKAY!
TODAY, LET'S AT LEAST FIND OUT WHERE HIS TREASURE IS HIDDEN BEFORE WE GO.
TREA-SURE? WHAT TREA-SURE?
IF WE'RE GOING TO CHANGE MADARAME'S HEART, WE HAVE TO FIND HIS TREASURE AND STEAL IT FIRST.
TO CHANGE HIS HEART ...?
OH YEAH. RIGHT. SO, UH, YEAH. THIS PLACE IS TECHNI-CALLY CALLED A PALACE.
IT'S SORTA LIKE ALL OF MADA-RAME'S DESIRES SOME-HOW WARPED INTO A BIG BUILDING, AND...
AUGH! FORGET IT! IT'S TOO CONFUS-ING!
ANYWAY, WHERE IS MADARAME LIKELY TO STASH THE STUFF HE REALLY CARES ABOUT?
I CAN'T SAY WHAT HE MIGHT TRULY CARE ABOUT ANYMORE, BUT THIS IS MADARAME.
IF THE ITEM LOOKS VALUABLE, HE WILL WANT TO PUT IT SOMEWHERE PROMINENT, TO DISPLAY IT.
MOST LIKELY ...

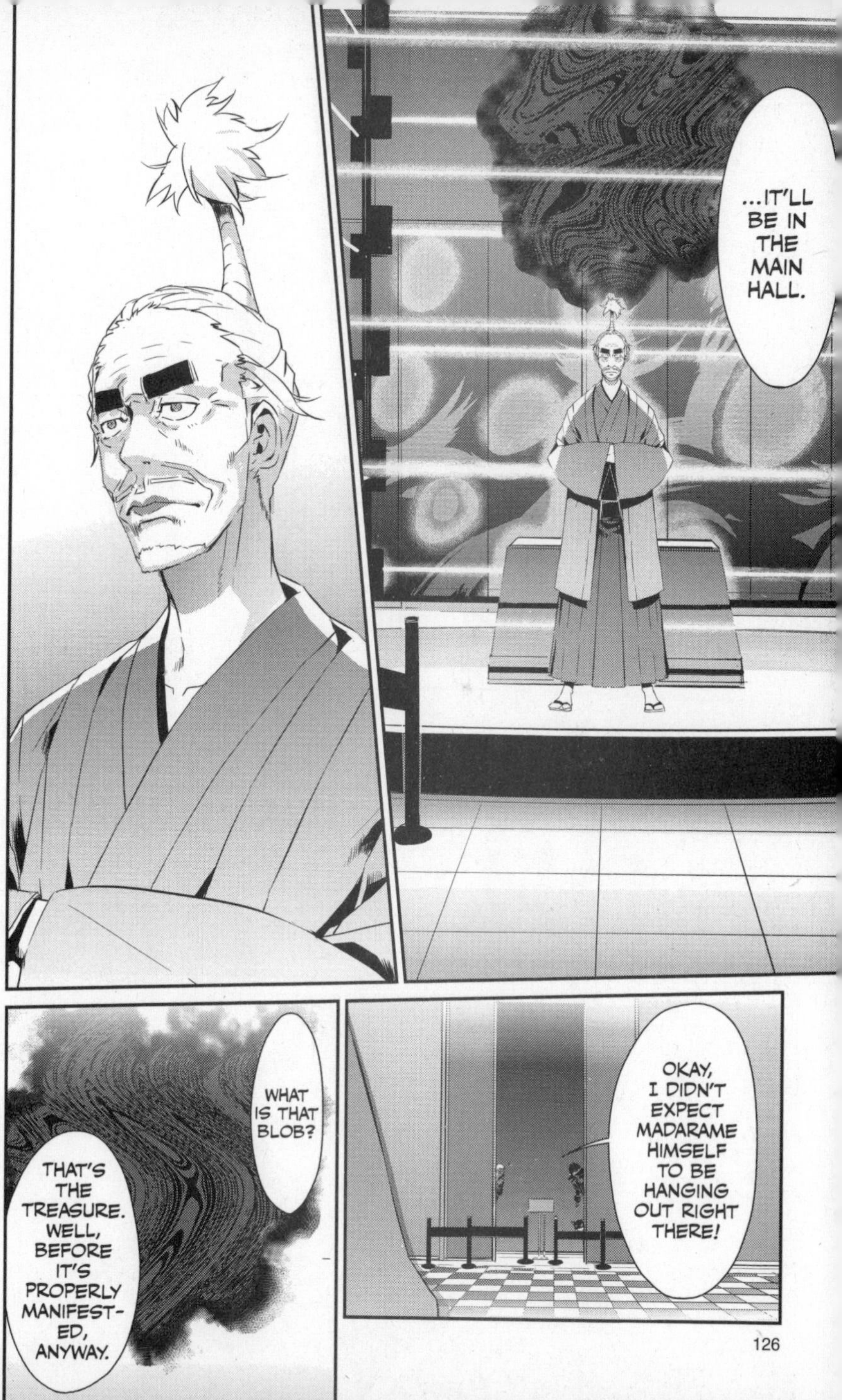
...IT'LL BE IN THE MAIN HALL.
OKAY, I DIDN'T EXPECT MADARAME HIMSELF TO BE HANGING OUT RIGHT THERE!
WHAT IS THAT BLOB?
THAT'S THE TREASURE. WELL, BEFORE IT'S PROPERLY MANIFEST-ED, ANYWAY.

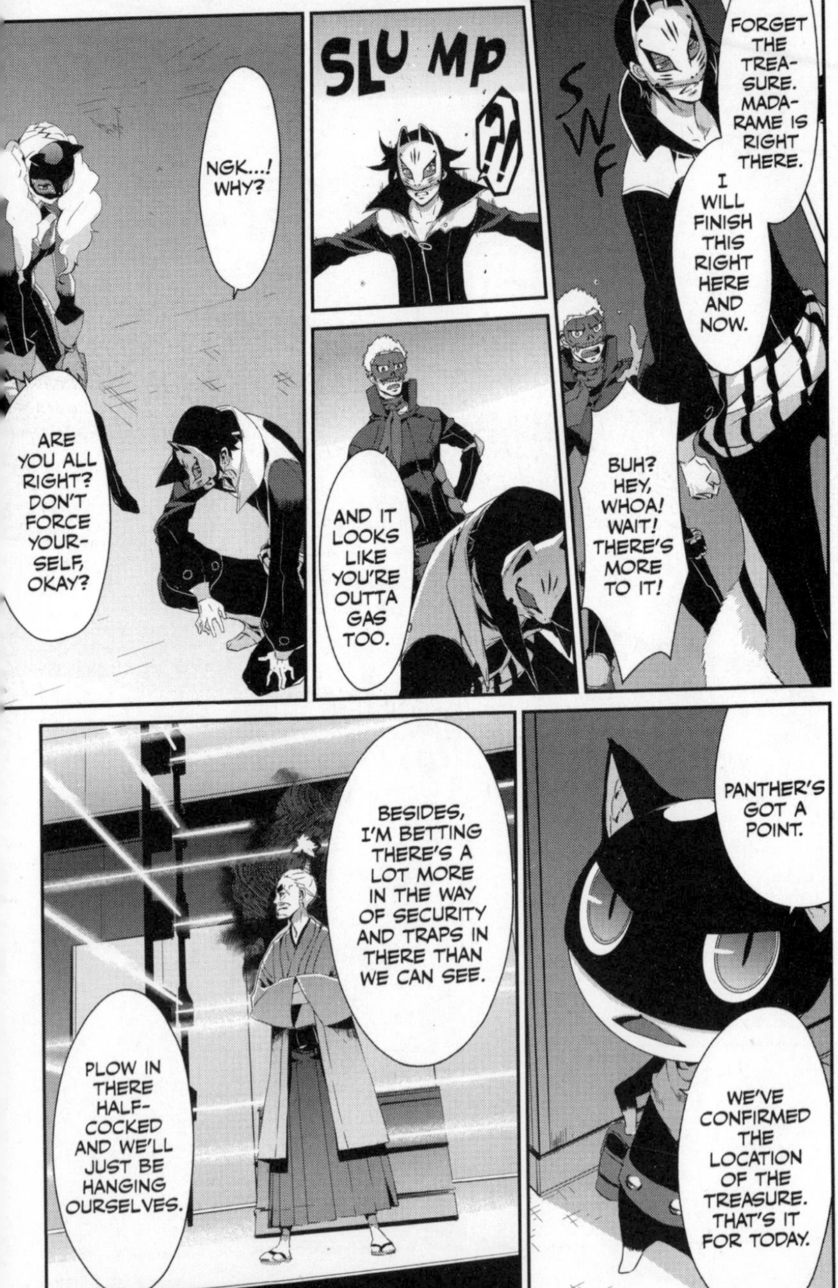
SWF
FORGET THE TREASURE. MADARAME IS RIGHT THERE.
I WILL FINISH THIS RIGHT HERE AND NOW.
BUH? HEY, WHOA! WAIT! THERE'S MORE TO IT!
SLUMP
?!
AND IT LOOKS LIKE YOU'RE OUTTA GAS TOO.
NGK...! WHY?
ARE YOU ALL RIGHT? DON'T FORCE YOURSELF, OKAY?
PANTHER'S GOT A POINT.
WE'VE CONFIRMED THE LOCATION OF THE TREASURE. THAT'S IT FOR TODAY.
BESIDES, I'M BETTING THERE'S A LOT MORE IN THE WAY OF SECURITY AND TRAPS IN THERE THAN WE CAN SEE.
PLOW IN THERE HALF-COCKED AND WE'LL JUST BE HANGING OURSELVES.

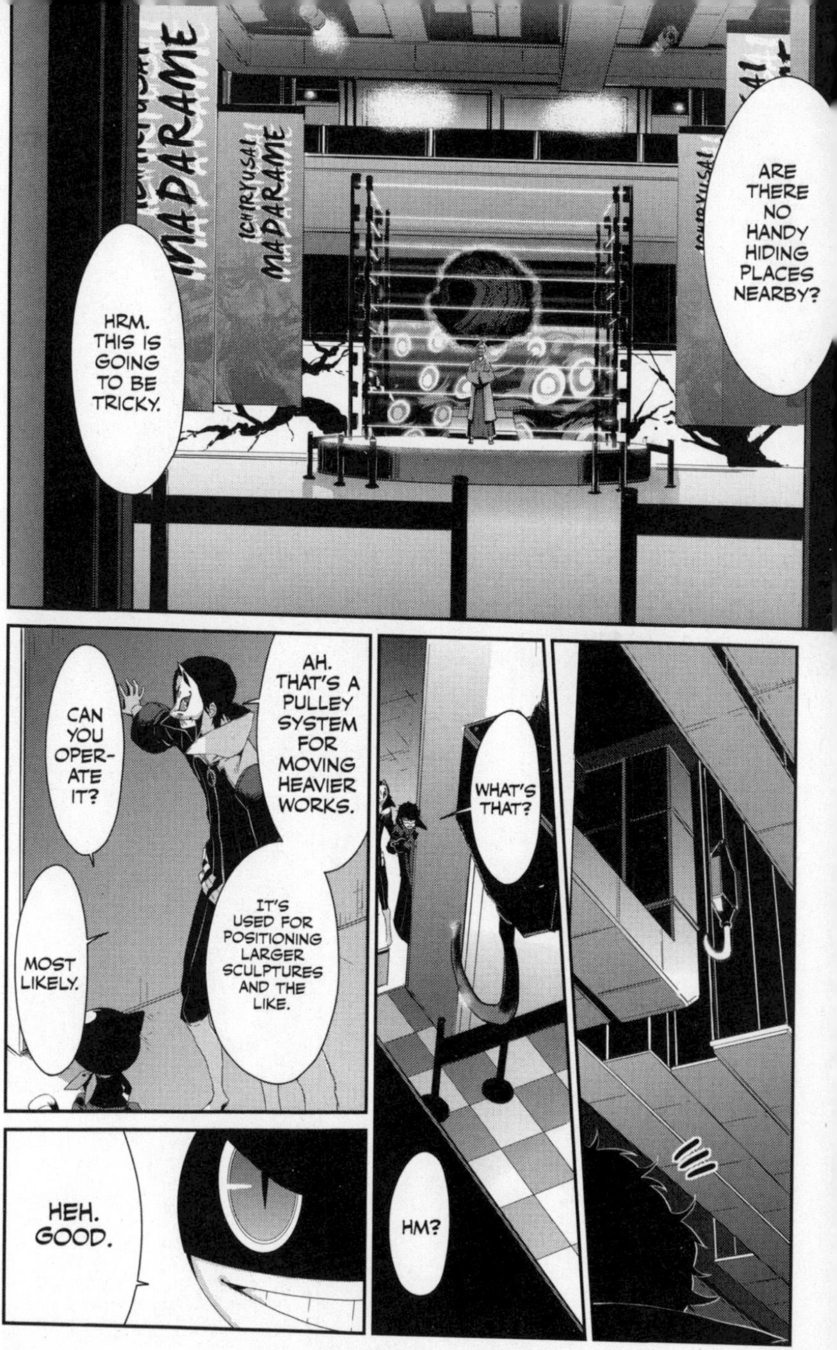
ICHIRYUSAI MADARAME
ICHIRYUSAI MADARAME
ICHIRYUSAI
ARE THERE NO HANDY HIDING PLACES NEARBY?
HRM. THIS IS GOING TO BE TRICKY.
WHAT'S THAT?
HM?
AH. THAT'S A PULLEY SYSTEM FOR MOVING HEAVIER WORKS.
IT'S USED FOR POSITIONING LARGER SCULPTURES AND THE LIKE.
CAN YOU OPERATE IT?
MOST LIKELY.
HEH. GOOD.

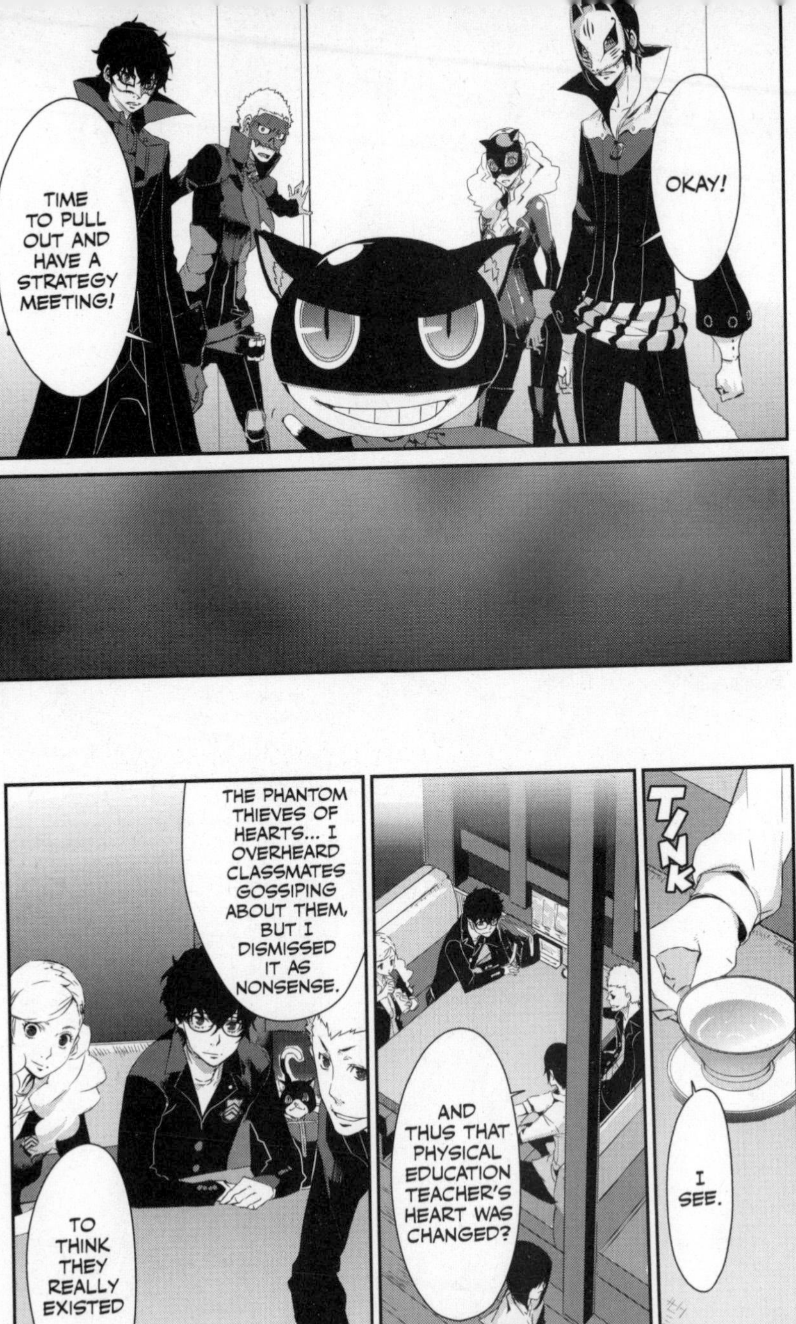
OKAY!
TIME TO PULL OUT AND HAVE A STRATEGY MEETING!
TINK
I SEE.
AND THUS THAT PHYSICAL EDUCATION TEACHER'S HEART WAS CHANGED?
THE PHANTOM THIEVES OF HEARTS... I OVERHEARD CLASSMATES GOSSIPING ABOUT THEM, BUT I DISMISSED IT AS NONSENSE.
TO THINK THEY REALLY EXISTED ...

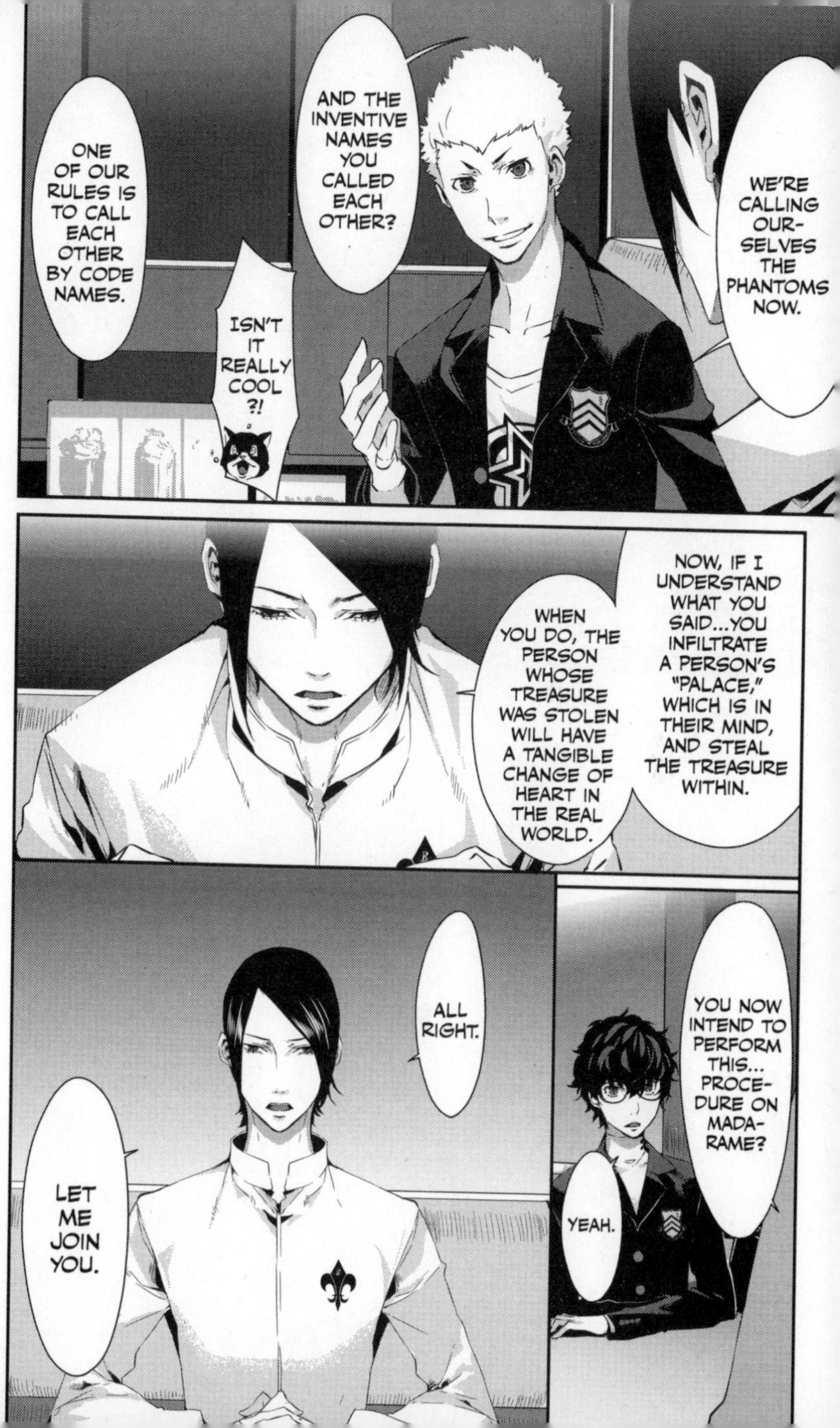
WE'RE CALLING OUR-SELVES THE PHANTOMS NOW.
AND THE INVENTIVE NAMES YOU CALLED EACH OTHER?
ONE OF OUR RULES IS TO CALL EACH OTHER BY CODE NAMES.
ISN'T IT REALLY COOL ?!
NOW, IF I UNDERSTAND WHAT YOU SAID...YOU INFILTRATE A PERSON'S "PALACE," WHICH IS IN THEIR MIND, AND STEAL THE TREASURE WITHIN.
WHEN YOU DO, THE PERSON WHOSE TREASURE WAS STOLEN WILL HAVE A TANGIBLE CHANGE OF HEART IN THE REAL WORLD.
YOU NOW INTEND TO PERFORM THIS... PROCE-DURE ON MADA-RAME?
YEAH.
ALL RIGHT.
LET ME JOIN YOU.

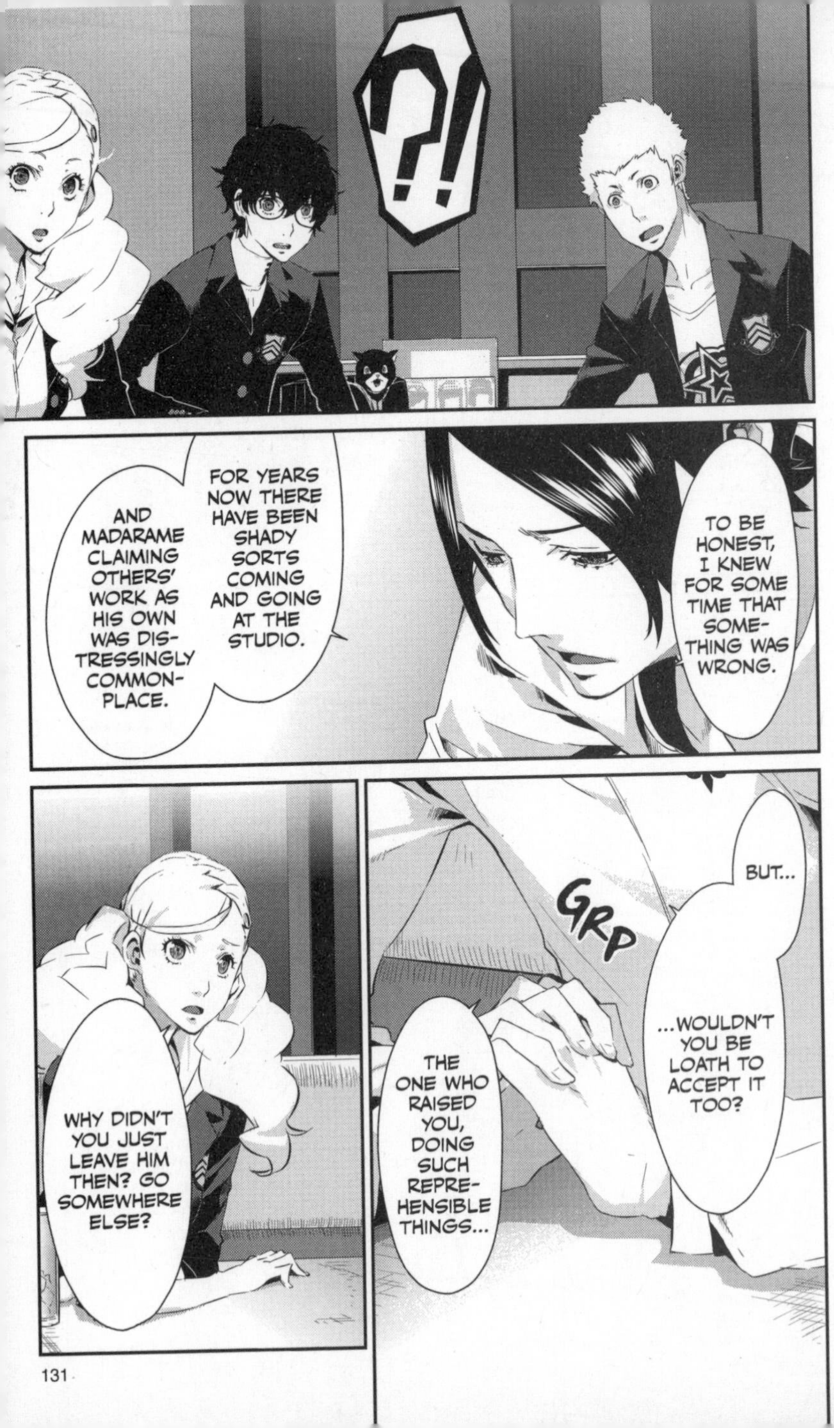
?!
TO BE HONEST, I KNEW FOR SOME TIME THAT SOME-THING WAS WRONG.
FOR YEARS NOW THERE HAVE BEEN SHADY SORTS COMING AND GOING AT THE STUDIO.
AND MADARAME CLAIMING OTHERS' WORK AS HIS OWN WAS DIS-TRESSINGLY COMMON-PLACE.
BUT...
GRP
...WOULDN'T YOU BE LOATH TO ACCEPT IT TOO?
THE ONE WHO RAISED YOU, DOING SUCH REPRE-HENSIBLE THINGS...
WHY DIDN'T YOU JUST LEAVE HIM THEN? GO SOMEWHERE ELSE?

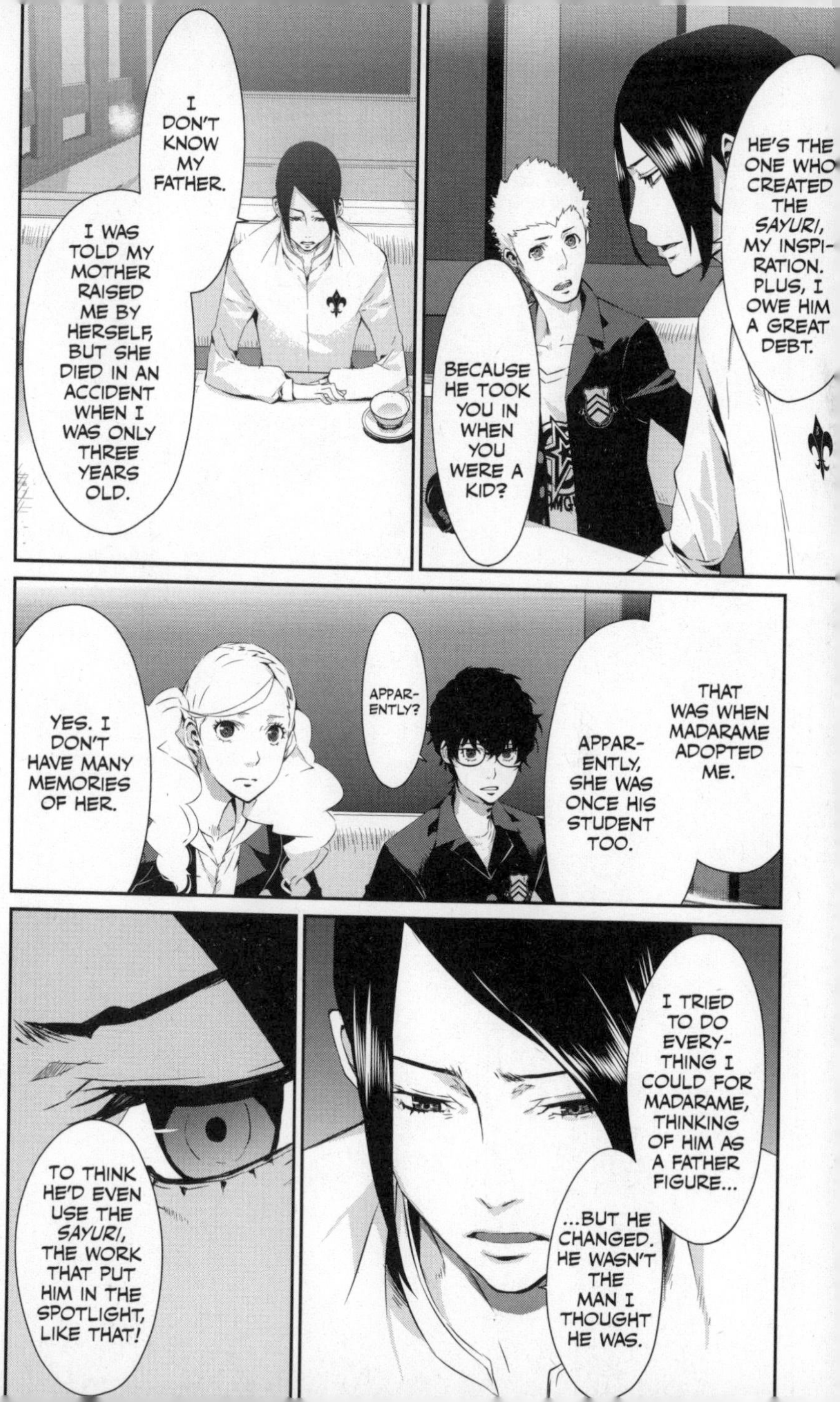
HE'S THE ONE WHO CREATED THE *SAYURI*, MY INSPIRATION. PLUS, I OWE HIM A GREAT DEBT.
BECAUSE HE TOOK YOU IN WHEN YOU WERE A KID?
I DON'T KNOW MY FATHER.
I WAS TOLD MY MOTHER RAISED ME BY HERSELF, BUT SHE DIED IN AN ACCIDENT WHEN I WAS ONLY THREE YEARS OLD.
THAT WAS WHEN MADARAME ADOPTED ME.
APPARENTLY, SHE WAS ONCE HIS STUDENT TOO.
APPARENTLY?
YES. I DON'T HAVE MANY MEMORIES OF HER.
I TRIED TO DO EVERYTHING I COULD FOR MADARAME, THINKING OF HIM AS A FATHER FIGURE...
...BUT HE CHANGED. HE WASN'T THE MAN I THOUGHT HE WAS.
TO THINK HE'D EVEN USE THE *SAYURI*, THE WORK THAT PUT HIM IN THE SPOTLIGHT, LIKE THAT!

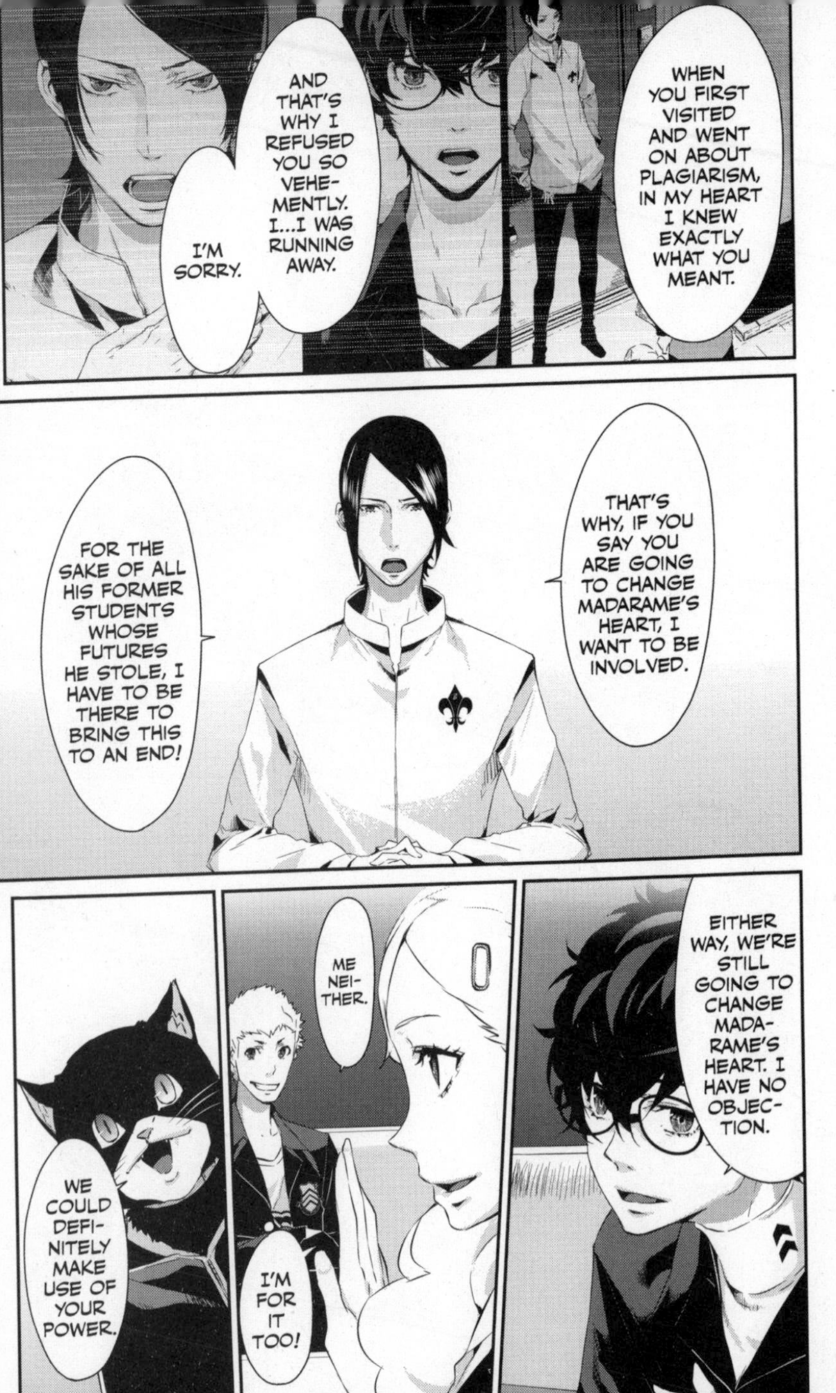
WHEN YOU FIRST VISITED AND WENT ON ABOUT PLAGIARISM, IN MY HEART I KNEW EXACTLY WHAT YOU MEANT.
AND THAT'S WHY I REFUSED YOU SO VEHEMENTLY. I...I WAS RUNNING AWAY.
I'M SORRY.
THAT'S WHY, IF YOU SAY YOU ARE GOING TO CHANGE MADARAME'S HEART, I WANT TO BE INVOLVED.
FOR THE SAKE OF ALL HIS FORMER STUDENTS WHOSE FUTURES HE STOLE, I HAVE TO BE THERE TO BRING THIS TO AN END!
EITHER WAY, WE'RE STILL GOING TO CHANGE MADARAME'S HEART. I HAVE NO OBJECTION.
ME NEITHER.
I'M FOR IT TOO!
WE COULD DEFINITELY MAKE USE OF YOUR POWER.

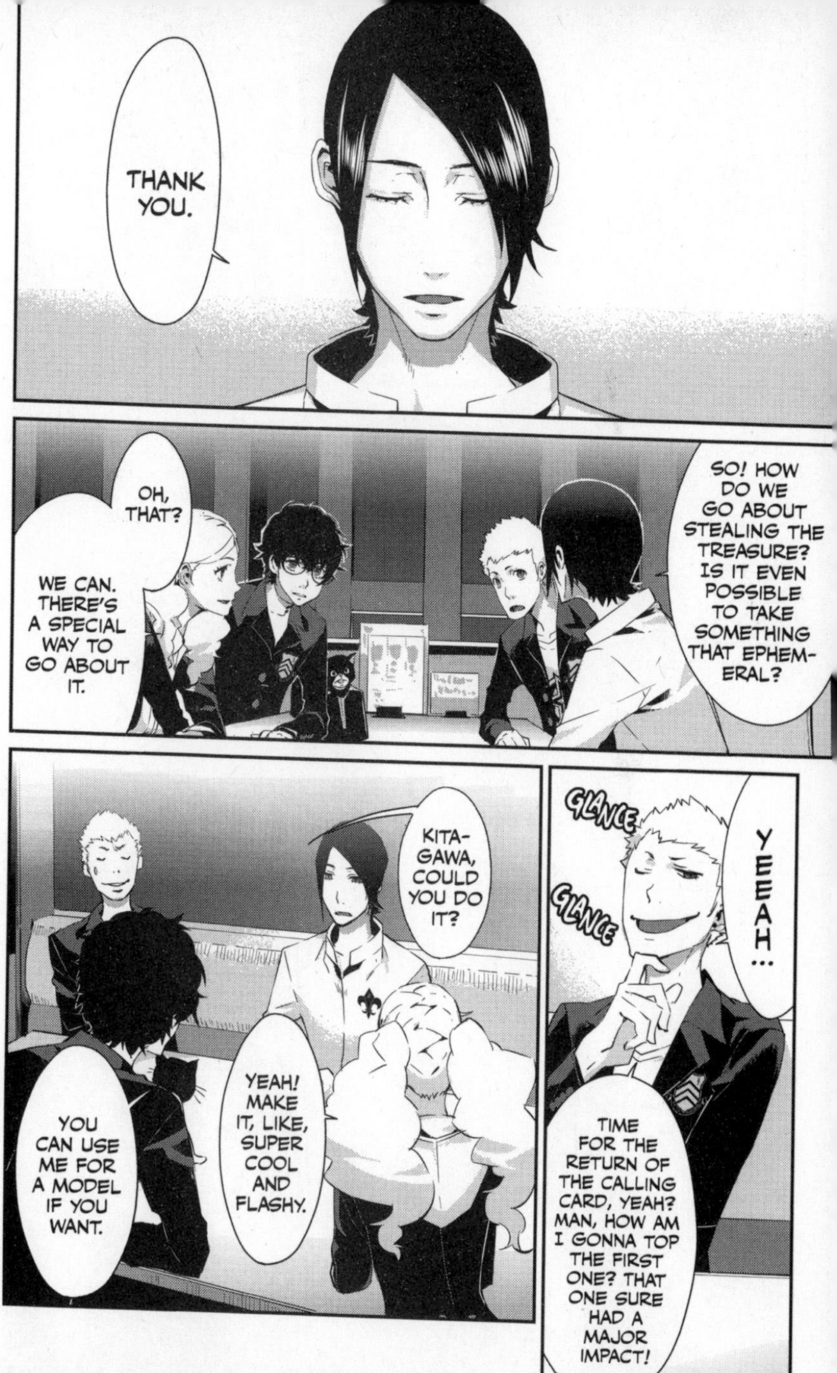
THANK YOU.
SO! HOW DO WE GO ABOUT STEALING THE TREASURE? IS IT EVEN POSSIBLE TO TAKE SOMETHING THAT EPHEM-ERAL?
OH, THAT?
WE CAN. THERE'S A SPECIAL WAY TO GO ABOUT IT.
GLANCE
GLANCE
YEEAH...
TIME FOR THE RETURN OF THE CALLING CARD, YEAH? MAN, HOW AM I GONNA TOP THE FIRST ONE? THAT ONE SURE HAD A MAJOR IMPACT!
KITA-GAWA, COULD YOU DO IT?
YEAH! MAKE IT, LIKE, SUPER COOL AND FLASHY.
YOU CAN USE ME FOR A MODEL IF YOU WANT.

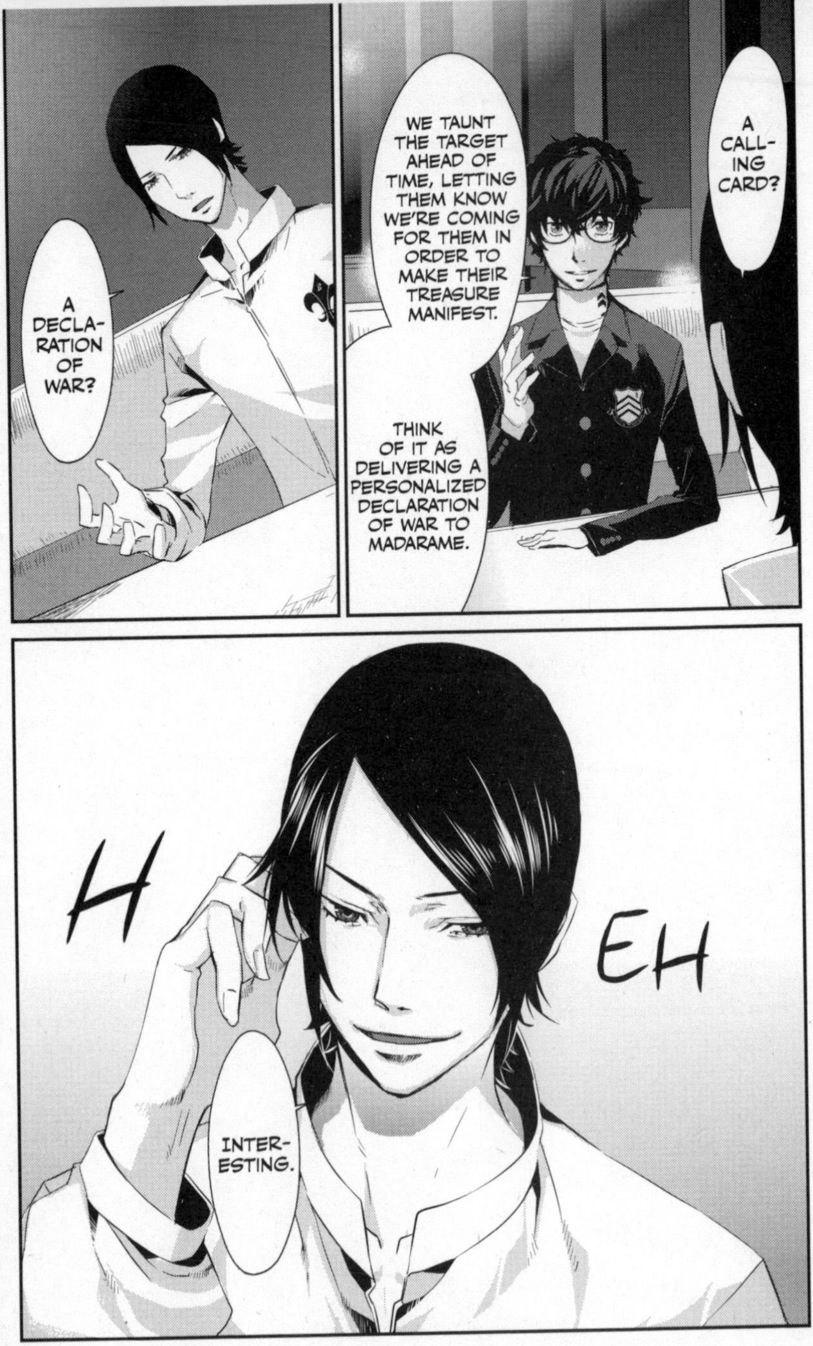
A CALLING-CARD?
WE TAUNT THE TARGET AHEAD OF TIME, LETTING THEM KNOW WE'RE COMING FOR THEM IN ORDER TO MAKE THEIR TREASURE MANIFEST.
THINK OF IT AS DELIVERING A PERSONALIZED DECLARATION OF WAR TO MADARAME.
A DECLARATION OF WAR?
HEH
INTERESTING.

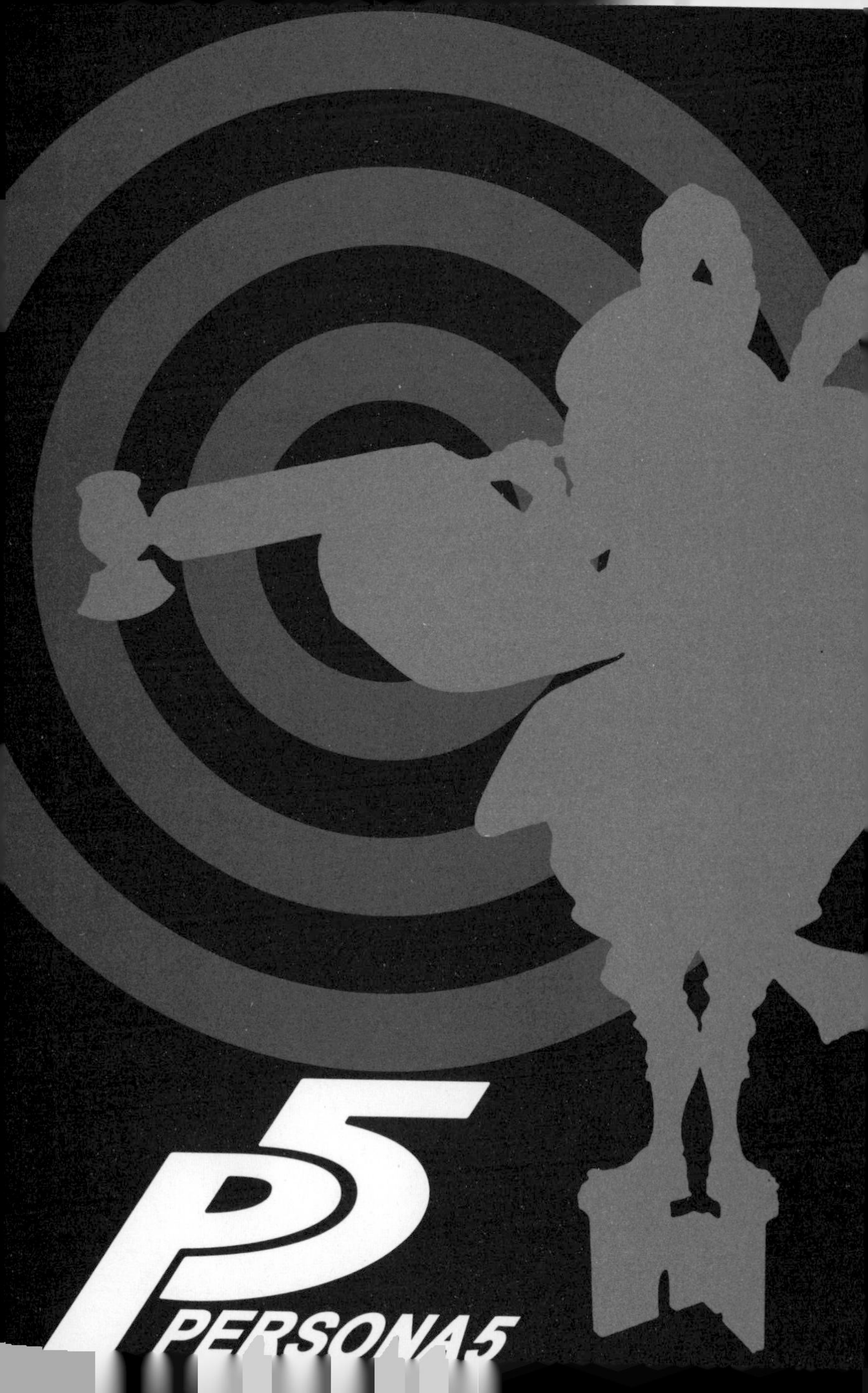
P5
PERSONA5

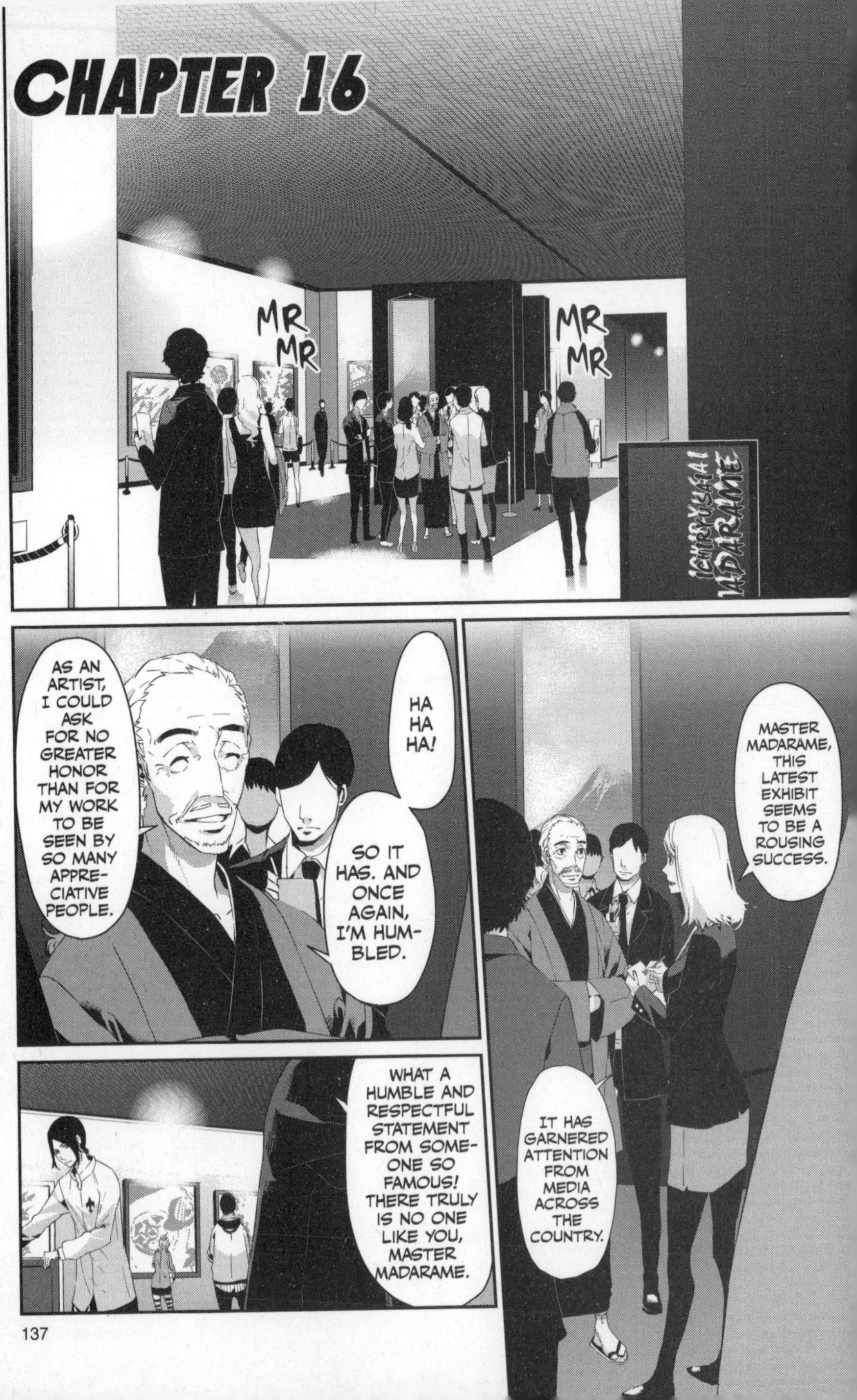

CHAPTER 16
MR MR
MR MR
ICHIRYUSAI MADARAME
MASTER MADARAME, THIS LATEST EXHIBIT SEEMS TO BE A ROUSING SUCCESS.
IT HAS GARNERED ATTENTION FROM MEDIA ACROSS THE COUNTRY.
SO IT HAS. AND ONCE AGAIN, I'M HUM-BLED.
AS AN ARTIST, I COULD ASK FOR NO GREATER HONOR THAN FOR MY WORK TO BE SEEN BY SO MANY APPRE-CIATIVE PEOPLE.
HA HA HA!
WHAT A HUMBLE AND RESPECTFUL STATEMENT FROM SOME-ONE SO FAMOUS! THERE TRULY IS NO ONE LIKE YOU, MASTER MADARAME.

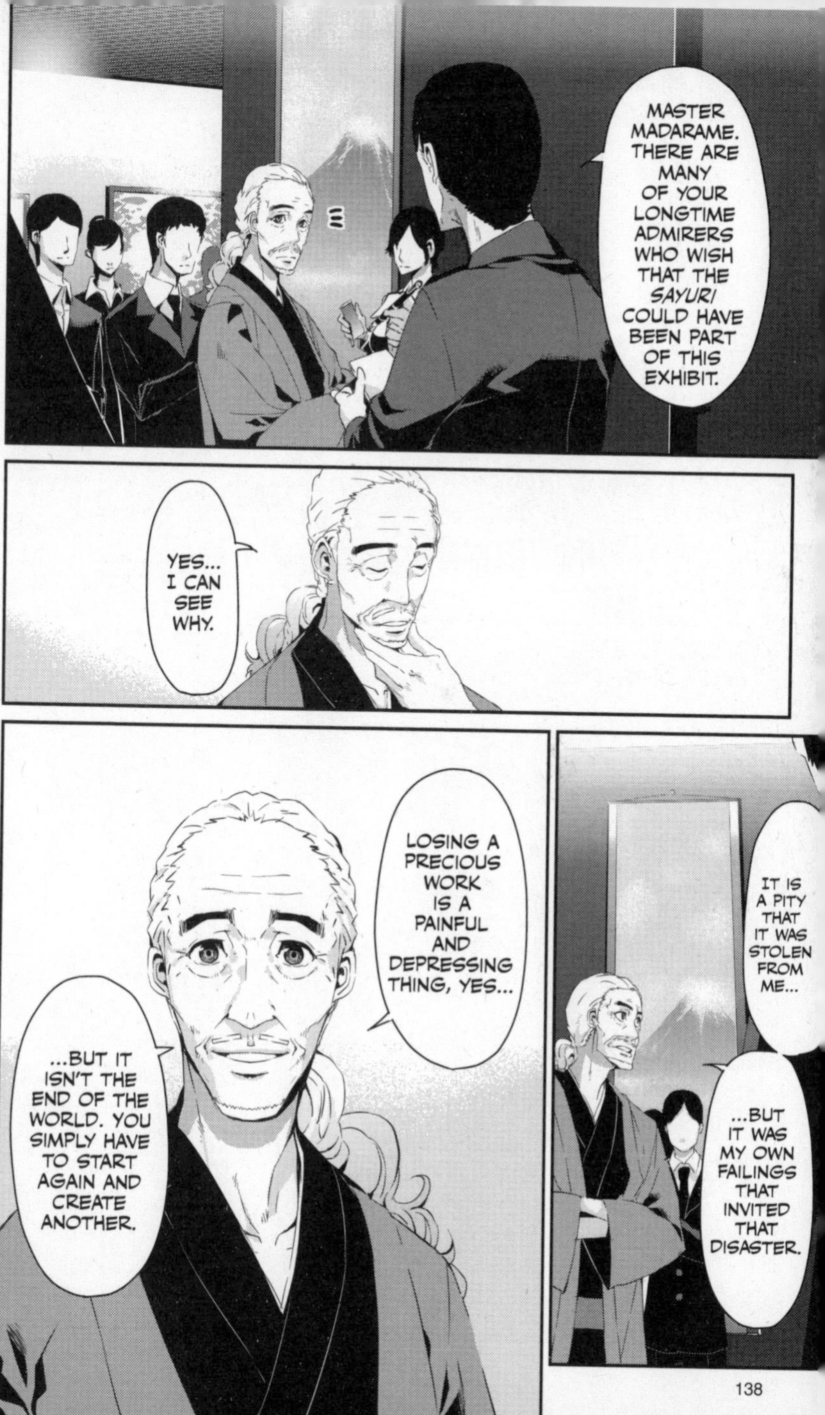
MASTER MADARAME. THERE ARE MANY OF YOUR LONGTIME ADMIRERS WHO WISH THAT THE *SAYURI* COULD HAVE BEEN PART OF THIS EXHIBIT.
YES... I CAN SEE WHY.
IT IS A PITY THAT IT WAS STOLEN FROM ME...
...BUT IT WAS MY OWN FAILINGS THAT INVITED THAT DISASTER.
LOSING A PRECIOUS WORK IS A PAINFUL AND DEPRESSING THING, YES...
...BUT IT ISN'T THE END OF THE WORLD. YOU SIMPLY HAVE TO START AGAIN AND CREATE ANOTHER.

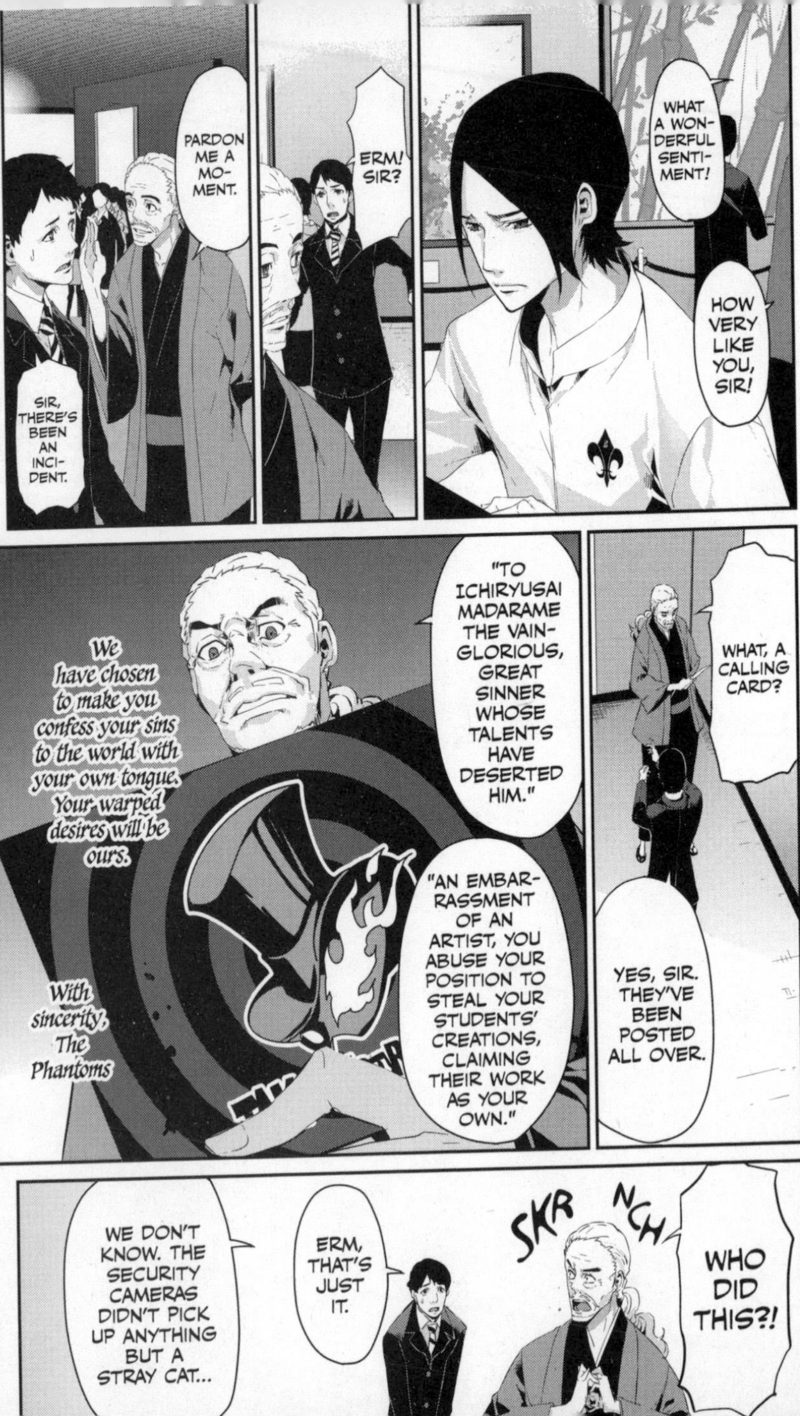
WHAT A WONDERFUL SENTIMENT!
HOW VERY LIKE YOU, SIR!
ERM! SIR?
PARDON ME A MOMENT.
SIR, THERE'S BEEN AN INCIDENT.
WHAT, A CALLING CARD?
YES, SIR. THEY'VE BEEN POSTED ALL OVER.
"TO ICHIRYUSAI MADARAME THE VAINGLORIOUS, GREAT SINNER WHOSE TALENTS HAVE DESERTED HIM."
"AN EMBARRASSMENT OF AN ARTIST, YOU ABUSE YOUR POSITION TO STEAL YOUR STUDENTS' CREATIONS, CLAIMING THEIR WORK AS YOUR OWN."
We have chosen to make you confess your sins to the world with your own tongue. Your warped desires will be ours.
With sincerity, The Phantoms
SKRNCH
WHO DID THIS?!
ERM, THAT'S JUST IT.
WE DON'T KNOW. THE SECURITY CAMERAS DIDN'T PICK UP ANYTHING BUT A STRAY CAT...

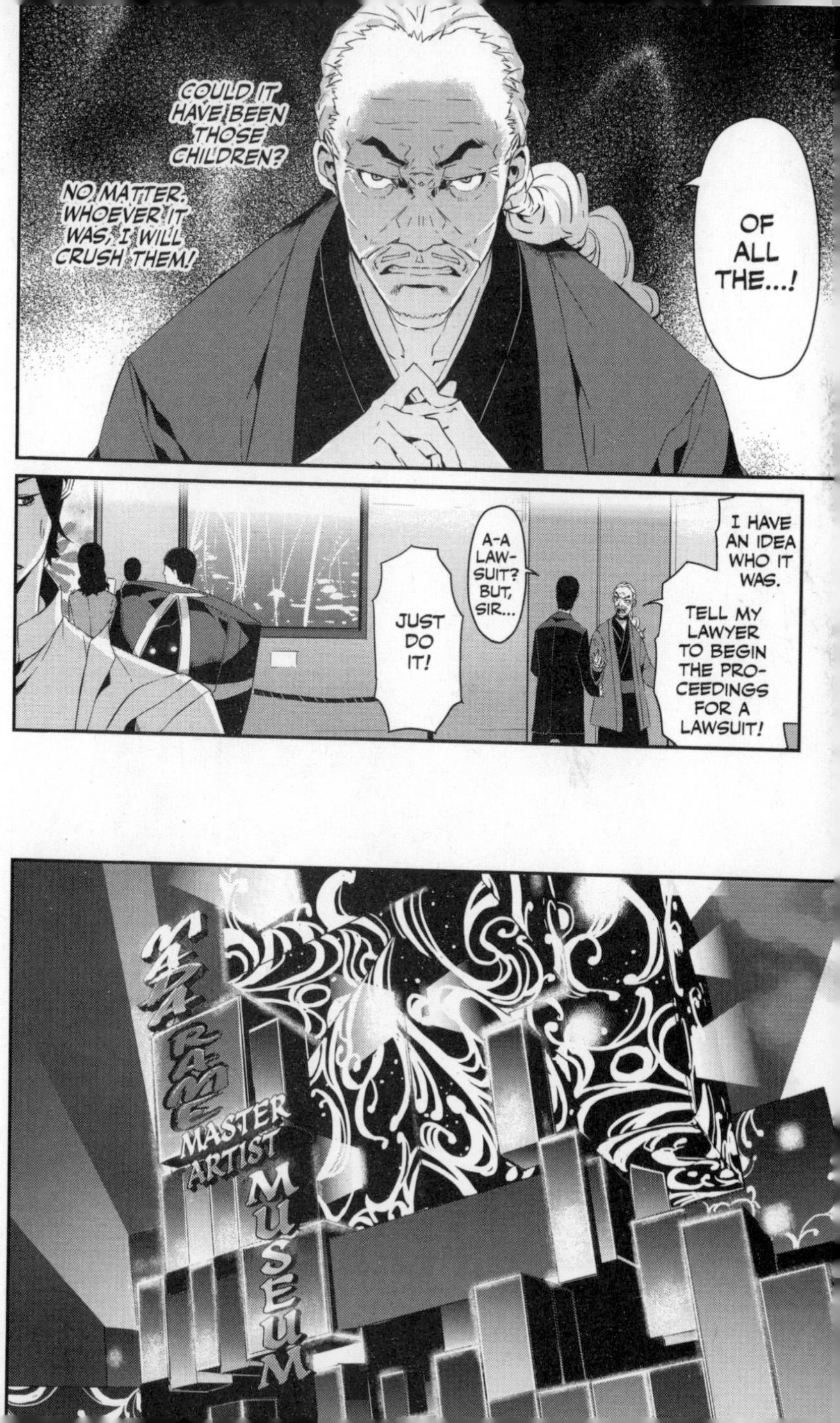
OF ALL THE...!
COULD IT HAVE BEEN THOSE CHILDREN?
NO MATTER. WHOEVER IT WAS, I WILL CRUSH THEM!
I HAVE AN IDEA WHO IT WAS.
TELL MY LAWYER TO BEGIN THE PRO-CEEDINGS FOR A LAWSUIT!
A-A LAWSUIT? BUT, SIR...
JUST DO IT!
MASTER ARTIST
MUSEUM

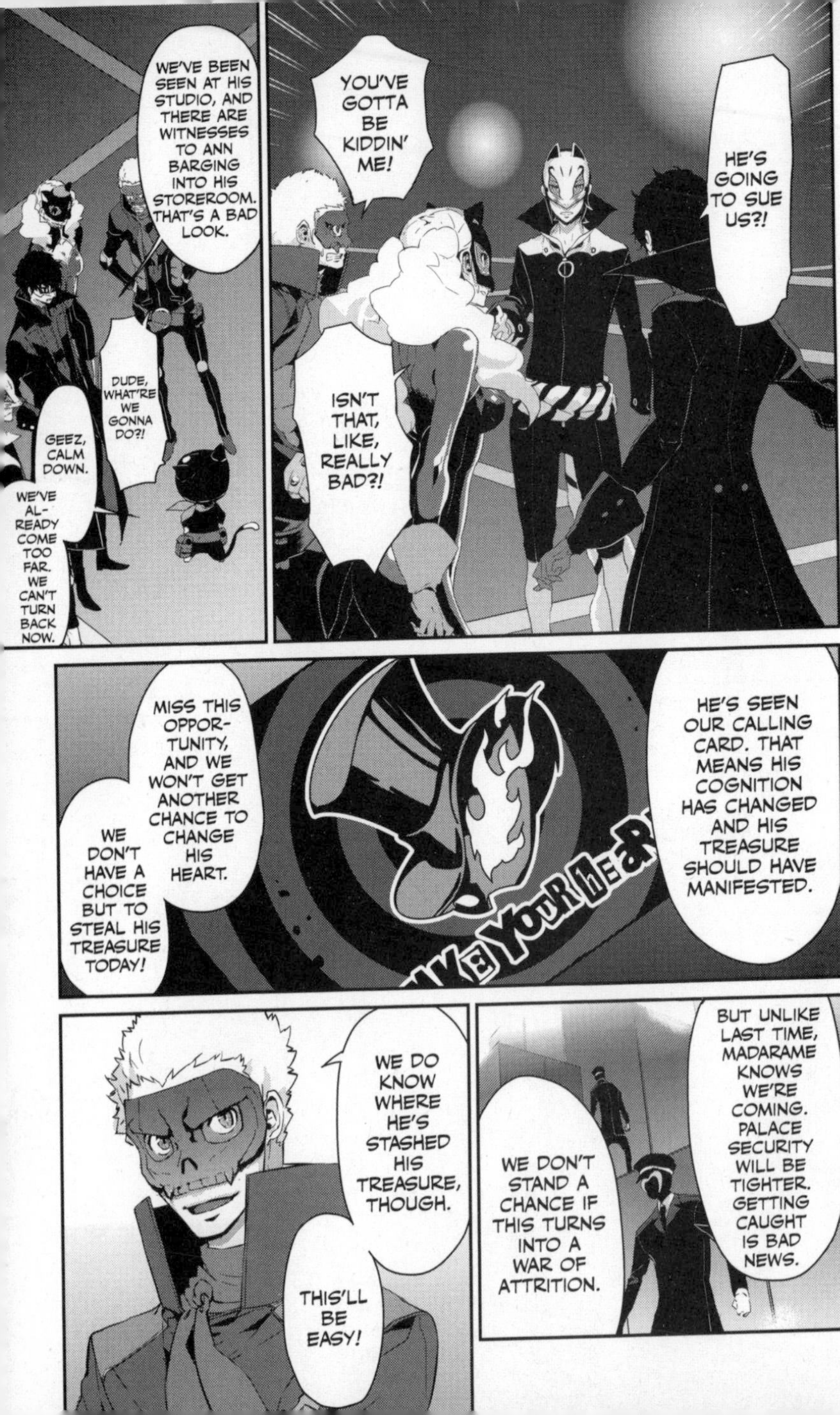
HE'S GOING TO SUE US?!
YOU'VE GOTTA BE KIDDIN' ME!
ISN'T THAT, LIKE, REALLY BAD?!
WE'VE BEEN SEEN AT HIS STUDIO, AND THERE ARE WITNESSES TO ANN BARGING INTO HIS STOREROOM. THAT'S A BAD LOOK.
DUDE, WHAT'RE WE GONNA DO?!
GEEZ, CALM DOWN.
WE'VE AL-READY COME TOO FAR. WE CAN'T TURN BACK NOW.
HE'S SEEN OUR CALLING CARD. THAT MEANS HIS COGNITION HAS CHANGED AND HIS TREASURE SHOULD HAVE MANIFESTED.
MISS THIS OPPOR-TUNITY, AND WE WON'T GET ANOTHER CHANCE TO CHANGE HIS HEART.
WE DON'T HAVE A CHOICE BUT TO STEAL HIS TREASURE TODAY!
BUT UNLIKE LAST TIME, MADARAME KNOWS WE'RE COMING. PALACE SECURITY WILL BE TIGHTER. GETTING CAUGHT IS BAD NEWS.
WE DON'T STAND A CHANCE IF THIS TURNS INTO A WAR OF ATTRITION.
WE DO KNOW WHERE HE'S STASHED HIS TREASURE, THOUGH.
THIS'LL BE EASY!

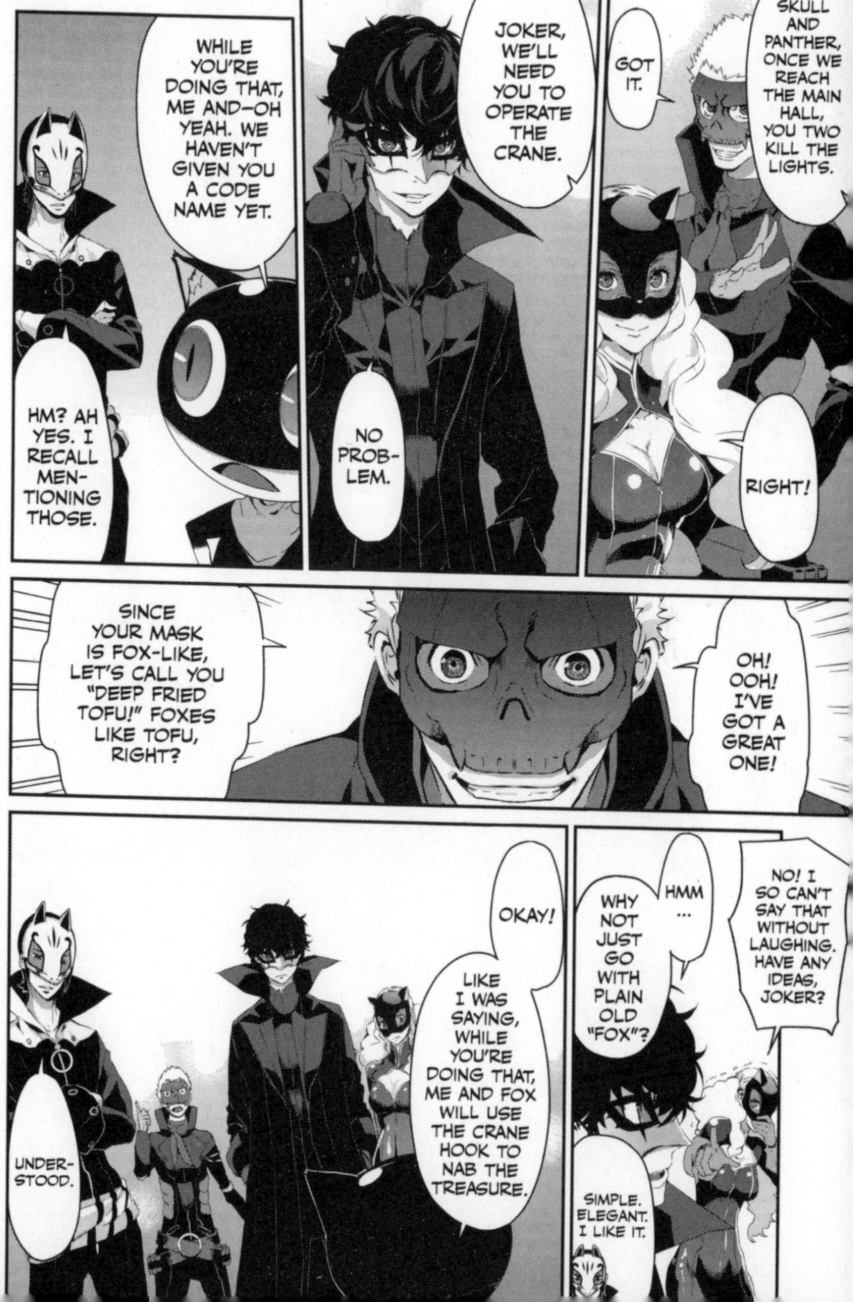
SKULL AND PANTHER, ONCE WE REACH THE MAIN HALL, YOU TWO KILL THE LIGHTS.
GOT IT.
RIGHT!
JOKER, WE'LL NEED YOU TO OPERATE THE CRANE.
NO PROB-LEM.
WHILE YOU'RE DOING THAT, ME AND—OH YEAH. WE HAVEN'T GIVEN YOU A CODE NAME YET.
HM? AH YES. I RECALL MEN-TIONING THOSE.
OH! OOH! I'VE GOT A GREAT ONE!
SINCE YOUR MASK IS FOX-LIKE, LET'S CALL YOU "DEEP FRIED TOFU!" FOXES LIKE TOFU, RIGHT?
NO! I SO CAN'T SAY THAT WITHOUT LAUGHING. HAVE ANY IDEAS, JOKER?
HMM ...
WHY NOT JUST GO WITH PLAIN OLD "FOX"?
SIMPLE. ELEGANT. I LIKE IT.
OKAY!
LIKE I WAS SAYING, WHILE YOU'RE DOING THAT, ME AND FOX WILL USE THE CRANE HOOK TO NAB THE TREASURE.
UNDER-STOOD.

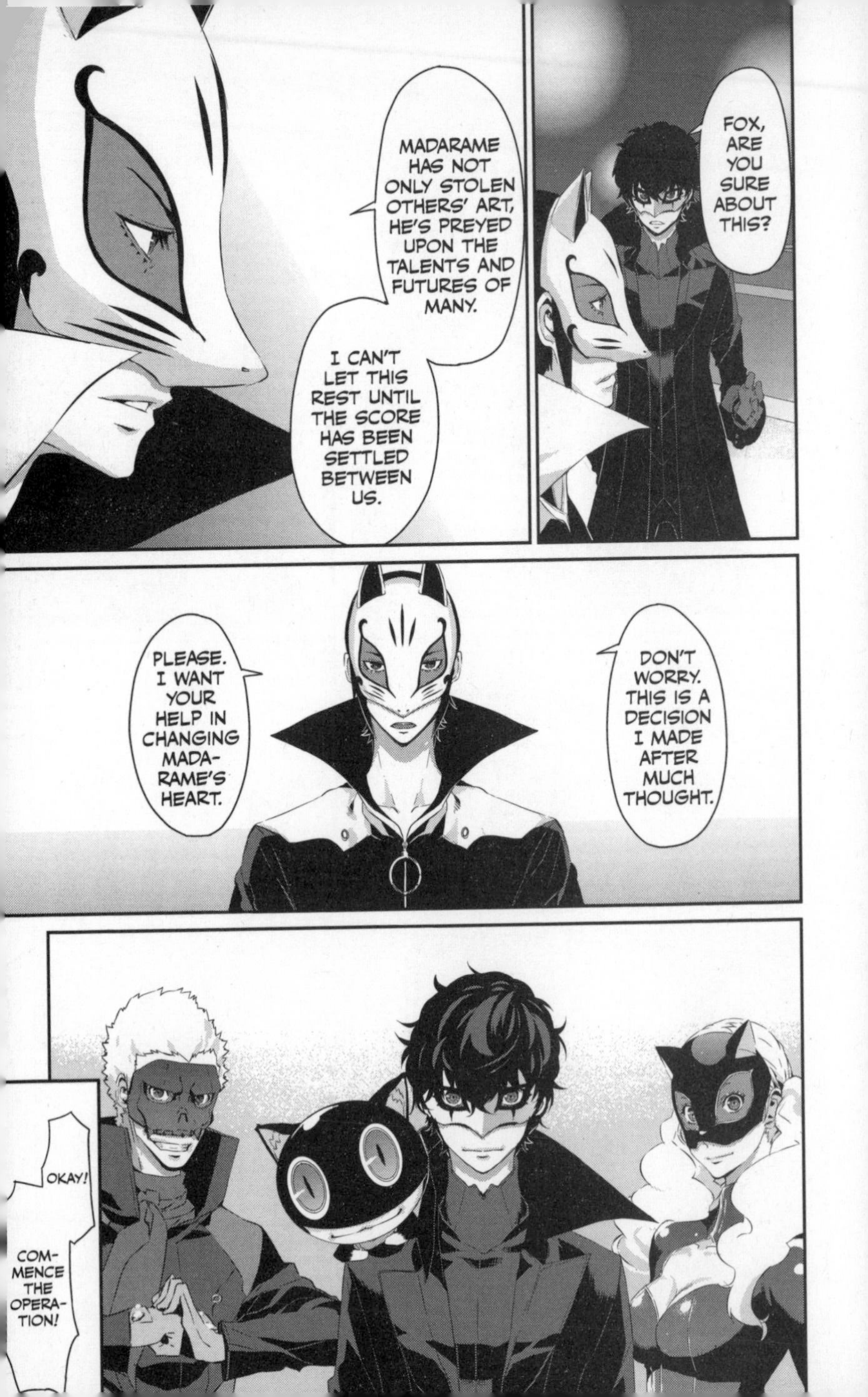
FOX, ARE YOU SURE ABOUT THIS?
MADARAME HAS NOT ONLY STOLEN OTHERS' ART, HE'S PREYED UPON THE TALENTS AND FUTURES OF MANY.
I CAN'T LET THIS REST UNTIL THE SCORE HAS BEEN SETTLED BETWEEN US.
DON'T WORRY. THIS IS A DECISION I MADE AFTER MUCH THOUGHT.
PLEASE. I WANT YOUR HELP IN CHANGING MADA-RAME'S HEART.
OKAY!
COM-MENCE THE OPERA-TION!

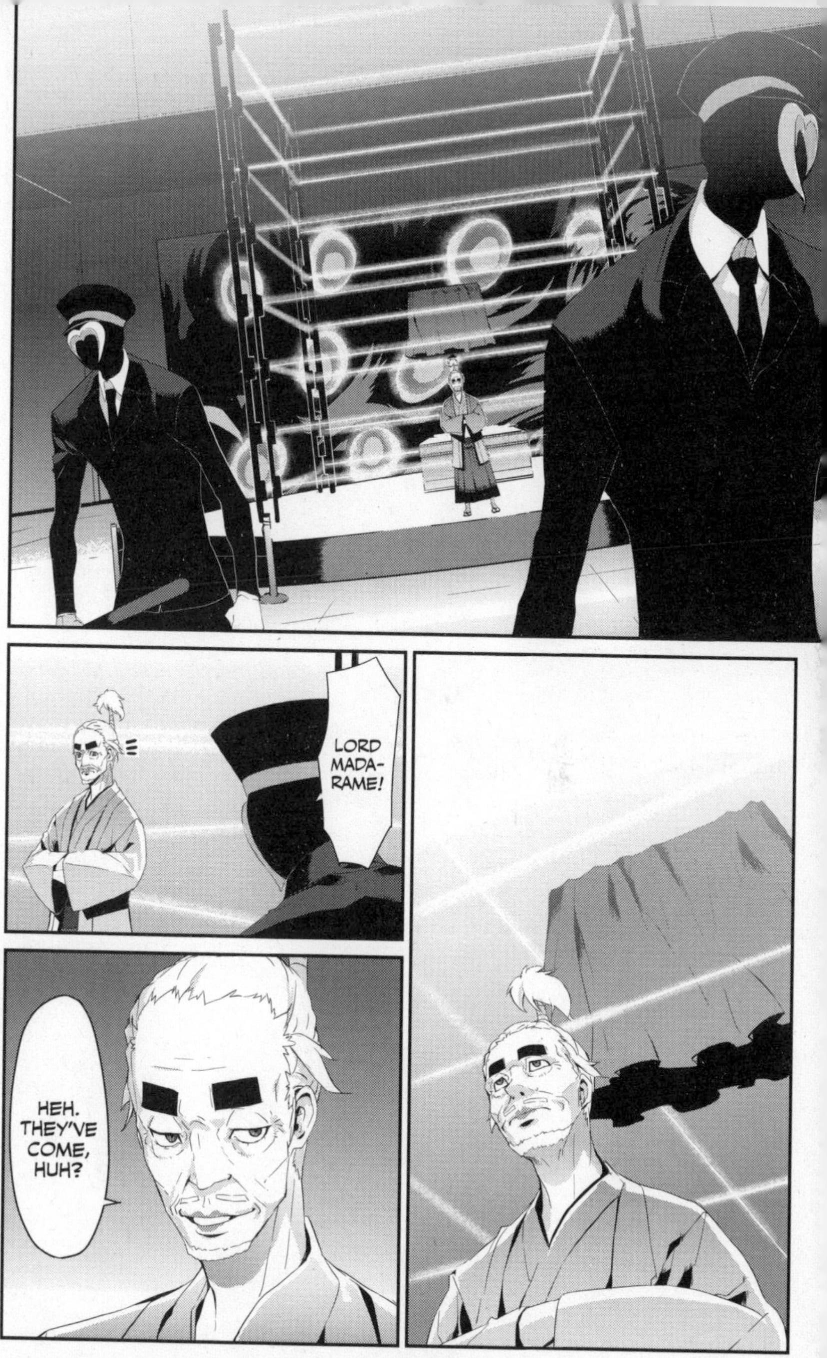
LORD MADA-RAME!
HEH. THEY'VE COME, HUH?

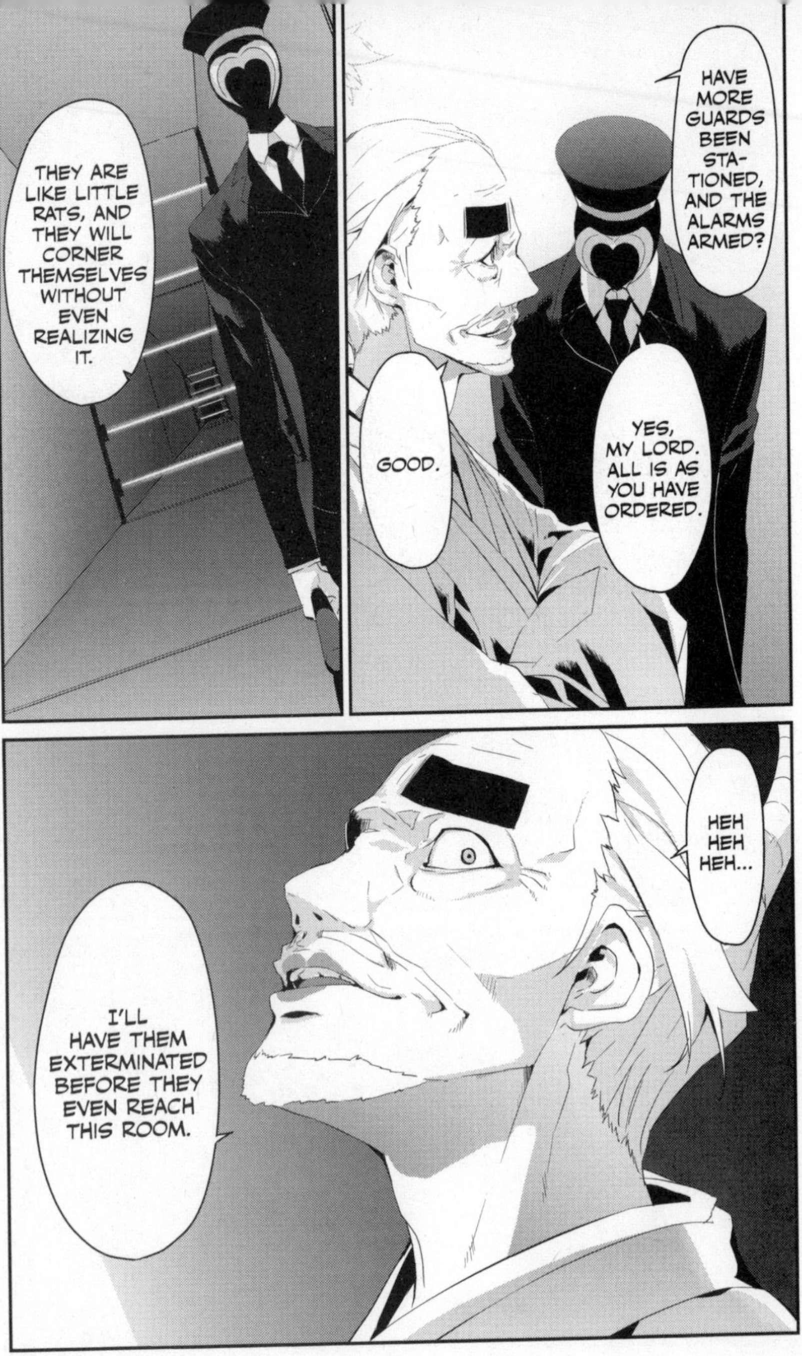
HAVE MORE GUARDS BEEN STATIONED, AND THE ALARMS ARMED?
YES, MY LORD. ALL IS AS YOU HAVE ORDERED.
GOOD.
THEY ARE LIKE LITTLE RATS, AND THEY WILL CORNER THEMSELVES WITHOUT EVEN REALIZING IT.
HEH HEH HEH...
I'LL HAVE THEM EXTERMINATED BEFORE THEY EVEN REACH THIS ROOM.

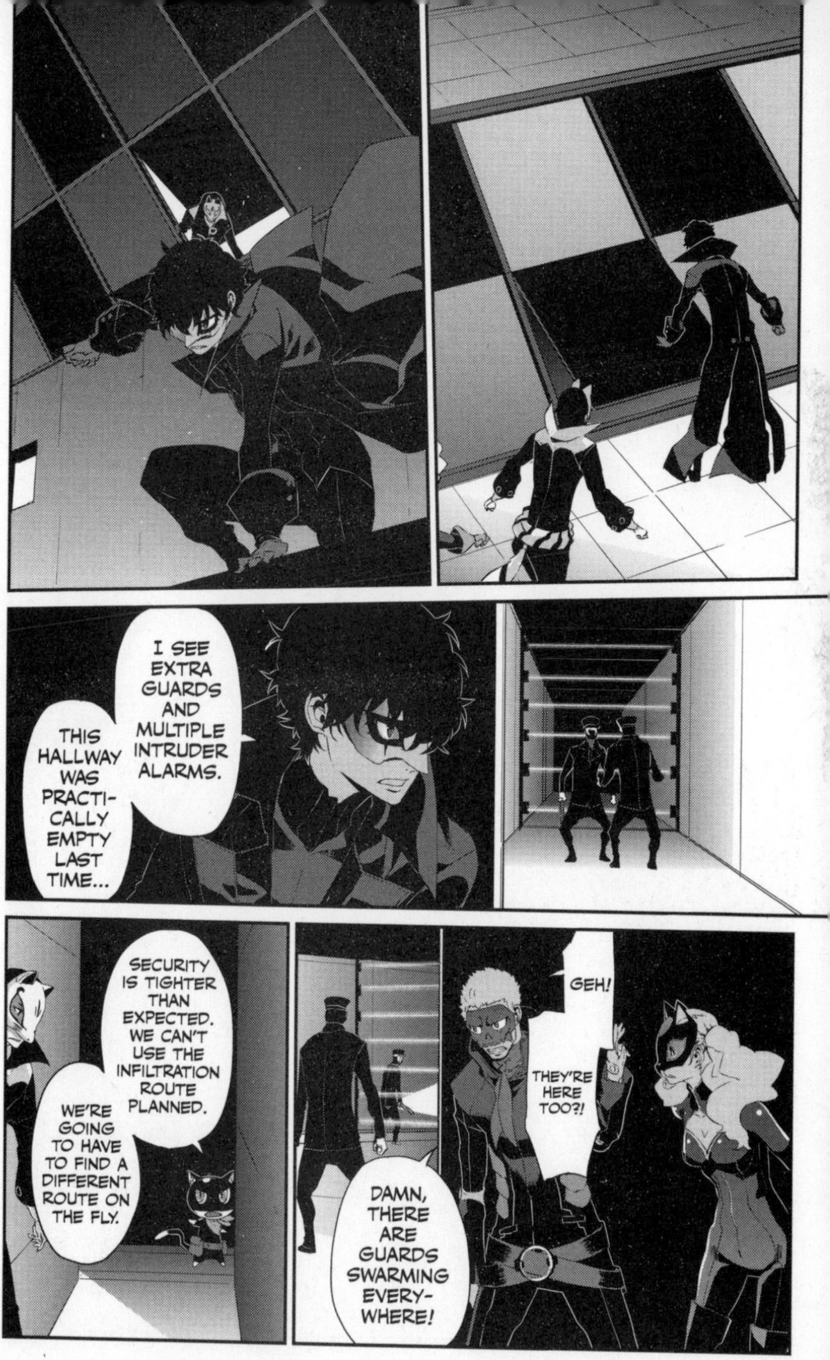
I SEE EXTRA GUARDS AND MULTIPLE INTRUDER ALARMS.
THIS HALLWAY WAS PRACTI-CALLY EMPTY LAST TIME...
GEH!
THEY'RE HERE TOO?!
DAMN, THERE ARE GUARDS SWARMING EVERY-WHERE!
SECURITY IS TIGHTER THAN EXPECTED. WE CAN'T USE THE INFILTRATION ROUTE PLANNED.
WE'RE GOING TO HAVE TO FIND A DIFFERENT ROUTE ON THE FLY.

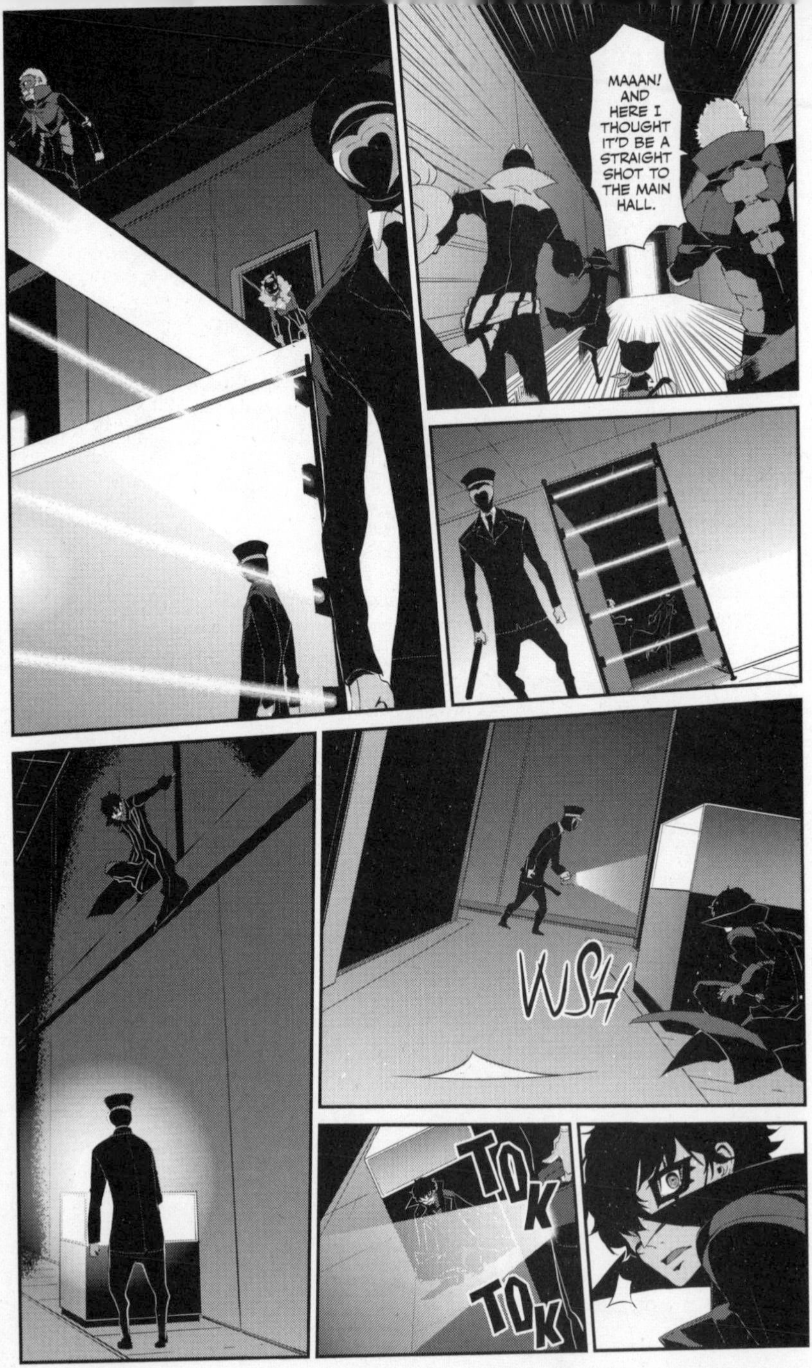
MAAAN! AND HERE I THOUGHT IT'D BE A STRAIGHT SHOT TO THE MAIN HALL.
WSH
TOK
TOK

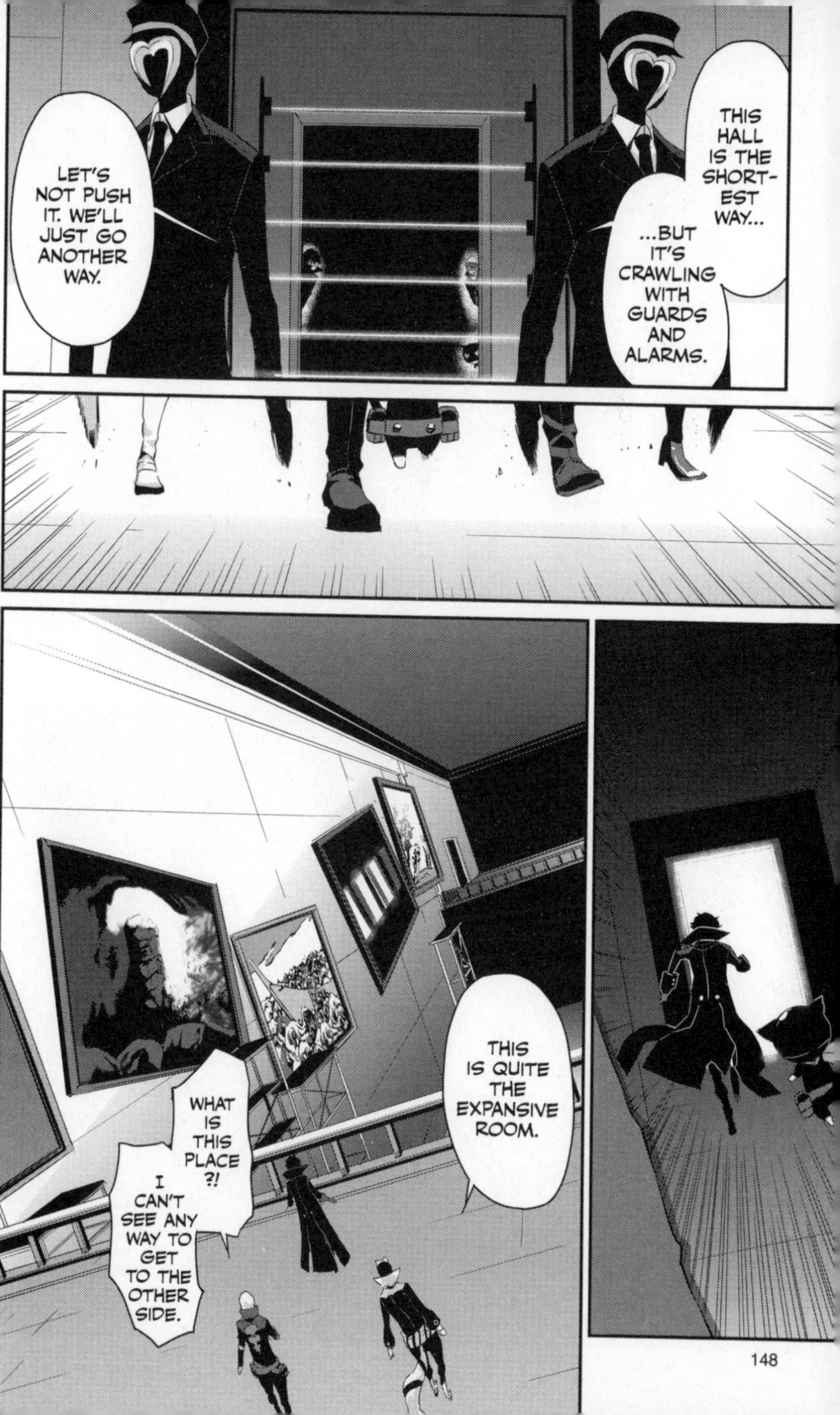
THIS HALL IS THE SHORTEST WAY...
...BUT IT'S CRAWLING WITH GUARDS AND ALARMS.
LET'S NOT PUSH IT. WE'LL JUST GO ANOTHER WAY.
THIS IS QUITE THE EXPANSIVE ROOM.
WHAT IS THIS PLACE?!
I CAN'T SEE ANY WAY TO GET TO THE OTHER SIDE.

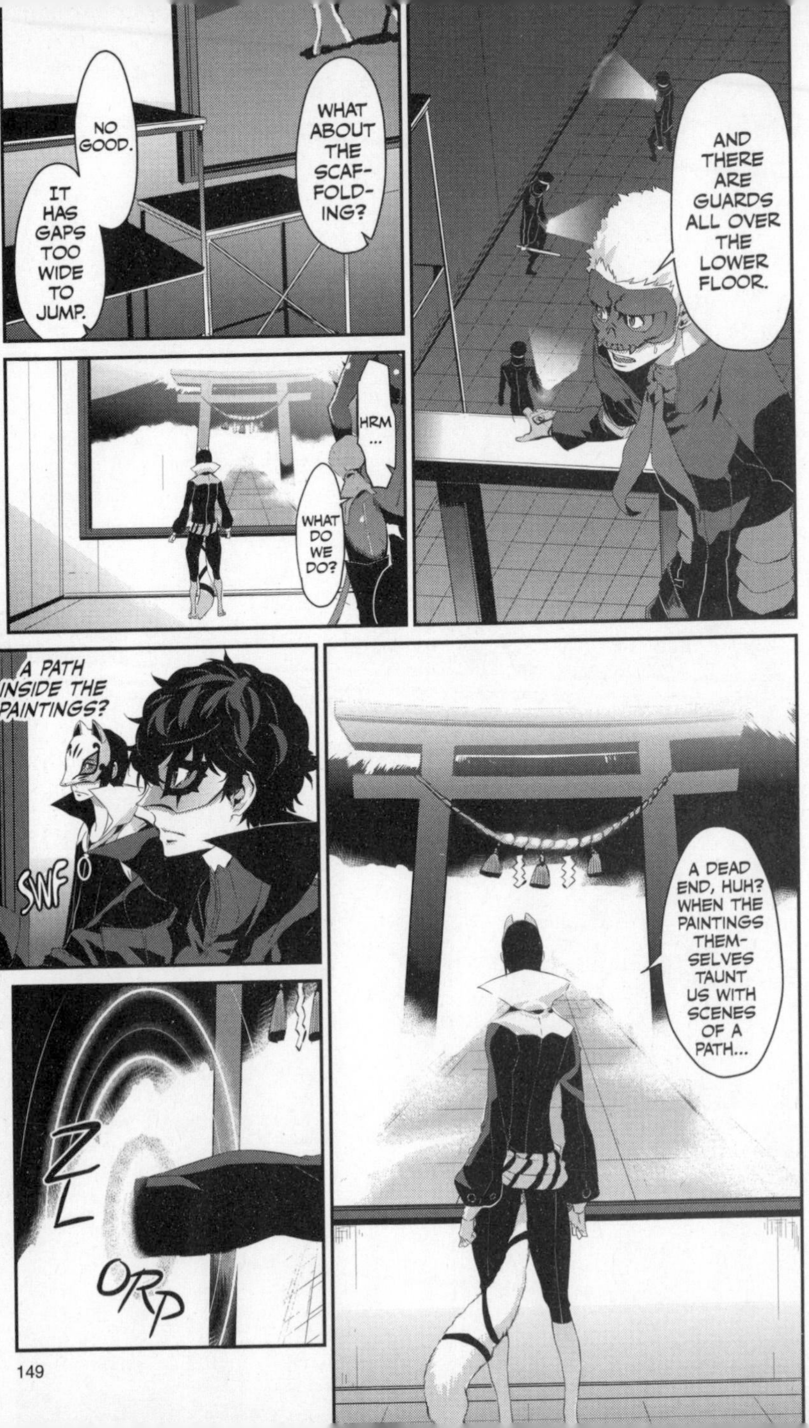
AND THERE ARE GUARDS ALL OVER THE LOWER FLOOR.
WHAT ABOUT THE SCAFFOLDING?
NO GOOD.
IT HAS GAPS TOO WIDE TO JUMP.
HRM ...
WHAT DO WE DO?
A DEAD END, HUH? WHEN THE PAINTINGS THEMSELVES TAUNT US WITH SCENES OF A PATH...
A PATH INSIDE THE PAINTINGS?
SNF
ZLORP

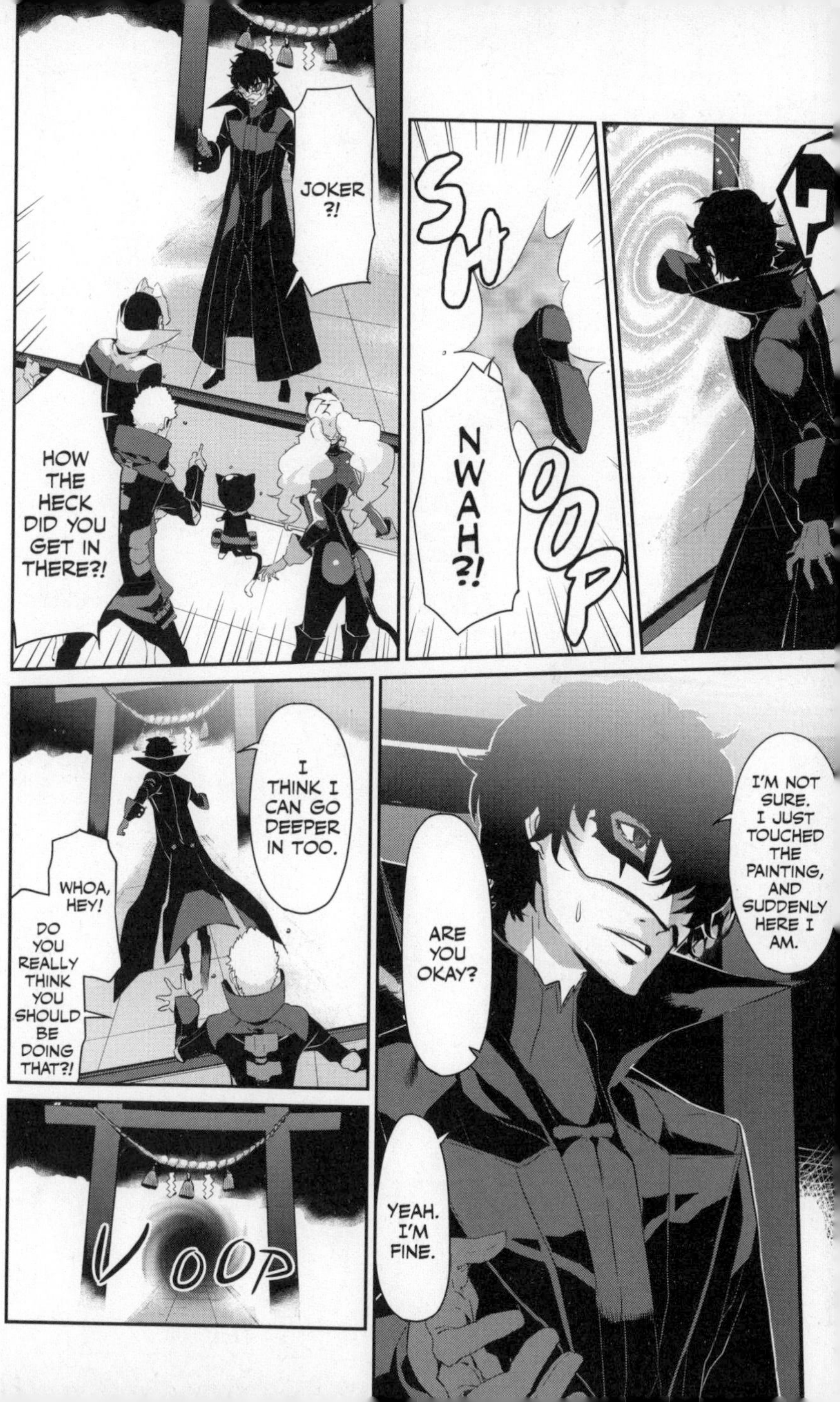
?
SHOOP
NWAH?!
JOKER?!
HOW THE HECK DID YOU GET IN THERE?!
I'M NOT SURE. I JUST TOUCHED THE PAINTING, AND SUDDENLY HERE I AM.
ARE YOU OKAY?
YEAH. I'M FINE.
I THINK I CAN GO DEEPER IN TOO.
WHOA, HEY!
DO YOU REALLY THINK YOU SHOULD BE DOING THAT?!
VOOP

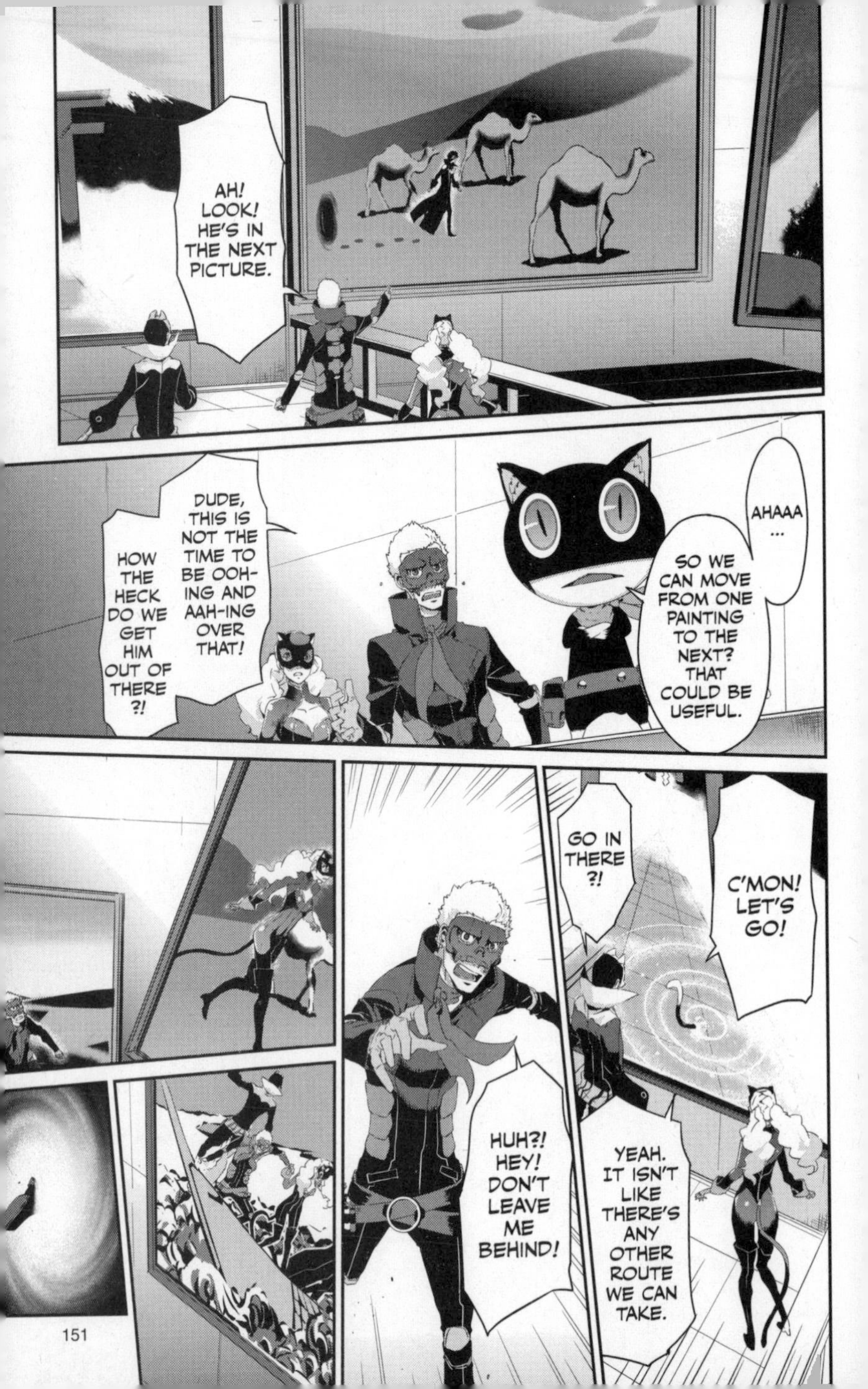
AH! LOOK! HE'S IN THE NEXT PICTURE.
AHAAA ...
SO WE CAN MOVE FROM ONE PAINTING TO THE NEXT? THAT COULD BE USEFUL.
DUDE, THIS IS NOT THE TIME TO BE OOH-ING AND AAH-ING OVER THAT!
HOW THE HECK DO WE GET HIM OUT OF THERE?!
C'MON! LET'S GO!
GO IN THERE?!
YEAH. IT ISN'T LIKE THERE'S ANY OTHER ROUTE WE CAN TAKE.
HUH?! HEY! DON'T LEAVE ME BEHIND!

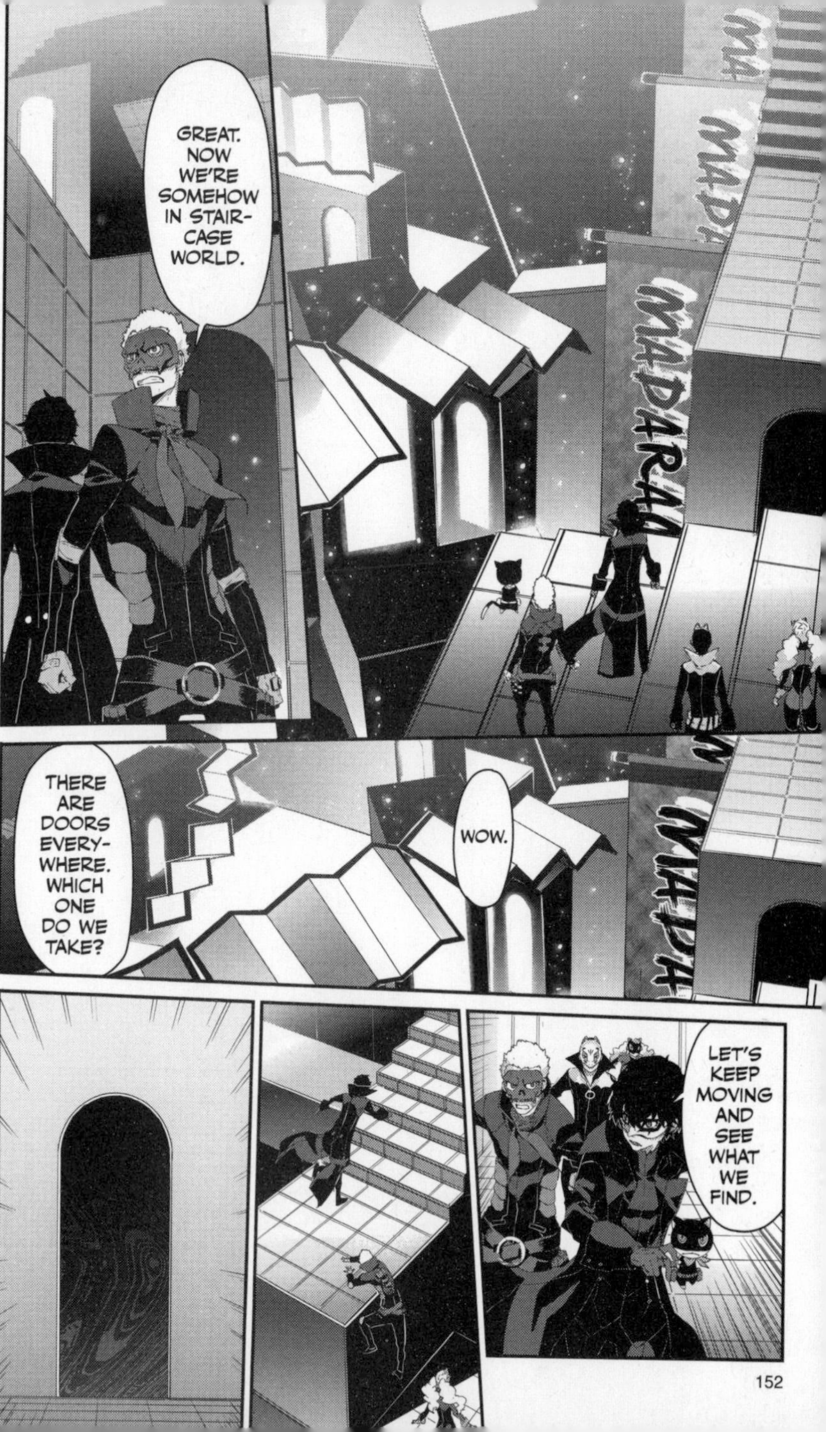
GREAT. NOW WE'RE SOMEHOW IN STAIR-CASE WORLD.
MADARAM
WOW.
THERE ARE DOORS EVERY-WHERE. WHICH ONE DO WE TAKE?
LET'S KEEP MOVING AND SEE WHAT WE FIND.

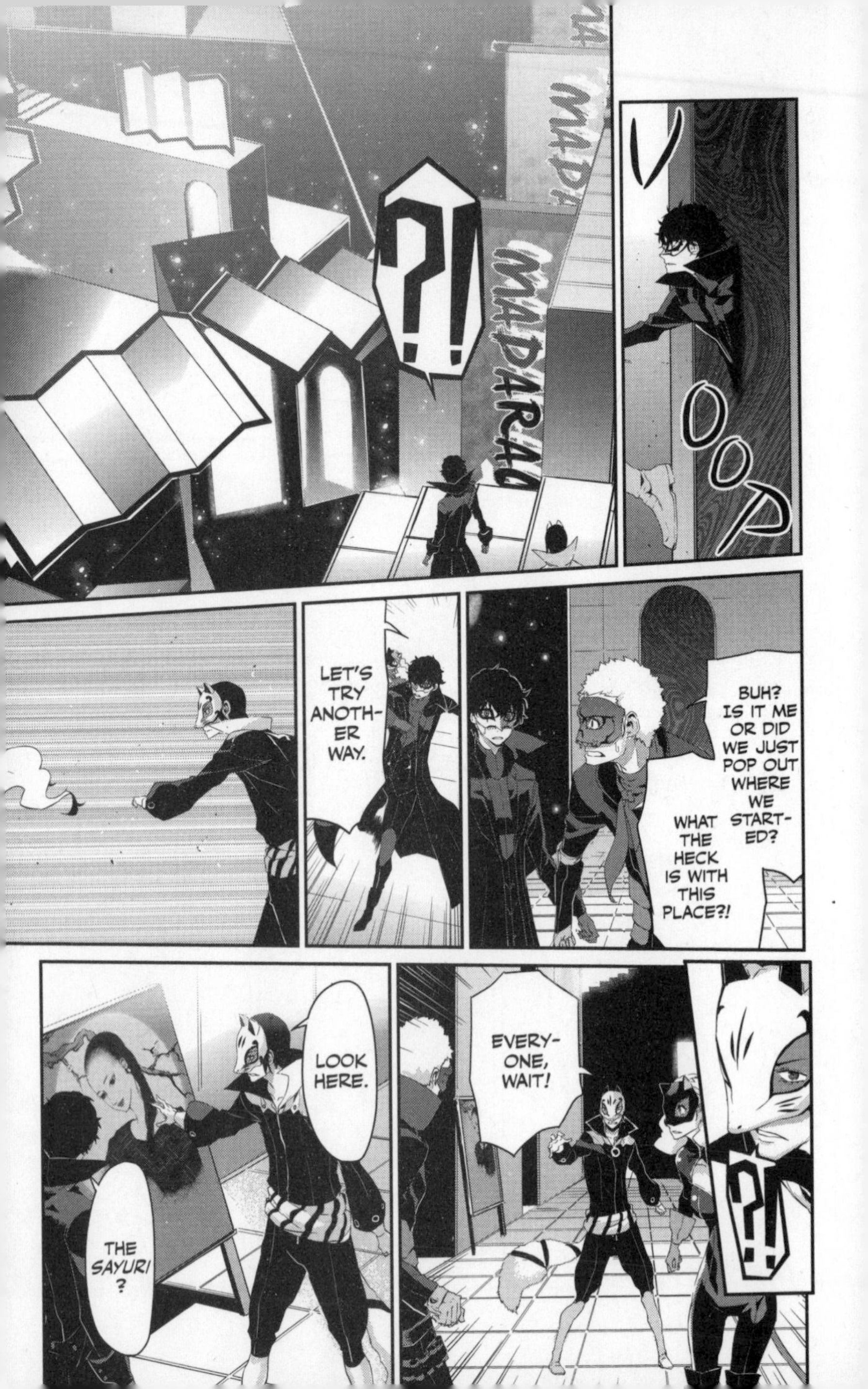
VOOOP
?!
BUH? IS IT ME OR DID WE JUST POP OUT WHERE WE STARTED?
WHAT THE HECK IS WITH THIS PLACE?!
LET'S TRY ANOTHER WAY.
?!
EVERYONE, WAIT!
LOOK HERE.
THE SAYURI?

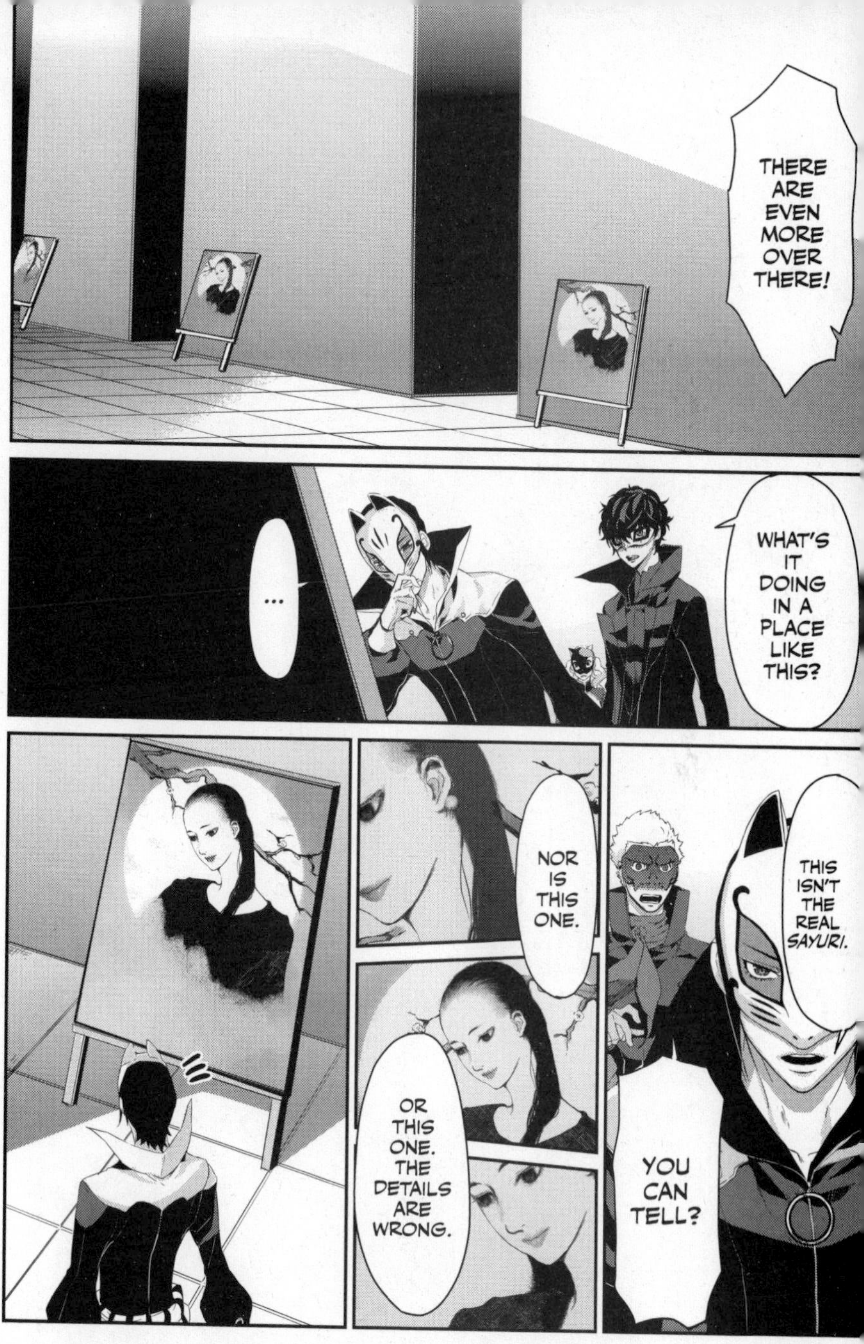
THERE ARE EVEN MORE OVER THERE!
WHAT'S IT DOING IN A PLACE LIKE THIS?
...
THIS ISN'T THE REAL *SAYURI*.
YOU CAN TELL?
NOR IS THIS ONE.
OR THIS ONE. THE DETAILS ARE WRONG.

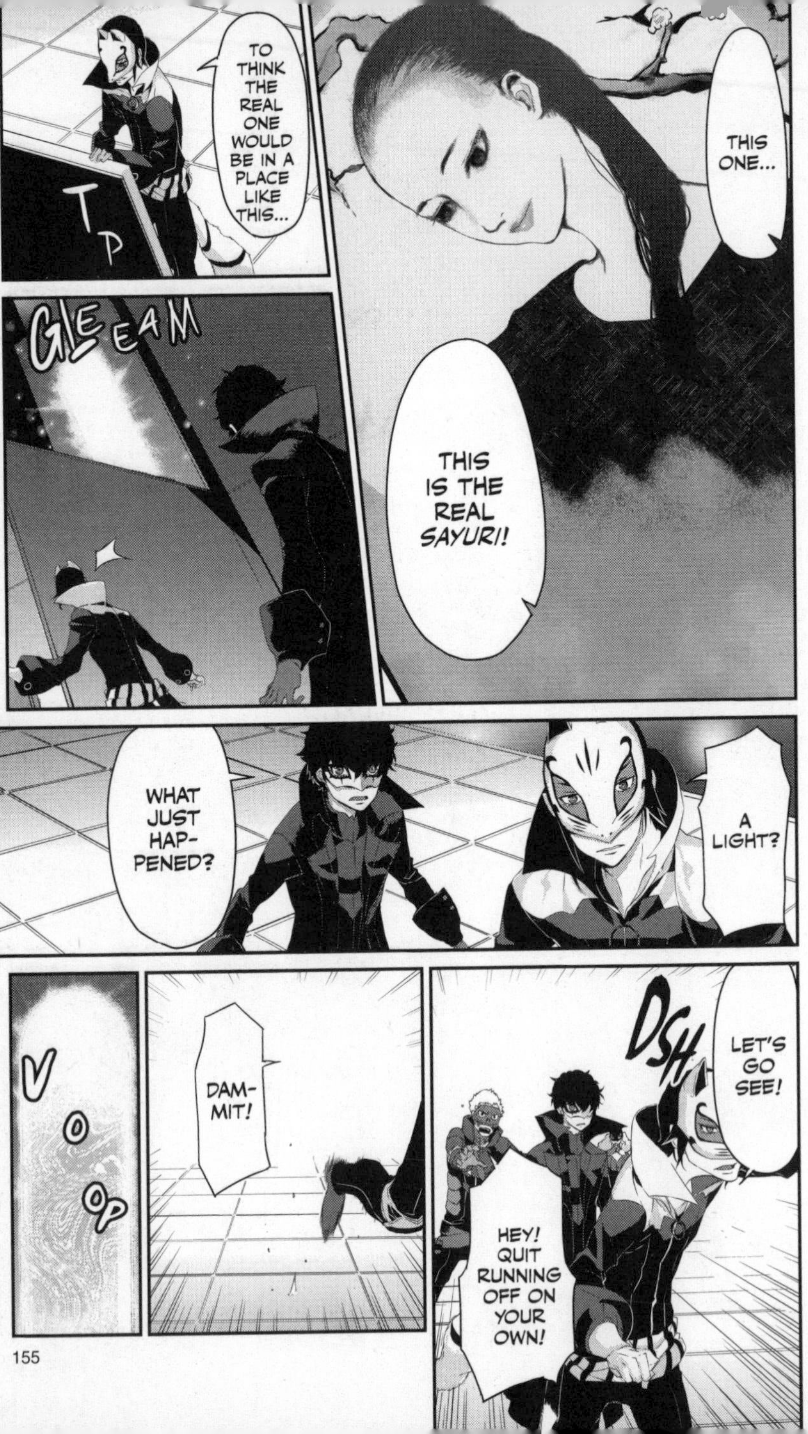
THIS ONE...
THIS IS THE REAL SAYURI!
TO THINK THE REAL ONE WOULD BE IN A PLACE LIKE THIS...
TP
GLEAM
A LIGHT?
WHAT JUST HAP-PENED?
LET'S GO SEE!
DSH
HEY! QUIT RUNNING OFF ON YOUR OWN!
DAM-MIT!
VOOP

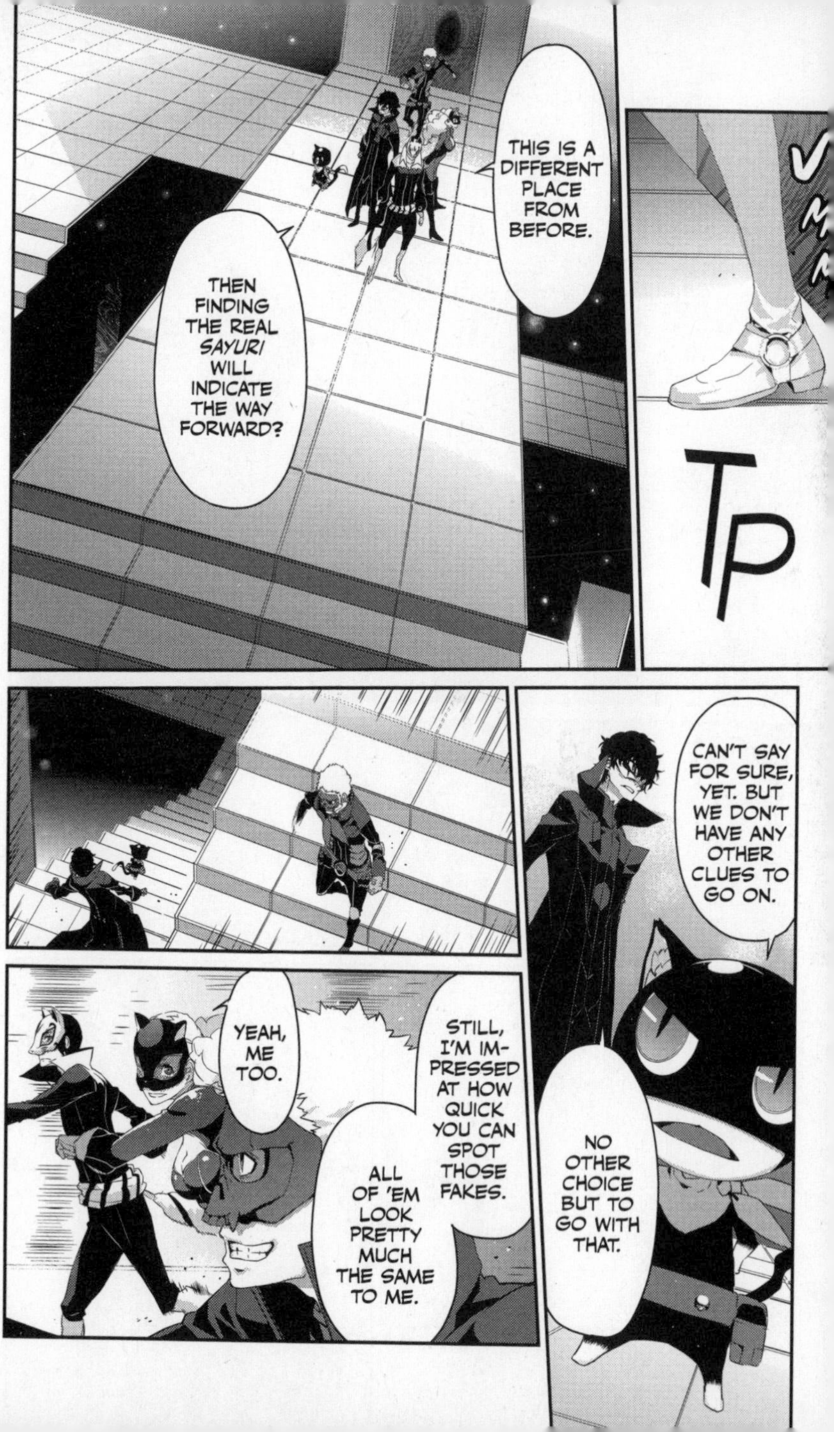
TP
THIS IS A DIFFERENT PLACE FROM BEFORE.
THEN FINDING THE REAL *SAYURI* WILL INDICATE THE WAY FORWARD?
CAN'T SAY FOR SURE, YET. BUT WE DON'T HAVE ANY OTHER CLUES TO GO ON.
NO OTHER CHOICE BUT TO GO WITH THAT.
STILL, I'M IM-PRESSED AT HOW QUICK YOU CAN SPOT THOSE FAKES.
ALL OF 'EM LOOK PRETTY MUCH THE SAME TO ME.
YEAH, ME TOO.

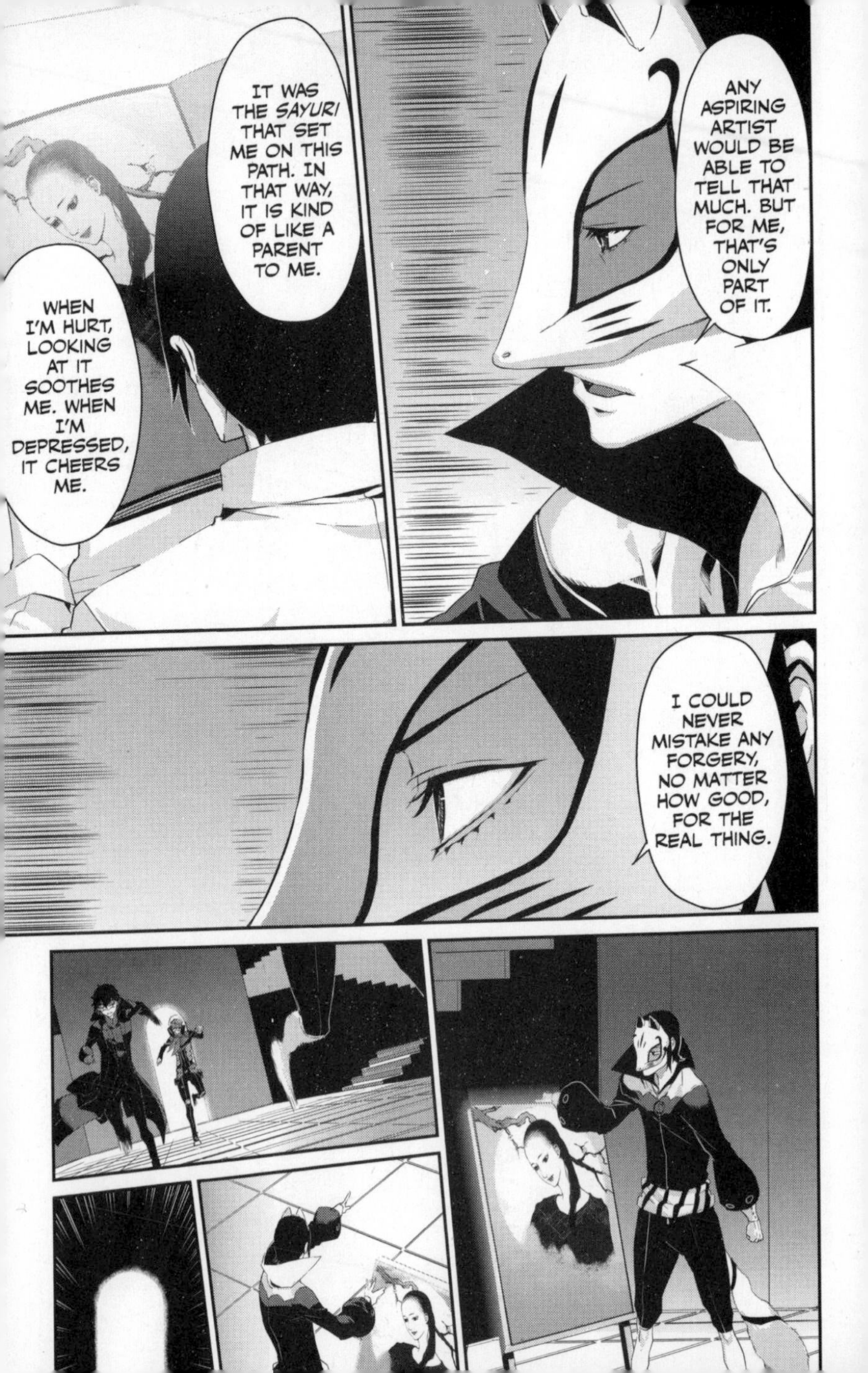
ANY ASPIRING ARTIST WOULD BE ABLE TO TELL THAT MUCH. BUT FOR ME, THAT'S ONLY PART OF IT.
IT WAS THE *SAYURI* THAT SET ME ON THIS PATH. IN THAT WAY, IT IS KIND OF LIKE A PARENT TO ME.
WHEN I'M HURT, LOOKING AT IT SOOTHES ME. WHEN I'M DEPRESSED, IT CHEERS ME.
I COULD NEVER MISTAKE ANY FORGERY, NO MATTER HOW GOOD, FOR THE REAL THING.

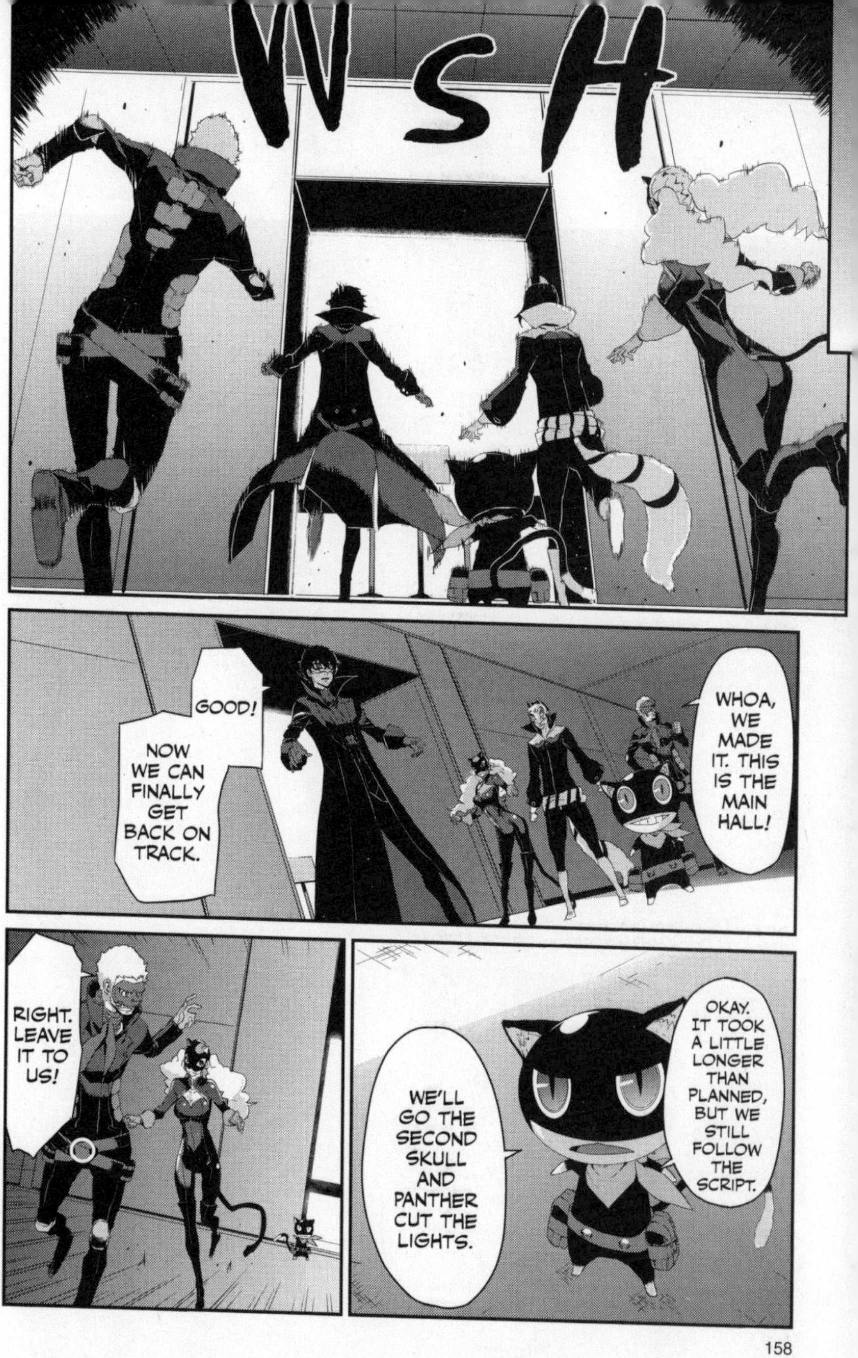
WSH
WHOA, WE MADE IT. THIS IS THE MAIN HALL!
GOOD!
NOW WE CAN FINALLY GET BACK ON TRACK.
OKAY. IT TOOK A LITTLE LONGER THAN PLANNED, BUT WE STILL FOLLOW THE SCRIPT.
WE'LL GO THE SECOND SKULL AND PANTHER CUT THE LIGHTS.
RIGHT. LEAVE IT TO US!

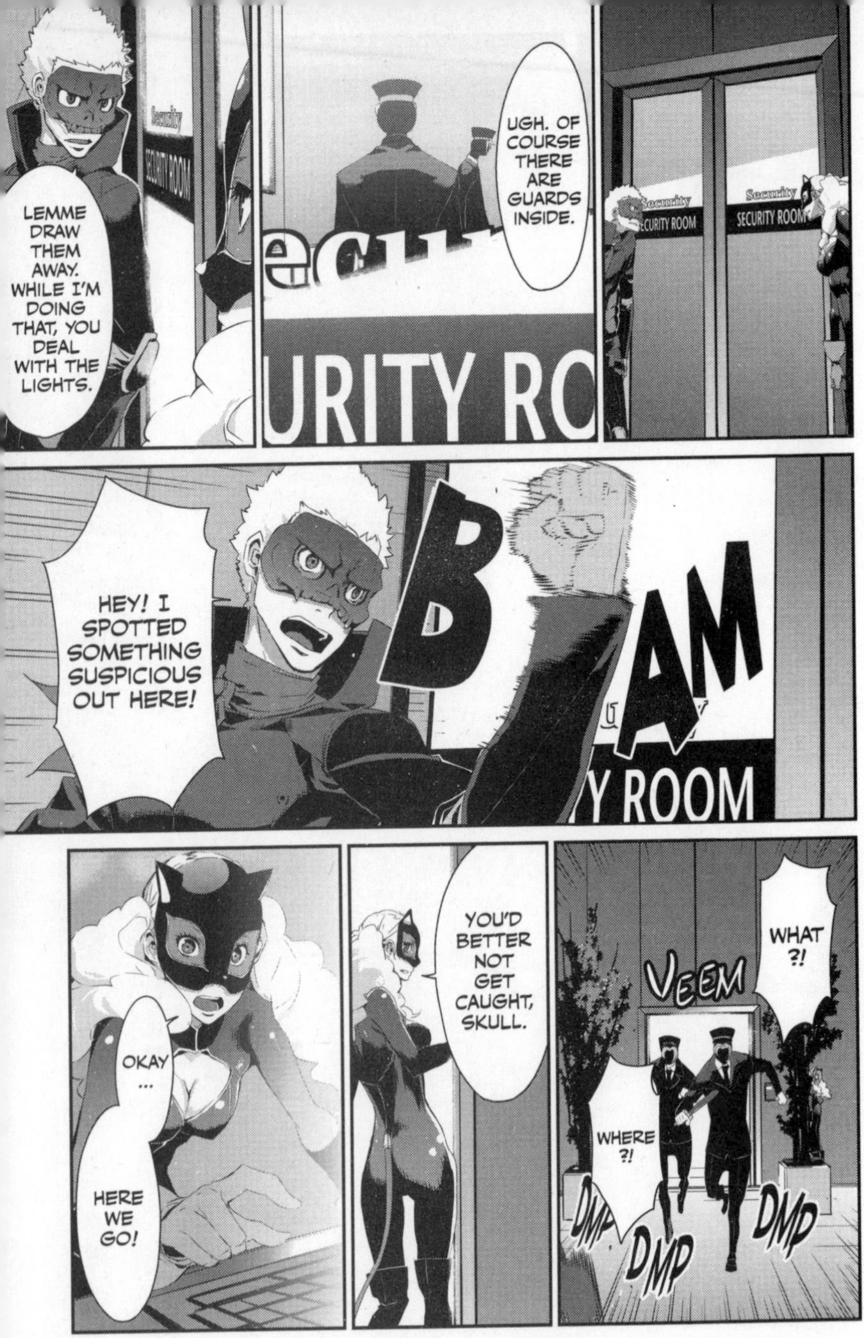
Security
SECURITY ROOM
Security
SECURITY ROOM
UGH. OF COURSE THERE ARE GUARDS INSIDE.
URITY RO
Security
SECURITY ROOM
LEMME DRAW THEM AWAY. WHILE I'M DOING THAT, YOU DEAL WITH THE LIGHTS.
BAM
HEY! I SPOTTED SOMETHING SUSPICIOUS OUT HERE!
Y ROOM
WHAT?!
VEEM
WHERE?!
DMP
DMP
DMP
YOU'D BETTER NOT GET CAUGHT, SKULL.
OKAY...
HERE WE GO!

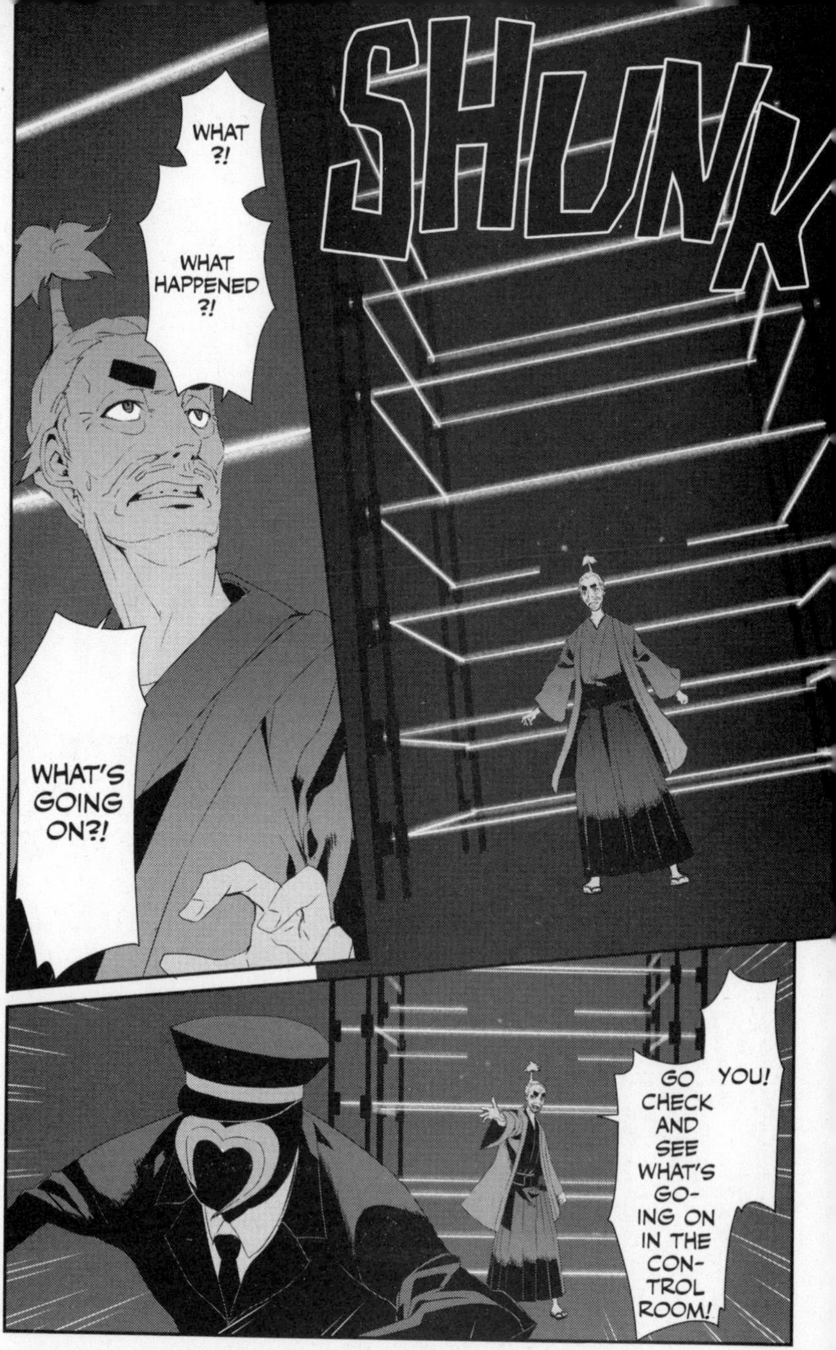
SHUNK
WHAT ?!
WHAT HAPPENED ?!
WHAT'S GOING ON?!
YOU! GO CHECK AND SEE WHAT'S GO-ING ON IN THE CON-TROL ROOM!

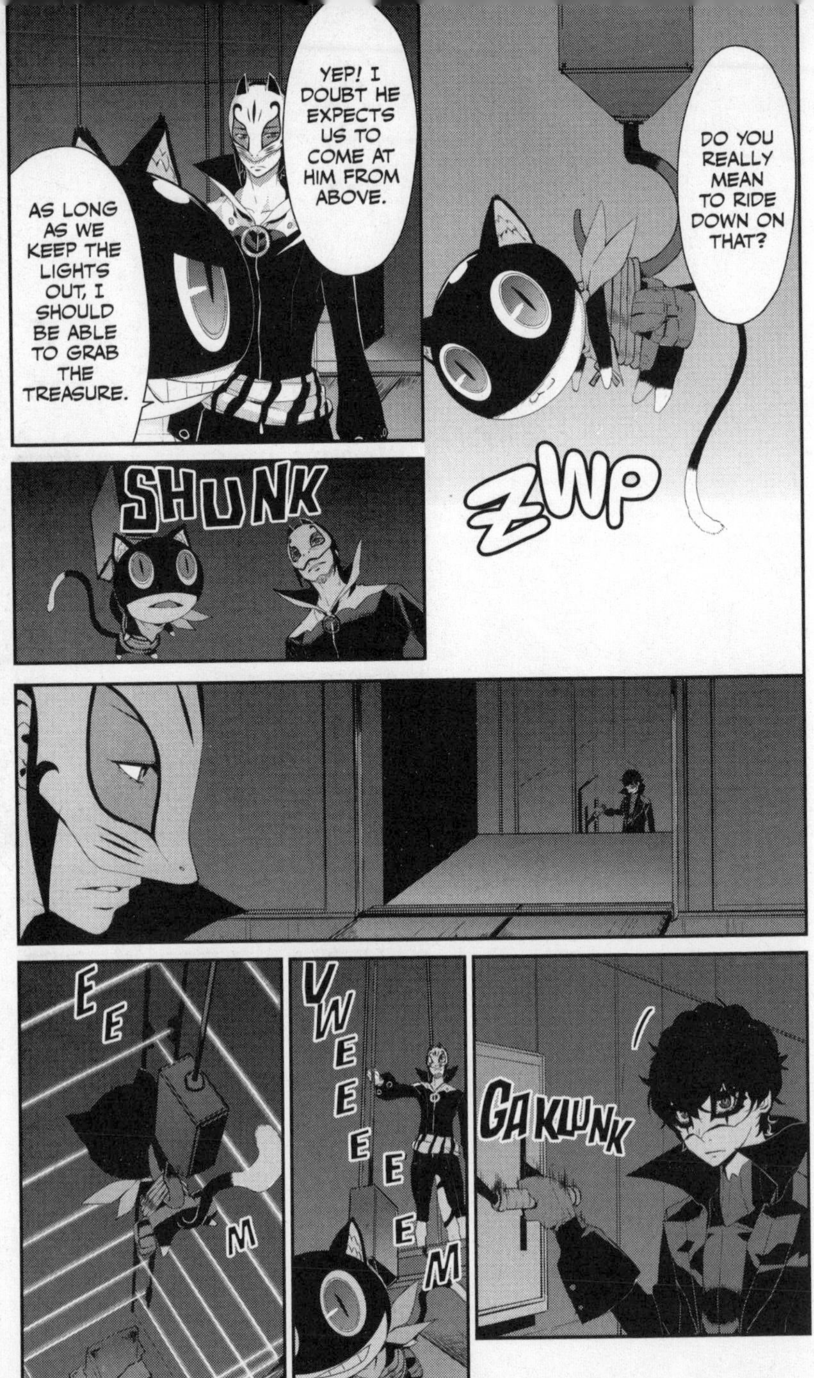
DO YOU REALLY MEAN TO RIDE DOWN ON THAT?
ZWP
YEP! I DOUBT HE EXPECTS US TO COME AT HIM FROM ABOVE.
AS LONG AS WE KEEP THE LIGHTS OUT, I SHOULD BE ABLE TO GRAB THE TREASURE.
SHUNK
GAKLUNK
VWEEEEEEM
EEM

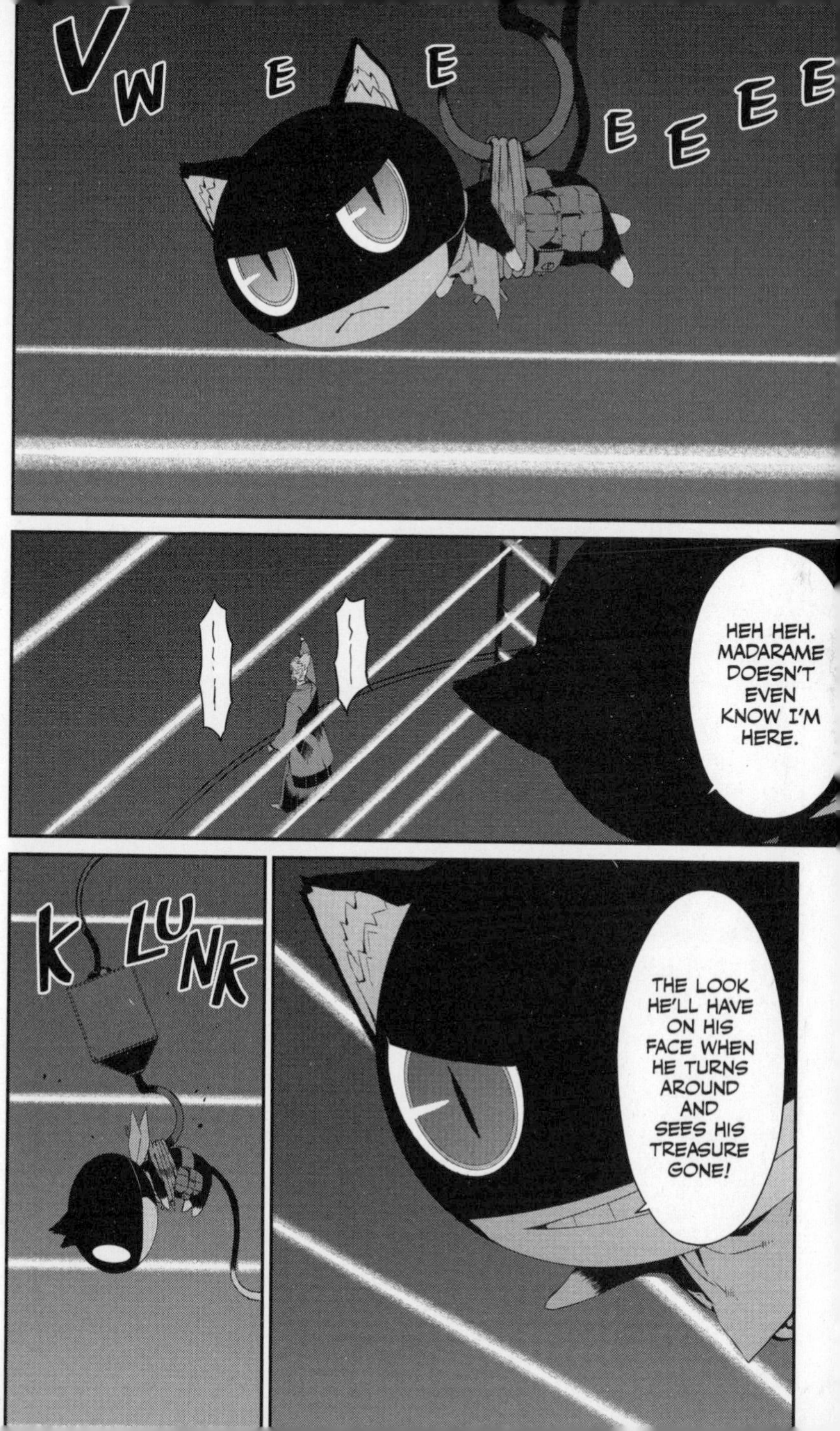
VWEEEEEEEE
HEH HEH. MADARAME DOESN'T EVEN KNOW I'M HERE.
!
...!
THE LOOK HE'LL HAVE ON HIS FACE WHEN HE TURNS AROUND AND SEES HIS TREASURE GONE!
KLUNK

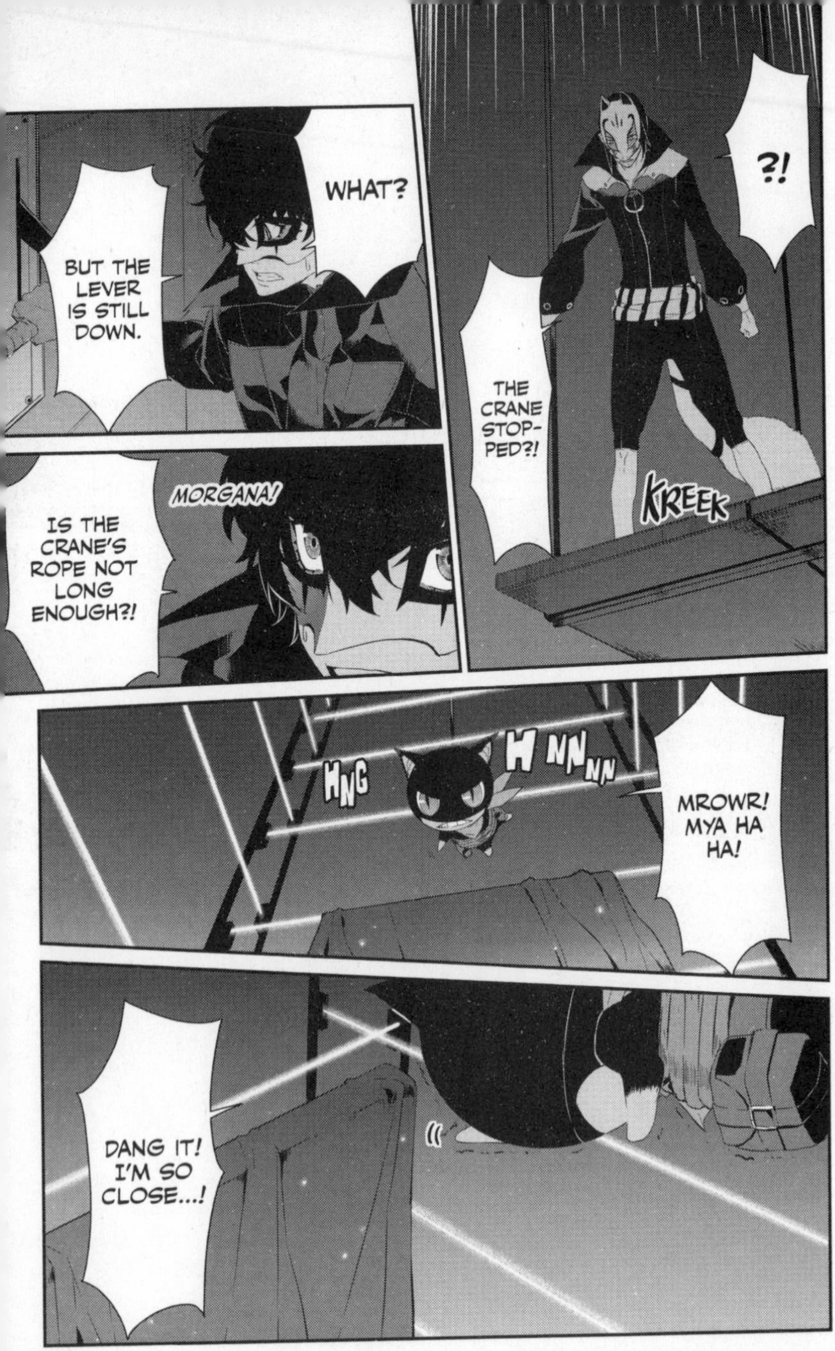
?!
THE CRANE STOP-PED?!
KREEK
WHAT?
BUT THE LEVER IS STILL DOWN.
MORGANA!
IS THE CRANE'S ROPE NOT LONG ENOUGH?!
MROWR! MYA HA HA!
HNNNN
HNG
DANG IT! I'M SO CLOSE...!

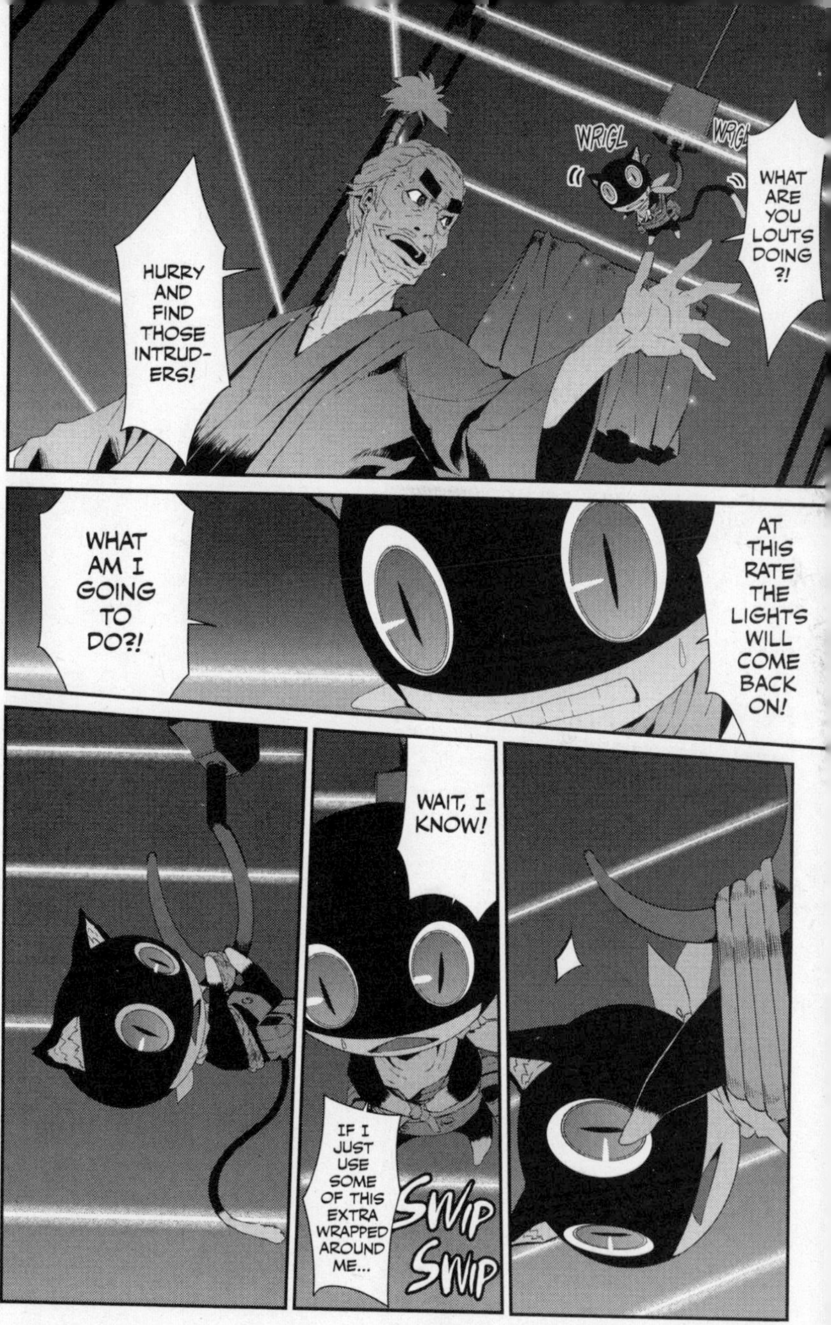
WHAT ARE YOU LOUTS DOING?!
WRIGL
WRIGL
HURRY AND FIND THOSE INTRUDERS!
AT THIS RATE THE LIGHTS WILL COME BACK ON!
WHAT AM I GOING TO DO?!
WAIT, I KNOW!
IF I JUST USE SOME OF THIS EXTRA WRAPPED AROUND ME...
SWIP
SWIP

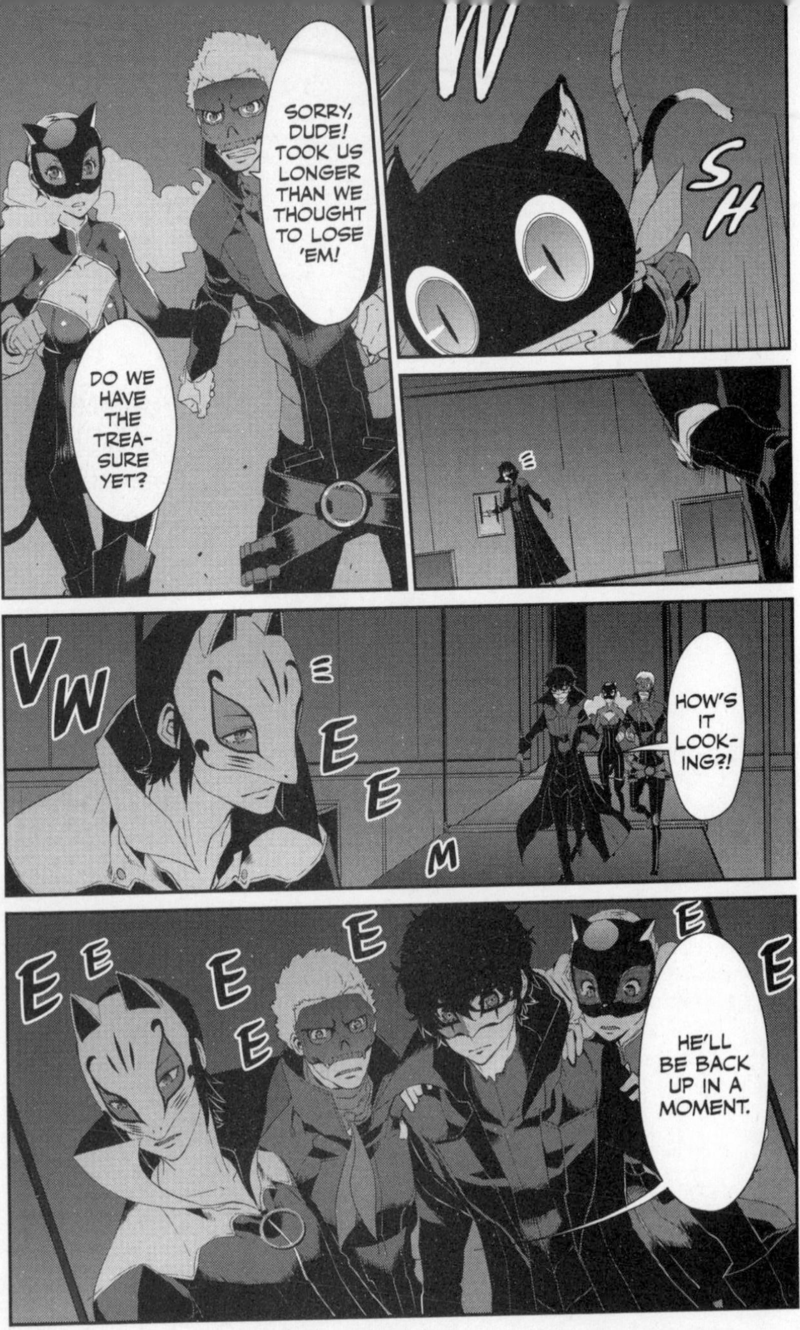
W
SH
SORRY, DUDE! TOOK US LONGER THAN WE THOUGHT TO LOSE 'EM!
DO WE HAVE THE TREA-SURE YET?
HOW'S IT LOOK-ING?!
VW
E
E
M
HE'LL BE BACK UP IN A MOMENT.
E
E
E
E
E
E
E
E

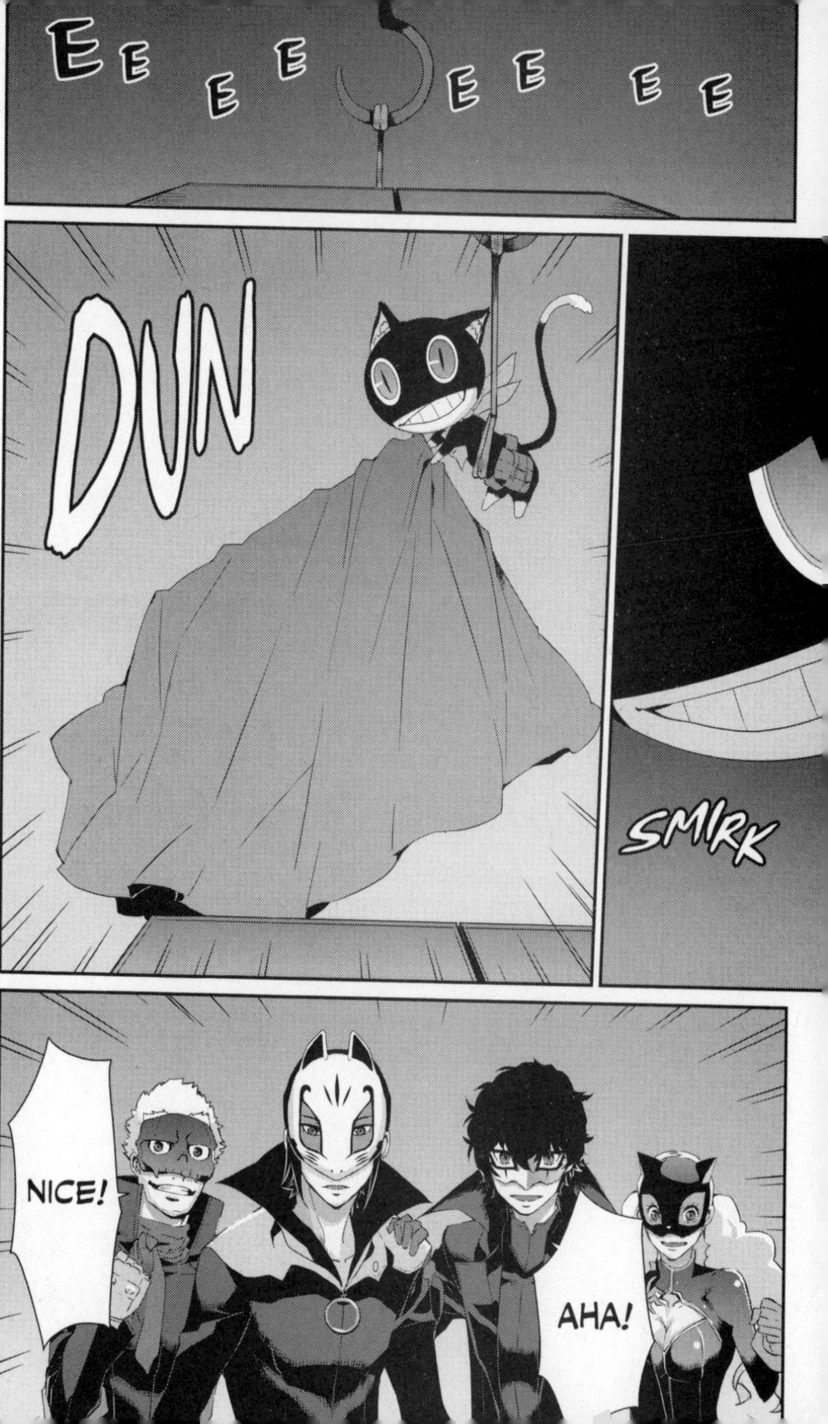
EEEEEEEEE
SMIRK
DUN
NICE!
AHA!

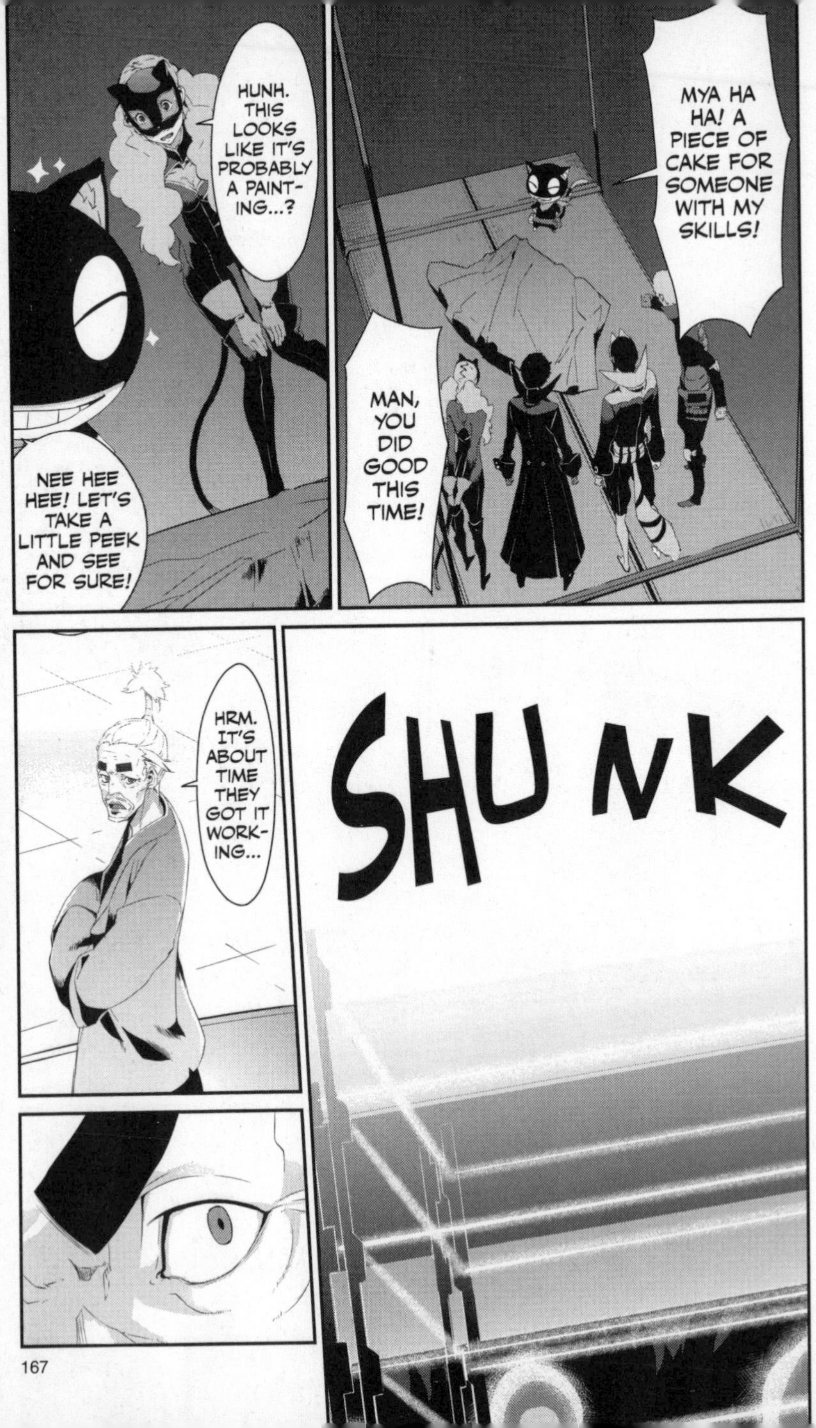

MYA HA HA! A PIECE OF CAKE FOR SOMEONE WITH MY SKILLS!
MAN, YOU DID GOOD THIS TIME!
HUNH. THIS LOOKS LIKE IT'S PROBABLY A PAINTING...?
NEE HEE HEE! LET'S TAKE A LITTLE PEEK AND SEE FOR SURE!
SHUNK
HRM. IT'S ABOUT TIME THEY GOT IT WORKING...

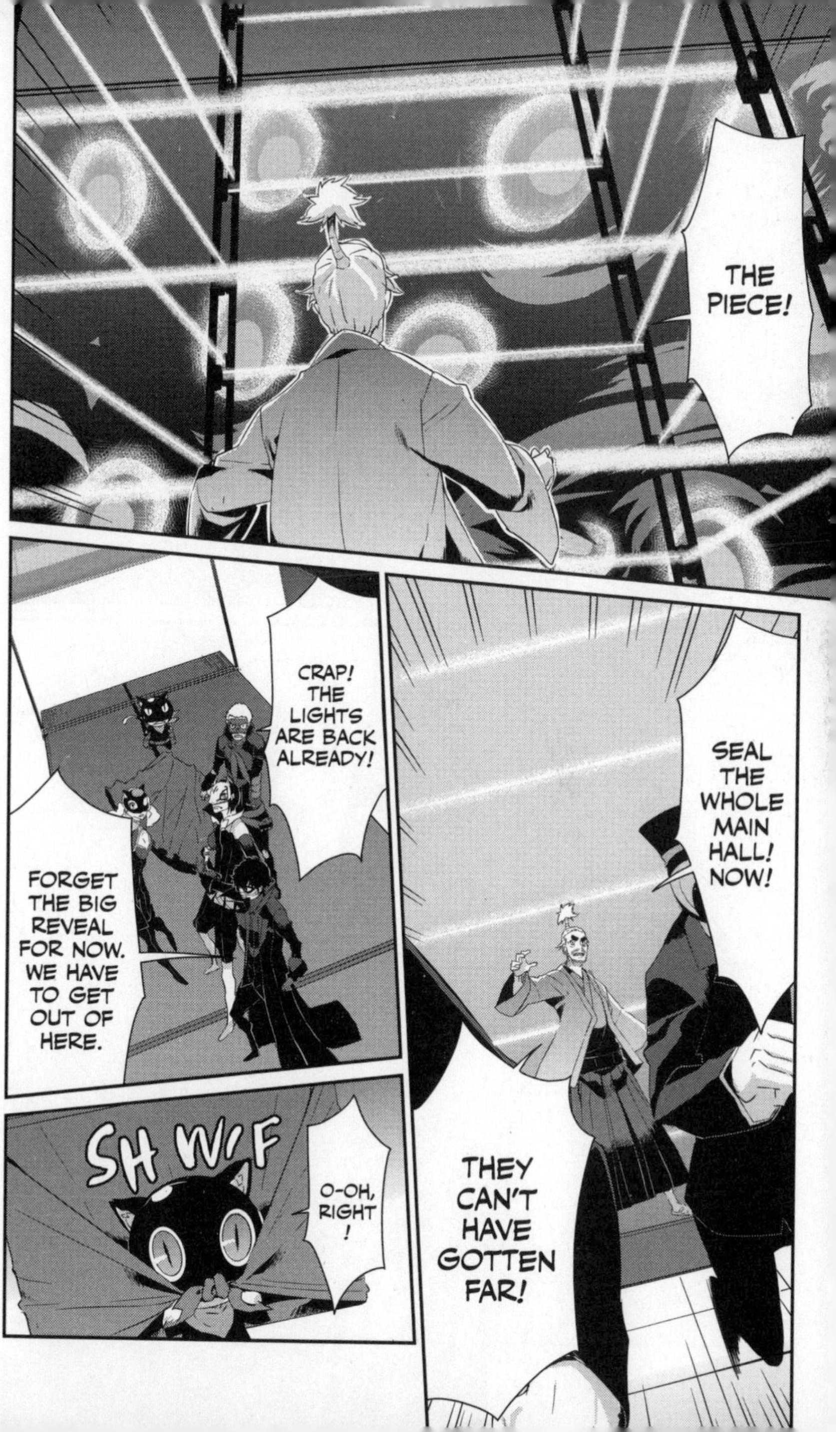
THE PIECE!
SEAL THE WHOLE MAIN HALL! NOW!
THEY CAN'T HAVE GOTTEN FAR!
CRAP! THE LIGHTS ARE BACK ALREADY!
FORGET THE BIG REVEAL FOR NOW. WE HAVE TO GET OUT OF HERE.
SHWIF
O-OH, RIGHT!

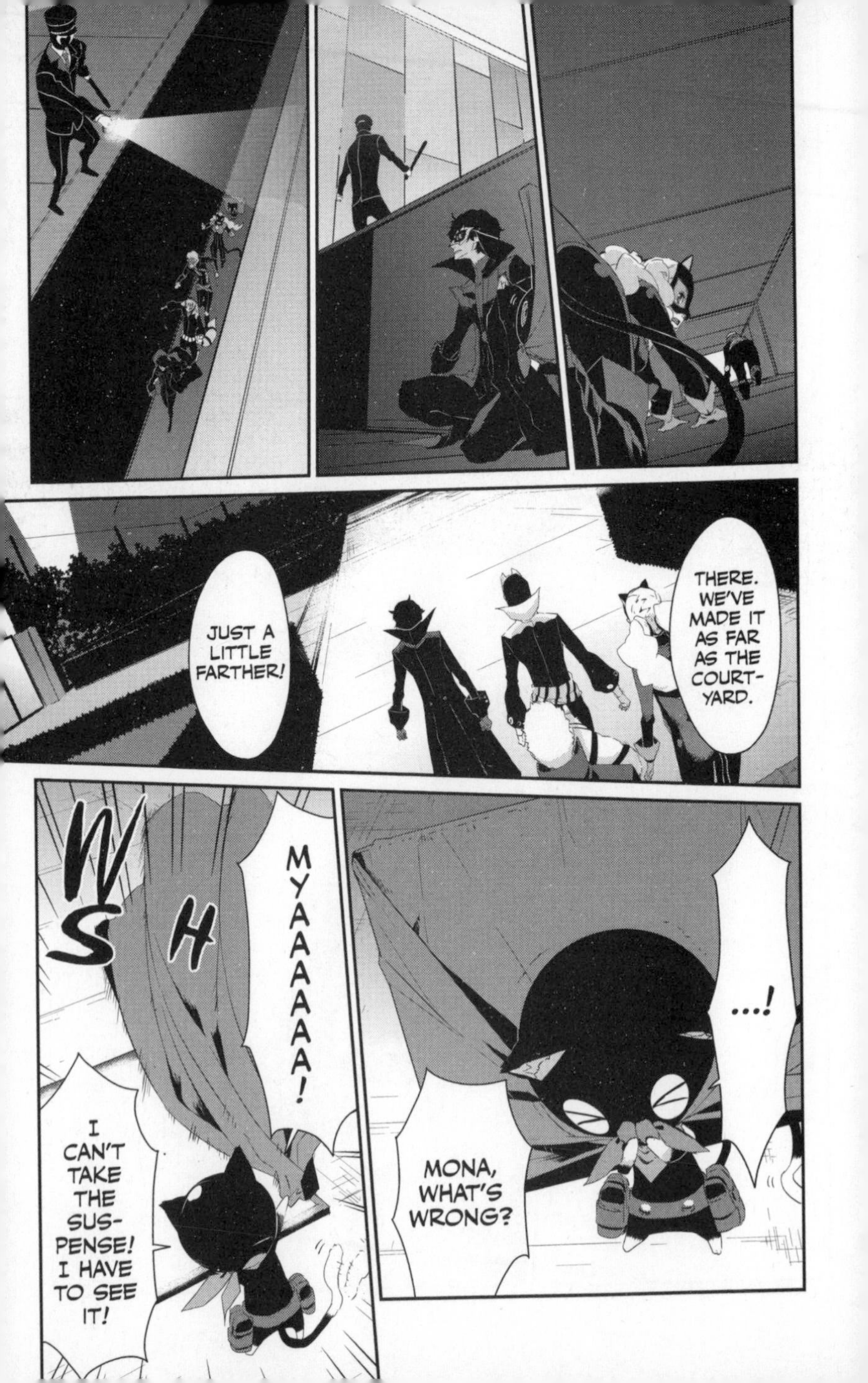
THERE. WE'VE MADE IT AS FAR AS THE COURT-YARD.
JUST A LITTLE FARTHER!
...!
MONA, WHAT'S WRONG?
MYAAAAAAA!
WHSH
I CAN'T TAKE THE SUS-PENSE! I HAVE TO SEE IT!

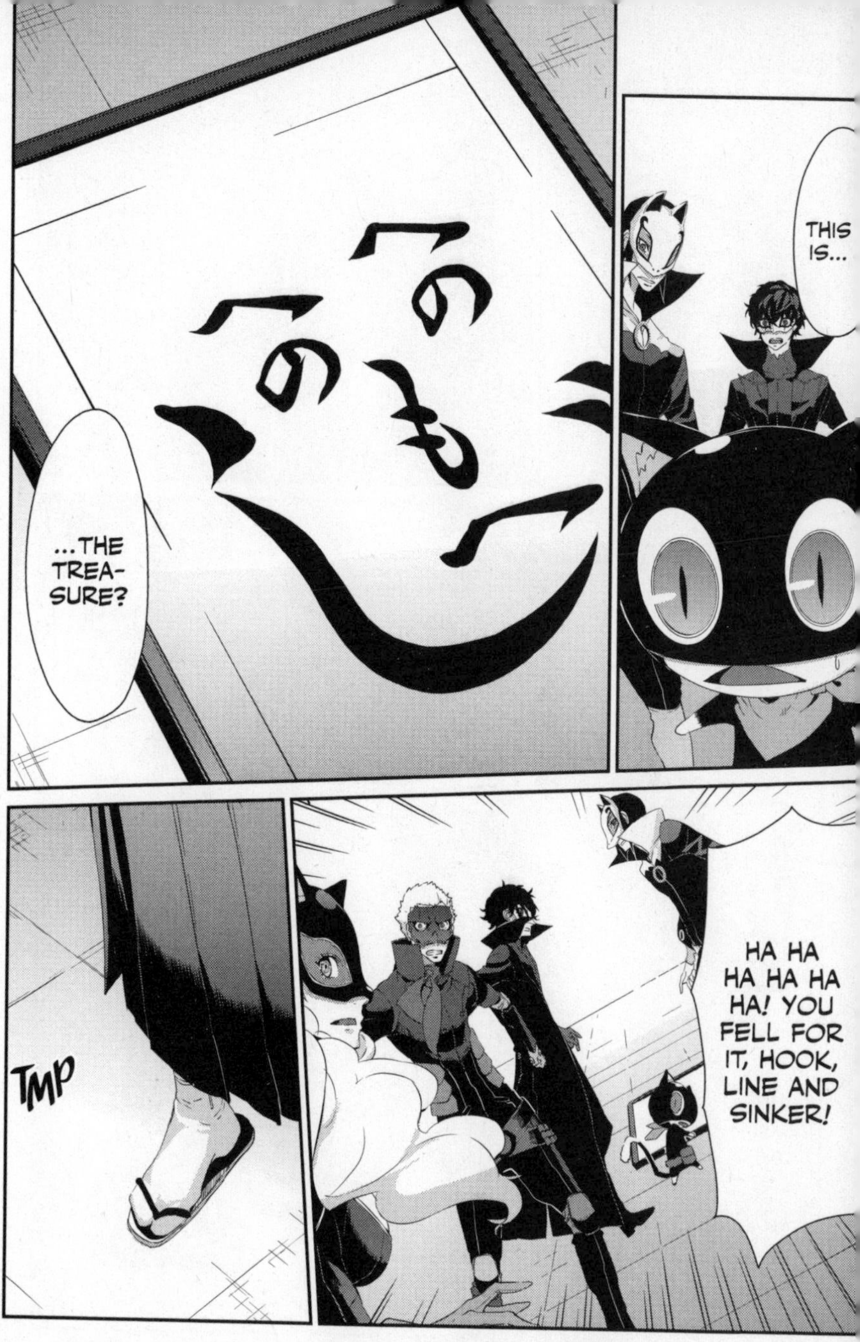
THIS IS...
へのへのもへじ
...THE TREASURE?
HA HA HA HA HA HA! YOU FELL FOR IT, HOOK, LINE AND SINKER!
TMP

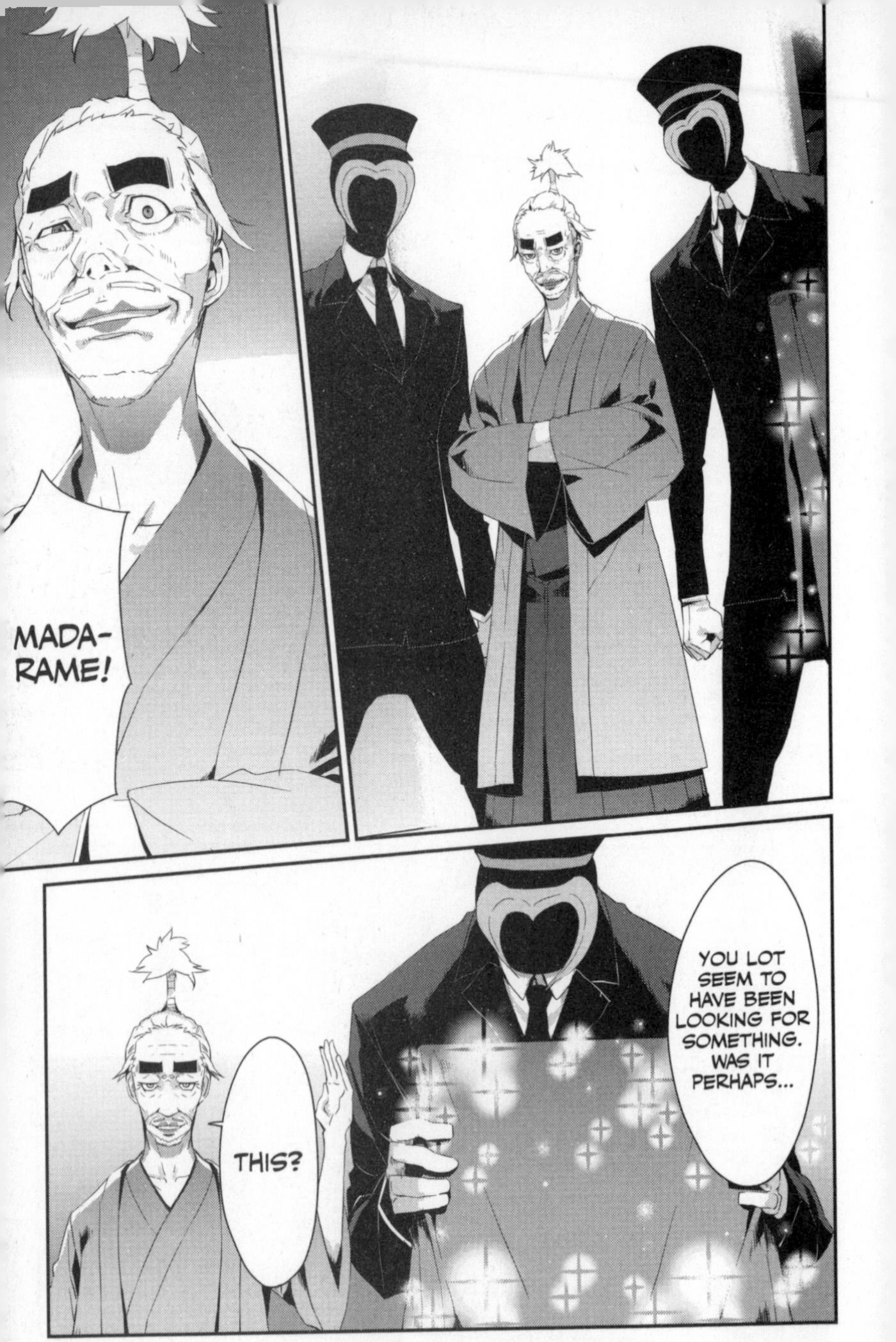
MADA-
RAME!
YOU LOT SEEM TO HAVE BEEN LOOKING FOR SOMETHING. WAS IT PERHAPS...
THIS?

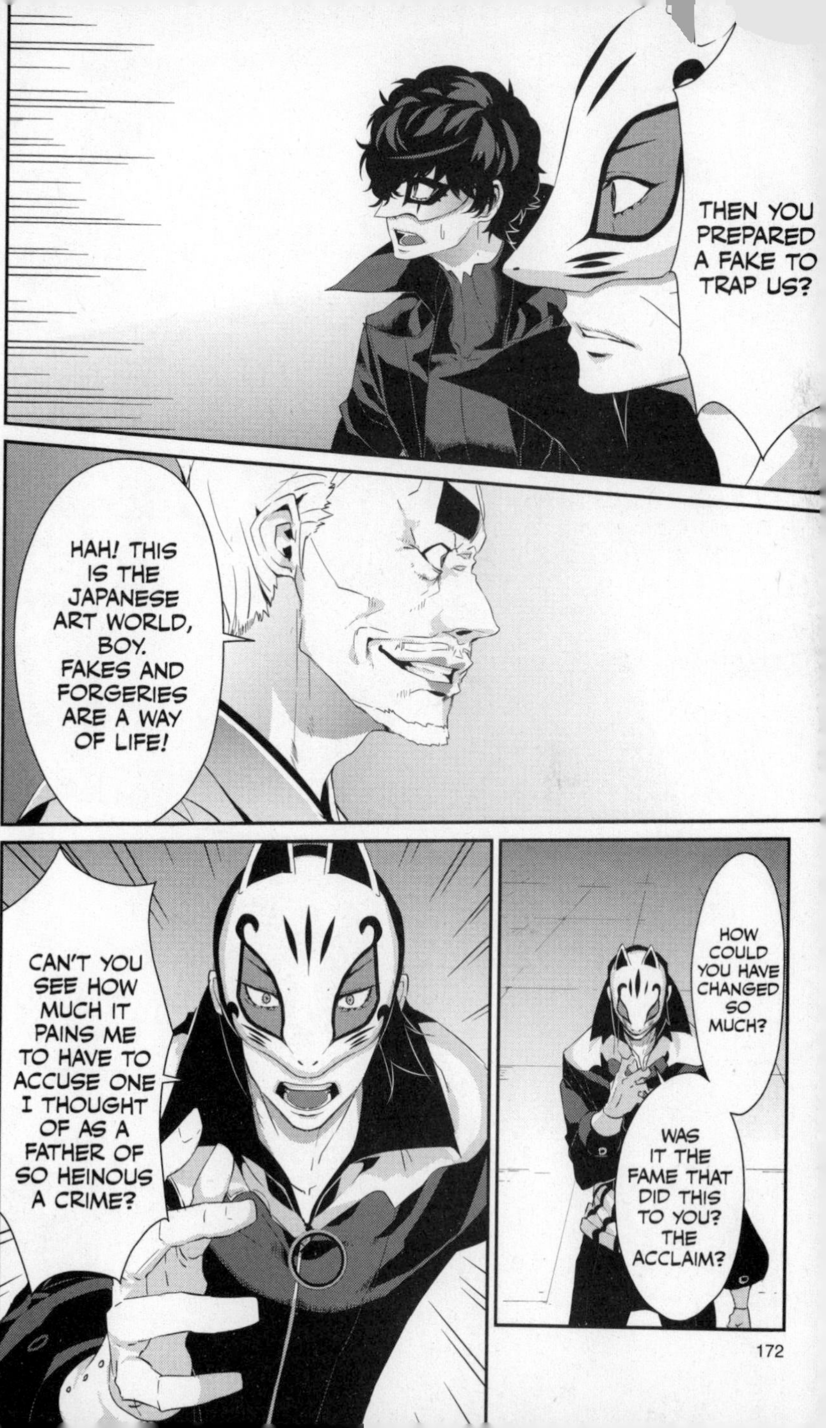

THEN YOU PREPARED A FAKE TO TRAP US?
HAH! THIS IS THE JAPANESE ART WORLD, BOY. FAKES AND FORGERIES ARE A WAY OF LIFE!
HOW COULD YOU HAVE CHANGED SO MUCH?
WAS IT THE FAME THAT DID THIS TO YOU? THE ACCLAIM?
CAN'T YOU SEE HOW MUCH IT PAINS ME TO HAVE TO ACCUSE ONE I THOUGHT OF AS A FATHER OF SO HEINOUS A CRIME?

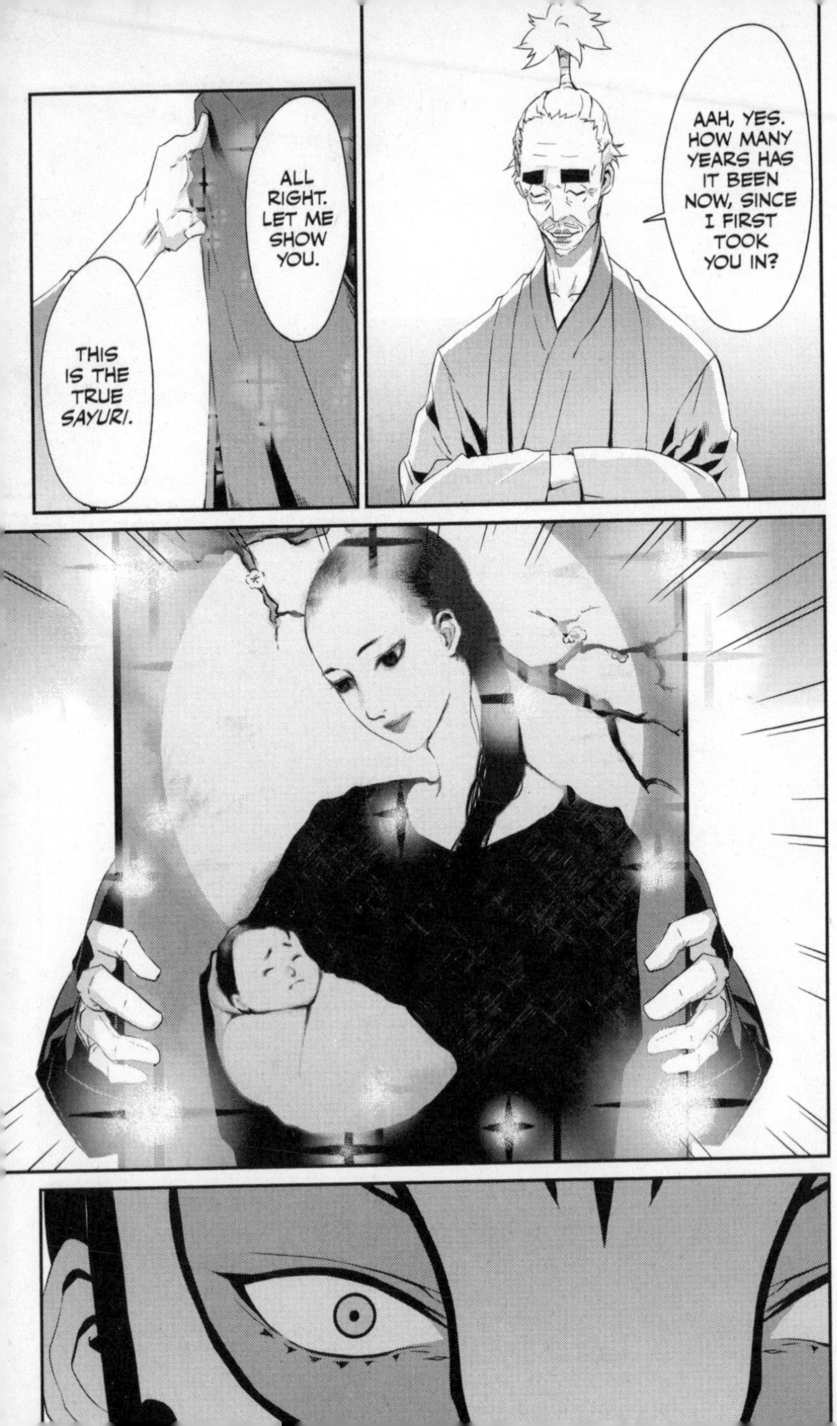
AAH, YES. HOW MANY YEARS HAS IT BEEN NOW, SINCE I FIRST TOOK YOU IN?
ALL RIGHT. LET ME SHOW YOU.
THIS IS THE TRUE *SAYURI*.

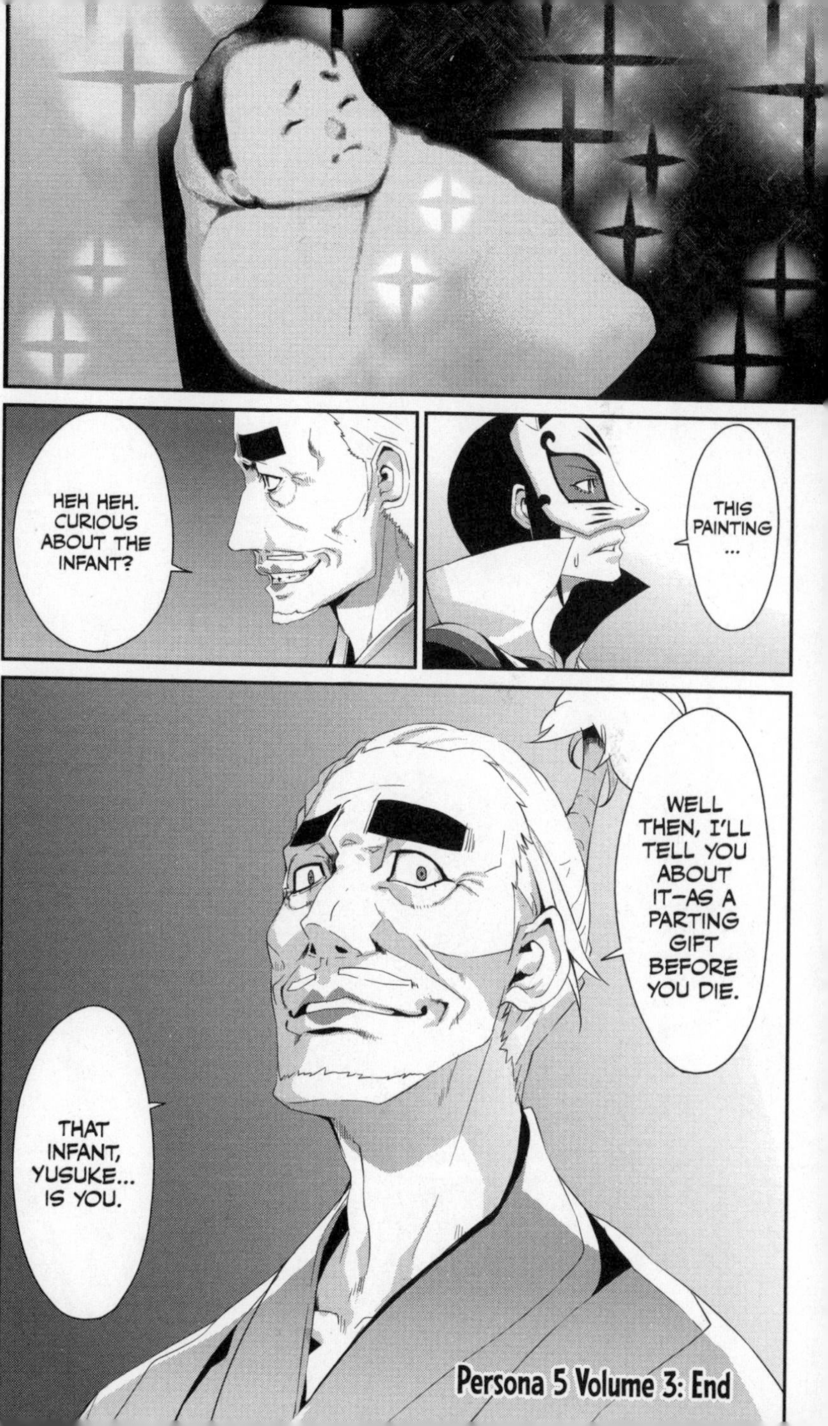
THIS PAINTING ...
HEH HEH. CURIOUS ABOUT THE INFANT?
WELL THEN, I'LL TELL YOU ABOUT IT—AS A PARTING GIFT BEFORE YOU DIE.
THAT INFANT, YUSUKE... IS YOU.

Persona 5 Volume 3: End

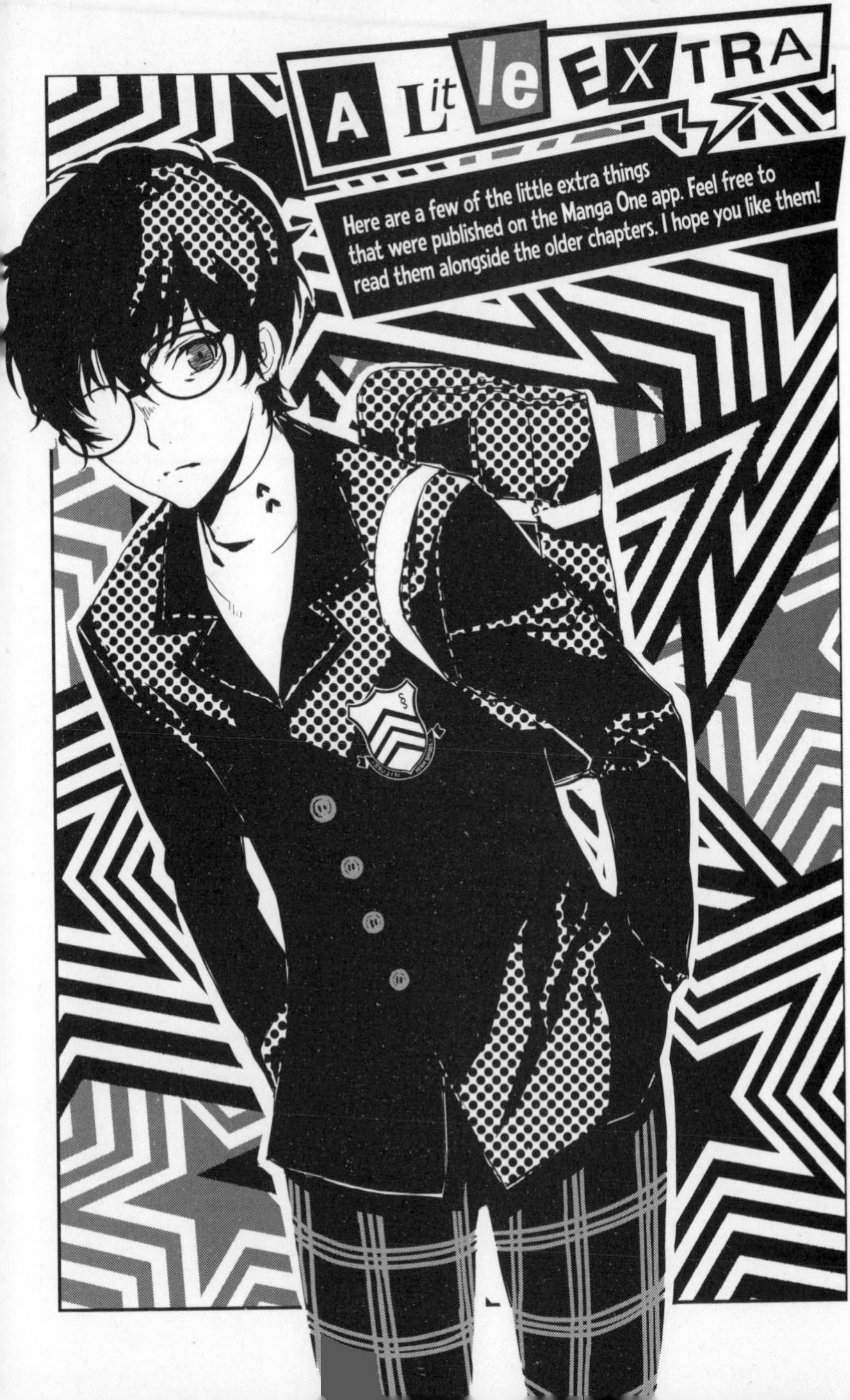
A Little EXTRA
Here are a few of the little extra things that were published on the Manga One app. Feel free to read them alongside the older chapters. I hope you like them!

Published 10/15/2016

HOODS

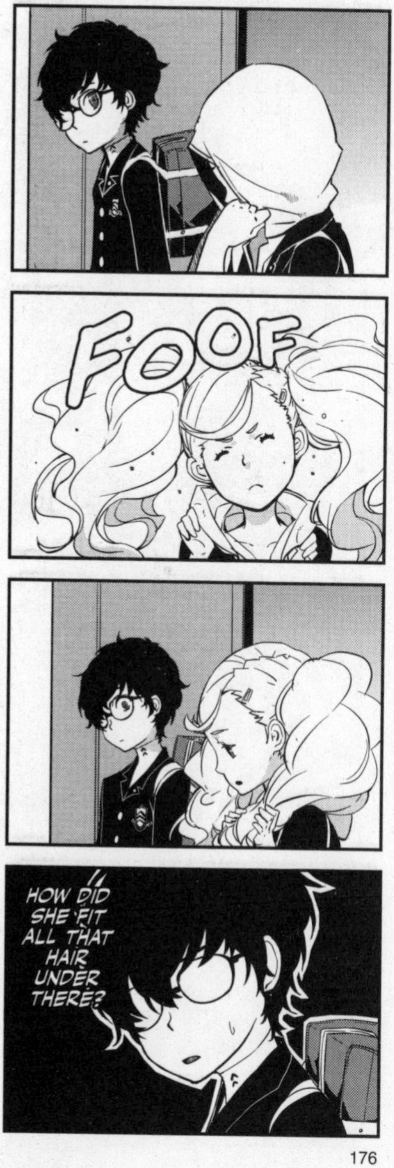
FOOF
HOW DID SHE FIT ALL THAT HAIR UNDER THERE?

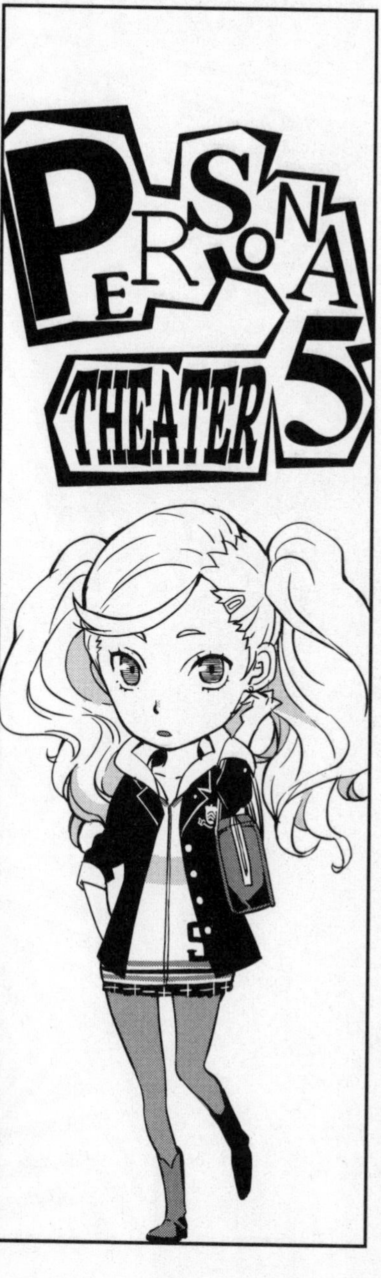
PERSONA
THEATER 5

Published 10/15/2016

COSPLAY

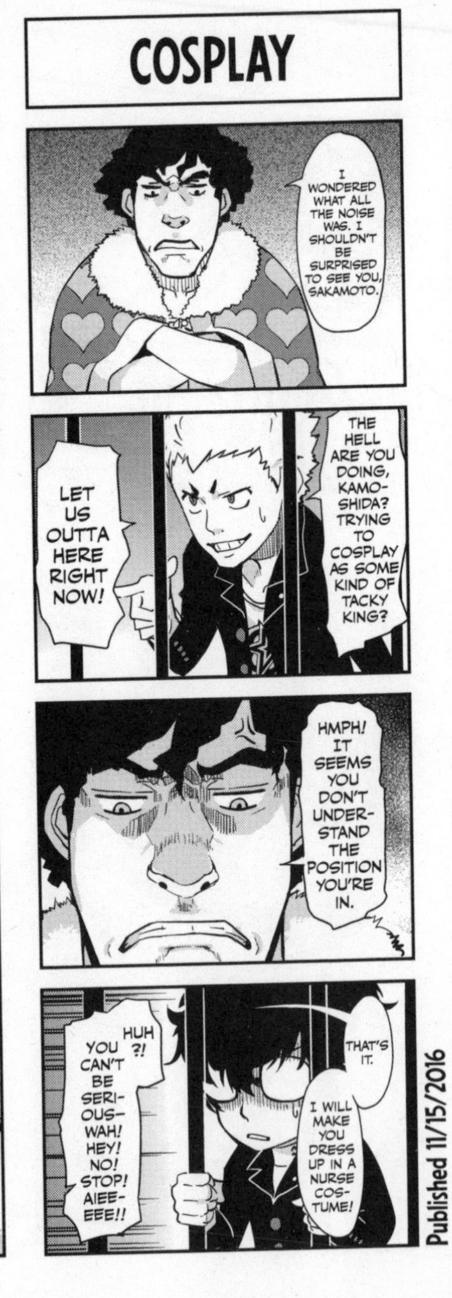
I WONDERED WHAT ALL THE NOISE WAS. I SHOULDN'T BE SURPRISED TO SEE YOU, SAKAMOTO.
THE HELL ARE YOU DOING, KAMOSHIDA? TRYING TO COSPLAY AS SOME KIND OF TACKY KING?
LET US OUTTA HERE RIGHT NOW!
HMPH! IT SEEMS YOU DON'T UNDER-STAND THE POSITION YOU'RE IN.
THAT'S IT.
I WILL MAKE YOU DRESS UP IN A NURSE COS-TUME!
HUH ?!
YOU CAN'T BE SERI-OUS-WAH! HEY! NO! STOP! AIEE-EEE!!

Published 11/15/2016

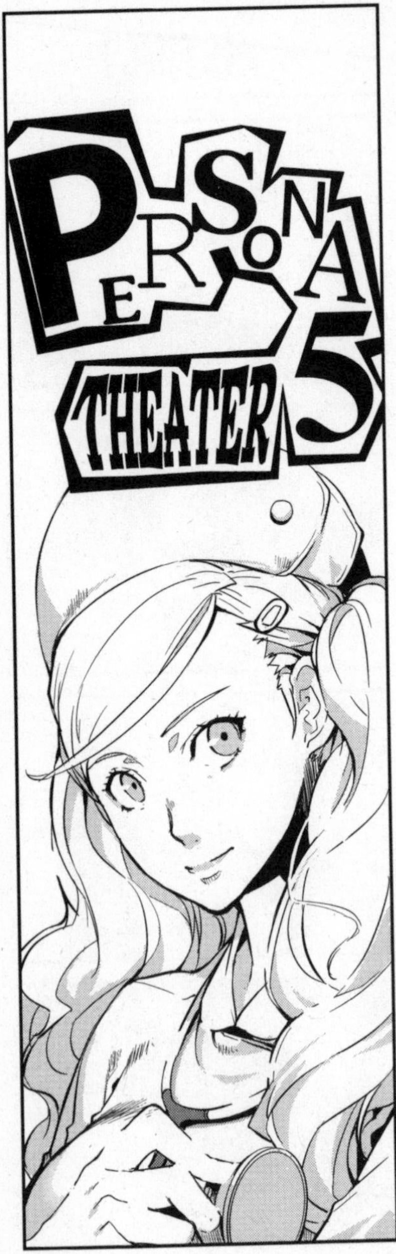
PERSONA 5
THEATER

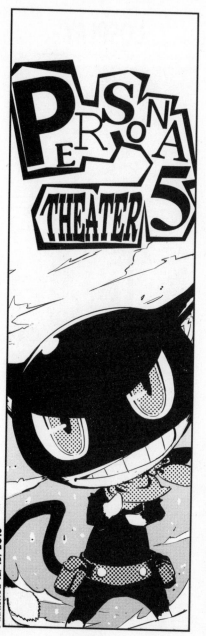

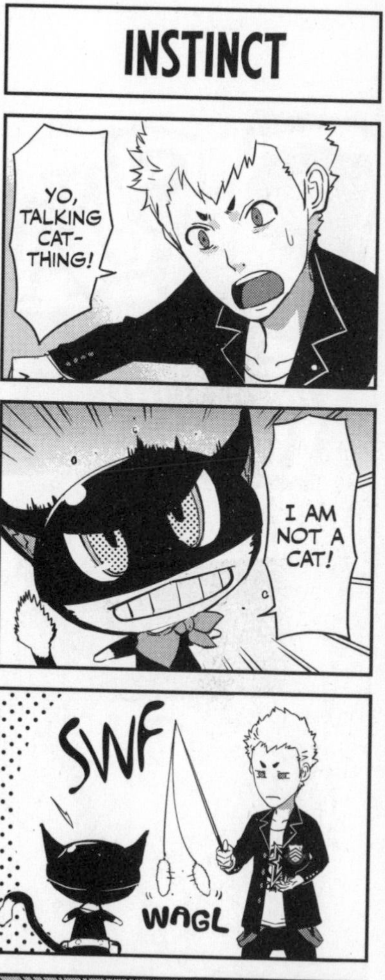
INSTINCT
YO, TALKING CAT-THING!
I AM NOT A CAT!
SWF
WAGL
I-I TOLD YOU... I'M NOT A...A CAT...!

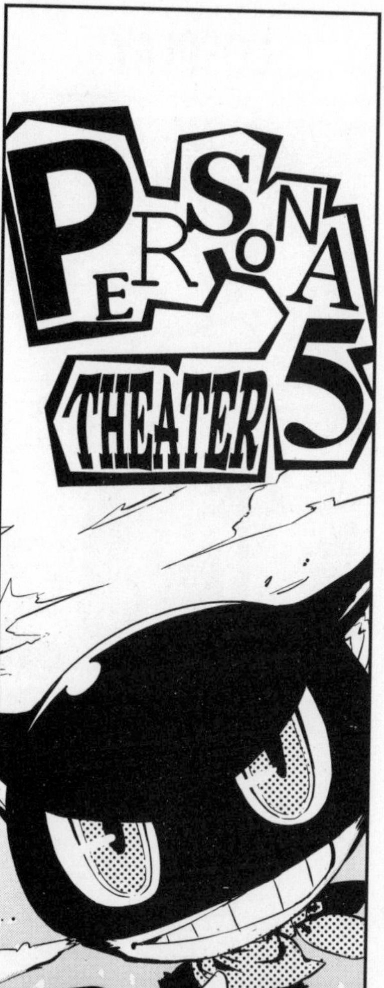
PERSONA 5
THEATER

Published 12/15/2016

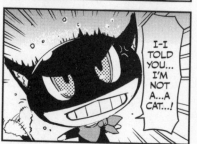

RUMORS

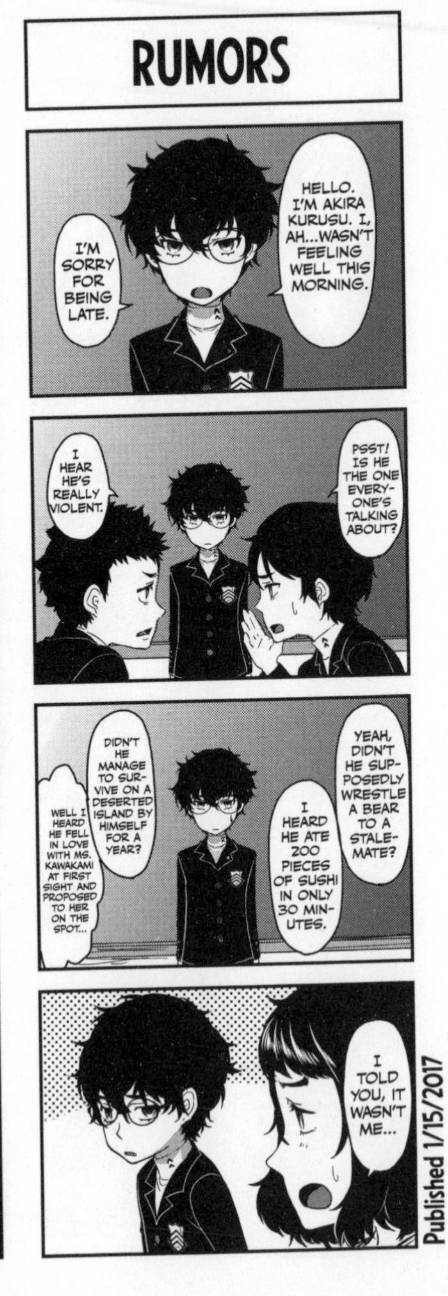
HELLO. I'M AKIRA KURUSU. I, AH...WASN'T FEELING WELL THIS MORNING.
I'M SORRY FOR BEING LATE.
PSST! IS HE THE ONE EVERYONE'S TALKING ABOUT?
I HEAR HE'S REALLY VIOLENT.
YEAH, DIDN'T HE SUPPOSEDLY WRESTLE A BEAR TO A STALEMATE?
I HEARD HE ATE 200 PIECES OF SUSHI IN ONLY 30 MINUTES.
DIDN'T HE MANAGE TO SURVIVE ON A DESERTED ISLAND BY HIMSELF FOR A YEAR?
WELL I HEARD HE FELL IN LOVE WITH MS. KAWAKAMI AT FIRST SIGHT AND PROPOSED TO HER ON THE SPOT...
I TOLD YOU, IT WASN'T ME...

Published 1/15/2017

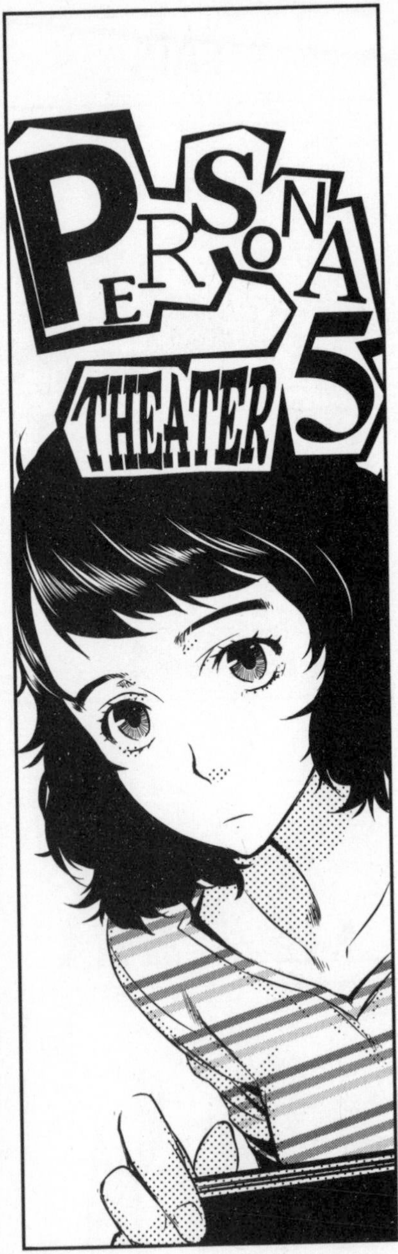
PERSONA
THEATER 5

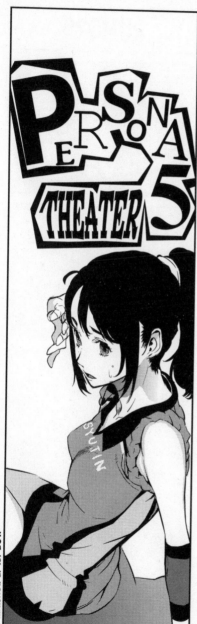

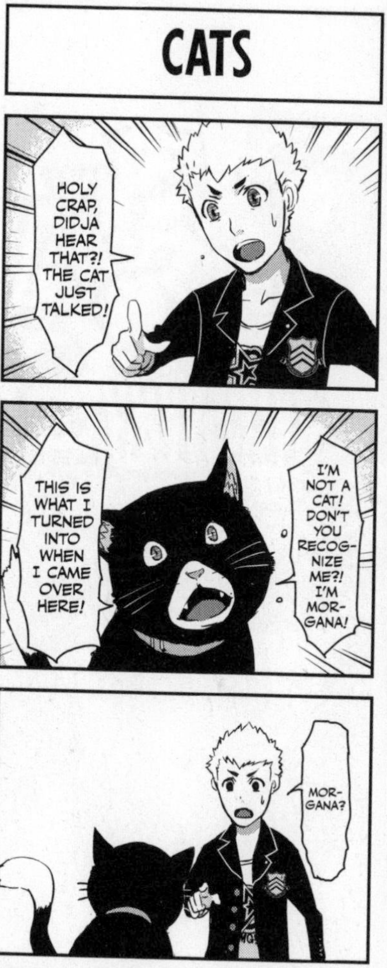
CATS
HOLY CRAP, DIDJA HEAR THAT?! THE CAT JUST TALKED!
I'M NOT A CAT! DON'T YOU RECOG-NIZE ME?! I'M MOR-GANA!
THIS IS WHAT I TURNED INTO WHEN I CAME OVER HERE!
MOR-GANA?
UM! I-I TO-TALLY KNEW IT WAS YOU.
Right?
Mew!
THAT'S A REAL CAT!
YOU DIDN'T KNOW AT ALL, DID YOU!

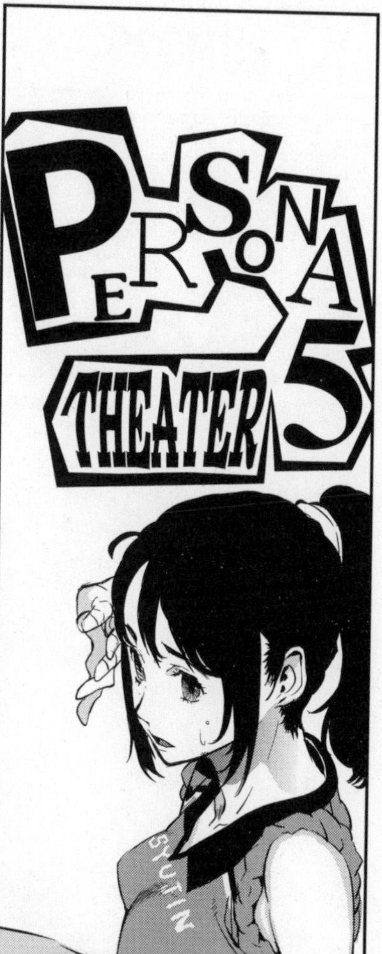
PERSONA 5
THEATER
SYUTIN

Published 2/15/2017

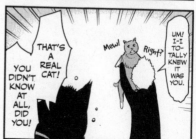

MY TURN

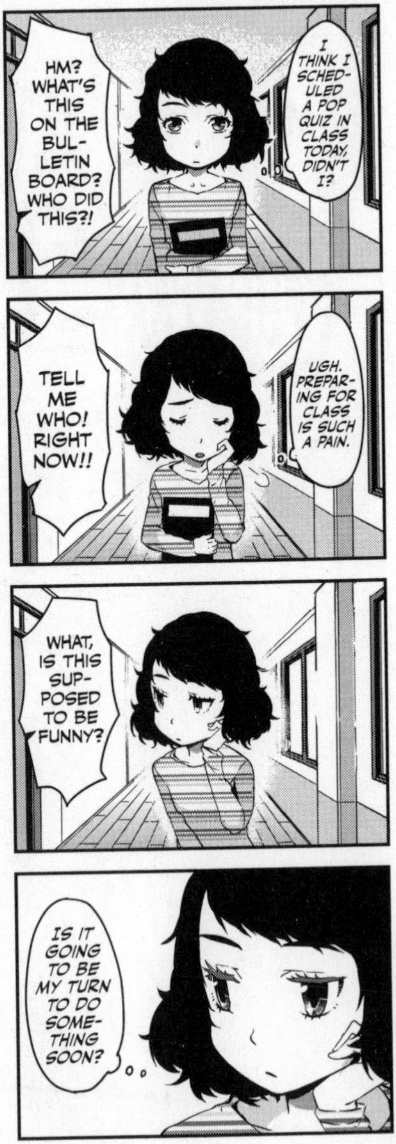
I THINK I SCHEDULED A POP QUIZ IN CLASS TODAY, DIDN'T I?
HM? WHAT'S THIS ON THE BULLETIN BOARD? WHO DID THIS?!
UGH. PREPARING FOR CLASS IS SUCH A PAIN.
TELL ME WHO! RIGHT NOW!!
WHAT, IS THIS SUPPOSED TO BE FUNNY?
IS IT GOING TO BE MY TURN TO DO SOMETHING SOON?

Published 3/15/2017

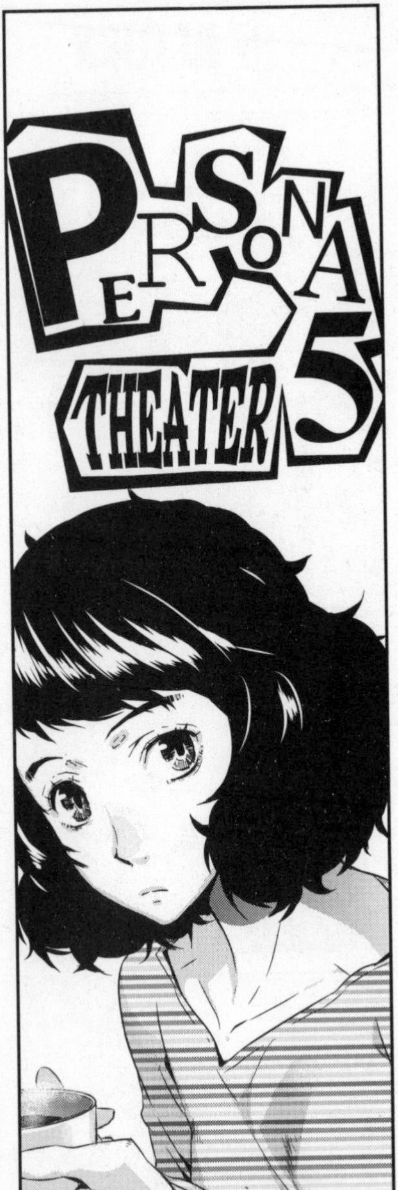
PERSONA 5
THEATER

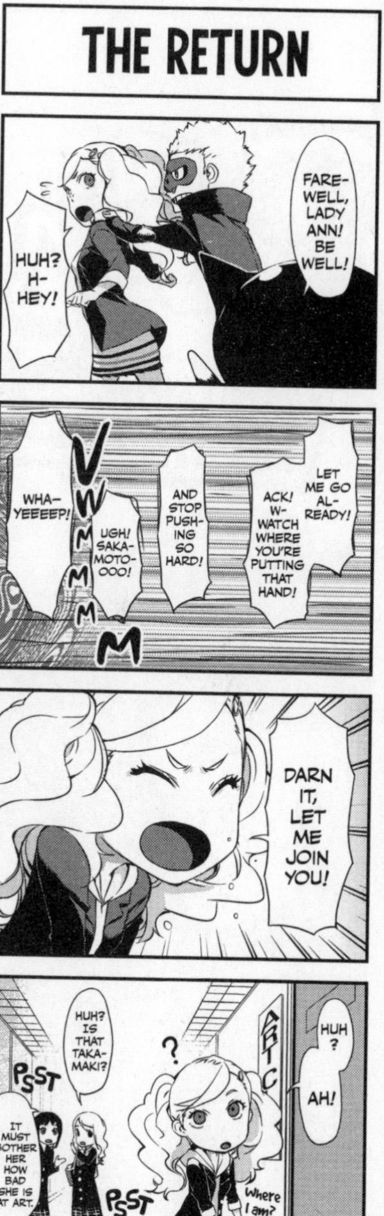
THE RETURN
FAREWELL, LADY ANN! BE WELL!
HUH? H-HEY!
LET ME GO ALREADY!
ACK! W-WATCH WHERE YOU'RE PUTTING THAT HAND!
AND STOP PUSHING SO HARD!
UGH! SAKAMOTO-OOO!
VWWMMMM
WHA-YEEEEP!
DARN IT, LET ME JOIN YOU!
HUH? AH!
ART C
?
HUH? IS THAT TAKAMAKI?
PSST
IT MUST BOTHER HER HOW BAD SHE IS AT ART.
PSST
Where I am?

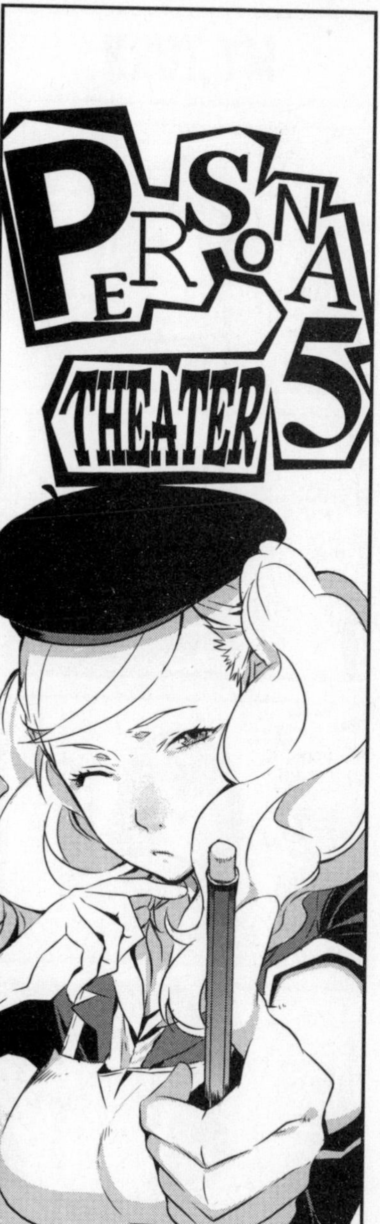
PERSONA 5
THEATER

Published 6/3/2017

A CAT...?

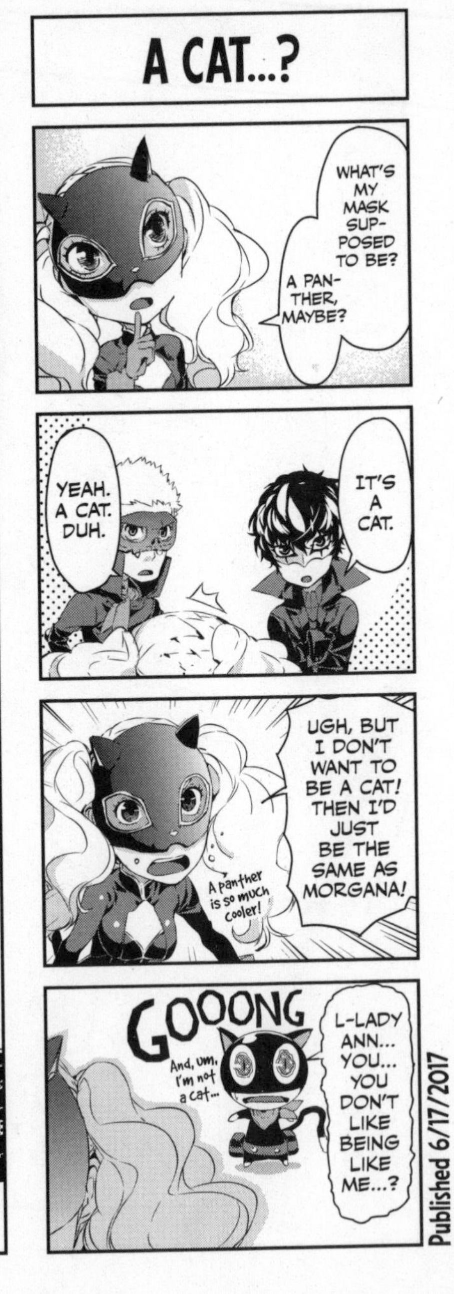
WHAT'S MY MASK SUP-POSED TO BE?
A PAN-THER, MAYBE?
IT'S A CAT.
YEAH. A CAT. DUH.
UGH, BUT I DON'T WANT TO BE A CAT! THEN I'D JUST BE THE SAME AS MORGANA!
A panther is so much cooler!
L-LADY ANN... YOU... YOU DON'T LIKE BEING LIKE ME...?
GOOONG
And, um, I'm not a cat...

Published 6/17/2017

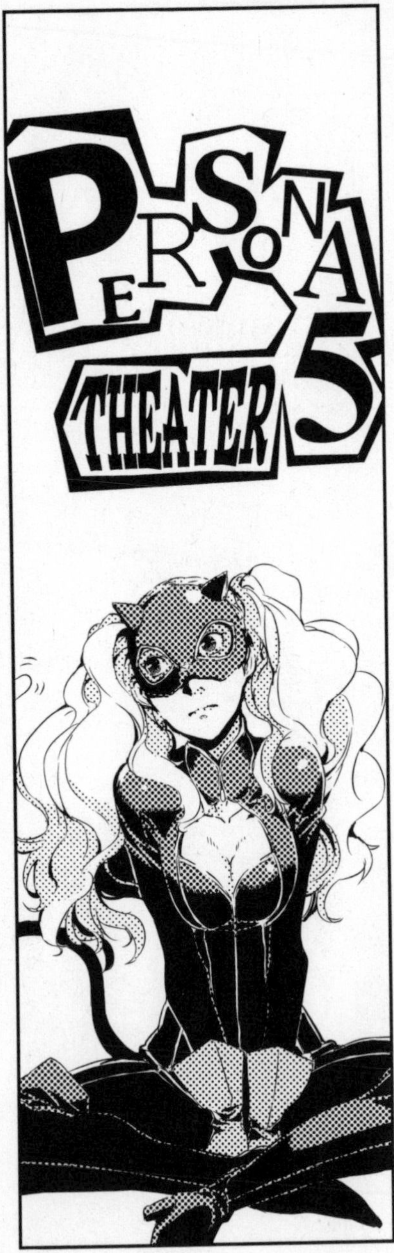
PERSONA THEATER 5

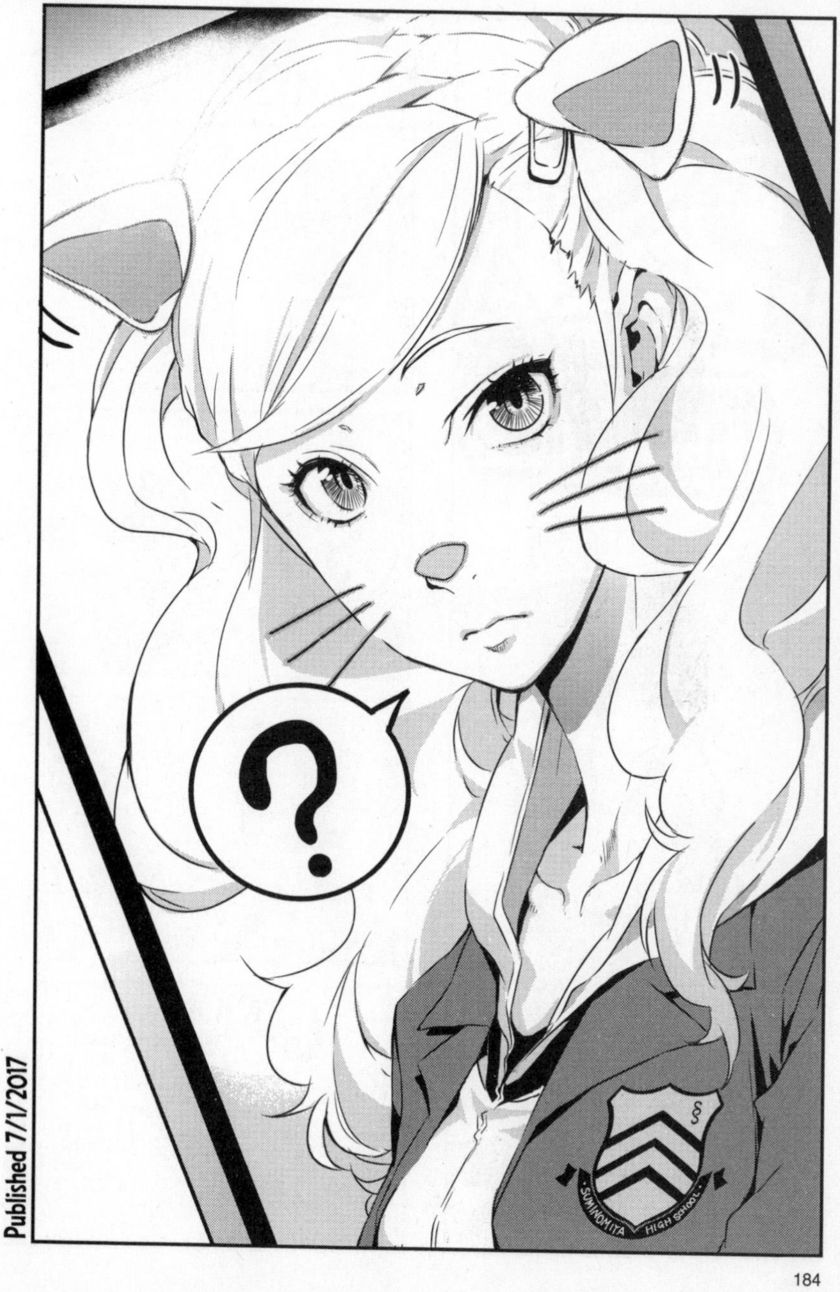
?
SUMINOMITA HIGH SCHOOL

Published 7/1/2017

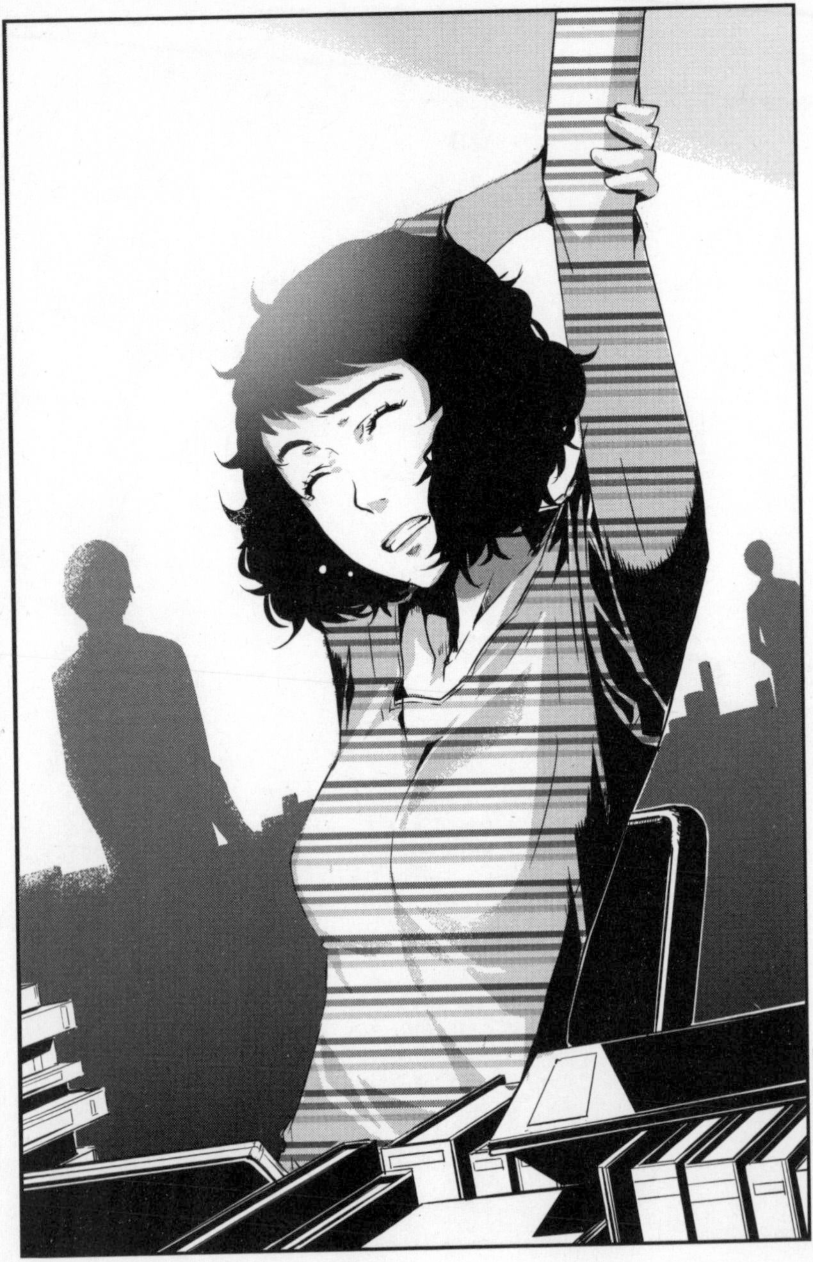

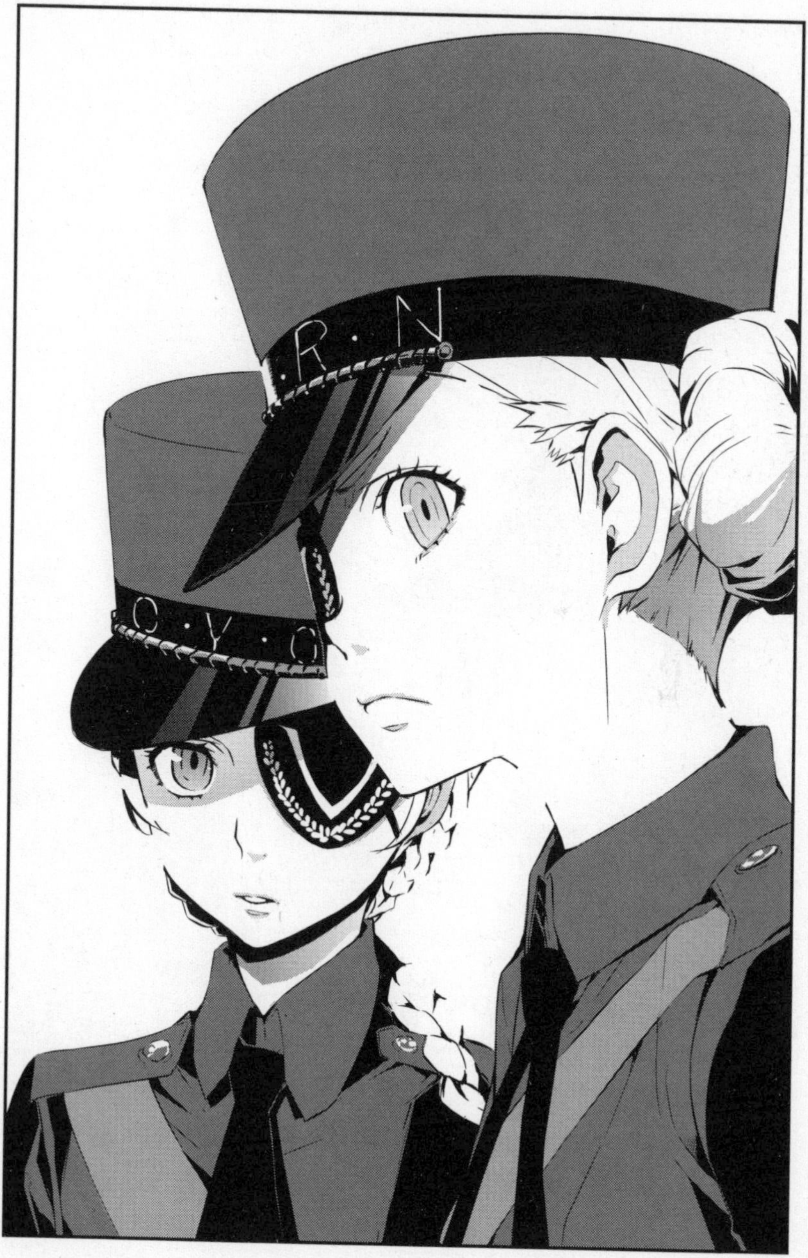
R · N
C · Y · C

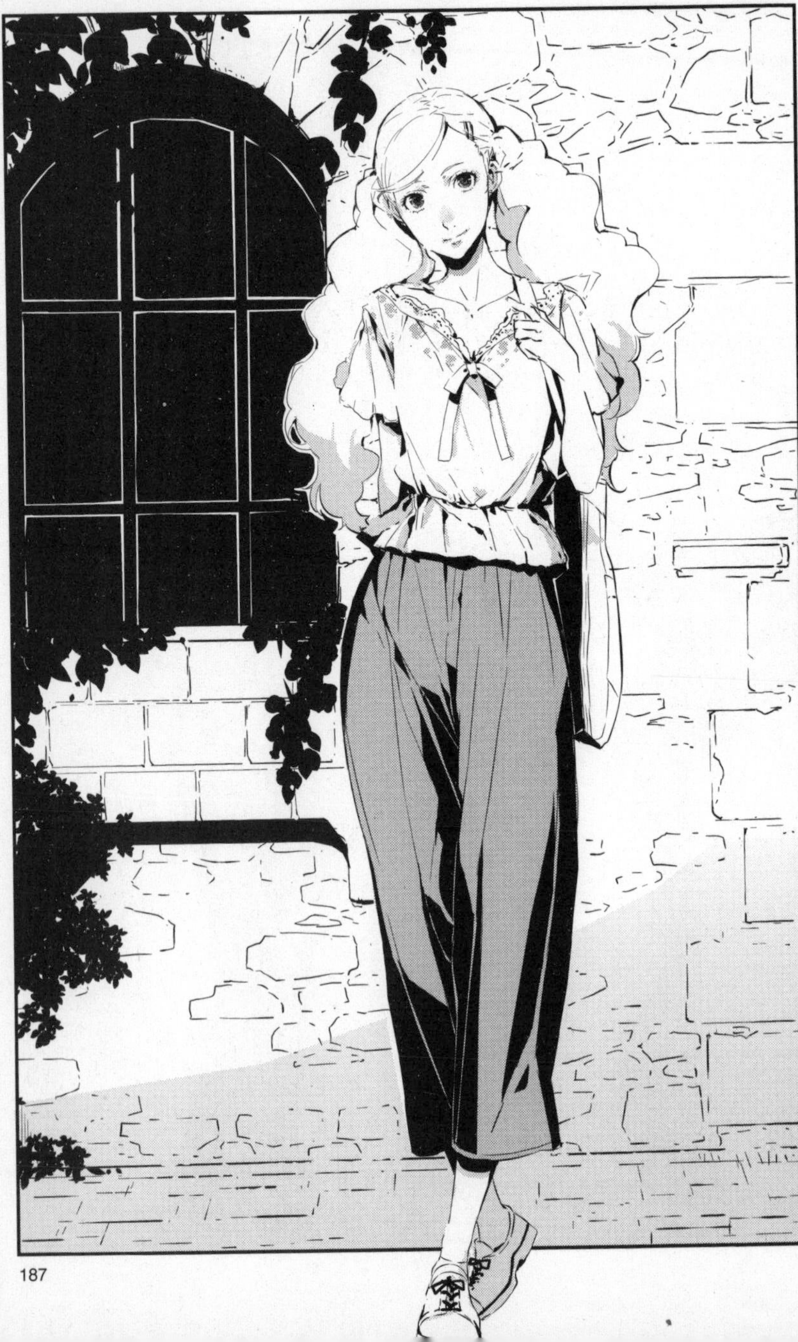

Published 8/26/2017

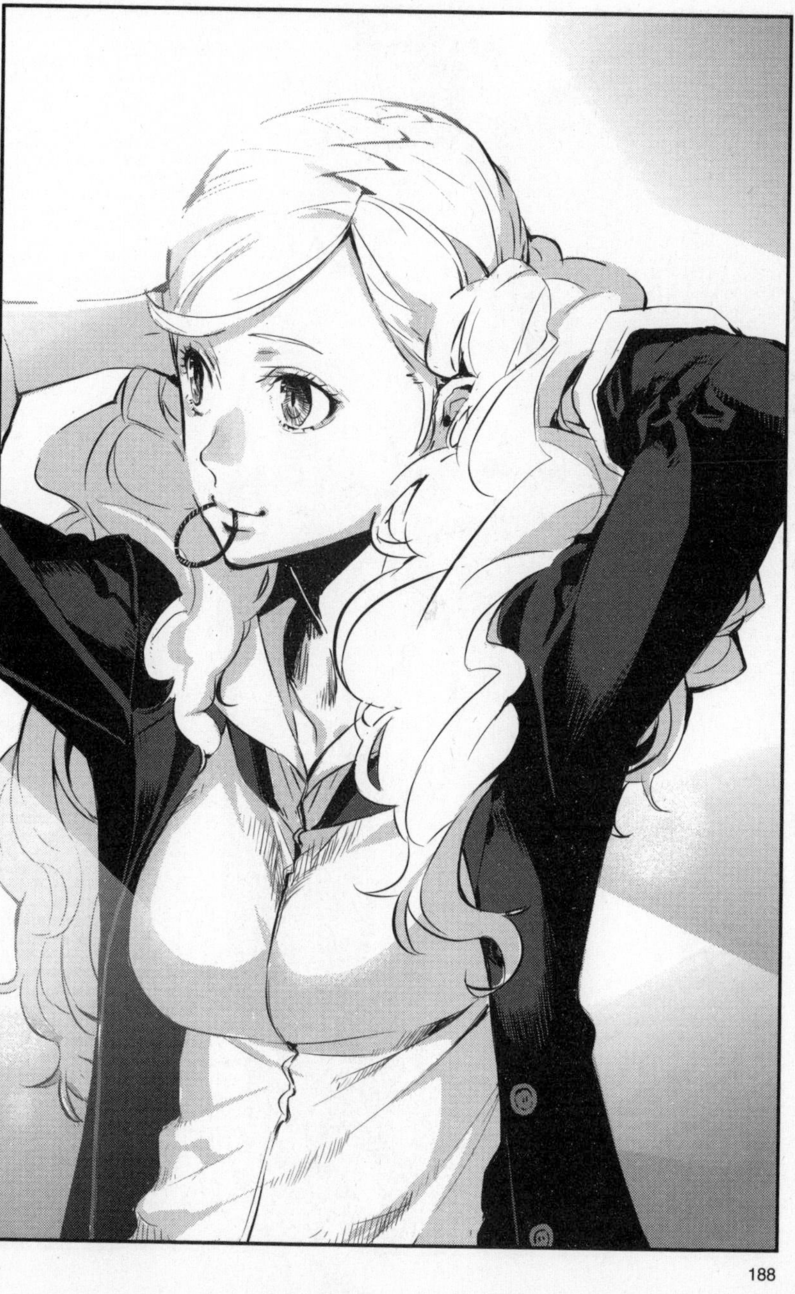

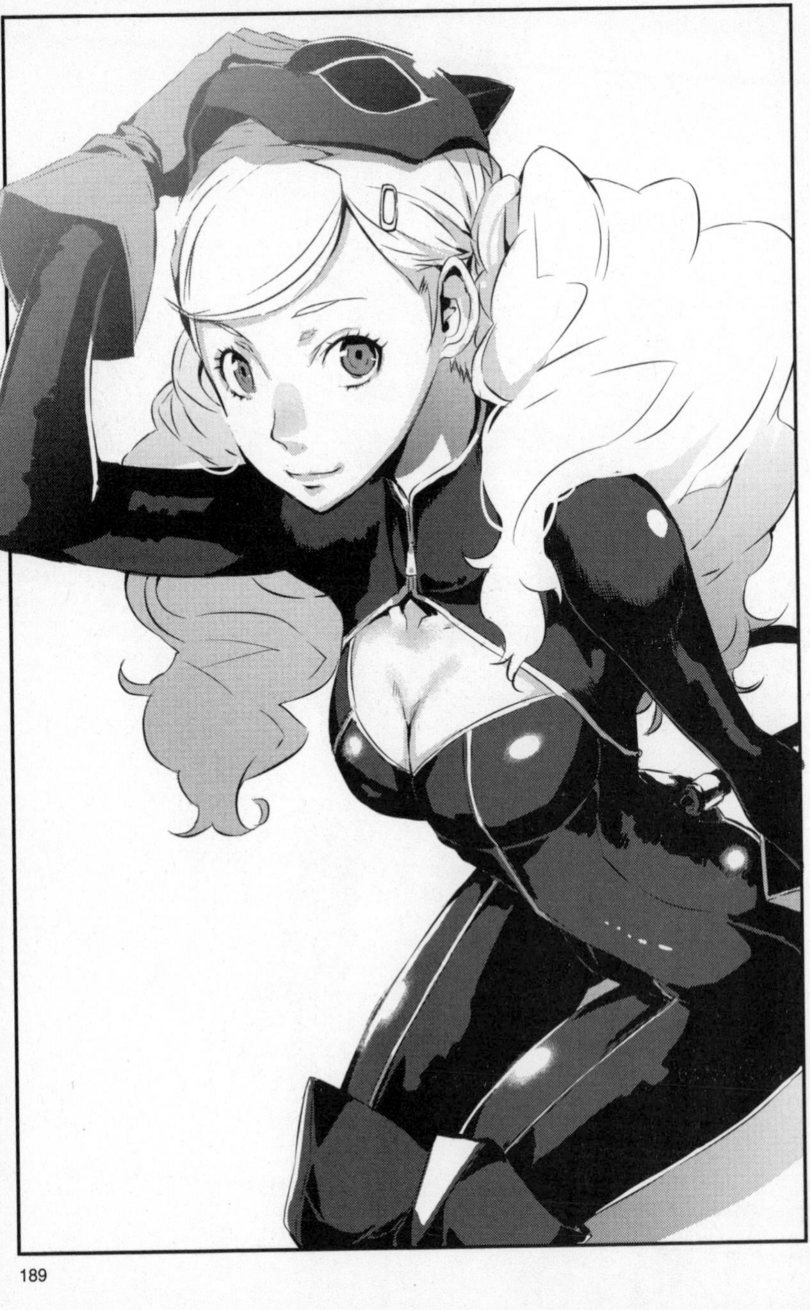

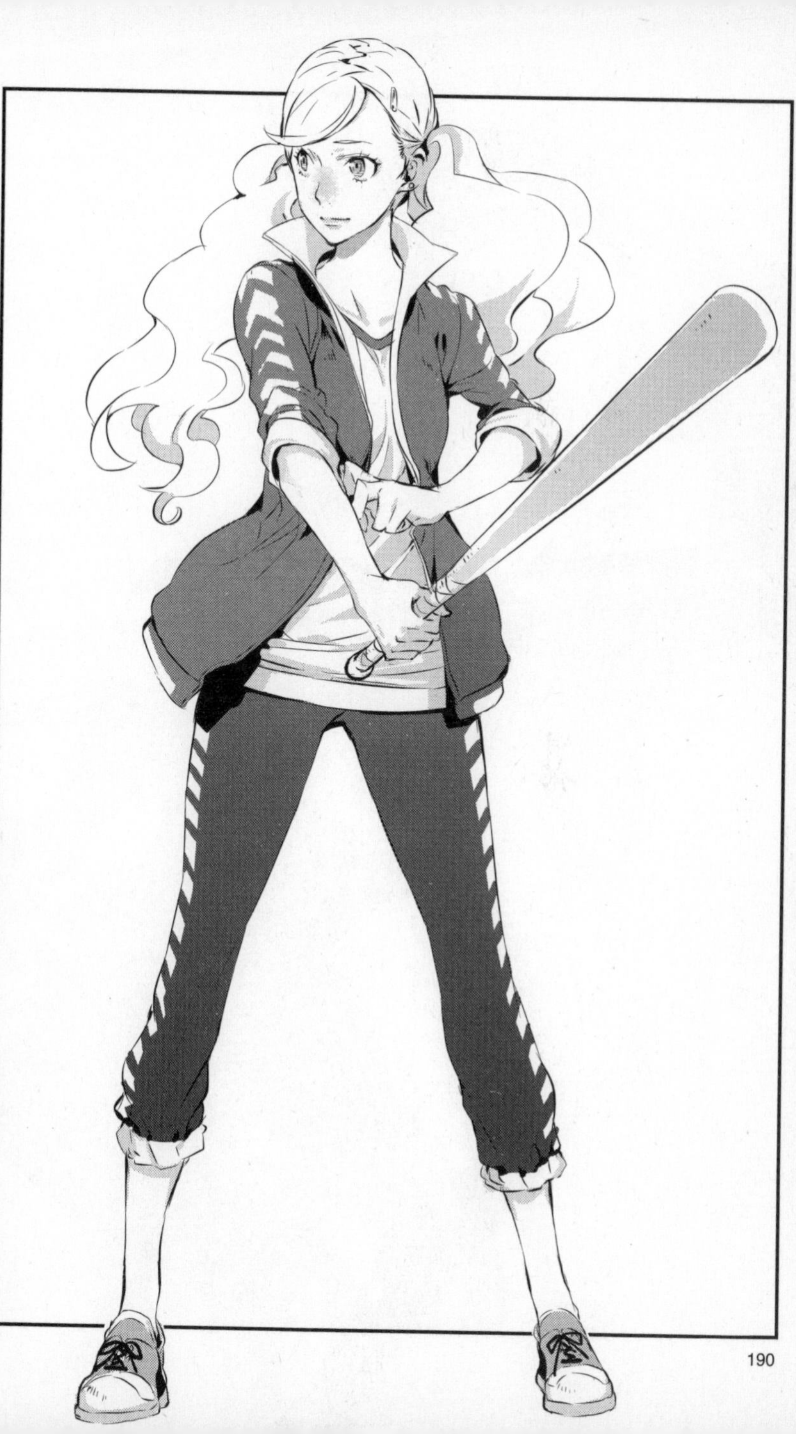

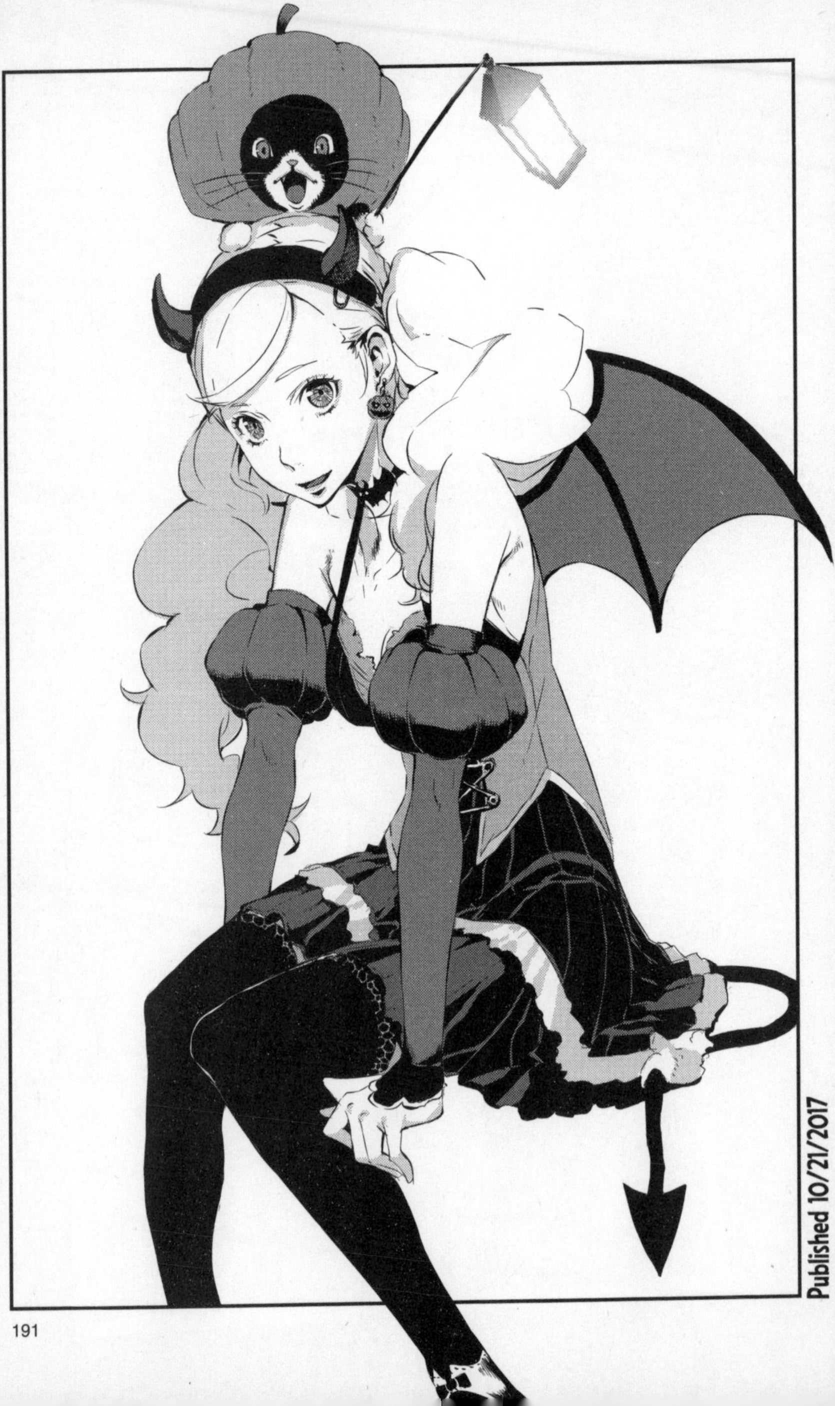

Published 10/21/2017

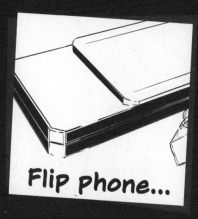

Flip phone...

HiSaTo MuRAsAKi

With its anime series* starting soon, the *Persona 5* franchise is heating up even more! I'm going to do my best to make the manga series even more fun and exciting to match!

*In Japan

Hisato Murasaki is a manga artist and illustrator from Japan. He has created illustrations for a number of manga and novel series, including *Hyakume no Kishi* (*Knight of 100 Eyes*), *The Case-Book of ENA*, the *D-Crackers* series, *Bravely Archive: D's Report*. He also wrote the manga, *Boku no Mawari no Uchuujin* (*The Alien Around Me*). He started work on *Persona 5* in 2016.

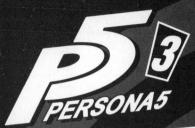

ART AND STORY BY
HISATO MURASAKI
ORIGINAL CONCEPT BY ATLUS

Translation/Adrienne Beck
Touch-Up Art & Lettering/Annaliese Christman
Design/Kam Li
Editor/Marlene First
Approval Cooperation/Shinji Yamamoto (ATLUS),
Miki Iwata (ATLUS)

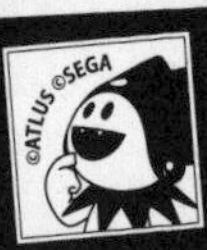

PERSONA 5 Vol.3
by Hisato MURASAKI
Original Concept by ATLUS
© ATLUS © SEGA All rights reserved.
© 2017 Hisato MURASAKI
All rights reserved.
Original Japanese edition published by SHOGAKUKAN.
English translation rights in the United States of America, Canada, the United
Kingdom, Ireland,Australia and New Zealand arranged with SHOGAKUKAN.

Original Cover Design: Kenro YOKOYAMA (Beeworks)

Printed in the U.S.A.

Published by VIZ Media, LLC
P.O. Box 77010
San Francisco, CA 94107

10 9 8 7 6 5 4 3 2
First printing, July 2020
Second printing, November 2020

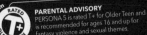

VIZ MEDIA

viz.com

PARENTAL ADVISORY
PERSONA 5 is rated T+ for Older Teen and
is recommended for ages 16 and up for
fantasy violence and sexual themes.

RATED **T+** OLDER TEEN
ratings.viz.com

NieR:Automata

ニーア オートマタ

NOVELS

Written by Jun Eishima and Yoko Taro

Original Story by Yoko Taro

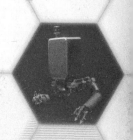

EXPERIENCE THE WORLD AND CHARACTERS OF THE HIT VIDEO GAME FRANCHISE!

NieR:Automata
LONG STORY SHORT
NieR:Automata
LONG STORY SHORT
Written by Jun Eishima
Original Story by Yoko Taro
VIZ
NieR:Automata
SHORT STORY LONG
NieR:Automata
SHORT STORY LONG
Written by Jun Eishima and Yoko Taro
Original Story by Yoko Taro
VIZ

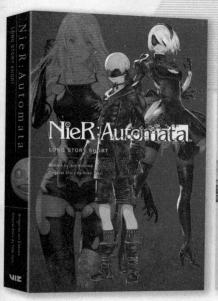

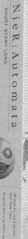

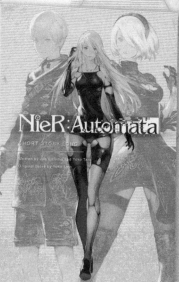

When alien forces invade with an army of Machines, the remnants of humanity must depend on Androids of their own design—the placid 2B and the excitable 9S—to survive.

VIZ

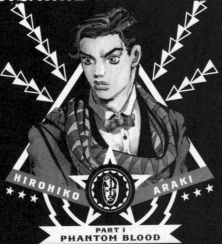
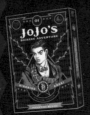
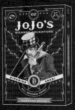
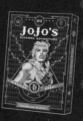

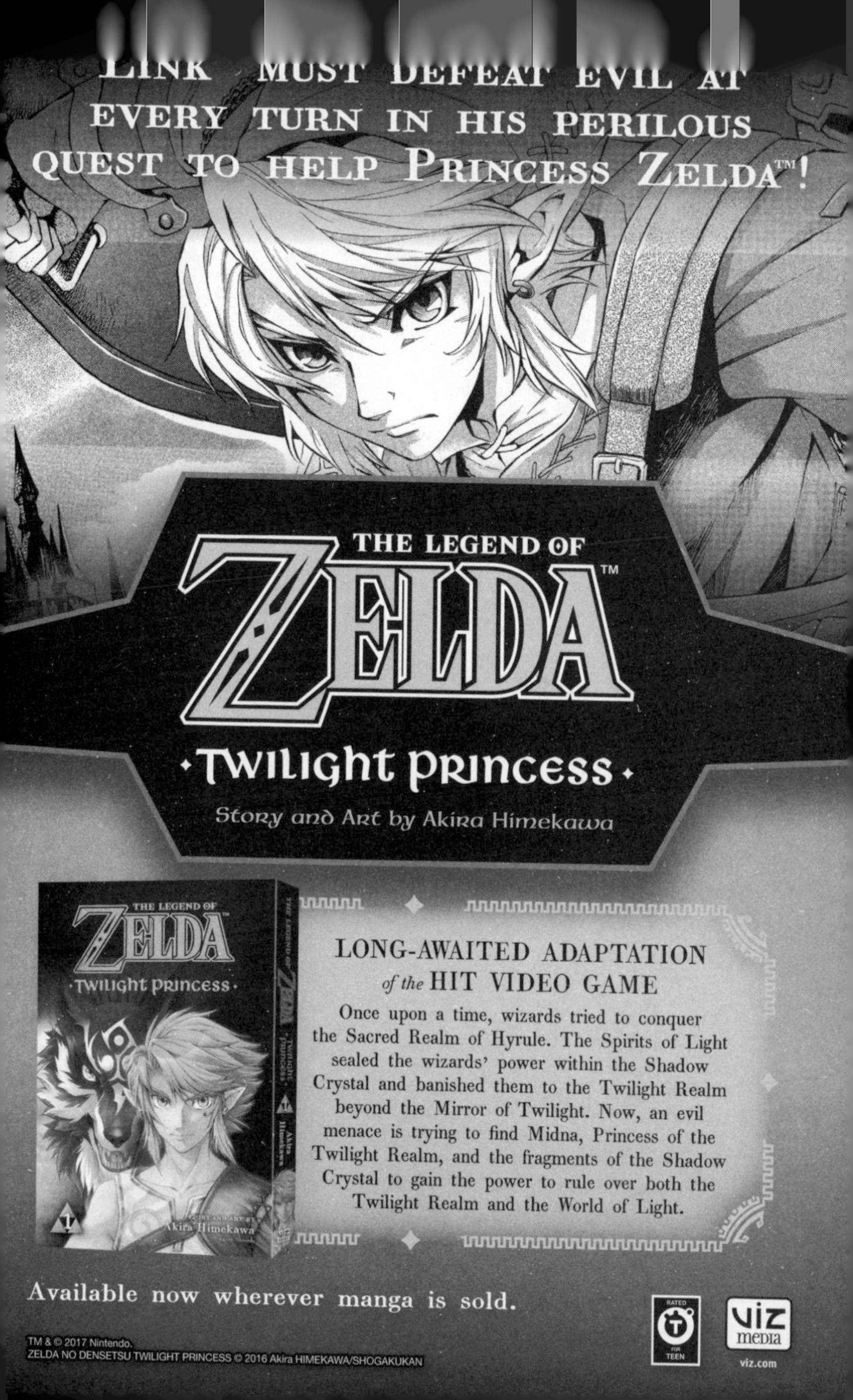
LINK MUST DEFEAT EVIL AT EVERY TURN IN HIS PERILOUS QUEST TO HELP PRINCESS ZELDA™!
THE LEGEND OF ZELDA™
·TWILIGHT PRINCESS·
Story and Art by Akira Himekawa
LONG-AWAITED ADAPTATION of the HIT VIDEO GAME
Once upon a time, wizards tried to conquer the Sacred Realm of Hyrule. The Spirits of Light sealed the wizards' power within the Shadow Crystal and banished them to the Twilight Realm beyond the Mirror of Twilight. Now, an evil menace is trying to find Midna, Princess of the Twilight Realm, and the fragments of the Shadow Crystal to gain the power to rule over both the Twilight Realm and the World of Light.
Available now wherever manga is sold.
RATED T FOR TEEN
VIZ media
viz.com
TM & © 2017 Nintendo.
ZELDA NO DENSETSU TWILIGHT PRINCESS © 2016 Akira HIMEKAWA/SHOGAKUKAN

THE LEGEND OF ZELDA

LEGENDARY EDITION

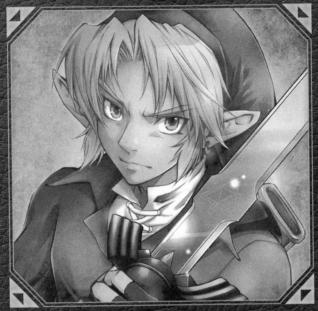

STORY AND ART BY
AKIRA HIMEKAWA

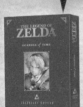 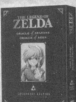 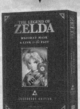 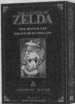 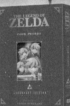

The Legendary Editions of *The Legend of Zelda*™ contain two volumes of the beloved manga series, presented in a deluxe format featuring new covers and color art pieces.

VIZ

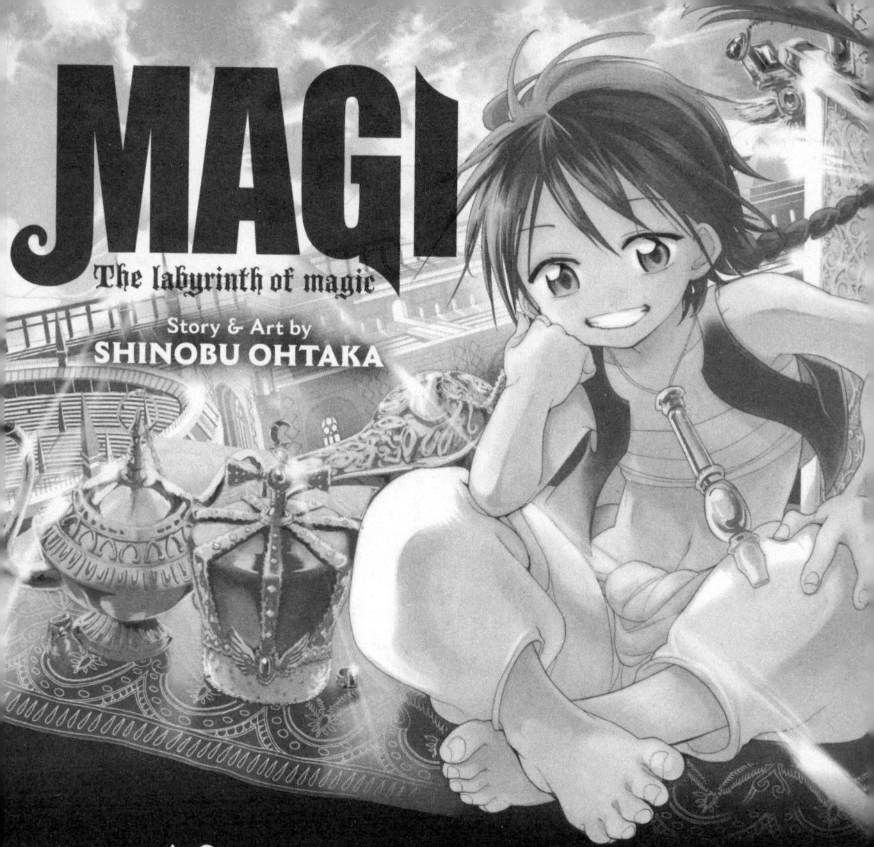
MAGI
The labyrinth of magic
Story & Art by
SHINOBU OHTAKA

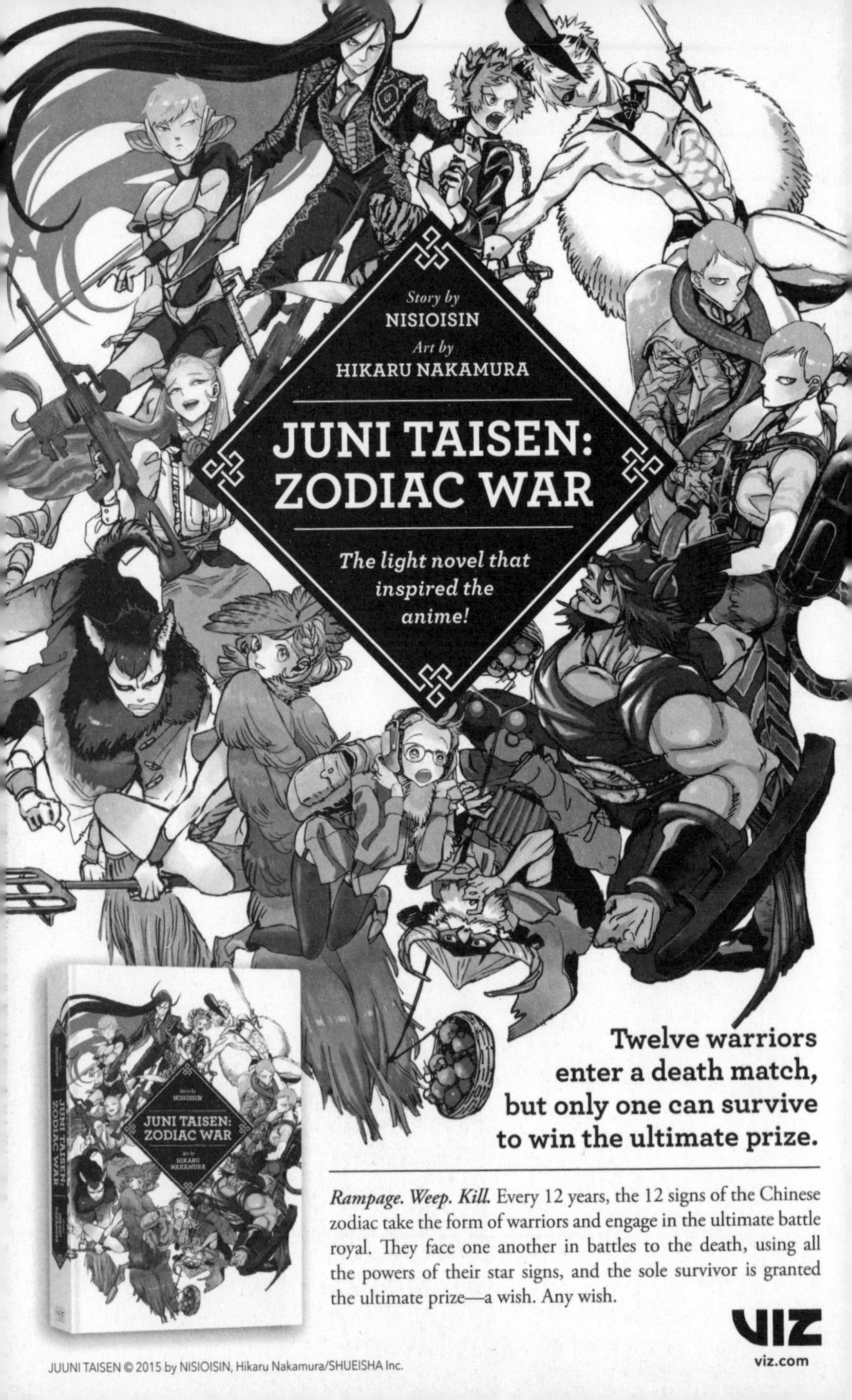
Story by
NISIOISIN
Art by
HIKARU NAKAMURA
JUNI TAISEN:
ZODIAC WAR
The light novel that inspired the anime!
Twelve warriors enter a death match, but only one can survive to win the ultimate prize.
Rampage. Weep. Kill. Every 12 years, the 12 signs of the Chinese zodiac take the form of warriors and engage in the ultimate battle royal. They face one another in battles to the death, using all the powers of their star signs, and the sole survivor is granted the ultimate prize—a wish. Any wish.
VIZ
viz.com
JUUNI TAISEN © 2015 by NISIOISIN, Hikaru Nakamura/SHUEISHA Inc.

This is the LAST PAGE!

You're Reading the WRONG WAY!

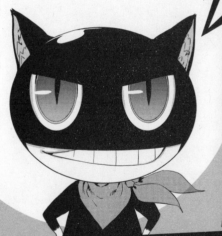

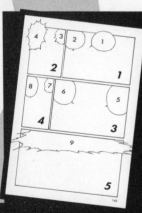

PERSONA 5 reads from right to left, starting in the upper-right corner. Japanese is read from right to left, meaning that action, sound effects, and word-balloon order are completely reversed from English order.